CITIZENS WITHOUT RIGHTS

Aborigines and Australian Citizenship

JOHN CHESTERMAN
and
BRIAN GALLIGAN

PUBLISHED BY THE PRESS SYNDICATE OF THE UNIVERSITY OF CAMBRIDGE
The Pitt Building, Trumpington Street, Cambridge CB2 1RP, United Kingdom

CAMBRIDGE UNIVERSITY PRESS
The Edinburgh Building, Cambridge CB2 2RU, United Kingdom
40 West 20th Street, New York, NY 10011–4211, USA
10 Stamford Road, Oakleigh, Melbourne 3166, Australia

First published 1997

Printed in Australia by Brown Prior Anderson

Typeset in Baskerville 10/12 pt

National Library of Australia Cataloguing in Publication data

Chesterman, John, 1967– .
Citizens without rights : Aborigines and Australian citizenship.
Bibliography.
Includes index.
ISBN 0 521 59751 X (pbk.).
ISBN 0 521 59230 5.
1. Aborigines, Australian – Legal status, laws, etc. 2. Aborigines, Australian – Citizenship. I. Galligan, Brian, 1945– . II. Title.
323.119915

Library of Congress Cataloguing in Publication data

Chesterman, John, 1967–
Citizens without rights : Aborigines and Australian citizenship / John Chesterman and Brian Galligan.
p. cm.
Includes bibliographical references and index.
ISBN 0-521-59230-5 (alk. paper). – ISBN 0-521-59751-X (alk. paper)
1. Citizenship – Australia. 2. Australian aborigines – Civil rights. I. Galligan, Brian, 1945– . II. Title.
KU2140.C48 1997
342.94'083–dc21 97–17467

A catalogue record for this book is available from the British Library

CITIZENS WITHOUT RIGHTS

Contents

Tables

Acknowledgments

In writing this book we are grateful to have had the support of many colleagues and friends and the generous assistance of a number of Australian research institutions. Tom Clarke, in particular, did much of the Commonwealth archival research on which this book is based, and he was joint author of two earlier journal articles that appeared in the *Australian Journal of Political Science* and *Australian Historical Studies.* These articles have been incorporated into chapter 4, of which Clarke is a co-author. In addition to the prior publication of chapter 4, we have published an earlier version of chapter 3 in the *Public Law Review.* We thank the editors and anonymous referees of all of these journals, both for their editorial assistance, and for their permission to use material published earlier by them. We are also indebted to Terry Garwood and Peter Russell, who provided advice on some parts of the manuscript, and especially to Henry Reynolds, who read and commented upon the final draft.

We also extend grateful thanks to the staff at the following institutions: Australian Archives in Canberra and Melbourne, the Queensland State Archives, the Victorian Public Record Office, and the Victorian State Library. We would especially like to thank the following archivists: Moira Bligh, Doreen Mahony, Margaret Reid and Monika Skladowski. In our own workplace, Kate Robb has provided generous administrative support. We are grateful to the following individuals and institutions for permission to reproduce copyright material: F. Lancaster Jones; the editors of the *Federal Law Review*; the Mitchell Library, State Library of New South Wales; and the Commonwealth of Australia, for allowing us to quote material from the 1961 'Report From the Select Committee on Voting Rights of Aborigines' and the 1974 'Aboriginal Land Rights Commission, Second Report'.

This book would not have been written without the support of several institutions. The Australian National University's Research School of Social Sciences, and the University of Melbourne, through its professorial establishment fund, provided generous support for the initial research. An Australian Research Council Large Grant on the 'institutional definition and development of Australian citizenship' was awarded in 1995 and funded the completion of the research for and writing of this book.

JOHN CHESTERMAN and BRIAN GALLIGAN

Abbreviations

AA	Australian Archives
ADB	Australian Dictionary of Biography
ATSIC	Aboriginal and Torres Strait Islander Commission
CLR	Commonwealth Law Reports
CPD	Commonwealth Parliamentary Debates
CRS	Commonwealth Record Series
QPD	Queensland Parliamentary Debates
QPP	Queensland Parliamentary Papers
QSA	Queensland State Archives
VPD	Victorian Parliamentary Debates
VPP	Victorian Parliamentary Papers
VPRO	Victorian Public Record Office
VPRS	Victorian Public Record Series
WAPD	Western Australia Parliamentary Debates

For my parents, Shirley and Peter,
a selfless teacher and a reflective preacher

John Chesterman

For Briony and Justin,
citizens of the future

Brian Galligan

Introduction

A citizen, according to Aristotle's famous definition which has shaped western political thinking, is one who shares both in ruling and in being ruled. Citizens as rulers exercise collectively the political prerogatives of authoritative power over the polity, while the self-same body of individuals are the subjects of such rule. This ideal was severely limited in practice for Aristotle and other ancient thinkers, because they thought that most people lacked either the qualities necessary for participating in political life or the privileged circumstances of a leisured life that would enable cultivation of such qualities and make political participation feasible.

The democratisation of politics in modern times has entailed a fundamental reaffirmation of the ancient ideal of citizenship. Democracy entails free and equal individuals forming themselves into a political community in which they, the people, have final authority to rule and in which they constitute government accordingly. As Rousseau expressed it succinctly, the individual is equally a member of the sovereign body that makes fundamental law and a member of the subject body that obeys it. This virtuous circle of citizenship links both sides of the political equation, restraining and civilising political authority on the one hand and on the other ennobling civil obedience because the citizen is obeying the will of a larger collective of which she or he is an active member.

The adoption of the principle of representation in modern times made democracy feasible for large political societies, even if it lowered the ideal of citizenship, for in representative democracies citizens do not participate directly in ruling but only indirectly through voting for those who exercise governmental power. Nevertheless, participation in the process of governing in this indirect way is fundamentally significant for any individual or group of people, and the denial of the right to participate entails a basic restriction. In a *constitutional* representative democracy like that of Australia, citizens also share the primary role of sanctioning the very system of government, including its key structures and offices, through which they are governed. At the political level, exclusion from citizenship means being cut off from membership of the sovereign body of people and from the ongoing process of collective self-rule. While those who are excluded may be treated well or badly, depending on the benevolence of the regime, they are denied realisation of the fundamental human fulfilment of sharing in the political rule of a self-governing community of people. In other words, citizenship itself is the important thing, not how well non-citizens might be treated. And, in any case, the best guarantee of proper treatment for individuals and groups is full entitlement to, and sharing in, citizenship rights and privileges.

Australia provides a rich political continent for studying citizenship in a modern constitutional democracy. Despite its unpromising beginning in this regard in the late eighteenth century as a series of isolated European penal colonies established by an imperial power through occupation and conquest of the original Aboriginal peoples, Australia, along with New Zealand, soon became something of a laboratory for democratic politics. Transportation of convicts was terminated, colonial self-government easily achieved, democratic innovations such as the secret ballot pioneered and, beginning with South Australia in 1894, female franchise implemented. In the closing decade of the nineteenth century, the Australian Commonwealth Constitution was drafted by elected delegates and endorsed by the people in referendum before being formally passed by the imperial parliament at Westminster. While links with Britain and the formal vestiges of monarchy were retained by deliberate choice, Australia had become one of the most progressive and innovative democracies in the world.

However, the most ignoble side of Australian politics was the treatment of Aboriginal peoples. Under the introduced law, they, by virtue of being born here, were British subjects. Similarly, from 1948, when Commonwealth legislation created the legal entity of 'Australian citizen', Aborigines, along with other Australians, automatically became citizens. However, even though subject to being ruled by the early British and colonial regimes and, after federation, by Commonwealth and State governments, Aboriginal peoples were denied a share in ruling. They had no say about being subjected to such rule, which was imposed by force, and no share in the rights and entitlements that ordinary citizens enjoyed. This book tells the institutional story of how Aboriginal peoples were subjected to being ruled but were denied a share in citizenship rights and entitlements; how they were treated as citizens without rights in their own land.

As we approach the centenary of federation, which is doubly significant as the centenary of the nation and the centenary of the Constitution, there has been much discussion about the establishment of a republic with an Australian head of state and about formally terminating the monarchic link. This issue has generated a surprising amount of heat and stimulated a good deal of historical investigation and argument about why Australia remained a formal monarchy at federation and what continuation of that status entails. Less prominent, but in our view much more significant than the issue of formal monarchic head of state, is that of Australian citizenship and the treatment of Aboriginal peoples as citizens without rights for most of our colonial and national history.

True, the reconciliation process has been in place for some time and has been given impetus by the 1992 landmark High Court decision in *Mabo v. Queensland*, which recognised native title, and the subsequent passage of the *Native Title Act*. And there is currently a burst of public and scholarly interest in civic education and in the concept of Australian citizenship. There has been a major gap, however, in understanding the institutional definition and development of Australian citizenship. How could Aborigines have been systematically excluded from the key rights and privileges of citizenship while having its formal shell? What is it about Australian citizenship that allowed Aborigines to be citizens without rights and, prior to the 1948 *Nationality and Citizenship Act*, subjects without the normal citizenship rights that other Australian subjects enjoyed?

Understanding the shameful status of Aboriginal people as citizens without rights for much of our political history is not simply a prerequisite for proper reconciliation as we approach the constitutional centenary. It is also necessary for understanding Australian citizenship *per se*. In order to be citizens without rights, as Aboriginal people were, citizenship had to be an empty category, and it was. The Australian founders eschewed putting any core positive notion of citizenship in the Constitution precisely to allow the States to perpetuate their discriminatory regimes and to enable the new Commonwealth parliament to implement a national regime of discrimination. As subsequent chapters show, the States not only continued but tightened up their discriminatory practices while the Commonwealth similarly availed itself of the opportunity by excluding Aborigines from voting and from receiving basic welfare benefits and entitlements.

Citizenship has traditionally been an exclusory category because citizens have basic rights and privileges that non-citizens do not share. The divide between citizens and non-citizens has often depended not so much on geography as on the fact of belonging to a particular race, religion or class, or some combination of these. With the expansion of regimes and the movement of peoples, original inhabitants have at times increased their power and wealth by precluding newcomers from citizenship. The early modern Italian republics like Venice operated in this way, as do some of the modern Arab nations. In such regimes the key divide is between citizens and non-citizens, those who enjoy full political rights and those who do not. In egalitarian Australia, however, subjecthood or citizenship was easily acquired – one simply had to be born here – but at the same time one's formal status as a citizen meant very little. The crucial divide was between those citizens who had rights and privileges and those who were denied them. Particular rights and privileges, from the crucial political right of voting to the social right of mothers to receive the maternity allowance, were controlled by separate legislation and administered by regimes that were characterised by their standard disqualification of 'aboriginal natives' of Australia and 'aboriginal natives' of other Asian and Pacific Island countries.

So, however rich Australia's democratic tradition and political culture may have been, Australian citizenship was empty and barren at its core and blatantly discriminatory in its parts. While such a flawed heritage obviously provides no positive standard for modern citizenship practice, its recognition is essential for mature reflection on Australia's past development as a nation and on its future. Moreover, the institutional definition and development of Australian citizenship that excluded Aboriginal people for so long is a central part of Australian political history and practice which needs to be known and appreciated. This is not a 'black armband' view of history; rather it is the reality of how Australian citizenship was structured and how Aboriginal peoples were systematically excluded. We need to understand and appreciate these realities if we are to have a mature appreciation of our nation, which has been at least partly defined by such practices.

Australians, or at least the majority of Australians who have enjoyed its benefits, have been inclined to take citizenship for granted. Our study of Aborigines and Australian citizenship shows just how precious it is, and how its denial can be a fundamental deprivation for those who are excluded. The Australian case illustrates only too well the significance of each of T.H. Marshall's three elements of modern democratic citizenship – civil, political and social – and how they are interrelated.

According to Marshall's influential account, which has shaped modern thinking on citizenship, there are three main components of citizenship, or three kinds of human rights, which have developed cumulatively during the last three centuries: the civil element, which developed largely in the eighteenth century, consisted of the rights necessary for individual freedom, such as the right to freedom of speech and the right to own property; the political element, which largely arose during the nineteenth century, entailed the right to take part in political processes, most importantly as a voter; and the social element, which has received its greatest definition during the twentieth century, was the third and least easily defined category, to which Marshall most closely connected the educational system and social services. This social element covered a range of rights, from one's right to a modicum of economic security to the 'right to share to the full in the social heritage and to live the life of a civilised being according to the standards prevailing in the society'.[1]

Our account of Aborigines and Australian citizenship, which is a political and institutional one focusing on the constitutional system, legislation, regulations and public administration, explores how Aborigines have been specifically excluded from certain rights in all three of Marshall's categories. We do so not on the assumption that this is the only way to write about the topic of Aborigines and citizenship. A number of writers in Australia have recently been considering the ways in which developments in the recognition of Aboriginal rights may inform new understandings of citizenship.[2] Their work adds to a growing body of literature that is broadening the study of citizenship by concentrating on its less formal aspects.[3] While these less formal social and cultural aspects of citizenship and community structures, practices and values are crucially important and an integral part of the total picture, we leave their articulation to other writers.

Nor do we pretend to speak for Aboriginal people or to give their account of what it was like to be treated as citizens without rights in their own land. It would be inappropriate for us to do so and it is not a task that we have set ourselves. At the same time, it is essential for any student of Australian history to engage with indigenous perspectives on this issue, and this is becoming an easier task, with the growing body of excellent literature that is being written by Aboriginal authors.

This literature, as with Aboriginal perspectives, is diverse. It ranges from the memoirs of political agitators, such as Faith Bandler, Roberta Sykes, Kevin Gilbert and Charles Perkins,[4] to more reflective pieces on what it has meant to grow up Aboriginal in Australia. Books in the latter category often detail moving personal testimonies about the devaluation of Aboriginal identity that the regimes discussed in this book were so centrally implicated in bringing about. Most famous among these would be Sally Morgan's *My Place,* but others include Margaret Tucker's *If Everyone Cared,* Ruby Langford Ginibi's *Don't Take Your Love to Town* and *Real Deadly,* and most recently Wayne King's *Black Hours.*[5] In addition, Aboriginal academics are now coming through university departments (although still in insufficient numbers) and are contributing to academic debates both in their teaching and writing.[6]

Our focus is on government institutions and practices, combining insights from an interdisciplinary approach that draws from political science, history, law and public policy. We aim to give an account of the public articulation of citizenship and the treatment of Aborigines through constitutional provision, legislative definition, administrative practice and judicial determination.

Citizenship in Australia is complicated because of the multiplicity of governments involved. Prior to federation, the various colonies had established their own regimes to govern Aboriginal people which, although there was a good deal of similarity and copying, differed in important respects, as chapters 1 and 2 on Victoria and Queensland show. For example, Victoria drew a sharp distinction between 'aboriginal natives' and those it accorded the offensive, but administratively much-used label of 'half-castes'. The Victorian government provided meagre sustenance for those in the former category on special stations and forced the latter to merge into white society. Queensland, in contrast, defined 'aboriginal natives' more broadly. If Queensland's treatment was less divisive among Aborigines, it was politically more oppressive because Queensland legislated to preclude Aborigines from voting while Victoria did not. The Commonwealth Constitution was designed to allow this mosaic of discriminatory but somewhat divergent colonial practices to remain in place, as chapter 3 shows.

Federation added a new sphere of national government with large but by no means exclusive citizenship powers. Although the national government lacked a specific power to pass laws with respect to Aboriginal people, the Commonwealth might have enhanced the status of Aborigines by including them in all the rights and entitlements that it controlled, such as the Commonwealth franchise, sickness and disability pensions and maternity benefits. Moreover, it could have used its ample taxing and spending powers to provide for Aboriginal people directly or to leverage better treatment for them from the States. Or when it took over the administration of the Northern Territory from

South Australia in 1911, the Commonwealth could have put in place a model regime for the States to emulate. It did none of these.

Rather, as chapter 4 explains, one of the first and most significant acts of the new Commonwealth parliament was its passing of the *Commonwealth Franchise Act 1902.* This legislation is justly famous for enfranchising women but, and this is not so well known, it barred Aboriginal people from the vote. Instead of adopting the best State practice of the time, as it did in following South Australia and Western Australia to enfranchise women, the Commonwealth followed Queensland and Western Australia in adopting the worst practice by excluding Aborigines from the vote.

This exclusion was championed by senators from Western Australia and Queensland and was achieved through an amendment to the franchise bill which eventually won support in both houses of parliament. Such exclusion went further than the policy in the other four States, as was forcefully pointed out by the government spokesman, Richard O'Connor, whose rhetoric stands as an indictment of Australia's treatment of its Aboriginal people for the next sixty years:

> It would be a monstrous thing, an unheard of piece of savagery on our part, to treat the aboriginals, whose land we were occupying, in such a manner as to deprive them absolutely of any right to vote in their own country, simply on the ground of their colour, and because they were aboriginals ... Although the aboriginals in New South Wales, Victoria, Tasmania, and South Australia, had the right to vote through all these years ... now under the Commonwealth, with the liberal views we are supposed to entertain and to bring into the legislative field, we are asked to take away from the sons of those people for ever the right to vote.[7]

Yet, despite such rhetoric, the Commonwealth did precisely that and set the legislative paradigm for excluding 'aboriginal natives' from subsequent citizenship rights and entitlements.

The Constitution was not to blame for such exclusion of Aboriginal people, as chapter 3 explains. Out of deference for the ongoing democratic practice that would determine such matters, the Constitution was drafted so as not to encroach unduly on the established regimes of the States, and it provided no positive standard against discrimination. The Constitution barely mentioned Aboriginal people, and the two occasions on which it did were by way of exclusion – from the section 51(26) race power and the section 127 census count. Contrary to widespread misunderstanding, such exclusion did not require or entail exclusion from citizenship. That was done through normal legislation and administrative practices by successive parliaments, governments and bureaucrats and was undone by amending and changing those discriminatory laws and practices, a process that largely occurred in the 1960s. Just as Aboriginal people were prevented from voting by the 1902 *Commonwealth Franchise Act*, they were granted the Commonwealth vote by 1962 amendments to the successor electoral Act.

After federation, as chapter 5 shows, the States tightened their discriminatory regimes and became increasingly more authoritarian in dealing with Aborigines. This was particularly the case in the 1930s, when it became clear that the Aboriginal race was not going to die out. The emphasis in Aboriginal policy shifted from protecting the last members of an ancient people to confining and regulating what white society considered to be an undesirable racial minority. Powers to remove Aboriginal people to reserves and keep them there under tight controls were increased. There was also more concern with merging or absorbing 'half-castes' into white society, as procedures for taking children from their mothers and communities were refined.

In response to such increased oppression, Aboriginal people became more effective in organising and demanding their rights in the 1920s and 1930s. But achieving the ordinary rights of citizenship was a slow and arduous process that was complicated by the patchwork of Commonwealth, State and Territory jurisdictions, as chapter 6 documents. Gaining formal 'Australian citizenship', along with other Australians in 1948, entailed no acquisition of basic citizenship rights for Aborigines. As Garfield Barwick pointed out in reiterating the legal structure of citizenship, there were 'nine different "citizenships" in Australia' and each had its own set of qualifications and disqualifications which were enshrined in discrete pieces of legislation. The States varied in the extent of their oppressive laws and harsh discretionary powers, with Western Australia, Queensland and the Northern Territory (under Commonwealth administration) having the largest Aboriginal populations and the most severe regimes. Moreover, the States often controlled, either formally or informally, the exercise of Commonwealth rights. For example, in 1949 the Commonwealth vote was extended to those Aborigines entitled to vote in the States, but of course this excluded Aborigines in Western Australia and Queensland. Many other Aborigines in those States – such as those officially labelled as 'half-castes' and, after 1949, those who were or had been members of the defence force – were entitled to the Commonwealth franchise in their own right, but were never enrolled. The 1961 House of Representatives Select Committee, whose report led to the Commonwealth's enfranchisement of all adult Aborigines in 1962, found that only 57 out of 659 Torres Strait Islanders who served in the Torres Strait Islands Regiment were enrolled in a local electoral division.

As chapter 6 also shows, the 1967 referendum provided no legal watershed in the citizenship status of Aborigines. While its passage was broadly contemporaneous with the removal of various restrictive measures – a factor that has probably led to much of the myth that surrounds the 1967 referendum – the referendum did not grant Aborigines citizenship. All voting restrictions, for instance, had already been dismantled when the referendum was passed. The referendum merely altered the Constitution's two references to Aborigines, giving the Commonwealth the power to pass laws specifically for Aborigines and requiring Aborigines to be counted in census statistics. While of more limited legal significance than many commentaries upon it suggest, the 1967 referendum was still symbolically very significant both for Aborigines, who worked tirelessly for its success, and for Australians generally, who voted overwhelmingly for it. With the support of just over 90 per cent of voters this was far and away the most popular referendum ever carried. The full dismantling of restrictions to citizenship rights and entitlements for Aborigines, however, was a much more painstaking and drawn-out process.

In our final chapter we consider how the recent recognition of indigenous rights – particularly native title to land – represents a political step forward for Aborigines, beyond the citizenship rights belatedly obtained by them. This political step forward is still far from being a social step forward, but it has already been subject to criticisms that, as we show, have bordered on the hysterical. Whether this latest development in the rights of Aborigines will, like the legislation for the first federal franchise, see the Commonwealth government in its least noble light, remains to be seen.

Our book gives a detailed account of the institutional definition and development of Australian citizenship as it has applied to Aborigines from colonial times, through federation and up to the present time when indigenous rights to land have been recognised and claims to self-determination are being debated. Our study examines the patchwork of variegated State and Commonwealth regimes, and shows how Aborigines were citizens without rights for much of this time, and were subjected to discriminatory practices of quite extraordinary severity and detail. The sheer amount of legislative ingenuity and administrative effort that went into devising and maintaining these discriminatory regimes is truly astonishing, and the formalised injustice and inhumanity that they embodied is shameful. Researching and documenting these regimes has taken years of painstaking work, even though our study is by no means comprehensive.

Our purpose in so doing is first and foremost the scholarly one of giving an account of this important topic. While the story of Australia's treatment of its Aboriginal peoples as citizens without rights is deeply shameful, this is not a good reason for not knowing about it or acknowledging it. As Australians take stock of a century of nationhood in the closing decade of the twentieth century, we can be justly proud of many achievements as a democratic and decent nation. But we must also recognise the terrible injustice that has been done to Australia's indigenous people through conquest and discrimination. This is so fundamental a political truth about Australian citizenship and Australia's founding as a nation that its omission or concealment entails distortion or gross dishonesty. The challenge for the twenty-first century – our second century of nationhood – is to recognise the special status of indigenous people and their rights not only to land but also to self-determination within the Australian nation.

A central theme of the book is that the citizenship of all Australians is interconnected with that of Aborigines. Treating Aborigines as citizens without rights fundamentally compromised Australian citizenship in the past because, to allow such discrimination, citizenship had to be an empty concept, even a deeply hypocritical one. Working out a satisfactory system of self-determination for indigenous people provides Australians with a rich opportunity to redefine democratic citizenship so that active sharing in ruling, which is the nobler part of citizenship, is enhanced not only for Aboriginal people but for all Australians.

CHAPTER 1

The Citizenship Divide in Colonial Victoria

> At the close of . . . seven years, [the half-castes] should have no further claim on the Board or Government, but be accounted in all respects free and equal citizens of the colony.[1]
>
> *Victorian Board for the Protection of the Aborigines, 1884*

One of the lowest points in the history of race relations in Australia came in 1902 when, in a late amendment to the franchise bill, every 'aboriginal native of Australia' was excluded from the federal franchise. This exclusionary clause, as we will show in chapter 4, was systematically defined and refined by the federal bureaucracy, and utilised by successive federal governments for over six decades to deny Aboriginal Australians citizenship rights and benefits, including the maternity allowance, invalid and old-age pensions, and even overseas travel.

A federal political system such as Australia's entails two levels of government and dual citizenship.[2] Consequently, the rights and benefits of citizenship are not the sole preserve of the federal government. The States, with their residual powers over areas such as health, education, land, and civil and criminal law, are significant in determining citizenship rights and entitlements. Moreover, since the States predated the Commonwealth as self-governing colonies, their established colonial citizenship regimes were influential in shaping the design of the new Commonwealth Constitution. Indeed, a major reason for the new federal government not being given a specific constitutional power to make laws with respect to Aboriginal people was the consideration that Aboriginal people were already sufficiently 'taken care of' under State laws.

In this chapter, we concentrate on the policies of one colony, Victoria, during the period leading up to federation and shortly afterwards, when a *de facto* – if not until 1948 *de jure* – citizenship policy was first being formulated and implemented federally in Australia.

Central to the new Commonwealth's approach to citizenship was the term 'aboriginal native'. People who came within that category were denied, in addition to the franchise, basic benefits such as the maternity allowance and invalid and old-age pensions. This exclusionary regime was meticulously enforced to keep Aboriginal people as non-citizens for more than half a century. From the very beginning, however, those of mixed ethnicity, who were given the offensive name 'half-castes', were considered not to be 'aboriginal natives' and hence were not denied federal citizenship rights and benefits.

We show in this chapter that colonial Victoria in 1886 pioneered the sharp distinction made federally between 'aboriginal natives' and 'half-castes'. In the Victorian case, the distinction was used ruthlessly to exclude 'half-castes' from special stations where the rest of Victoria's Aboriginal people were given modest support by the Board for the Protection of Aborigines.[3] Perversely, 'half-castes' were forcibly removed from stations and denied supporting benefits in the name of making them 'free and equal citizens', a status denied to 'aboriginal natives'.

In this chapter, we pay particular attention to the formulation and implementation of the 1886 'merging of the half-castes' policy in Victoria, a policy that saw an administrative board draw a rigid line to separate one group of Aborigines ('aboriginal natives') from another ('half-castes'). For these latter Aborigines, the State, despite the injustices of the preceding decades, would now deny that it owed them any special responsibility.

We have chosen to focus initially on Victoria for two important reasons. First, as several authors have noted, Victoria was the first colonial government to enact a comprehensive scheme to govern the administration of Aboriginal affairs.[4] The fact that it was the first colony to seek comprehensively to regulate the lives of its Aboriginal inhabitants alone makes it a worthy subject of study. But, furthermore, Victoria, with its relatively small number of Aborigines, was and remains a State whose policies towards them could never really pose a serious threat to the State's finances, election outcomes, or land use.

Noel Butlin has estimated that the Victorian Aboriginal population prior to 1788 may well have been in excess of 50,000. Others suggest the figure was a more modest one of between 5000 and 15,000.[5] Disease, violence, and incomplete census methods resulted in the official Aboriginal population in Victoria in 1836 being recorded as between 6000 and 7000.[6] By 1863 the official figure was 1908, and by 1877 only 1067. The *Victorian Year-Book* reported that as few as 565 Aborigines resided in Victoria in 1891, a figure that gradually increased over the next twenty years.[7]

Even if it is accepted that these figures represent an underestimation, Victorian policies towards Aborigines could hardly be said to have been motivated by the fears entertained in States like Western Australia and Queensland, where Aborigines were more numerous. The fear generated about Aborigines in Western Australia was manifested during the final debates leading to the fixing of the federal franchise in 1902, when the belief that Aborigines would outnumber whites in some Western Australian electorates was enough to persuade wavering politicians to exclude Aborigines from the federal franchise. As one member of the House of Representatives put it:

> While it may be admitted that in New South Wales and Victoria the black vote is a negligible quantity, of no consequence one way or the other, it is a very serious matter in the northern parts of Western Australia, where the state of affairs is such that no democrat could for one moment tolerate the extension of the franchise to the aboriginals.[8]

Even notable liberals like Senator Richard O'Connor, who argued strongly if unsuccessfully against excluding Aborigines from the franchise, modified their once firm stance in order to secure the passage of the franchise bill. O'Connor said:

> I took a very strong view that an aboriginal ought to be allowed to have his vote . . . But the other House has taken the opposite view . . . for the reason that, while in New South Wales, Victoria, and other States there are a large number of aboriginals who may be very well intrusted with the franchise which they possess, in Western Australia there are a large number who, living in a state of semi-civilization . . . might become registered.[9]

It is well known that Queensland and Western Australian governments enacted oppressive regimes to deal with their large Aboriginal populations. Given the above considerations, one might have expected Victoria's policies around the turn of the century to have been relatively more generous and liberal towards Aboriginal people. Indeed, Victoria's approach to the administration of Aboriginal affairs should have provided the more positive influence on federal policy. But it did not. Indeed, our argument is that Victorian policies towards Aborigines, despite one significant exception, were entirely congruous with the policy of exclusion that was implemented by the federal government in the first decades of this century.

The Franchise: Exclusion by Other Means

Victoria did differ from States like Queensland and Western Australia in never specifically excluding Aborigines from the franchise. Theoretically, Aboriginal men could vote in Victorian elections from 1856, following the adoption of the Victorian Constitution the year before. The Constitution and subsequent electoral Acts made no mention of any exclusion of Aboriginal voters. Similarly, Aboriginal women theoretically could have voted from 1908, when the *Adult Suffrage Act* which enfranchised Victorian women also made no exceptions for Aboriginal voters.[10]

However, other obstacles stood in the way. From 1856 and through the period under discussion in this chapter, anybody in receipt of relief as an 'inmate' of a charitable institution was not eligible to be put on an electoral roll.[11] Consequently, one would have thought that Aboriginal men who lived on stations or received provisions from depots would have been ineligible to vote. Despite all this, Diane Barwick claims that Aborigines on the Ramahyuck Aboriginal station were enrolled in 1878, but, unfortunately, does not cite her evidence for this claim.[12] Other evidence from the late nineteenth century suggests that Aborigines rarely voted. John Murray, who would become Premier of Victoria, said in the Legislative Assembly in 1895 that Aborigines did not have the vote, and no-one stood to contradict him.[13] A similar scenario occurred in the federal parliament only a few years later, when Sir William Lyne argued that Victorian Aborigines did not have the vote.[14] Our own limited search of Victorian electoral records reveals evidence of only a very small number of Aborigines voting around the turn of the century.[15]

Suffice it to say that an Aboriginal man in nineteenth century Victoria would need to have been very determined to vote, first to contradict the popular perception that he was not entitled to vote, and then to convince an electoral officer that he was not in receipt of charitable relief. Further, there is every reason to doubt that Aboriginal men would have felt inclined to vote anyway. Compulsory voting did not exist in Victoria until 1926, and one can well imagine that the combination of institutional obstruction and personal disaffection would have deterred most Aborigines from voting.[16]

Whether or not Aboriginal men were actually on the Victorian electoral roll prior to 1901 would become crucial in determining whether they could vote federally. In a provision designed to protect the rights of the women who had already won the vote in some States, section 41 of the Commonwealth Constitution provided that people who had the vote at State level could not be prevented from voting federally. Accordingly, the *Commonwealth Franchise Act*, which otherwise excluded Aborigines, gave the vote to those Aborigines who had the vote at State level (by means of an exception required by section 41 of the Constitution). But, as Pat Stretton and Christine Finnimore have shown, this provision was defined narrowly to mean that only those voters actually enrolled at the State level prior to 1902 were entitled to the protection of section 41.[17] For Aboriginal men in Victoria, this meant that they could only exercise the federal franchise if they were enrolled in Victoria prior to 1902. According to an estimation prepared by the Commonwealth Electoral Office in 1922, less than 100 Victorian Aborigines had taken advantage of the protection offered by section 41 and enrolled federally.[18]

While it is clear that most Victorian Aborigines did not vote at federal or State elections, their eligibility to vote in Victoria does represent a significant difference between Victorian law and the contemporary franchise laws in force in some other Australian jurisdictions. Restrictions on Aboriginal voters were not removed until 1962 at the Commonwealth level, in Western Australia, and in the Northern Territory, whereas Queensland Aborigines did not get the vote until 1965. But the formal difference between Victoria and other jurisdictions was minimised in practice because so few Aboriginal men after 1856, and Aboriginal women after 1908, voted. The reason for Victoria's non-exclusion of Aborigines from the franchise appears to have been rather less than worthy: their numbers were not significant enough to bother excluding them from the franchise, and those in receipt of government support were excluded anyway.

Notwithstanding the eligibility of Aboriginal men to vote, the last decades of the nineteenth century saw Victorian Aborigines specifically excluded from the rights and benefits of citizenship in much the same way that all Aboriginal Australians would be excluded in the new Commonwealth of Australia. A policy of segregation, followed in 1886 by a ruthless policy that divided 'half-castes' from 'aboriginal natives', saw the term 'aboriginal native', and its analogues 'pure blood' and 'full blood', become the key point of division between those included and those excluded from citizenship. Moreover, as would happen at the federal level, the responsibility for devising and implementing Victorian policies towards Aborigines predominantly lay not with parliament, but with an extraordinarily meticulous and driven bureaucratic regime.

The Victorian Regime: Creating a Citizenship Divide

From the time of European settlement in Victoria in 1834, the Port Phillip Protectorate (1838–49) and the actions of subsequent Victorian governments sought to remove Aborigines to isolated areas. Aborigines were not systematically rounded up, as in other colonies, but inducements were offered, and some level of sanctuary from white society was provided, by the dozen or so reserves, stations and missions established in Victoria.[19] These became special precincts where Aborigines were supported materially by the State. The price for this support was a tight regulatory regime that denied basic citizenship rights and privileges enjoyed by other Victorians.

From the establishment of the protectorate, Aborigines in Victoria occupied the special position of 'protected persons' rather than citizens. Although Aborigines were, by virtue of birth in one of the King's dominions, British subjects who were subject to the law, they were not entitled to the benefits of citizenship. Aborigines, according to this philosophy, needed to be protected from the evils of settlement. This philosophy informed the establishment of reserves and stations, and it also justified other measures, such as the passing of laws preventing the sale of alcohol to Aborigines.[20]

The year 1860 marked a significant turning point in the governance of Aborigines in Victoria. By this stage four Aboriginal stations were in operation. Following the report of a select committee in 1858, parliament decided to reserve land for several tribes and provide funds for food and clothing.[21] Overseeing the implementation of this was, from 1860, a 'Central Board Appointed to Watch over the Interests of the Aborigines'. The first Board was appointed by the Governor and consisted of seven members, of whom three were members of parliament.[22] In its first annual report, the Board recommended that permanent reserves be set aside for Aborigines and that 'they should be confined as closely as possible to those reserves'. The Board also recommended that parliament legislate to enable it to order where Aborigines should reside.[23]

Nine years later, Victoria became the first colonial government to establish a comprehensive system of Aboriginal administration. In 1869 the Victorian parliament passed *An Act to Provide for the Protection and Management of the Aboriginal Natives of Victoria.* The Act gave the Governor the power to prescribe where Aborigines could live, and to distribute money granted by parliament. The Act also gave legislative basis to the Board, which would now be titled the 'Board for the Protection of Aborigines'. The Act defined 'aboriginal' to include 'every aboriginal native of Australia and every aboriginal half-caste or child of a half-caste, such half-caste or child habitually associating and living with aboriginals'.[24] Already, the term 'aboriginal native' was being used in contradistinction to 'half-caste'.

For the next ninety years, the Board for the Protection of Aborigines oversaw the operation of Victoria's Aboriginal stations. The Board's

Chairman was the Chief Secretary of Victoria, who was also the Minister responsible for Aborigines. He rarely attended the Board's fortnightly (and later monthly) meetings, which were usually presided over by the Vice-Chairman. The Board's day-to-day representatives were the Secretary and the General Inspector, two positions that were merged for much of the period under discussion and performed by one person in full-time public service employment. Managers of the Aboriginal stations, and local guardians in areas without stations, were appointed by the Board, whose budget was voted annually by parliament. During the years 1880 to 1910, parliamentarians generally made up a minority of the Board's members.[25] As shall be seen later, the General Inspector and Secretary was the most significant determinant of Board policy, and was responsible for ensuring the compliance of station managers with the Board's policy.[26] By 1874 the Board controlled six Aboriginal stations: Coranderrk, situated close to Healesville; Framlingham, near Warrnambool; Lake Condah, to the north of Portland; Lake Hindmarsh (or Ebenezer), in the Wimmera; Ramahyuck (or Lake Wellington); and Lake Tyers, both situated in Gippsland. Around 500 Aborigines lived at these stations, roughly half the Aboriginal population of Victoria.[27]

During the first thirty years of the Board's existence, Aborigines were governed by an extraordinary level of regulation. The Governor's power to prescribe the place where Aborigines could reside was vested in the Board and used to control individuals. The following type of order commonly appeared in the *Victorian Government Gazette*:

> In pursuance of the power given . . . the Governor in Council has made an Order prescribing the Aboriginal Station at Coranderrk as the place where the aboriginal native named 'Baird' shall reside.[28]

The first comprehensive series of regulations governing Aborigines was gazetted in 1871. Nineteen regulations established, among other things, the Board's power to govern the conditions on which any Aboriginal could be employed in Victoria. The regulations set out the requirements to be completed in any contracts of employment lasting longer than three months. The contracts had then to be submitted to the Board for its approval. Alternatively, Aborigines were able to enter their own binding contracts of employment, but only if they first received a certificate from the Board. The certificate listed the age, height, and any distinguishing features of the holder.[29]

Testimony to the extraordinary level of control exercised over the lives of Aborigines was this regulation of 1880:

> Every aboriginal male under 14 years of age, and also all unmarried aboriginal females under the age of 18 years, shall, when so required by the person in charge of any station in connection with or under the control of the [Board for the Protection of Aborigines], reside, and take their meals, and sleep in any building set apart for such purposes.[30]

The citizenship divide, which is the focus of this chapter, was introduced into the Victorian administration of Aboriginal affairs in 1886, when the Victorian parliament amended the 1869 Act with what became known as the 'merging the half-castes' Act.[31] This Act was significant because it drew a sharp divide between citizens and non-citizens. Equally significant was the fact that the new policy, adopted in the Act, was the creation of an administrative board, rather than a government department or responsible minister.

The central provision in the 1886 Act was section 4, according to which the category of 'aboriginals' was defined much more narrowly than it had been in 1869. Those who were deemed to be 'half-caste' were now excluded from the definition, with a couple of exceptions: if the 'half-caste' was thirty-four years of age or older and lived or associated with Aborigines; if, in the case of a woman, she was married to an Aboriginal; or, if the individual had been granted a licence by the Board. All those people now excluded from the definition were to be provided with rations for three years, and the Board was given power to 'exercise care and oversight in the management or condition of half-castes' for seven years.[32] The 1869 and 1886 Acts were consolidated, with no relevant changes, into a new *Aborigines Act* in 1890.

Effectively, the 1886 Act put in place a policy of merging 'half-castes' into the white community, while 'aboriginal natives' would spend their remaining years on stations and reserves. The object of the legislation, Alfred Deakin explained in the Legislative Assembly, was to carry out certain recommendations of the Board. The legislation 'was not a Government Bill; it was the Bill of the Board; and it was introduced chiefly with the object of making the half-castes useful members of society, and gradually relieving the State of the cost of their maintenance'. Indeed, the Board had wanted to go much further than the Act ultimately did. An original clause, removed just prior to the passing of the bill, had provided that:

> Any able-bodied half-caste found lodging, living, or wandering in company with any aboriginal, and not being able to give a good account of himself, should be deemed an idle and disorderly person, and liable to imprisonment for any time not exceeding twelve months, with or without hard labour.[33]

Another clause, struck out at the last minute, would have continued the power that enabled a Justice of the Peace to decide, simply by looking at someone, whether or not they were Aboriginal or 'half-caste'.[34]

This swift and major change in policy had been masterminded by the Board for the Protection of Aborigines. The earliest documented evidence of the Board's policy to merge 'half-castes' is a letter from the Board's secretary to the Victorian Chief Secretary, dated 8 June 1881. According to the letter, the Board hoped 'to get rid of all the half-castes who are capable of providing for themselves'.[35] Less than a month later, on 6 July, the Board adopted the new policy.[36] As Michael Christie and others have shown, this new policy was contrary to the Board's stated position in its report for 1881, and was also contrary to the recommendations made by a Royal Commission only four years earlier. The Royal Commissioners had carried out an inquiry into the 'present condition of the Aborigines', and had reported that: 'The semblance of attention to outward appearance, and a ready conformity to conventional rules, have probably led to the misapprehension that any sound distinction could be drawn between the Aboriginal native and the half-caste.'[37]

Three factors motivated the Board's change in policy. The first, as indicated above, was the financial saving to be made by preventing Aborigines with some European ancestry from drawing on the funds administered by the Board. In a statement that was virtually an early draft of the 1886 legislation, the Board argued: 'The object aimed at is that the process of merging should be completed as soon as possible, after which all responsibility of the Government as regards [the half-castes] would cease – *finality* being thus attained.'[38] The second factor informing the Board's change in policy was the social Darwinist view that the Aborigines were a 'dying race'. European racial attitudes increasingly came to view 'full blood' Aborigines as belonging to a race that would disappear within a few generations. Meanwhile, the philosophy held that people of mixed descent would in a short time be able to pass as white. An article in the *Age* newspaper in January 1888 summed up this view:

> It may be doubted whether the Australian aborigine would ever have advanced much beyond the status of the neo-lithic races in which we found him, and we need not therefore lament his disappearance. All that can be expected of us is that we shall make his last days as free from misery as we can.

But this obligation did not extend to those of mixed descent:

> Parliament has sought to provide against the growth of a permanent pauper class by directing the gradual elimination of the half-caste element from the native settlements and its gradual absorption in the general population.[39]

By isolating 'full bloods' on reserves and forcing 'half-castes' to merge with white society, the Board was playing its part to ensure that 'finality' would be achieved.[40] The third and most direct concern driving the Board is revealed by the timing of its change in policy, which coincided with a parliamentary inquiry into the operations of the Coranderrk station. Michael Christie has shown how the threatened break-up of Coranderrk, and the dismissal of the station's manager, led to considerable unrest at the station during the 1870s and early 1880s. On several occasions, Aborigines walked the forty miles to Melbourne to put their protest to parliament, and they wrote letters to newspapers in support of their cause. Most of the 100 or so Coranderrk Aborigines were of mixed descent, and Christie has convincingly argued that the Board's policy was designed to silence them.[41] When a deputation from Coranderrk came to Melbourne to outline their concerns to the Chief Secretary, the *Argus* newspaper recorded the official line: that the station had been turned into a 'nursery for half-castes, giving employment to a few, but entailing great expense on the country'. The Board's new policy would 'apply Coranderrk to the legitimate purpose for which it had been established'.[42]

There is a gap in current historical understanding regarding the implementation and significance of the 'half-caste' policy in Victoria. Michael Christie's book is an excellent account of the administration of Victorian Aboriginal affairs in the years 1835 to 1886. Peter Corris' insightful work also stops with the passing of the 1886 Act. Jan Critchett has written a thesis that provides some analysis of the way the new policy impacted upon Aborigines at two stations. This has since been generalised and published as a history of the Framlingham station. Diane Barwick and Linda Wilkinson have also considered the effect of the Act on residents at Framlingham. Meanwhile, Phillip Pepper and Tess De Araugo have looked at the Act's impact on Aborigines in Gippsland. Further, Bain Attwood, in his 1989 *The Making of the Aborigines,* considers the background to the 1886 Act, but remarks that the full story of the Act's implementation remains to be told.[43]

In our view, this Victorian policy of separating 'Aborigines' from 'half-castes', and merging the latter into white society as 'free and equal citizens of the colony',[44] was an important precursor to national citizenship practices. By investigating the meticulous and callous implementation of the Victorian policy, we can preview the way in which the Commonwealth definition and administration of citizenship would develop in the early federation years.

Implementation: Making 'Free and Equal Citizens'

In its first annual report after the enactment of the new policy, a policy which for 'a long time the Board had been urging', the Board reported that it had already carefully explained the policy to all the 'half-castes' to whom the law applied. Letters had been written to station managers requesting them to acquaint the 'half-castes' with the provisions of the Act, and to give them notice that they must look out for employment or homes among the white population. Already, 60 out of the 233 people to whom the legislation applied had been moved off stations.[45]

Having succeeded in turning its policy into law, the Board was responsible for enforcing a division, which even it admitted was arbitrary, between 'Aboriginal' and 'half-caste'.[46] An earlier suggestion had been that the term 'mixed blood' be used instead of 'half-caste' in order that all who were not 'pure blacks' would come under the operation of the definition.[47] This was rejected in favour of the complex definition of 'half-caste' outlined earlier. The clinical and offensive racial analysis that this involved saw, on one occasion, one of the station managers, the General Inspector of the Board, and the Victorian Chief Secretary's office, engaged in a debate about whether a man who appeared to have some African heritage should be deemed a 'half-caste'.[48]

Unfortunately, only the written evidence of the Board's work remains. One can well imagine that most of the Board's uncompromising dealings with individuals were never documented. But the surviving records alone suggest that the Board was ruthless in implementing its policy. The following become a typical entry in the minute books of the Board: 'Mrs Rawlings applied for permission to allow her half-caste daughter with her child to live at Framlingham and to grant the usual supply of rations to them ... The Board refused to grant the application.'[49] The broad aim of the Board was spelt out in its meeting of February 1888:

> It was intended to place all the half-castes out as opportunity offered: and it was expected that by the end of six years the majority would have obtained employment. The pure aboriginals, of which there are about 300, will be kept until the end of their days: but the opinion of the

> board is that in the course of a very few years the whole of them will have passed away.[50]

According to the Board, 'pure aboriginals' were to be maintained until they died out. The Board's role would be to smooth the pillow of a dying race. Meanwhile, Aborigines with any European heritage would be forced into a new relationship with the State. Regardless of the life opportunities that had been denied them, and regardless of the inherent difficulties they faced in obtaining employment, housing and education in white society, these people would now be treated by the State as though they were not Aborigines. In pursuing this policy, the State effectively denied that it owed them any special responsibility.

The Board regularly sent letters to the managers of the stations saying that they could no longer legally support 'half-castes'.[51] Not satisfied with the level of compliance with the legislation, the Reverend Friedrich Hagenauer – a Moravian missionary and formerly religious superintendent at several Victorian stations, and now the Board's General Inspector and Secretary – wrote to the Chief Secretary requesting information as to what legal steps could be taken to remove these people from stations. The response was that they were trespassers, who should be given the appropriate notice.[52] After requesting police to post the 1886 Act at their police stations, the Board regularly requested them to remove Aborigines from stations.[53]

The Board often refused simple requests for rations, with little or no discussion of the predicament of the particular applicant.[54] Such an approach was exemplified in December 1889, when the Board simply told station managers that: 'Rations to those Half-Castes who come within the meaning of the Act must cease at the end of the present month.'[55]

When pushed to justify its apparent cold-heartedness, the Board had the temerity to state that it was 'carrying out an Act of Parliament not its own policy'.[56] The Board's disingenuousness is revealed by a letter from Hagenauer to Alexander Morrison, the Vice-Chairman of the Board, in which Hagenauer confessed that he had reluctantly approved the provision of rations to some 'half-castes' at Framlingham. But he had only done so, he wrote, because on the previous day members of parliament had said that the rations had to be given.[57] As this letter suggests, the Board applied a vigour to the implementation of its policy that was neither desired nor expected by politicians. Nor can the centrality of the policy to the Board's operations be understated. Morrison had written to the Chief Secretary recommending that Hagenauer, who had been acting General Inspector and Secretary since July 1889, be permanently appointed to the position, since there was no-one else 'who can so efficiently deal with the half-caste question'.[58] Morrison himself was aware of the politically sensitive nature of the Board's work, telling the Chief Secretary a month later that the Board was carrying out two important measures, 'the amalgamation of the half-castes among the general population of the Colony and the amalgamation of stations for the pure blacks'. The former was being rapidly accomplished, but the latter was being proceeded with 'very cautiously, so that there may not be the appearance . . . of any hardship'.[59]

When confronted with the possibility that some Aborigines, having attempted life off the station, might wish to return, the Board was adamant in its stance. Some of these people, according to the Board:

> who are too lazy to work, are endeavouring to return to the stations, which the Board under no circumstances can allow, as it would be entirely against the wise enactment of Parliament, and at the same time do great harm to the people themselves.[60]

Any Aborigines on stations who were thought to be sharing their rations with those who had been expelled were threatened with having their own rations stopped.[61] Equally, the Board was adamant that its line of division not be crossed in other ways. When residents of one station chose to go off the station and mix with Aborigines who had previously been removed, the Board threatened to transfer them to other stations if they did not return.[62]

From 1890, the lives of Aborigines would become even more regulated than ever before. In May 1890, twenty-six 'Regulations Relating to Half-Castes' were gazetted. These regulations prescribed, among other things, the conditions on which 'half-castes' could be licensed to reside at stations, the precise poundage of the rations they were to receive each week if they were so licensed, and the precise wording for the forms to be used when their children were sent out as apprentices or servants. These regulations subsequently formed part of the forty-six regulations gazetted in September 1890, following the enactment of the consolidating *Aborigines Act* in 1890.[63]

Nowhere was the intrusiveness and complexity of the Board's policy more apparent than in its regulation of marriage. In response to one query about whether a couple would have to leave their station after marrying, the General Inspector of the Board replied that had the couple married before 1 January 1887 the woman would have been deemed to be Aboriginal, but that since they had not married before that date she would have to be treated as a 'half-caste'.[64] Therefore, they could not marry and stay at the station. While the Board did not legally have the power to prevent people from marrying, it could and did exercise this power by threatening to remove people from stations and deny them rations if their marriage contravened the Board's policy.[65] The Board reported in 1888 that 'half-caste girls' should be discouraged from marrying 'pure blacks' because the 1886 legislation was 'framed to merge the half-caste population into the general community; by *encouraging* the intermarriage of blacks and half-castes that point would not be attained'.[66]

Jan Critchett writes about Tokas Johnson, a 'full-blood' Aboriginal, who wrote to Friedrich Hagenauer requesting permission to marry Ina Lancaster, a 'half-caste' woman. Upon being refused permission, Johnson wrote to the Chief Secretary of Victoria, who asked Hagenauer to explain. Hagenauer had told Johnson that he ought to marry either of two widowed 'half-caste' women, Mrs Saunders or Mrs Cousins. As Hagenauer later wrote, Mrs Saunders' age put her outside the operation of the new law. Were Johnson to marry Ina Lancaster, 'she will be considered in the eyes of the Law as a white woman, and an Aboriginal marrying such an one cannot claim rations nor reside with the Aborigines'. Johnson waited for six years after his request was made for permission to marry Lancaster, and never married her.[67]

The success of the Board in implementing its policies cannot be disputed. In 1892 the Board announced that while 233 'able-bodied half-castes' had resided on stations in 1886, as many as 224 had already left stations in the six years since the adoption of the new policy. The Board argued that in 'cases of real want or sickness . . . help is given to those who are in need of it'.[68] But even this minimalist claim is not supported by the existing record, which reveals little evidence of compassion or flexibility. On the contrary, the archive for the period leading up to federation, a period of crippling depression, is replete with examples of the Board's pedantic and clinical adherence to its policy. By 1895 the Board could announce that, in the space of six years, it had halved the Government's expenditure on Aborigines, and this without 'interfering with their comfort'.[69]

Removing Adolescents and Children: Facilitating 'Finality'

Without doubt the most offensive aspect of the 1886 policy was the Board's separation of adolescents and later children from their parents. The Board did not allow familial relationships to deter it from pursuing a rigid line of division between 'Aborigines' and 'half-castes'.[70]

After 1886, 'half-caste' adolescents aged fourteen and over who remained on stations were, with increasing force, told to leave. The Governor had power to prescribe the conditions on which 'half-caste infants' could be licensed or apprenticed out.[71] In the space of a few years, the Board was using this power to tell Aborigines, once they reached fourteen, that they would have to look after themselves.[72] In one instance, the Board asked the constable in charge of the Woodford depot to inform one woman that her daughter, having reached fourteen years of age, had now to provide for herself.[73] This letter to John Ross at Framlingham evidenced the Board's approach:

> In accordance with the Act of Parliament for the merging of Half-Castes with the white people of the Colony and the Regulations passed by the Governor in Council, your children over the age of 14 years [are to] be at once placed out to service among white people . . . Under no circumstances can rations be granted to you, if you will not carry out the established law of the land.[74]

The Board's policy was simply that 'half-caste children should be away from the influence of Blacks residing at the stations'.[75] The Board believed that idleness on the stations was detrimental to the children, and that the solution was to remove the children. Five Aborigines cogently disputed this in a letter to the *Warrnambool Standard*, where they argued that their children would not grow up idle if they had land of their own.[76]

By the turn of the century, the Board was no longer sending fourteen-year-olds out to service.[77] But, as we shall see, this was only because other methods had ensured that these and younger children had already been removed from stations, and from the care of the Board.

The Board took a little longer to develop a system under which it could separate children younger than fourteen years of age from their parents. Ever since 1871 the Governor had been empowered to send 'any aboriginal child neglected by its parents, or left unprotected' to an industrial or reformatory school. And, from 1886, the Governor was able to regulate for the transfer of any 'half-caste' orphan to the Department for Neglected Children or any other institution for orphan children. The Board regularly made use of this power, and it did not always wait for parents to die before sending their children to orphanages.[78]

According to the intricate definition of 'Aboriginal' contained in the relevant legislation from 1886, 'half-caste' children on stations who were unable to earn their own living were deemed to be Aboriginal. Thus, from 1886, the Board could pursue its policy of division and remove 'half-caste' children from stations as long as they were either orphans or could be deemed neglected.[79] The Board's minutes and correspondence files contain several references to mothers being told that their children could not live with them. One woman was told that her children were at an industrial school and were well, but she could not even be told where they were.[80] In a concise statement of the Board's approach, Hagenauer told one inquirer:

> The Board cannot grant rations to Henry Albert and family, as they are half castes, but every assistance will be given to place their children into the Industrial Schools and get them boarded out to respectable families.[81]

In 1896, Hagenauer told a policeman that he regretted that one child legally had to be returned to her parents because there was evidence that she and her siblings were not destitute. The children could not be sent to industrial schools.[82] Three years later, such evidence was no longer a barrier.

Late in 1899 a remarkable new regulation was gazetted that was even broader in its discretionary ambit:

> The Governor may for the better care custody and education of any aboriginal child order that such child be transferred to the care of the Department for Neglected Children or the Department for Reformatory Schools.[83]

Gone was the requirement that the child be neglected. Within a year the Board had decided that all 'half-caste' children on stations would be sent to industrial schools once they reached twelve years of age.[84] In its 1900 report, the Board stated:

> In connexion with the merging of the half-castes with the general population, the question of giving the boys and girls a suitable industrial training, in order that they may be enabled to earn their own living, has been well considered by the Board, and, after careful inquiry, the practice of transferring these half-caste children on leaving the station schools to the Department for Neglected Children has been adopted; and the system of training the boys on the farm at Bayswater, and the girls at the home for domestic service, has been working remarkably well. All the children already transferred are happy in their new surroundings, and there seems every likelihood of them becoming useful members of the community.[85]

The manager of the Lake Condah station, the Reverend Stähle, was satisfied with this new approach. In his report to the Board, he wrote that: 'As the blacks are dying out, and the Board removes the half-caste boys and girls by handing them over to the Industrial Schools Department, *finality is greatly facilitated*, and will, doubtless, be attained within a few years.'[86]

The Head of the Department for Neglected Children reported that by the end of 1900 two girls and eight boys, of whom one had since died, had been transferred to his department under the new regulation. He was glad to have been able to assist the Board to resolve an 'anxious and difficult problem, viz., how best to dispose of their young wards when paternal claims conflict with the higher welfare and interest of their children'.[87]

Clearly, the number of children affected by the new regulation was not significant, although, of course, the repercussions for the individuals were enormous. For our purposes, the significance of the new regulation is that it testifies to the length to which zealous administrators would go in ruthlessly extending the 1886 policy in pursuit of a certain 'finality' for Victoria's Aboriginal people. The regulation gave an administrative board a relatively unfettered power to remove children from their parents. Indeed, the fact that the architect and enforcer of such a program was an administrative board presents a disturbing commentary on the workings of responsible government in Victoria.[88]

Closing the Stations

The corollary to the removal of Aborigines from stations was the Board's desire to reduce the number of stations and thereby reduce the State's expenditure on Aborigines. As early as 1879 the Vice-Chairman of the Board had written that the Board anticipated that 'ultimately the last of the Victorian natives' would be gathered on two stations: Ebenezer and Lake Tyers.[89] Ten years later, the Board officially embraced this aim:

> As the number of pure blacks is very small, the Board unanimously adhere to their general policy with regard to the amalgamation of stations, with the twofold object of first and primarily improving the condition and comfort of the full blacks themselves, and in the second place of reducing the annual expenditure.[90]

Once again, the Board led parliament in the pursuit of this aim. The Board was soon referring to its policy of 'the amalgamation of the half-castes ... and the amalgamation of stations', and told the government that it would be glad to meet to arrange the return of land.[91]

Late in 1889 the Board decided to close Framlingham station. Jan Critchett has shown how the Board's plans for achieving the closure of Framlingham even outraged the Chief Secretary, who warned that force was not to be used by the Board in removing the Framlingham residents. Had parliament, and particularly the local member John Murray, not intervened, it seems likely that most of the Framlingham land would have been surrendered. Instead, twenty-five out of the ninety-four residents remained on what was now a reserve, without the facilities provided by a station.[92]

By 1902 the Board was able to report to the Chief Secretary that in the fifteen years since the 1886 Act was passed, it had reduced expenditure on Aborigines from £12,328 to below £5000, and had surrendered 12,000 acres of land. It reluctantly reported that its expenditure could not be reduced much further since it still had responsibility for over 400 Aborigines. But it could now announce its unanimous decision that Ebenezer should close.[93]

Two months later, the Board revealed the extent to which it considered itself responsible for Aboriginal policy in Victoria. The Chief Secretary, William Trenwith, had appeared in the papers advocating that the Ramahyuck station in Gippsland, which he had recently visited, be closed immediately. The Board took great offence, and told Trenwith so. The Board wrote that it was reluctant to believe the reports about Trenwith's statements because it was reluctant to believe that such a step would be taken without consulting it, the Board, which had been 'especially appointed to watch over and protect the Aborigines, to manage the stations set apart as their homes, and to give advice to the Government on all subjects connected with the original owners of the soil'. The Board then assured Trenwith that it was the best qualified body to decide which stations should be closed.[94]

The Board's reasons why Ramahyuck should not yet be closed were entirely financial. Cottages would need to be built at Lake Tyers, where the sixty Ramahyuck residents would be forced to move. In addition, the State would incur a heavy debt to the Presbyterian Church, which had built cottages at Ramahyuck on the agreement that compensation would be paid should the station be closed.[95]

The Board eventually oversaw the closure of Ramahyuck in 1907, some four years after it closed Ebenezer.[96] During the next decade two more stations, Lake Condah and Coranderrk, would cease to operate as Aboriginal stations, leaving only Lake Tyers.[97] To be sure, the closure of most stations did not proceed smoothly. Indeed, the level of opposition mounted by Aborigines to prevent and delay the closure of their stations was such that this whole episode marks a significant point in the history of Aboriginal political struggle in Australia. While not germane to our discussion, this is a subject about which a great deal can and should still be written.[98]

The Division Collapses

In the early years of the twentieth century the Board continued its attempts to merge 'half-castes' and reduce government expenditure. But it is evident from the extant documentation that members of the Board began to question the success and value of their once definitive policy. In February 1908 the Board undertook to find out how many 'half-castes congregated at various centres in the State' and in what condition they lived.[99] A memorandum from the Acting Secretary reveals the Board's growing disaffection. After referring to a group of 'half-castes' living near the Framlingham camp, who were living in a 'wretched state', he noted:

> The provisions of the 'Aborigines Act 1890', do not apply to these men, who are not aborigines, and consequently had to leave the stations in compliance with the law. There are about 250 people in the State who have been residents on the Aboriginal Stations, and it is not within the power of the Board to provide for their maintenance. The conditions under which they could be granted food and clothing terminated many years ago. Consequently when they were compelled to merge with the white population, they were obliged to provide for their own support. In order that these people be maintained, it would be necessary to amend the Act, and to increase the Annual Vote . . . [100]

Those Aborigines with European heritage who were game enough to ask the Board for assistance were still generally refused, unless they were dying or disabled.[101] But gradually the exceptions were becoming more common. In 1909 John Murray became Premier and Chief Secretary. For years Murray had sympathised with the position of the Framlingham Aborigines, using his seat in parliament to publicise their inadequate treatment. He had once, for instance, criticised the Board for providing insufficient quantities of meat to the Framlingham Aborigines, and had labelled their treatment by the Board 'an infamous scandal to humanity'.[102]

Murray had been Chief Secretary, and thus formally the Chairman of the Board, from 1902 to 1904, and returned to this position in 1909. Unlike most other Chief Secretaries, he did not see himself as a mere figurehead. Murray took a personal interest in the well-being of some Aborigines, successfully encouraging the Board to break with its policy and provide them with rations.[103] In response, the Board was quick to let the Premier know that its expenses had increased, mainly as a result of its 'support of half-castes'.[104]

By June 1910 the Board's arbitrary division between 'half-castes' and 'pure blacks' was collapsing, ironically at the very time that New South Wales was adopting Victoria's 1886 model.[105] The Board now found it necessary to assist 'destitute half-castes', and sought legislative authority to do so. The Board told the Premier that:

> The half caste is invariably the child of a black mother and is reared by her amongst the aborigines. Although not pure blacks, such half-castes are practically aboriginals . . . it is just as essential to assist them as the pure blacks.[106]

In July 1910 the Board decided to continue supplies to 'half-castes' for three months. Soon after, the Board met with Murray, who subsequently moved a new two-clause Aborigines bill that effectively abolished the artificial divide that had anchored the administration of Victorian Aboriginal policy for a quarter of a century. The Board was once again empowered to 'exercise in the case of any half-caste all or any of the powers conferred on the Board with regard to aboriginals'.[107] Murray told parliament that:

> It was thought [in 1886] that the half-castes would in time merge in the rest of the population, and that they would be able to help themselves, but our experiences have not confirmed that expectation.[108]

Conclusion

In creating and implementing the 'half-caste' policy, many of the Board's members had, no doubt, attempted in a paternal manner to 'do real good to the Black people'.[109] Instead, they succeeded only in causing unspeakable harm to many. The Board put 'half-castes' on one side of a contrived citizenship divide by forcibly removing them from protective stations and State support. This was the means through which they would become 'free and equal citizens'. Meanwhile, the Board imposed an increasingly intrusive regulatory regime on 'full-blood' Aborigines who received modest State support on stations. These people continued to be denied basic citizenship rights such as freedom of movement, the freedom to marry, and the freedom to rear children.

The period from 1880 to 1910 in Victoria provides an illuminating context and precedent for federal citizenship policy. The Commonwealth Constitution largely ignored Aborigines, and excluded them from the census, which meant in turn that they would not be factored into the representation calculus or financial distribution formulas of the new Commonwealth. The first and subsequent Commonwealth parliaments and the federal administration defined citizenship negatively, excluding 'aboriginal natives' from rights and benefits. We have shown that this policy was not simply the result of fear generated by the representatives of States with large numbers of Aboriginal inhabitants. For in Victoria, a colony and then State with one of the smallest Aboriginal populations, an entirely congruous citizenship policy was pursued in the decades either side of federation.

CHAPTER 2

Under the Law: Aborigines and Islanders in Colonial Queensland

When we admit any person to citizenship along with us, we presume that he is fit to come into our company. What are the qualifications for citizenship of the aboriginals?

Senator Stewart, Queensland
1902 Commonwealth Parliamentary Debates[1]

Having investigated the position of Aboriginal Victorians in the years either side of federation, it is now appropriate to examine the policies of a colony and then State which had a relatively large Aboriginal population. Queensland was home to an estimated 100,000 Aborigines in 1788. By 1901 the official figure had fallen to 26,670, yet Queensland's Aboriginal population remained the largest of any State, and at federation was about 50 times the size of Victoria's.[2]

Queensland has been the most recalcitrant State in conferring citizenship rights upon Aborigines. Restrictions on Aboriginal voters in Queensland elections remained in place until as recently as 1965, three years after the Commonwealth and West Australian governments removed similar restrictions. Earlier on, at the Commonwealth Constitutional Conventions and in debates on the fixing of the federal franchise, Queensland politicians were at the fore in ensuring that Aborigines were excluded from citizenship at both State and federal levels.[3] Senator Stewart from Queensland made the remarks quoted above during the debates on the Commonwealth franchise bill. He also said:

It was surprising to hear [Senator Neild] utter so trite a remark as that the aboriginals of Australia were entitled to the franchise because they were the original owners of the country . . . But even if the aboriginals were the

> former owners of Australia, what possible use is there in giving them the franchise?[4]

Many people thought that their relatively small numbers made it somewhat superfluous for Aborigines to be specifically excluded from the franchise. But another Queensland Senator was concerned to refute this. He cited one source that suggested that Queensland's Aboriginal population numbered 70,000. He accepted that the true figure was less than this, but commented that:

> It can readily be seen what a far-reaching effect their enfranchisement will have upon the representation of [Queensland] in the Federal Parliament. The passage of the Bill as it stands would be antagonistic to the sentiments of public opinion in the State I represent.[5]

Needless to say, Queensland's State politicians were of similar mind to their federal representatives.

In this chapter, to complete our selective inspection of State Aboriginal administrations at the turn of the twentieth century, we shall consider the policies pursued by Queensland governments. The most noticeable difference between the situation in Queensland and that already considered in Victoria was the far greater prevalence of violence, sexual assault and exploitation of labour suffered by Aborigines and Torres Strait Islanders. While few official statistics on these issues exist, the anecdotal evidence, to which we shall make reference, is overwhelming. In response to this difference, the Queensland government sought to 'protect' Aborigines by enacting more restrictive legislation than existed in Victoria. Our key concern will be the enactment and implementation of the *Aboriginals Protection and Restriction of the Sale of Opium Act 1897* (Qld). Along with the *Commonwealth Electoral Act 1962* and the *Native Title Act 1993* (Cwlth), this would surely be one of the most significant Aboriginal affairs Acts ever passed by an Australian legislature. With this Act, the colony with reputedly the largest Aboriginal population in Australia announced that there was no need for any federal intervention into the realm of Queensland Aboriginal affairs. For by the Act, the colony would put Aborigines, and those who dealt with them, under the law.

Our argument will be that the Queensland government, through the 1897 Act and through a range of regulatory provisions, ensured that Aboriginal Queenslanders were denied basic citizenship rights. While continuing to be excluded from the franchise, Aborigines would now be heavily restricted in other ways: in their movement, in their employment, in their freedom to marry, in the rearing of their children, and generally in their freedom to exercise any substantial degree of personal autonomy.

Most of the restrictions on citizenship rights emerged under the rubric of 'protection', and this signified an important shift in governmental and administrative thinking. From 1897 Aborigines were increasingly less likely to be killed by white people, and the legislative and administrative initiatives were largely responsible for this. Yet these provisions put into place a citizenship exclusion that had previously operated only on an informal level. The restrictions existed both at a public level, in legislation and regulation, and, less visibly, in the exercise of the extraordinary discretionary power granted to those administrators appointed to implement the provisions. Once control over Aborigines had rested in the guns of settlers. After 1897, it increasingly rested in the determinations of administrators.

Pre 1897

The history of race relations in Queensland prior to the protection era renders this period as surely one of the most disgraceful in Australian history.[6] Indiscriminate killings of Aborigines accompanied their forced removal from any lands considered useful to settlers. In the absence of the rule of law, settlers largely determined the manner in which they would deal with Aborigines. Often this perceived freedom was attended by the belief that Aborigines simply had no rights, and were free to be treated as sub-humans.[7]

As a number of studies has shown, Queensland Aborigines were not always passive victims of violence. C.D. Rowley argues that Aborigines in Queensland came closer than they did elsewhere to guerilla warfare, killing settlers and stock. But as the title of his book, *The Destruction of Aboriginal Society,* indicates, it was Aborigines who suffered in exponentially greater numbers.[8] Through disease, white violence, and the incongruous agency of the Native Police Force, the Aboriginal population of Queensland in 1897 numbered one-third of its pre-settlement figure. This compared with around 850 settler deaths at the hands of Aborigines.[9]

After its introduction into northern Queensland in 1848, the Native Police Force was the principal means by which whites attempted to take control of Queensland. The force consisted of armed Aborigines under the control of white officers. Although it never numbered more than 250, it was responsible for the deaths of innumerable Aborigines, and the outrages it committed led to an investigation in 1861 by a Legislative Assembly Select Committee.[10] The Native Police Force was officially sanctioned in 1859, the year in which Queensland became self-governing. One author has argued that the sanctioning of the force amounted to the first Aboriginal policy of the Queensland government.[11]

Aborigines were British subjects by birth, and their murder made their killers legally liable to be hanged. But the general silence of those whites at the 'frontier' about atrocities committed upon Aborigines, the use of euphemisms such as 'disperse' rather than 'kill' when reference in public was occasionally made to conflicts with Aborigines, and the adoption of the metaphor of war to cover indisputable acts of violence, removed the actions of settlers and the Native Police from the public gaze.

Many Aborigines who escaped death at the hands of white settlers suffered in other ways, through the exploitation of their labour, and the exploitation of Aboriginal and Islander women by white men.

The extension of white settlement into inland Queensland, often referred to as the 'opening up of the Queensland frontier', would have presented many more problems for white settlers had it not been for the use of Aboriginal trackers. Steadily, from the 1870s onwards, settlers began to make use of Aboriginal labour in other ways. Previously, settlers had sought to drive Aborigines from their stations and pastoral runs, but economic need and labour shortages, partially resulting from the gold rushes of the 1870s, made Aboriginal labour attractive.[12] At the same time, Aboriginal women were increasingly used as domestic servants.

Further to the land frontier was the 'sea frontier', which was a prime site for the exploitation of Aboriginal and Islander labour. The coast of North Queensland was rich in bêche-de-mer and pearl shell, and white fishermen keenly exploited this. A range of practices, from the use of cheap labour to outright kidnapping, saw up to 500 Aborigines employed in the northern fisheries in the 1880s and 1890s.[13]

Two of the earliest pieces of Aboriginal protection legislation in Queensland principally concerned the opening up of the sea frontier. The *Native Labourers' Protection Act 1884* required the employment of all 'native labourers' on ships in Queensland waters to be documented in an 'Agreement of hiring', which required the nature of the work and the rate of payment to be set out. A 'Native Labourer' was defined as 'any Aboriginal Native of Australia or New Guinea, or of any of the islands adjacent thereto'.[14] The *Pearl-Shell and Bêche-de-mer Fishery Act 1881* was amended in 1886 so that all workers in this flourishing industry were required to have written employment agreements.[15]

C.D. Rowley argues that the *Native Labourers' Protection Act 1884* was in part the result of the British presence in New Guinea (the British protectorate there was proclaimed in 1884).[16] Noel Loos argues that both Acts were motivated more by concern about the collection of revenue and the protection of Queensland's reputation and self-governing status than by the desire to protect indigenous workers. Prior to these Acts, the Queensland and Imperial parliaments had used 'protection' legislation in a bid to regulate the Pacific Islander labour trade, which was a slave trade in all but name. The *Polynesian Laborers Act 1868* set minimum wage and ration levels which employers were required to provide for Polynesian employees. This Act also required a certificate to be drawn up verifying that the labourer had voluntarily come to work. Meanwhile, Imperial Acts such as the *Pacific Islanders Protection Act 1872* and the *Pacific Islanders Protection Act 1875* made the forced recruitment (kidnapping) of Islanders a felony. A further Queensland Act, the *Pacific Island Labourers Act 1880*, required all employment agreements concerning Pacific Islanders to be in a specified form.[17]

Most of these legislative initiatives were motivated less by concern with the position of Aboriginal and Islander workers than with the threat that their labour posed to white society. The cheap labour directly threatened white labour, and had at least to be regulated. Not surprisingly, most of the legislative arrangements failed to adequately 'protect' Aboriginal and Islander labourers.[18]

From the beginnings of European settlement in Australia white men engaged in sexual relations with Aboriginal and Islander women that might variously be described as prostitution, exploitation, and unambiguous rape. Unsurprisingly, there is little written evidence to support this claim. The institutions that might have given us historical sources on this issue, particularly the courts and the police, were the ones that ignored and thereby sanctioned the abuse of Aboriginal women and girls. We do know that the white population was largely male, that sexual diseases were prevalent among white and Aboriginal communities, and that there was an ever-increasing population of people of mixed-race ethnicity.[19] Other evidence, such as the recorded comments of parliamentarians, points to the prevalent and frequent abuse of Aboriginal women and girls.[20] Such as it is, the evidence supports the fairly uncontentious conclusion that Aboriginal women and girls were regularly and often systematically abused by white settlers, who were usually immune from any legal consequences.

Central to their widespread exploitation were the legal obstructions faced by Aborigines. Were it not for these obstructions, courts might more readily have punished settlers for atrocities committed upon Aborigines. Principal among these legal obstructions was the inadmissibility of Aboriginal evidence in courts. Aborigines were considered incapable of understanding the nature of an oath, and this belief was used to render their testimony inadmissible. In 1876 legislation was passed to allow Aborigines to give evidence in court by making a promise and declaration, but this practice, with a couple of exceptions, continued to see Aboriginal evidence excluded. Courts regularly found that the promise and declaration was as inappropriate for an Aboriginal to give as an oath. Only in 1884, with the passage of the *Oaths Act Amendment Act,* was Aboriginal evidence generally able to be admitted in court, although it still carried less weight than white evidence. Nor was this minor change in policy motivated solely by the injustice that preceded it. The change was made to ensure the reach of the law over all Queenslanders, because 'many serious crimes, committed in the western districts and the interior of the colony, would go unpunished if the evidence of blackfellows was not admitted'.[21]

Another legal obstruction was, of course, the ineligibility of Aborigines to vote. In 1885 the *Elections Act* stated that 'No aboriginal native of Australia, India, China, or of the South Sea Islands shall be entitled to be entered on the roll except in respect of a freehold qualification'. The faint chance that an Aboriginal might satisfy the freehold requirement and vote was guarded against in 1905, when the Queensland legislation was amended to make it almost identical to the Commonwealth exclusion. From 1905 the Queensland exclusion read: 'No aboriginal native of Australia, Asia, Africa, or the Islands of the Pacific shall be entitled to have his name placed on an Electoral Roll'.[22] In chapter 4 we shall consider the extraordinary lengths to which the federal bureaucracy would go in interpreting an identical clause. In 1905 the Queensland government sought advice as to whether 'half-castes' were permitted to vote federally, and received the response that 'half-castes are not disqualified, but the children of a half-caste and an aboriginal native are precluded'.[23] There is little evidence as to whether this thinking was then applied to the workings of the almost identical State franchise legislation. It would seem that Queensland 'half-castes' who came within the definition of 'Aboriginal' in the 1897 Act were prevented from exercising the State franchise, although this was not made specific until 1930.[24]

Missions and Reserves

Not all white Queenslanders considered Aborigines and Islanders to be there for their physical and economic exploitation. Indeed, many of the missionaries who arrived from the 1870s onwards saw their role to be as much about protecting Aborigines from white violence as it was about Christianizing them. This protection was generally well-intentioned, and it certainly contributed to a reduction in the open violation of Aborigines and Islanders. But the missions in many ways served to replace one system of oppression with another.

In 1897 there were six mission stations in Queensland, of which five received some government assistance. Friedrich Hagenauer, the Moravian missionary and General Inspector of the Victorian Board for the Protection of the Aborigines, had visited the north of Queensland during 1885, and had argued that missions were needed there.[25] A year later, three missions were set up in the north by the Lutheran church: Marie Yamba (near Proserpine), Cape Bedford (later Hopevale, north of Cooktown), and Bloomfield (south of Cooktown). In 1891 the Presbyterians established Mapoon, near the Cape York Peninsula. The Church of England set up Yarrabah (near Cairns) in 1892 and Deebing Creek (near Ipswich) the year after. In addition, two government reserves were established in the south. The first, Bogimbah, on Fraser Island, had originally been established as a Methodist mission in 1873. The other reserve was in Durundur, near Caboolture. Rather than establish reserves in the north, the government made use of the mission stations there and gave funds to most of them.[26] The missions and reserves would become central to the government's Aboriginal policy, with the Queensland government applying to them most of the resources it set aside for Aboriginal affairs.[27] The government also provided funds to fifteen depots, which distributed food and tobacco. But even the motivations for this initiative were dubious. Dawn May has argued that the provision of rations was designed more to stop Aborigines from killing cattle than to improve their health.[28]

The establishment of the missions and reserves ushered in the period of protection, which the government fully embraced from 1897. Both the religious initiatives and the protection legislation enacted by the State resulted in a highly regulated Aboriginal administration, and engaged what we would call the central protection injustice. Both were responsible for diminishing the amount of violence suffered by Aborigines, and yet both worked to restrict the kind of lives Aborigines were able to lead.[29] Although Aborigines were now less likely to be shot or die of starvation, they were also far less likely to be able to maintain their cultural roots.

Background to the *Aboriginals Protection and Restriction of the Sale of Opium Act 1897*

Three reports commissioned by the Queensland government were central to the framing of the *Aboriginals Protection and Restriction of the Sale of Opium Act 1897*. Archibald Meston, a former member of the Legislative Assembly who was widely regarded as an expert on Aboriginal issues, compiled two reports at the request of the Home Secretary, Horace Tozer.[30] The first, completed in 1895, addressed the manner in which the government should treat Aborigines. A year later Meston was made a Special Commissioner, and he prepared a more specific report on the mission stations and depots in the north. His brief was to examine the effect of government assistance to these missions. The third significant report was prepared in 1897 by William Parry-Okeden, the Queensland Commissioner of Police. He had been asked to report on the Aborigines in northern Queensland, and to inquire into the operations of the Native Police.

Meston argued in his 1895 report that the only way the Aboriginal race could be preserved was by total exclusion from white society. He rejected the theory that the Aboriginal race was a doomed one, and argued that the reserves would soon be able to finance themselves.[31] For his 1896 'Report on the Aboriginals of Queensland', Meston travelled 5000 miles over four months. He attributed the 'miserable contests' between the black and white races in Australia to misunderstanding, although he labelled most of the murders of bêche-de-mer fishermen by Aboriginals 'acts of justly deserved retribution'. He called for the total prohibition of Aboriginal labour on pearl-shell, bêche-de-mer and tortoise-shell fishing boats, or, alternatively, the most stringent regulation of the industry. Meston also made some reference to the regular abuse of Aboriginal women and children, arguing that stringent legislation was required to curb this. His principal consideration was that:

> There is no prospect of any satisfactory or permanent good without the creation of suitable reserves, the establishment of 'Aboriginal Settlements', chiefly, if not altogether, self-supporting, and *absolute isolation* from contact with whites except those specially appointed to guide them . . . [32]

Here Meston couched his call for the isolation of Aborigines in economically attractive terms, one of the factors that seems to have made his scheme favourable to parliamentarians.[33]

Meston was absolute in his recommendations, calling for: the total abolition of the Native Police; the removal from townships of all Aborigines, except those in registered employment agreements with whites; and the imprisonment of anyone found selling alcohol or opium to Aborigines. Meston also called for the creation of Aboriginal reserves, and the appointment of a Chief Protector of Aborigines in the north, and an Assistant Protector in the south.[34] Although Meston's proposals were not uniformly adopted, several of them were followed when the legislation was enacted.[35]

William Parry-Okeden's report differed somewhat from Meston's. He acknowledged and condemned the Native Police's current operations, but, unlike Meston, did not call for its abolition. Indeed, Parry-Okeden wanted several detachments strengthened. Otherwise, the police force would need to recruit members from the north, from a class among whom were 'wretches who have wrought deeds of appalling wickedness and cruelty'.[36] Like Meston, Parry-Okeden believed that society would be best served if Aborigines could be protected, and the way to do this was through legislation. Parry-Okeden's rhetoric is to some extent made hollow by consideration of the draft bill he appended to his report. Many of the eighteen clauses dealt with regulating the employment of Aborigines, but one clause would have enabled a senior police officer, with the consent of the head Protector, to ban Aborigines from approaching a township. Another clause held that:

> Upon report by the Protector that venereal or other contagious or infectious diseases prevail among the aboriginals of any locality, the Commissioner of Police may cause all affected aboriginals to be mustered and removed to some island or other place appointed for the purpose, to be there detained until cured.[37]

It could be said that the reserve system made such a draconian power a reality, and that only the terminology would be softened. But Parry-Okeden's draft bill and recommendations, save for those regarding the Native Police, were largely passed over in favour of Meston's.[38]

The 1897 Act

The *Aboriginals Protection and Restriction of the Sale of Opium Act 1897* (Qld) was the first Queensland Act to regulate comprehensively the lives of Aboriginal Queenslanders. Prior to this Act, one author has written, Queensland's official policy towards its Aboriginal inhabitants might be said to have resided in its undertaking to distribute one blanket to every Aboriginal each year.[39] The Act, the same author has argued, was the first comprehensive Aboriginal protection Act in Australia, a claim that takes no account of the earlier Victorian legislation considered in the last chapter. The Queensland Act certainly was to prove far more restrictive than the existing Victorian legislation.[40] This debate aside, the Queensland Act was significant on a national level. It remained the principal expression of Queensland government policy for forty years, and was more or less replicated in three jurisdictions.

In Western Australia, the *Aborigines Act 1905* was largely derived from the Queensland Act.[41] Later, the South Australian parliament passed two similar pieces of legislation: one for the Northern Territory, just prior to the Territory's formal separation from South Australia; and one for the governance of South Australian Aborigines. The *Northern*

Territory Aboriginals Act 1910 (SA) and the South Australian *Aborigines Act 1911* were drawn largely from the Queensland and West Australian Acts. As with the Victorian legislation considered in chapter 1, all of these Acts drew a legal distinction between 'Aborigines' and 'half-castes', all of them empowered administrators (usually called protectors) to remove Aborigines to designated reserves, and all of the Acts vested an extraordinary level of regulatory power in the relevant Minister.[42] Our concentration in this chapter is specifically on the position in Queensland, but many of the considerations are applicable to other jurisdictions.

The 1897 Queensland Act had two main objectives: to 'protect' Aborigines from the worst excesses of white violence by enabling their removal to isolated missions and reserves, and to curtail the thriving opium trade and restrict its sale, and the sale of alcohol, to Aborigines.[43] The Act was subtitled 'An Act to make provision for the better protection and care of the Aboriginal and Half-caste inhabitants of the Colony, and to make more effectual provision for restricting the sale and distribution of opium'. The key part of the Act was section 9, which permitted the relevant Minister to remove and keep 'every aboriginal within any District . . . [on] any reserve situated within such District, in such manner, and subject to such conditions, as may be prescribed'. The Minister could also move Aborigines from one reserve to another, a power used often in Victoria to prevent any unified resistance to the governance of stations. Aboriginal women who were married to non-Aboriginal men, and Aborigines who were lawfully employed or were the holders of special permits, were exempted from the operation of section 9. 'Aboriginal' was defined to include a 'half-caste' who lived as the wife, husband or child of an Aboriginal, or, alternatively, a 'half-caste' who habitually lived or associated with Aborigines. The term 'half-caste' was itself defined as referring to a person whose mother was Aboriginal but whose father was not. In 1901 the category 'Aboriginal' was expanded to include a 'half-caste child whose age does not in the opinion of a Protector exceed sixteen years'.[44] Then, in 1904, Torres Strait Islanders, who previously had not been subject to the 1897 Act and whose labour continued to be exploited, were brought under the Act.[45]

Although both the Queensland and Victorian legislation drew a legal distinction between Aborigines and 'half-castes', the division between the two groups was not pursued with anything approaching the same vigour in Queensland as it was in Victoria. Unlike the strictly legislated divide in the 1886 Victorian Act, the regulatory ambit granted in the 1897 Act enabled the Queensland Minister to decide whether 'half-castes' were to be treated the same or differently from Aborigines. The final section of the Act made this power clear, enabling the Minister to issue any 'half-caste' a certificate exempting him or her from the operations of the Act. Such an exemption could not be granted to an Aboriginal.[46]

The Act created the title 'Protector of Aboriginals', which would be adopted over the next ten years by dozens of men and one woman who, in the main, were police officers. By 1907 there were 24 protectors in Queensland. Protectors were responsible for overseeing the employment of Aborigines and female 'half-castes'. In order for Aborigines to be employed, a written agreement, witnessed by either a Justice of the Peace or a police officer, had to be approved by a protector.[47]

The most extraordinary aspect of the 1897 Act was the breadth of regulatory power it ascribed to the Governor in Council. Section 31 enabled regulations to be made in no less than seventeen areas, including: the manner in which Aborigines were moved to reserves; the powers of protectors; the care, custody and education of children; the transfer of orphaned or deserted 'half-caste' children into orphanages; the conditions on which children could be placed out to service; the maintenance of discipline on reserves and the imprisonment for up to three months of any Aboriginal or 'half-caste' in breach of disciplinary regulations; the authorisation for a protector to summarily imprison an Aboriginal or 'half-caste' for up to fourteen days for committing a crime or for being grossly insubordinate; the prohibition of Aboriginal rites or customs that, in the opinion of the Minister, 'are injurious to the welfare of aboriginals living upon a reserve'; and the provision 'for all other matters and things that may be necessary to give effect to this Act'.[48] Henry Reynolds and Dawn May have argued that the scope for regulation contained in the Act was such that decision-making powers effectively passed from politicians to public servants. C.D. Rowley comments that no matter what the intention was behind it, the Act was so broad in ambit that its implementation would ultimately reflect the attitudes of those empowered to enforce it.[49] Indeed, such was the breadth of discretion afforded to the superintendents over their reserves, and the protectors over their districts, that the Act provided very little restraint on their exercise of power.

Noel Loos argues that the Act, which basically embodied Queensland government policy until 1965, introduced the 'era of protection and segregation', when Aborigines and Torres Strait Islanders 'lost their legal status as British citizens and became, in effect, wards of the state'.[50] Certainly, after the 1897 Act, the relationship between Aborigines and the state was analogous to that between parent and child, or state and ward. But that did not entail Aborigines and Torres Strait Islanders losing their legal status as British subjects (not citizens).

Even so, the fact that Aborigines and Torres Strait Islanders remained British subjects did not assist them. For, as we shall argue in the ensuing chapters, one's status as a British subject prior to 1948, and indeed as an Australian citizen after 1948, was meaningless on its own. The Australian people have never, at the colonial, State or Commonwealth level, adopted a constitutional or legislative statement outlining the rights and responsibilities of British subjecthood or Australian citizenship. Rather, 'British subject' and then 'Australian citizen' have been empty categories to which citizenship rights and entitlements have been attached, or in the case of 'aboriginal natives' denied, in supplementary legislation.

The 1897 Queensland Act was one significant piece of supplementary legislation that determined the citizenship status of Aborigines; administrators became legally empowered, without the need for any further parliamentary debate, to restrict the movement of Aborigines, to summarily punish them, and to regulate their employment. Regardless of the moral considerations guiding Queensland's legislators in 1897, this outcome was a clear and absolute statement that Aborigines would not be citizens of the state in any meaningful sense.[51]

A Flicker of Liberalism

During November 1897 the members of Queensland's Legislative Assembly took part in a rare display of contrition over the treatment received by Aboriginal Queenslanders at the hands of white men. One member recalled Aborigines being shot down for sport from the veranda at one station, and he stated his belief that a great many of the murders alleged to have been committed by Aborigines had not been committed by them at all. Another member responded by saying:

> I feel that there is a slur on Queensland that will remain for ever. No matter what we do we can never wipe out that slur, and to know that white men behaved in such a cruel, brutal, murdering manner towards a lot of poor wretches that had no opportunity of protecting themselves makes one feel ashamed . . . It is some comfort to know that at last an attempt is to be made to ameliorate the lot of the blacks after the long period of persecution they have had to endure.[52]

The Home Secretary, who would be responsible for implementing the Act, raised one issue that would not be fully debated for another eighty years. He acknowledged that the imprisonment of an Aboriginal for three years was generally as harassing as imprisonment for ten years was to a white man. At the same time, however, he adopted the most paternalistic attitudes soon to be enshrined in law. He stated that the bill's aims were analogous to those of a charitable organisation, and that Aborigines needed to be governed by a system of rules. It would be necessary, he said, to give reserve superintendents and protectors a minor power of punishment so that:

> If a person will not conform to the rules, I think the superintendent should be empowered to say, 'Go to your room'.[53]

The remorse shown about the treatment of Aborigines was the first detailed public acknowledgment of the atrocities committed by white settlers, and yet the members of the Queensland parliament were not about to redress the situation by granting citizenship rights to Aborigines. Nor was such an action even seriously considered. At one stage, a member of the Legislative Assembly refused to blame white men for the exploitation of labourers on the northern coast of Queensland. Another member questioned his omission, asking: 'Why don't you attack the white men also? Is it because they have got votes?'[54] But even the questioner was not about to go the next step and suggest giving the labourers votes.

One member of the Legislative Assembly thought that the power to remove Aborigines to reserves treated them as criminals.[55] This was a view which would gain more and more credence, particularly once it became clear that the administration of the Act would largely be the responsibility of the Police Department. Indeed, Police Commissioner Parry-Okeden was to become responsible for the implementation of the Act.[56] Gradually, the new administrative regime was established. Aside from the proclamation of districts and the appointment of protectors, the first series of regulations made under the Act were gazetted in September 1899. They created the positions of Northern and Southern Protectors. The former and more prestigious position was filled by Walter Roth, a physician who had come to Australia from England twelve years earlier.[57] Archibald Meston became the Southern Protector. Roth would later become Chief Protector of Aboriginals, when that position was created in 1904. By then, Roth would be an acknowledged expert in Aboriginal affairs, a fact highlighted by his appointment in 1904 to head a Royal Commission into the administration of Aboriginal affairs in Western Australia.[58]

Regulating Labour

One of the chief aspects of the 1897 Act was its regulation of Aboriginal employment. The Act provided that the employment of 'an aboriginal or female half-caste' needed to be approved by a protector, and that those who held work permits were exempt from the possibility of being sent to reserves.[59] The September 1899 regulations set out the manner in which applications were to be made for the employment of Aborigines and 'half-castes'. Anyone wishing to hire these people had to submit an application in prescribed form to the nearest police officer in charge of a station. The officer would comment on the application and forward it to the district protector, who would then decide whether or not to grant a permit. If granted, the applicant then had to complete a 'form of agreement', again in prescribed form, and remit a duplicate copy, signed by employer and employee, to the district protector.[60]

The requirement for work permits does not seem to have significantly lessened the demand for Aboriginal employees, even though permits for wages above five pounds attracted stamp duty.[61] Over 1100 permits were granted in the Cook District alone in the first six months of the Act's operation, while 60 applications were refused.[62] Some protectors were so overwhelmed by permit applications that newspaper advertisements were placed requesting applicants to apply to their nearest police stations.[63] The Northern Protector reported that around 1500 permits were granted in each year between 1901 and 1903. Meanwhile, in the South, permits were granted for 1475 Aborigines in the period 1897 to 1902.[64] But testimony to the extent to which Aboriginal labour was being put under the law was the opinion of the Crown Solicitor in 1906 that the employment of Aborigines engaged in the pearling industry had to be regulated according to both the 1897 Act and the *Pearl Shell Act* of 1886. Eight years prior the Crown Solicitor had, however, ruled that an Aboriginal employed under the provisions of the *Native Labourers Protection Act 1884* did not also need a permit under the 1897 Act.[65] By 1909 Aboriginal labour was so heavily under the law that a letter arrived at the Office of the Chief Protector from a man asking how he should go about hiring an Aboriginal boy to help him for a couple of hours to chop down an oak tree. Other potential employers were of the opinion that the Chief Protector's department actually hired out Aborigines to work.[66]

While some employers certainly threatened to sack Aborigines because of the new protection legislation, it is difficult to know the extent to which Aborigines were unable to gain employment because of the new requirements designed to 'protect' them.[67] Again, this engages the central injustice of the protection regime; for while the new requirements would have lessened the degree to which Aboriginal labour was exploited, it was only Aborigines who suffered for their protection.

When the 1897 Act was amended in 1901, employment permits were no longer able to be granted for Aborigines or 'half-castes' to work on boats outside Queensland waters, and a minimum wage was set for all Aborigines and 'half-castes'. Also from 1901, the district protectors were able to direct that the wages for Aboriginal and 'half-caste' females be paid to them, to be used for the workers' benefit.[68] Many white employers objected to the minimum wage requirement, a factor evidenced by a petition to parliament by fifteen men who sought the freedom to pay Aboriginal wages 'in accordance with the merit of the employee'. Other employers argued that as soon as an Aboriginal was employed, 'the Protector steps between employer and employed, causing annoyance and unpleasantness'.[69] Archibald Meston, the Southern Protector, put these comments in some perspective when he reported that some employers often gave items to workers instead of wages. Through protection legislation, Meston sought an end to this 'slave system'.[70]

Aboriginal labour was even more restricted from March 1904. Twenty new regulations continued the system governing the employment of Aborigines, and new minimum wages were set for Aboriginal and 'half-caste' women and girls. These wages could be increased 'at the discretion' of the district protector. As envisaged by the 1901 amendments to the Act, the new regulations provided that all the wages of Aboriginal and 'half-caste' females, save for 'pocket-money', would be paid to the district protectors. The protectors held the wages as trustees, and were entitled to spend the money for the worker as they saw fit.[71]

All of these regulations and restrictions must, of course, be understood in the context of a new Commonwealth legislature that was determined to protect jobs for white labour. The *Pacific Island Labourers Act 1901* (Cwlth) restricted the employment able to be undertaken in Australia by residents of most Pacific islands. Meanwhile, several pieces of Commonwealth legislation encouraged the use of white labour through the payment of bounties and the granting of exemptions from excise duties. These affected Queensland more than any other State, and included the *Post and Telegraph Act 1901* and the *Sugar Bounty Act 1903*.[72] The term 'white labour' was defined in Commonwealth regulations to exclude 'all forms of coloured labour, whether aborigines of Australia or not, and whether half-caste or of full blood'.[73]

Henry Reynolds and Dawn May have argued that while Police Commissioner Parry-Okeden wanted discretion to be exercised in the Act's implementation, Walter Roth was rigorous in ensuring that all Aboriginal workers had employment agreements. It was this rigour that Roth believed led to the considerable white opposition his work generated.[74] But despite the hostility to Roth, it soon became clear that the regulation of Aboriginal employment served white interests far more than it improved Aboriginal working conditions. As one employer wrote soon after the passage of the 1897 Act:

> I appreciate the usefulness of some permit-system under Government control: as I apprehend, besides protecting the aborigines, it will also protect white employers from the interference by other people, with their black servants.[75]

The use of formal agreements introduced and enforced western styles of work, protected white employers from interference with their workers, and did not generate substantial benefits to Aborigines. On remote cattle stations, for instance, Aborigines could effectively be segregated at no cost to the state, while their cheap labour could assist the viability of a struggling industry.[76]

Inter-racial Sex

It quickly became clear that the new administrative regime could work to prevent the number of Aboriginal deaths through violence, and also begin to lessen the degree to which Aboriginal and Islander labour was exploited. However, the widespread sexual violence suffered by Aboriginal women and girls showed no signs of abatement.

One of the objects of the 1897 Act, according to the Secretary for Agriculture, had been to prevent the abuse of women.[77] In an attempt to regulate sexual relations between white men and Aboriginal women, the Act made it an offence for a person to have an Aboriginal or female 'half-caste' on their property except as provided for by the Act.[78] Members of parliament appear to have thought that by prohibiting the 'harbouring' of Aborigines, by regulating their employment, and by empowering protectors to move Aborigines to reserves, the sexual exploitation of Aboriginal women and girls would be limited. But the administrators refused to turn their attention to the white men who were responsible for the violence.

In the late 1890s it became apparent that sexual assault remained widespread despite the operations of the Act. One station manager wrote of the regularity with which Aboriginal women were kidnapped, and then blamed for having 'chosen' a life of prostitution:

> [Aboriginal women] do not go and live with a white man of their own accord. They are often taken by force from their camps, and even kept in irons until they are too terrified to make any attempt to return to their own

> tribe, and then you are told sometimes that they are leading this life of prostitution from their own choice or their own free will.[79]

In his report for 1899, the Northern Protector, Walter Roth, described the difficulty of knowing how many 'half-caste' children there were in the north. Even more difficult to know were the numbers of 'half-castes' actually born, since many were routinely killed at birth. Roth continued to make arrangements to send 'half-caste' girls to mission stations, because:

> It is far better to know that all such are ultimately legally married and protected by the missionaries, and, through them, by the State, than to realise that as soon as they get old enough to be tampered with by unscrupulous whites – *the present normal condition of things* – they are sent back into their camps as bad girls and left there to ultimate disease and ruin.[80]

Roth wrote that the protectors had little power to prevent white men visiting Aboriginal camps, and that cases continued to come to his notice about girls under sixteen being 'criminally assaulted'. Rarely, however, was any action taken against white men. According to Roth, this was because 'in the absence of any legal proof of age, the futility of attempting to press for a conviction is apparent'. Roth did make a suggestion that legislation be enacted to put the onus of proof in such cases on the accused.[81] But this aside, Roth, as with all those in positions of power in the new regime, sought to remedy the situation by blaming the victim.

Roth believed that 'If left to themselves, the majority of the girl half-castes ultimately become prostitutes, and the boys cattle and horse thieves.' One solution would have been to ensure that these children were in fact left to themselves. But Roth's solution was to send them to mission stations and reformatories.[82] This is what happened to Dolly, a 'half-caste' who had been in service with the same employer for ten years. She had never received any wages, and only had the clothes she wore. Her employer moved away and did not want to take Dolly, who was then handed over to police. She was found to be seven months pregnant, and was ordered to go to Yarrabah station. Before Dolly arrived, she gave birth to a child, who died before she could resume her journey. Dolly was thirteen years old.[83]

To the extent that Roth and the administrative regime sought to limit the widespread sexual violence suffered by Aboriginal women and girls, they did so in two ways: by blaming the victim and removing all those thought to be in danger to mission stations; and by believing that if they could regulate marriage then they could regulate women's sexuality. Any thought that white men could be held responsible for their actions attracted significant opposition at all levels, as evidenced by this exchange in 1901 in the Legislative Assembly:

> Mr W. Hamilton: How is it possible to make a man go into the [witness] box and admit that he is the father of a half-caste child? I do not think that is a nice, or proper, or fair thing to do.
> The Home Secretary: Anything is fair with a man of that sort.
> Mr W. Hamilton: A half-caste may belong to a syndicate, and it is hard to tell who the father is.[84]

Despite such sentiments, one token gesture was introduced in 1901, requiring the father of a 'half-caste' child to contribute to his or her maintenance if the child was reliant on government support. However, paternity was always difficult to prove when the father contested it; all the more so when the legislation held that 'no man shall be taken to be the father of any such child upon the oath of the mother only'.[85] The cases where fathers did give their 'half-caste' children some measure of support were, according to Roth, exceptional.[86]

Rather than look to bring the white fathers to justice, parliamentarians in 1901 turned their attention to the victims. An amendment that year to the 1897 Act brought all 'half-caste' children who appeared to a protector to be under sixteen years of age within the definition of 'Aboriginal'. Thus, in order to remove such children to reserves, it was no longer necessary to prove that they were living as the children of Aborigines, or alternatively that they were habitually associating with Aborigines.[87] This was clearly a move designed to restrict the sexual violence committed upon Aboriginal girls. One district protector wanted all 'half-caste' girls to be moved onto mission stations once they reached fourteen, since: 'No matter how well they are watched, it is my experience that they are invariably got into trouble by some unprincipled white man, who only laughs at the poor unfortunate whom he has seduced.'[88]

Another provision, section 14, was also designed to regulate, if not prevent, sexual violence. It stated that where there was an allegation that a sexual offence had been committed upon an Aboriginal or 'half-caste' girl, there was no need to prove that she was under any specified age. During the parliamentary debates about the 1901 amendments, the Home Secretary told of one case where a girl under ten years of age had been 'violated'. Nothing had happened to the rapist, however, because there was 'no absolute legal proof that she was under the age of sixteen'. This scenario, he argued, necessitated the new provision. But the provision said more about what was permitted than it did about what was prohibited. For the last sentence provided that it was a defence to the charge if the girl had reached puberty.[89]

In many of the contemporary reports, sexual conduct was discussed under the euphemistic term 'marriage'. One member of the Legislative Assembly stated in 1901 that he thought most members 'have been long enough in the colony to know that in this climate young ladies become fit for the married state long before they arrive at the age of sixteen'.[90] By regulating marriage, however, one did not regulate sexual relations, a point that could hardly have been lost on legislators. Nevertheless, regulations on marriage were soon in place.

From 1901 the marriage of female Aborigines to non-Aborigines was prohibited unless permission in writing had been given by certain protectors.[91] Prior to the passage of the 1901 amendment Act, Walter Roth, the Northern Protector, recorded his belief that 'most, if not all' of the marriages between Aboriginal women and non-Aboriginal men had occurred in order to defy the 1897 Act, particularly the provision prohibiting the harbouring of Aboriginal women. As early as 1898 he had feared this would be the case, and at that stage had sought to regulate the marriage of white men to Aboriginal women. He wrote in 1901 that: 'Cases occurred where men of bad character, upon being warned against harbouring or employing native females, deliberately went and married them, and so defied the Protectors.'[92] Roth himself became the first protector authorised by the Home Secretary to give permission for Aboriginal females to marry non-Aborigines.[93] No regulatory system would be complete without a prescribed form, and such a form for inter-racial marriages came into existence in 1904.[94]

The number of non-Aborigines permitted to marry Aboriginal women was not large. In 1907, for instance, fifteen such marriages were permitted. Five of these marriages involved white or European men, while the rest mainly involved Islander men. The following year forty-one of these marriages were permitted, when most husbands were Pacific Islander and Malay men.[95] From extant reports it appears that the number of refused applications for 'mixed marriages' was also small. Less easy to identify is the extent to which Aboriginal women followed the general prescription behind the legislation, and simply did not seek to marry.

Nor was the proscription confined in its effect to the marriage of non-Aboriginal men to Aboriginal women. When two 'half-castes' sought to marry, the bureaucratic position was that if they 'associate with blacks [the] consent of [the] Chief Protector must be obtained'.[96] That the 1901 law regarding marriage infringed basic citizenship rights was not lost on all parliamentarians, one member of the Legislative Assembly commenting:

> Now, I maintain that we have no right to treat these aboriginals or half-castes as if they were slaves, and yet this Bill proposes to treat them as slaves . . . By a clause of this Bill we find that any person is absolutely prohibited from marrying either a half-caste or an aboriginal, no matter what age they may be, without the permission of the protector. I do not think that is a power that should be given either to the Home Secretary or the protector.[97]

Of course, this statement could be read as a lament that white men were now being restricted in their choice of wives. But the comments reveal an awareness of the discriminatory nature of the legislation, regardless of the rhetorical purposes to which the comments were put. The restriction on the marriage of Aboriginal women was a restriction upon their citizenship rights, which the architects of the restriction clearly knew.

Restricting Movement

One of the key limitations imposed upon Aborigines in Queensland was the restriction of their movement. Next to their exclusion from the franchise, this was the most clear statement of their citizenship status. This restriction, consistent with others already discussed, was done in the name of protection.

We have already considered section 9 of the 1897 Act, which gave a sweeping power to the Minister to move any Aboriginal to any reserve subject to any conditions considered necessary. On first inspection, that provision might equally be seen to be one aimed at protecting Aborigines as it was aimed at confining their movement. Placed in context with section 17 of the 1901 amending Act, however, one must lean toward the latter view. That section provided that protectors could direct 'any aboriginals or half-castes who are camped or are about to camp within or near the limits of any township to remove their camp or proposed camp to some place at such distance from such township' as the protector chose.[98] Exactly what constituted a 'proposed camp' is unclear. What is clear is that this provision gave protectors, in addition to their power to recommend the removal of Aborigines to reserves, a blanket power to disperse Aborigines. Furthermore, the fact that miners were able to enter Aboriginal reserves suggests that the protection of Aborigines was hardly the paramount consideration governing administrators.[99]

Once on a reserve, Aborigines were subject to further regulation. The use of divided dormitories meant that even families who went to a reserve together suffered some degree of separation and division. Typically, children were separated from their parents and slept in single-sex dormitories, a practice that was used as a form of social control.[100] According to one of the Royal Commissioners into Aboriginal Deaths in Custody, the dormitory system contributed to the erosion of traditional Aboriginal practices and authority structures. In place of power residing in Aboriginal elders, it now devolved to white administrators.[101]

By 1907 there were eight Aboriginal reserves in Queensland. In the north, these remained under mission administration. Of the eight missions and reserves that had existed ten years earlier, four had now closed. In the north, two of the Lutheran missions, Marie Yamba and Bloomfield, were now closed. Meanwhile, the Presbyterians had opened Weipa (on the west coast of the Cape) and Aurukun (on the Archer river), and the Church of England had opened the Mitchell River station in 1904. In the south, the Fraser Island and Durundur reserves were now closed. In their place, the reserve at Barambah (later called Cherbourg) became the State's southern reserve.[102]

It is extremely difficult to ascertain the numbers of Aborigines removed to missions and reserves under section 9 of the 1897 Act. Statistics exist for the numbers of Aborigines at missions and reserves each year, and for the number of Aborigines removed between 1914 and 1940, a figure which is said to have been at least 5,600.[103] But it is unclear how many people were rounded up by police and taken to missions and reserves in the early years of the Act.

Some figures do exist for forced removals in the south. According to a report prepared by Archibald Meston in 1903, around 600 Aborigines were sent to reserves between February 1897 (before the Act came into operation) and March 1903.[104] In the north, one must rely on attendance figures in order to make any reasonable estimation. In one sense this lack of information is not particularly significant. Whether Aborigines were physically forced to move, or simply told they would be forced if they did not remove themselves, is an arbitrary distinction. In 1901 the northern mission stations had only around 500 permanent residents, a seemingly small figure given the size of the State's Aboriginal population and the enthusiasm accompanying the broad powers given to administrators by the 1897 Act. It seems that the missions and reserves usually catered for twice the number of people actually living on them, with Aboriginal camps often being established nearby. All the same, there had been no instant and wholesale removal of Aborigines to reserves.[105]

One suspects that such a removal was never intended. Indeed, the fact that it was not casts some light upon the rhetorical use to which the idea of 'protection' was put. If Aborigines needed to be moved for their own protection, then, presumably, this needed to happen quickly. On this understanding, one must conclude that the protection of Aborigines was very slowly and poorly implemented. If, however, the power to move Aborigines to reserves was designed to empower protectors to move troublesome Aborigines out of the way, the slow removal would seem to make more sense. Large-scale removals were not intended because the principal aim could be met simply by the enactment of the power to move Aborigines.

One case serves to illustrate the thinking governing the removal of Aborigines. In 1902 Meston, the Southern Protector, ordered the removal of Annie, 'an aboriginal half-caste girl with a Chinese father'. She was diagnosed to be suffering from gonorrhoea, following her cure from which she sought Meston's permission to marry an Aboriginal man. Meston alleged that Annie was caught with another man soon after her marriage, and as soon as he heard this news, Meston sent Annie to Fraser Island.[106] Clearly it was not Annie's protection that Meston sought to secure. Rather, Annie had deviated from the life that Meston thought she should lead, and was promptly punished.

Other Restrictions

The restrictions placed on Aborigines were not limited to those made by parliament or the executive. Some of the missions established 'courts' which drew up their own regulations. At Yarrabah, for example, the adults on the mission annually elected twelve court members, who were required to be church communicants. These twelve Aborigines, together with the missionaries, formed the court, which was presided over by the Chief of the local Yarrabah (Gungganji) tribe. The court tried cases of misconduct and awarded punishments ranging from strappings to imprisonment. It is very difficult to know how much coercion, as opposed to self-determination, was involved in the operations of such courts. There is reason for considerable scepticism when the nature of the 'laws' made by the court are considered. The following are some of the laws in place around 1902:

> (c) Any one showing disrespect to . . . any Mission officer to be severely punished.
> (d) If any person creates a disturbance and refuses to stop, any member of the Government can order the court officers to lock the offender up at once.
> (e) All letters from and to members of the Mission to pass through the hands of the head of the Mission or his representative for perusal.[107]

Legislation and regulation remained, however, the main instruments of restriction. In addition to the restrictions already considered, other legislative and regulatory provisions limited the autonomy of Aborigines. For instance, district protectors were entitled to seize, retain or sell any property of an Aboriginal, and they could exercise in the name of an Aboriginal 'any power which the aboriginal might exercise for his own benefit'.[108] By a regulation gazetted in 1904, all letters from 'aboriginal inmates' of mission stations, reserves, reformatories, or schools were required to pass through the hands of the superintendents or officers-in-charge, who were authorised to withhold them from transmission.[109]

The following year, eleven 'Regulations for Maintaining Discipline and Good Order Upon a Reserve' were gazetted. These included:

3. Every inmate shall obey all reasonable instructions and commands of the superintendent . . .
6. A protector may inflict summary punishment by way of imprisonment not exceeding fourteen days upon aboriginals or half-castes living upon a reserve who, in his judgment, are guilty of any crime, serious misconduct, neglect of duty, gross insubordination, or wilful breach of these Regulations.

Other provisions enabled superintendents to inflict corporal punishment on children for attempting to leave reserves, and rendered any Aboriginal who attempted to leave a reserve, after having been ordered to reside there, liable to imprisonment for up to three months.[110]

In addition to these restrictions, Aborigines suffered in the provision of health and education services. An informal code regularly saw Aborigines denied access to hospitals, when they were brave enough to present themselves, and white parents often protested successfully if they discovered that their children were being educated with Aboriginal children.[111]

The Caste Divide

In the last chapter we considered how the Victorian Aboriginal administration pursued a strict line of division between 'full blood' Aborigines and 'half-castes'. The former were able to be removed to government stations, while the latter, in the name of making them 'free and equal citizens', were actively prevented from relying on state support. We have seen that the situation was not entirely congruous in Queensland, where there also existed a legal distinction between 'Aboriginal' and 'half-caste', but the Aboriginal administration was given power over both groups by legislation that can fairly be characterised as enabling rather than prescriptive. 'Half-caste' women were specifically targeted in the legislation in order to inhibit inter-racial sexual relations taking place on the pretext of employment, and this has led some authors to argue that 'half-caste' men were summarily excluded from the Act's operations.[112] But the Act's definition of 'Aboriginal' was so broad that 'half-caste' men could and were easily brought within its parameters. Rather than drawing a strict racial divide, as occurred in Victoria, the Queensland administration sought to base its division on criteria of employment and lifestyle.

As in Victoria, the power of bureaucrats to determine who was a citizen was at its most visible when decisions were made regarding 'half-castes'. To be sure, bureaucratic determinations regularly impacted upon the citizenship rights of all Queensland Aborigines, but 'half-castes' were the group whose citizenship status was most frequently and dramatically affected by administrators.

The power to determine whether a 'half-caste' came under the Act was simultaneously the power to determine who was a citizen. This was a complex process, as highlighted in 1900 by a note made by the Under Secretary of the Queensland Home Secretary's Department, when asked to rule on whether a 'half-caste' girl who was employed as a domestic servant came within the operation of the 1897 Act. His response outlined both the bizarre complexity of the racial categorisations, and the power attributed to administrators:

> She is not an 'aboriginal' within the meaning of the Act while so employed but . . . whenever any such half-caste returns to her people and resides with them . . . she becomes an 'aboriginal' within the meaning of the Act.[113]

Under the Queensland Act, 'half-castes' were able to be removed to reserves if they were the wife, husband or child of an Aboriginal, or if they habitually lived or associated with Aborigines. But Queensland Aborigines and 'half-castes' who were 'lawfully employed', and Aboriginal women who were married to non-Aborigines, could not be sent to reserves.[114] Thus, in effect, if a 'half-caste' lived a European lifestyle, or if any Aboriginal worked in a European-style employment relationship, he or she would not be subject to the principal clause of the 1897 Act. Prior to its enactment, this distinction was articulated by one member of the Legislative Assembly:

> There were two classes of half-castes, those who generally went with the blacks, and those who went with white people, and the provisions of the measure might very well be restricted to those half-castes who would come within the definition of an aboriginal – that was, those who habitually lived or associated with aboriginals.[115]

But inevitably the choice as to whether 'half-castes' lived European lives and remained outside the provisions of the Act was not theirs to make, a fact illustrated by one girl's very common fate. Deborah, a 'half-caste' girl of ten or twelve years of age, had been regularly abused in her work as a home servant. When her abuse came to the attention of administrators, she was 'committed' for seven years to the Industrial School at Mapoon. Had she not been sent to an Industrial School, Deborah might have been excluded from the operations of the Act once she turned sixteen. But the decision whether she stayed outside the operation of the Act was not hers to make.[116]

In 1904 Roth sought to clarify the legal status of 'half-castes', releasing a memo entitled 'Synopsis of the Law Relating to Half-Castes'. In the memo Roth divided 'half-castes' into four categories: children, men, women, and those irrespective of age who lived as the spouse of an Aboriginal or otherwise associated with Aborigines. For each group he set out the legal position. Roth's certainty about the law relating to 'half-castes' was, however, belied by his actions the following year when he sought to have a 'half-caste' woman removed to Barambah. He wrote in the following terms to the Under Secretary of the Home Office:

> As far as the law is concerned, she cannot . . . be dealt with under the Aboriginals Act. For the woman's own sake, if for nothing else, I would accordingly take the liberty of suggesting to the Minister the urgency of *stretching a point*, and signing the attached order for removal.

Suffice it to say that the request was granted and the woman was sent to Barambah.[117]

As if there was not already scope for the exercise of considerable discretion in the administration of the Act, an additional exit clause existed in the Act by which any 'half-caste' could be granted a certificate and exempted from the provisions of the Act. Such certificates were rarely applied for and rarely granted. At the end of 1903, for example, the Northern Protector had granted only two certificates, and had refused only two. In each of the years between 1907 and 1909, the number of certificates of exemption granted by the Chief Protector were five, sixteen and eleven. The Chief Protector wrote in 1909 that: 'Only half-castes who are civilised and have no intercourse with aboriginals can obtain them, and then only on satisfying the Department of their ability to manage their own affairs.'[118]

The fact that so few exemptions were sought or given is not surprising when one considers the discretionary nature of most of the Act's provisions. Most Queensland Aborigines were not moved to missions or reserves, and one suspects that those Aborigines who might have been eligible for exemptions never needed to apply for them in the first place.

Although the Queensland regime did not pursue a strict racial division between Aborigines and 'half-castes', a noticeable change began to emerge in the reports of the Chief Protector after 1905. Once, Roth had been of the opinion that 'half-caste' children were better served by being on reserves. Since 1865, 'any child born of an aboriginal or half-caste mother' had been deemed to be a 'neglected child' under the *Industrial and Reformatory Schools Act 1865*. In this, the most racist provision imaginable, all Aboriginal children were said to be neglected simply because of their race. This enabled any Aboriginal or 'half-caste' child to be sent to a reformatory or industrial school. Most Aboriginal missions had been proclaimed as industrial schools and reformatories by 1905, giving protectors another ground on which to remove Aborigines to missions and reserves.[119] In the five years to June 1905, at least 126 'half-caste' children – forty-five boys and eighty-one girls – under the age of sixteen were sent to northern missions under that power. In the eighteen months to June 1905, thirteen 'half-caste' boys and twenty-eight 'half-caste' girls were similarly dealt with in the south.[120] In his 1904 report, Roth wrote that it was not advisable that 'half-castes' should grow up without religion and education, and he asserted that they were well served by being at mission stations.[121] However, in his 1905 report, he changed his mind and wrote:

> It appears to me a matter of urgency that more stringent measures should be insisted on with a view to raising the social status of the half-caste children (both male and female), and with this object in view I can recognise no better plan than that, *in the future*, all such infants taken from the camps should be brought up as white children, and not in the aboriginal mission reformatories as black ones.[122]

The principal justification for this, however, was nothing vaguely noble. Roth was concerned to prevent 'the inbreeding of half-castes with full-bloods'.[123]

Here were the beginnings of an assimilation policy that would be embraced in the coming decades. Even the chief administrator of the 'protection' policy was now beginning to question its broad application.

Conclusion

During the era of protection, Queensland Aborigines and Islanders suffered restrictions on their employment, their movement, their ability to marry, and their right to personal autonomy. Through a series of deliberate legislative and regulatory actions, Aboriginal Queenslanders were legally excluded from the rights and benefits from which they had previously been informally excluded. This exclusion was enforced by dozens of protectors, who decided when their broad and largely unreviewable powers would be exercised. The extension of the rule of law in Queensland meant that Aborigines were less likely to face indiscriminate violence. But instead they had now become victims of the law.[124]

While Aboriginal Queenslanders were being formally excluded from the rights of citizenship, politicians from around the country were debating the kind of national government that Australia would adopt. This was to have profound implications for Aborigines, who had already been excluded from citizenship rights at the colonial level. In the next chapter we consider these federation debates and their outcome – the Australian Constitution – with a view to the impact they would have on the citizenship rights of Aborigines.

CHAPTER 3

Is the Constitution to Blame?

The constitutional treatment of Australia's Aboriginal people is cryptic and enigmatic. The Commonwealth Constitution, which formally created the Australian nation and set up its federal system of government in 1901, mentioned Aboriginal people only twice in its 128 sections. Moreover, both instances were by way of exclusion: section 51(26) excluded people of the Aboriginal race from the scope of the special race power given to the Commonwealth, while section 127 excluded Aboriginal natives from the census of national and State populations. The two sections read as follows:

> s. 51. The Parliament shall, subject to this Constitution, have power to make laws for the peace, order, and good government of the Commonwealth with respect to: . . .
>
> (xxvi) The people of any race, other than the aboriginal race in any State, for whom it is deemed necessary to make special laws.
>
> s. 127. In reckoning the numbers of the people of the Commonwealth, or of a State or other part of the Commonwealth, aboriginal natives shall not be counted.

What are we to make of such 'negativism of the Constitution', as Geoffrey Sawer termed it?[1] For many today, as in 1967 when overwhelming majorities of more than 80 per cent of the people in every State voted in referendum to delete both exclusionary clauses from the Constitution, the original constitutional treatment of Aboriginal people seems surprising and even shocking.

Such surprise and shock is conflated by a widespread assumption among historians and public figures that the Constitution, through these two sections, excluded Aboriginal people from citizenship. In a recent piece on 'Australian Citizenship, Rights and Aboriginal Women', historian Ann McGrath begins with the presumption that 'When Australia became a nation in 1901, its newly written constitution excluded all Aborigines, male and female, from citizenship.'[2] Addressing the National Press Club in August 1994, chair of the Centenary of Federation Advisory Committee and previously Premier of Victoria, Joan Kirner, asserted that 'Women had no formal role in drawing up the Constitution, which also formally excluded indigenous Australians from their rights of citizenship.'[3] The Kirner Committee's *2001 A Report from Australia* repeated the claim that 'Federation was a time when the indigenous people were to be formally excluded.'[4] This exclusionary view is picked up in a recently published text for secondary schools: 'When Australia federated in 1901, Australia's indigenous people were not included in the discussions, and *the Constitution did not recognise Aborigines and Torres Strait Islanders as citizens.*'[5]

Whether or not the Constitution excluded Aborigines from citizenship is an important question. If it did, as these authors and reports claim and many assume, that would be a serious indictment of the instrument and the founders might properly be saddled with a good deal of blame for the subsequent treatment of Aboriginal people. If it did not, the Constitution stands in a somewhat nobler light and we need to look elsewhere to account for the shameful exclusion of Aboriginal people from citizenship for more than half a century after federation.

This chapter explores the constitutional treatment of Aboriginal Australians: why they were barely mentioned in the Constitution, and then only by way of exclusion in the two sections cited above; and whether such treatment entailed exclusion from citizenship in the new nation. The answer to the first question follows on from the discussions of colonial regimes and mindsets presented in previous chapters on Victoria and Queensland. These were presupposed and evident in what was said and not said in the Federation Conventions. For the most part, the founders left Aboriginal policy as a State responsibility. The position of Aboriginal people in the various colonies at the time of federation helps explain this treatment in the new Commonwealth Constitution, and will be summarised shortly.

This chapter argues that the Constitution did not exclude Aboriginal people from citizenship in the new Australian nation. Such exclusion was achieved through parliamentary legislation beginning with the 1902 *Commonwealth Franchise Act.* Subsequent chapters show how successive governments and administrators, through legislative and administrative practices, routinely extended and embellished this exclusion of Aboriginal people from citizenship rights and entitlements. The exclusionary regime was not required or sanctioned by the Constitution, so it could be dismantled by simply changing legislation and administrative practices. This was done most notably in 1962, five years before the Aboriginal referendum, when amendments to the *Commonwealth Electoral Act* allowed all adult Aborigines to vote. The 1967 referendum was enormously significant as a symbolic act and for converting the section 51(26) races power into an effective Commonwealth power to pass laws with respect to Aboriginal people. It did not, however, restore Aborigines to citizenship because the Constitution had never excluded them.

Comparative Omission

Comparative analysis can help to highlight Australia's constitutional treatment of its Aboriginal people. This was in sharp contrast to that of the United States and Canada, whose federal constitutions were otherwise influential with the Australian founders. Whereas those federal countries gave their national governments substantial power over indigenous peoples, there was no such Commonwealth power in the Australian Constitution. Brief reference to these otherwise comparable North American federations brings out the Australian difference.

The United States Constitution includes Indian tribes in the key commerce clause, which is third in the list of eighteen heads of congressional power specified in section 8. That section reads: 'The Congress shall have Power . . . To regulate Commerce with foreign Nations, and among the several States, and with the Indian Tribes.' Other powers to wage war, raise and support armies, call forth the militia and make treaties were just as important during the next century in dealing with the Indian tribes who occupied vast western lands. They were used extensively because American Indians were a major force to be dealt with by the national government. This no doubt explains why such national powers featured in the United States Constitution.

The Canadian Constitution, adopted in 1867, has a more substantial Aboriginal power. In its list of national powers set out in section 91, subsection 24 confers upon the federal parliament the power to make laws in relation to 'Indians, and Lands reserved for the Indians'. To illustrate the double-headed nature of this power, the Canadian *Indian Act* made drunkenness an offence for any Indian off a reserve, while, under a different section, drunkenness was an offence for any person on a reserve. The power to make laws with respect to Indians and Indian lands was a key national power. The proclamation of 1763 recognised Indian ownership of vast areas of the lands ceded to Britain by

France, and required treaties with the crown before any of these lands could be settled upon.

Comparison with the United States and Canada helps emphasise the Australian Constitution's lack of a national power to deal with Aboriginal people. The situation of Australia's Aboriginal people and the jurisdiction of established settler colonies over land were also quite different. At the time of federation in both the United States and Canada, the national governments had responsibility for vast western territories and Indian lands from which new states – provinces in Canada's case – were carved. By the time of federation in Australia, Aboriginal people had been largely dispossessed of most of their land while administration of their affairs was under established regimes of the various colonies which entered federation as States. Nor did Australia's Aboriginal people pose a military threat that required national action via a national power, as was the case in the United States.

But this is not a sufficient explanation for the Australian founders' apparent lack of concern for the plight of Aboriginal people. Sawer cites two additional reasons given by the West Australian Chief Protector of Aborigines to the 1927–29 Royal Commission on the Constitution: gross underestimation of Aboriginal numbers because of the lack of reliable census data, and an assumption that they were a dying race.[6] Probably more important were the attitudes and political sensitivities of the founders who, as experienced colonial politicians, were fully aware of, and in part responsible for, the colonial treatment of Aboriginal people. They were also acutely aware that the draft Constitution would have to be endorsed by the people of the colonies in popular referendum.

Had the Australian founders been sensitive to the plight of Aboriginal people who had been dispossessed of their land and culture, brutalised on the fringes of white settler society and systematically denied rights and freedoms under the guise of colonial protection, they may have been moved to provide the Commonwealth with a power to improve their lot. But such 'if onlys' would seem to belie the attitudes and circumstances of the time. Moreover, as chapter 5 makes clear, the Commonwealth's administration of Aboriginal people in the Northern Territory after 1911 would be no different from that of the States.

Giving the Commonwealth a special power to deal with Aboriginal people would have been out of sync with the structural design of the federal system that was being put in place. Australia's constitutional founding was a complex amalgam of the old and the new, being designed by political leaders of the old who had some vision for the new. The old consisted of independent colonies with contiguous jurisdiction over the whole Australian land mass and established policy regimes for dealing with Aboriginal peoples. The colonies were incorporated as semi-independent States in the new federation and retained jurisdiction over all policy areas not specifically given to the new Commonwealth government. The Commonwealth was generally given concurrent rather than exclusive jurisdiction with the States, but the Commonwealth would have precedence in the event of conflict over matters of national significance, such as overseas and interstate trade, currency, immigration, and post and telegraph services. As Sawer has pointed out:

> The Commonwealth was not initially given any independent territory on the mainland and its ultimate acquisition of such territory, though likely, was by no means certain; general questions of land settlement, industrial development, employment relations and education were also left to the States, and few of the powers given to the Commonwealth had any obvious or direct relevance to aboriginal policy, so that a decision to leave aboriginal questions to the States was rationally defensible.[7]

Sawer adds: 'What is surprising is that the position of the Aborigines was never even mentioned'. According to the above analysis, however, that was not so surprising. In any case it is an overstatement since Aborigines were mentioned, albeit scantily, in the federation debates regarding the two sections in which they are specifically mentioned, sections 51(26) and 127.

They were also mentioned in two additional contexts to do with excluding and including categories of people: section 25, which excluded from the Commonwealth representational calculus 'persons of any race' disqualified from voting by a State; and section 41 which guaranteed the franchise in the new Commonwealth to any person with the right to vote in a State. Consequently, Aborigines in Queensland and Western Australia would not be included in reckoning the number of members of the House of Representatives for these two States under section 25. On the other hand, section 41 should have guaranteed Aborigines who had acquired the right to vote in a State, such as South Australia, that same right for the Commonwealth.

Both sections are evidence of the founders' respect for the States and state powers. More generally, the position of Aboriginal people in the colonies at federation goes a long way towards explaining their treatment in the Constitution. The following section reviews the position of Aborigines in the States at federation and provides the context for our subsequent discussion of the treatment of Aborigines in the Constitution.

Position of Aborigines in the States and Territory at Federation

Aborigines or 'aboriginal natives' comprised a special category of people in all of the colonies and the Northern Territory (over which South Australia had governance until 1911). Just how many Aborigines there were was a matter of rough estimation. An official figure is given in table 1, but is clearly an underestimation. Western Australia is credited with having only 5261 Aborigines, whereas Geoffrey Bolton argues that in Western Australia there were around 15,000 Aborigines 'inside the frontier' in 1898 and 6000 outside.[8]

How many Aborigines there were depended, obviously, on the definition of 'Aboriginal'. For the most part, colonial definitions of 'Aboriginal' referred to someone of 'pure' Aboriginal stock or 'full blood'. Since this was a legislative and administrative category of white-settler regimes, it was manipulated for policy purposes and extended to include some part Aborigines or 'half-castes' who were identified as belonging with Aborigines. Although there were broad similarities among States, each had its own regime and various idiosyncrasies, which are summarised in table 2.

As we have seen, Victorian legislation in 1901 defined 'Aboriginal' narrowly, so that only a small subgroup of 'half-castes' were officially recognised to be Aboriginal: females who were married to Aborigines; 'half-castes' who had reached thirty-four years of age by 1887 and who habitually associated with Aborigines; and children unable to earn their own income who had one Aboriginal parent. Victorian Aborigines could be forced to reside on reserves or elsewhere, and their employment was subject to formal regulation.[9] In Queensland, the term 'Aboriginal' was defined more broadly to include all 'half-castes' who were married to Aborigines and all 'half-castes' who habitually associated with Aborigines. This definition was further expanded in 1901 to include all 'half-caste' children. As we saw in the last chapter, those people who came within the definition were subjected to even greater restrictions on their personal freedom than were their Victorian counterparts.[10]

Table 1 Official Aboriginal population estimate, 1901

Vic.	*Qld*	*WA*	*NSW*	*SA*	*NT*	*Tas.*	*Aust.*
521	26,670	5261	8065	3070	23,363	0	66,950

Source: F. Lancaster Jones, *The Structure and Growth of Australia's Aboriginal Population*, 1970. All of these figures represent underestimations.

Table 2 Governance of Aboriginal affairs as at the beginning of 1901

	Definition of 'Aboriginal'	*Governing body*
Victoria	Aboriginal natives and small subgroup of 'half-castes'	Board for the Protection of Aborigines
Queensland	Aboriginal natives and 'half-castes' habitually associating with them	Northern Protector and Southern Protector
Western Australia	Aboriginal natives and 'half-castes' habitually associating with them	Aborigines Department (replacing the Aborigines Protection Board)
New South Wales	No relevant legislation	Board for the Protection of Aborigines
South Australia and the Northern Territory	No relevant legislation	Part-time Chief Protector of Aborigines
Tasmania	No relevant legislation	No relevant body

West Australian Aborigines in 1901 had been subjected to more individual pieces of legislation than had Aborigines in any other State. At the start of 1901, five pieces of legislation solely concerning Aborigines, which had been passed prior to Western Australia's first Aboriginal protection Act, remained valid. They concerned: the ability of Aborigines to give evidence without taking an oath; the use of Aboriginal interpreters in court proceedings; the 'enticing' of Aboriginal girls from their schools or services; the regulation of Aboriginal workers in the pearl-shell industry; and the summary trying of Aboriginal offenders. In addition, Aborigines were not permitted to possess alcohol.[11]

In 1886 the West Australian parliament passed the *Aborigines Protection Act 1886* (WA), thereby creating an Aborigines Protection Board and enabling the executive to appoint protectors of Aborigines. The Act, which defined as Aboriginal 'Every Aboriginal Native of Australia, and every Aboriginal half-caste or child of a half-caste, such half-caste or child habitually associating and living with Aboriginals', regulated Aboriginal employment and formally enabled justices to remove Aborigines who were 'found loitering' or who were not 'decently clothed from neck to knee' from townships.[12] An amendment to this Act in 1892 provided that Aborigines could be imprisoned for up to three months for breaching a contract of employment.[13]

In 1897 the West Australian Aborigines Protection Board was abolished, and was replaced by the Aborigines Department, which was responsible for managing and regulating Aboriginal reserves.[14] Legislation had been passed in 1889 giving the Governor the power to set crown lands aside for Aborigines. This power was reinforced by the *Land Act 1898* (WA), which permitted the Governor to lease crown lands to Aborigines and to establish Aboriginal reserves.[15] In 1901 there was no express power for protectors to send Aborigines to reserves, but such a power was clearly implied in the legislation.

The background to the abolition of the Aborigines Protection Board rests with the so-called 'section 70 compromise', which in part underpinned Western Australia's achievement of self-governing status. Western Australia was granted self-governing status in 1890 but was required to have a provision (section 70) in its Constitution that guaranteed a certain level of funding to cover the administration of Aboriginal affairs. When the West Australian Constitution was being drafted, the British government insisted upon the inclusion of a clause guaranteeing £5,000 or one per cent of the colony's revenue, whichever was greater, as an annual contribution to the Aborigines Protection Board. The Board was to remain autonomous from government control. In several sometimes farcical manoeuvres, the West Australian parliament sought to remove this clause almost from the time it embarked on self-government. It finally succeeded in abolishing the Board and the funding requirement in 1897.[16] It was not until 1905 that Western Australia had protection legislation similar to that already in existence in Victoria and Queensland.

In New South Wales, the only legislation passed in the nineteenth century that solely affected Aborigines concerned their giving of evidence in criminal cases, their possession of firearms, and the supply of alcohol to them.[17] In 1883 the New South Wales government created an Aborigines Protection Board to monitor religious initiatives into Aboriginal affairs and to oversee the distribution of rations.[18] The New South Wales legislature did not pass its first Aboriginal protection Act until 1909.

Similarly, in South Australia and the Northern Territory, no Aboriginal protection legislation had been passed at the time of federation. An 1844 Ordinance had enabled the South Australian government to regulate the 'up-bringing of orphans and other destitute children of the Aborigines', and had made a Protector of Aborigines the guardian of all 'half-caste' and Aboriginal children whose parents were dead or 'unknown'. The Ordinance had further provided that guardianship over 'half-caste' or Aboriginal children vested in the Protector when one parent signed over authority.[19] Other legislation concerning Aborigines permitted their unsworn testimony to be used in court, and made it illegal for them to buy alcohol and opium.[20] However, South

Australia's first protection legislation was not enacted until 1911. The part-time Chief Protector of Aborigines and a small group of sub-protectors, often police, took what little responsibility the colony assumed over Aborigines.[21] A protection bill was debated in 1899, with Aboriginal employment and inter-racial sexual relations receiving strong attention, but no agreement could be reached on the policy that the colony should pursue.[22]

In keeping with the officially sanctioned historical fiction that there were no Tasmanian Aborigines, there was no Tasmanian legislation that directly affected Aborigines in 1901.

In addition to the restrictions already outlined, specific legislation existed in Western Australia and Queensland in 1901 to prevent Aborigines from voting. The *Constitution Acts Amendment Act 1899* (WA) prevented Aborigines from voting (see table 3, p. 83) for either house of parliament. It provided that:

> No aboriginal native of Australia, Asia, or Africa, or person of the half-blood, shall be entitled to be registered [to vote], except in respect of a freehold qualification.[23]

Similarly in Queensland, the prevailing legislation in 1901, the *Elections Act 1885* (Qld), held that:

> No aboriginal native of Australia, India, China, or of the South Sea Islands shall be entitled to be entered on the roll except in respect of a freehold qualification.[24]

In neither colony is there evidence of Aborigines avoiding these restrictions by satisfying the freehold requirements. Both colonies subsequently removed the freehold exception.

Queensland and Western Australia were the only colonies to expressly prohibit Aborigines from voting. But other colonies had legislation which in effect led to the same result. In New South Wales, for instance, the franchise legislation prevented people in receipt of charitable aid from voting.[25] Aborigines on missions and reserves were considered to be in receipt of charitable aid and were thus excluded from the vote. Other Aborigines, one imagines, would have had a hard time convincing New South Wales electoral officers that they, first, were permitted to vote, and that they were not in receipt of charitable aid. As we mentioned in chapter 1, a similar situation prevailed in Victoria.

For Aboriginal women, the situation was doubly impossible. By 1901, only South Australia and Western Australia had enfranchised women at the State level. Thus all Aboriginal women, except those in South Australia, were formally prevented from voting in 1901 either because of their race as in Western Australia or because of their sex in the other States.

This colonial patchwork of special treatment and entrenched discrimination was preserved and the Constitution simply added an additional national level of governance. This included the full paraphernalia of national institutions and powers while the colonies were incorporated as States within the new federation. Many of their processes and established practices, including those governing the treatment of Aboriginal people, were respected and guaranteed.

Constitutional Exclusion

Those who claim that the Constitution excluded Aboriginal people from citizenship appeal to their exclusion from the section 51(26) race power and from the census in section 127. It is necessary, therefore, to examine why each of these exclusions was made. By reflecting upon the federation debates, which constitute one of the most complete records ever made of a constitutional drafting process, we can, to some extent, enter into the minds of the founders and appreciate their handiwork, even if finally we choose to find critical fault with what they did and did not do.

1891 Convention

For a start, it is worth keeping in mind the strong, even perverse, decentralist sentiment voiced by some at the beginning of the round of federal conventions. An extreme form was evident in views put by Captain Russell from New Zealand at the beginning of the 1891 Convention when general principles were being formulated and positions staked out:

> The reason why I think we should have a system of federation as loose as possible is this: that all the more outlying portions of Australasia must be allowed to work out their own destinies. When you think that we, in our own colony, have what may be termed a foreign policy, inasmuch as we deal with an alien race, that we have laws very materially affecting them, that the questions of native title are matters of very grave moment, and that any interruption in our relations with those people might be of the most serious importance to the colony, I think you will agree with me that we shall require to see that we have a safeguard in all such respects as these before we submit ourselves to a federal authority. And so, in the colonies of northern Australia, you yourselves may yet find that you have difficulties unforeseen to cope with. It is true that the native races of the more settled portions of Australia have given you but little trouble, and you have dealt with them summarily,

> but possibly when you go to northern Australia you will find there a race more resolute and more difficult to deal with.[26]

Russell's preference was for a loose Australasian federation incorporating 'countless islands throughout the Pacific', each with control over its own colonised peoples. This New Zealander's vision was rejected by leading Australian delegates, including those from northern Australia such as Griffith and Macrossan, who supported giving the Commonwealth an exclusive race power to deal with groups like the Kanakas in north Queensland. Nevertheless, Queenslanders remained deeply divided over this and other issues concerning federation so no delegates were sent to the second round of federation conventions in 1897–98. Nor did New Zealand participate after the abortive 1891 convention.

The opposite view to that of Captain Russell was put at an early stage of the 1891 convention by William McMillan from New South Wales, who made no bones about wanting 'a constitution created of such a character as will annihilate, not the localisms, but the nationalities of the different states'. Eliminating the nationalities of the different States required a strong central government with power to make policies towards people of different race:

> I want to see a central government, which will prove of immense service in welding together the different elements of the people of this country. I want to see a central government, which will deal with the black question in North Queensland, and with the great territories of Western Australia, as far as by influence and by common consent they can be dealt with. We should do now what is possible in that direction.[27]

The exclusion of people of a particular race from the electoral calculus was included from the outset, being part of the 1891 draft that Samuel Griffith introduced at the beginning of the convention. Until the new Commonwealth parliament provided otherwise, it was proposed that members of the House of Representatives be chosen by the people of each State. There would be one representative for every 30,000 people, with the qualification of electors being the same as that for the lower house of the parliament in each State. Griffith explained why:

> We did not see our way to provide for a uniform qualification in all cases. That would have involved a complete and elaborate electoral system, and it might have been suggested that it would interfere too much with the internal affairs of the states themselves. It is provided also that in any state where there is a race of people not admitted to a share in the representation there, it shall not be counted in reckoning the number of members to be elected to the parliament of the commonwealth.[28]

While this passage refers to the exclusion of 'people of any race' (eventually section 25 of the Constitution), it illustrates the founders' respect for the States' internal affairs that permitted discrimination on the basis of race.

Sensitivity to established State policy domains was also apparent in the larger issue of allocating powers between the Commonwealth and the States. Generally, 'national' powers were allotted to the Commonwealth level of government on a concurrent rather than exclusive basis. As Griffith explained, the State legislatures could go on exercising their existing powers until the Commonwealth decided to act: 'It is only when the federal parliament comes to the conclusion that it is necessary to make laws on those matters that the powers of the states will be excluded, and then only to the extent to which the federal legislature chooses to exercise its functions.' Griffith went on to explain that there was a small number of exclusive Commonwealth powers proposed, including a special race power. In so doing he paid tribute to Macrossan, his fellow Queensland delegate who died tragically only a short time before:

> It is proposed to give some exclusive powers to the legislature of the commonwealth. One of them is to deal with 'the affairs of people of any race with respect to whom it is deemed necessary to make special laws not applicable to the general community; but so that this power shall not extend to authorise legislation with respect to the aboriginal native race in Australia and the Maori race in New Zealand'. I am sorry that my late colleague and co-delegate for Queensland, Mr Macrossan, is not here to express his opinion on that proposal. I am satisfied, notwithstanding that during all his political career he was a representative of northern constituencies in Queensland – constituencies where the question of black labour was a burning one – that he would have most cordially supported the proposal, and would have insisted upon the necessity of that power being given to the legislature of the commonwealth of Australia, and not to the legislature of any particular state, because the introduction of an alien race in considerable numbers into any part of the commonwealth is a danger to the whole of the commonwealth, and upon that matter the commonwealth should speak, and the commonwealth alone.[29]

From this, the purpose of the race power and reason for excluding Australian Aborigines and New Zealand Maoris should be clear. The power was for dealing with people of other races such as the Kanakas in Queensland or Chinese, Indians or Malays who might be brought to Australia as indentured labourers. This was emphasised by Griffith:

> The intention of the clause is that if any state by any means gets a number of an alien race into its population, the matter shall not be dealt with by the state, but the commonwealth will take the matter into its own

> hands . . . What I have had more particularly in my own mind was the immigration of coolies from British India, or any eastern people subject to civilised powers. The Dutch and English governments in the east do not allow their people to emigrate to serve in any foreign country unless there is a special law made by the people of that country protecting them, and affording special facilities for their going and coming.[30]

In other words, this was a power to deal with, including to protect, alien races allowed into Australia. Aboriginal people were not in that category and were quite properly excluded from its application. While the wording of the clause was to change in 1897–98, its meaning and intention did not.

The other specific mention of Aboriginal people in the Constitution, section 127, which excluded them from being counted for purposes of electoral calculations, also originated in 1891. Griffith introduced the following 'new clause, dealing with the mode of reckoning the population' on April 8, late in the 1891 Convention: 'In reckoning the number of people of a state, or other part of the commonwealth, the aboriginal natives of Australia shall not be counted.'[31]

The clause was in and out of the 1891 draft but, because the drafting committees' sessions were secret and there was little time for discussion on the convention floor, its purpose was never made completely clear. The clause had not been in the draft bill prepared by the committee on constitutional machinery and presented by Griffith to the committee of the whole on March 31. Griffith's only explanation was that it had been in the original bill prepared by the drafting committee, but had been struck out by the general committee along with the clauses to which it referred. Since those clauses had been reinstated – Griffith did not say which clauses they were – it was 'necessary that this clause also should be reinserted'. Griffith moved the amendment, which was agreed to without debate on April 8.[32]

Probably the clauses referred to were financial ones dealing with apportionment of expenditure for the new Commonwealth among the States and the return of surplus revenue to the States. A *sine qua non* for federation was the establishment of a national customs union, which entailed turning over customs and excise, the colonies' main tax base at the time, to the Commonwealth as an exclusive power. That meant, at least for the transitional period until the Commonwealth parliament provided otherwise, that some method of apportioning commonwealth expenditure and dividing surplus revenue among the States had to be found. This proved extremely difficult. The finance committee had recommended that such apportionment be on a population basis, while the constitutional drafting committee altered this to a proportion of revenue contributed by the States. This in turn was reversed by the convention as a whole. If this was the reason, and the exclusion of Aboriginal people was for purposes of financial calculations, it suggests that Aborigines were considered marginal or insignificant for public expenditure purposes.

1897–98 Convention

While a new beginning was made in the 1897–98 series of conventions held in Adelaide, Sydney and Melbourne, the 1891 draft bill was used as a blueprint. Much of its institutional architecture and many of its actual clauses, including the two excluding Aboriginal people, were taken over and reworked. There was minimal discussion of the treatment of Aboriginal people, although occasional comments shed further light on what was intended. Moreover, a couple of significant changes were made: the race power, section 51(26), was made a concurrent, rather than an exclusive, Commonwealth power; and the census exclusion, section 127, was extended to the people of the Commonwealth as well as of the States.

The purpose of the race clause, which was initially reproduced verbatim from the 1891 draft, was reiterated in an exchange between Henry Higgins and Richard O'Connor. Higgins said he understood that the clause was 'to provide for the Parliament dealing with the kanaka question'. He was uneasy with the wording which purported to give the parliament power 'with respect to the affairs of the people of any race'. Higgins thought this was too broad and might imply that parliament was being given power to deal with the affairs of 'kanakas in their own islands', rather than simply their relations with Australia.[33] O'Connor interrupted him to point out that relations of Kanakas towards Australia were included in the powers over emigration and immigration, thus making it clear that the race power was complementary to the immigration power.[34] Higgins' reservation was later accommodated by the deletion of 'the affairs of' from the clause.

The exclusion of Aboriginal people from the census was also incorporated into the 1897–98 draft, initially as clause 120. An exchange at Adelaide brought out a crucial distinction between exclusion from the census statistics and exclusion from the franchise. This passage of the debates is worth quoting in full because three authoritative members of the convention, Edmund Barton, Richard O'Connor and Alfred Deakin, were involved in responding to Dr Cockburn from South Australia. The passage includes reference to both the electoral as well as financial consequences of the exclusion.

Clause 120 – In reckoning the numbers of the people of a State or other part of the Commonwealth aboriginal natives shall not be counted.

DR COCKBURN: As a general principle I think this is quite right. But in this colony, and I suppose in some of the other colonies, there are a number of natives who are on the rolls, and they ought not to be debarred from voting.

MR DEAKIN: This only determines the number of your representatives, and the aboriginal population is too small to affect that in the least degree.

MR BARTON: It is only for the purpose of determining the quota.

DR COCKBURN: Is that perfectly clear? Even then, as a matter of principle, they ought not to be deducted.

MR O'CONNOR: The amendment you have carried already preserves their votes.

DR COCKBURN: I think these natives ought to be preserved as component parts in reckoning up the people. I can point out one place where 100 or 200 of these aboriginals vote.

MR DEAKIN: Well, it will take 26,000 to affect one vote.

MR WALKER: I would point out to Dr Cockburn that one point in connection with this matter is, that when we come to divide the expenses of the Federal Government per capita, if he leaves out these aboriginals South Australia will have so much the less to pay, whilst if they are counted South Australia will have so much the more to pay.[35]

This exchange brings out a number of key points. The most important one is that exclusion from the census did not entail denial of the right to vote. Dr Cockburn was perfectly right: that 'as a matter of principle' Aboriginal natives with voting rights should not have been excluded from the reckoning of numbers of people of a State for purposes of determining the quota of members for the State. But the founders were not driven entirely by principle and its logical consequences. Since the denial of the right to vote at the Commonwealth level was not in jeopardy – in fact, as O'Connor pointed out, that had been preserved by a previous amendment (the current section 41) – the census exclusion was sanctioned on pragmatic grounds. The numbers were too small to affect the representational calculus (Deakin); and South Australia would pay less as a result of the exclusion (Walker).

Deakin's response that the representational calculus would not be affected held only if the Aborigines concerned were the relative few, '100 or 200', according to Cockburn, who actually voted. The tens of thousands of Aborigines in Queensland and Western Australia would have made a difference had they been counted, and even the several thousand recorded in South Australian estimates would have been significant (table 1). Perhaps the best sense we can make of this important exchange is that Aborigines who actually had the vote in a State, most notably the ones referred to in South Australia, were considered part of the political community or civil society. Their right to vote was preserved by section 41 and was not in jeopardy by the exclusion of 'aboriginal natives' from census calculations. Enfranchised Aborigines, however, were the insignificant minority. The majority of Aborigines were outside the colonial political communities: most were based in Queensland and Western Australia, where they were denied the right to vote, and in the Northern Territory, where the lack of a specific exclusion far from equated with enfranchisement.

Other Relevant Sections

Another section potentially significant to Aboriginal people was the broader race exclusion, which is still in the Constitution as section 25 and reads as follows:

> For the purposes of the last section, if by the law of any State all persons of any race are disqualified from voting at elections for the more numerous House of the Parliament of the State, then, in reckoning the number of the people of the State or of the Commonwealth, persons of that race resident in that State shall not be counted.

It is not clear from the federation debates, however, whether it was intended that Aborigines were to be included in this broader race disqualification. In an 1897 exchange, Joseph Carruthers said they were: 'What was intended was to exclude from the computation aboriginals, or others who might be expressly disqualified by parliamentary enactment'. Barton affirmed that it was a matter for determination by the States, but equated 'race' with 'alien race', a category that could not apply to Australian Aborigines: 'A race not entitled to vote is such an alien race as may exist in the community to whom the state in which they live has not conceded the privilege of voting.'[36] On this analysis, and indeed on the reasoning that had seen Australian Aborigines excluded from the race power conferred by section 51(26), Australian Aborigines ought not to have been caught by section 25. But the adjective 'alien' did not appear in section 25, theoretically making the phrase 'persons of any race' applicable to Australian Aborigines.

Not surprisingly, there was some confusion between this earlier section excluding people on the basis of race (section 25) and the later exclusion of 'aboriginal natives' from the census (section 127). After the preliminary draft had gone back to State parliaments for consideration, the Legislative Council of New South Wales proposed to broaden the later exclusion (section 127) by adding to 'aboriginal natives' the amendment 'and aliens not naturalized'. In recommending the rejection of such an amendment, Barton insisted that the two sections were quite different, but his explanation of the difference was not clear. The earlier section dealt with the reckoning of the number of electors for determining representation in both houses of the Commonwealth parliament, Barton said, whereas the later section dealt with counting people of the States for financial and other purposes.[37] In the latter instance, he variously claimed that 'it would not be considered fair to include the aborigines' and, subsequently, that 'where the provision is merely for statistical purposes, it is only considered necessary to leave out of [the] count the aboriginal races'.[38] There was little debate on the matter and both sections were retained. The delegates' lack of concern for the political interests of Aboriginal people meant that they could simply be left out of the count.

However, section 41, which guaranteed that those on State electoral rolls could also vote in Commonwealth elections, would suggest a different view insofar as it applied to Aboriginal people. Section 41 was potentially more significant for Aboriginal rights, although its purpose was to protect female suffrage. Section 41 states:

> No adult person who has or acquires a right to vote at elections for the more numerous House of the Parliament of a State shall, while the right continues, be prevented by any law of the Commonwealth from voting at elections for either House of the Parliament of the Commonwealth.

The wording of the section suggests an open-ended requirement that the Commonwealth franchise respect the State franchise qualifications. This was not intended by those who proposed and supported the clause, although it was raised as an alarming possibility by those who opposed it. Section 41 merits careful attention because of its potential significance for protecting the franchise of those Aboriginal people who won it in the States.

Potential Inclusion

The purpose of section 41 was clearer than its actual wording. That purpose was to protect at the Commonwealth level the voting rights of women who had already won the franchise in the States, as had occurred in South Australia a few years previously in 1894. It came onto the constitutional agenda as a fall back to the bold but unsuccessful move to entrench a universal franchise, although the concern was with female rather than Aboriginal suffrage.

On 15 April 1897 Frederick Holder from South Australia moved to include the guarantee that 'every man and woman of the full age of twenty-one years, whose name has been registered as an elector for at least six months, shall be an elector'. This was by way of amendment to the clause specifying the qualification for electors of members of the

House of Representatives. Holder proclaimed the 'purpose I have in view is simply to give effect to the desire that many of us cherish, that women as well as men should be recognised as electors of this great Commonwealth'.[39] This was opposed on the grounds that the matter was one for State determination until the federal parliament was formed and passed its own national franchise law. Defending the majority view, Bernhard Wise explained: 'The franchise is a matter to them in one sense of Federal interest, but until the Federal Parliament is formed, it is a matter of purely local interest.'[40]

In the ensuing discussion there was more delicacy shown towards State sensitivities than women's suffrage. If women's suffrage was such a good idea, Wise contended, it would spread from the example of New Zealand and South Australia. But so far there was a reserve in the other colonies that ought to be respected.[41]

Barton and O'Connor, both members of the constitutional drafting committee, opposed Holder's amendment. O'Connor claimed that it would make 'it a condition that the whole Commonwealth will accept woman suffrage'.[42] Barton was concerned that 'a uniform suffrage of this kind should be forced upon the Commonwealth, and . . . whether the Bill would stand even a fair chance of being carried in the various colonies if this proposal were adopted'.[43] On the other hand, the South Australians championed female suffrage, with Kingston asserting:

> I think those who believe in female suffrage should advance it by voting for it whenever they get the chance. I have no sympathy with those who say they are in favour of it, but when they have an opportunity of extending it throughout Australia they will have nothing to do with it. I believe in a uniform franchise.[44]

Holder's initial motion was lost twenty-three votes to twelve, but he immediately proposed a somewhat more restrictive version in the negative form: 'no elector now possessing the right to vote shall be deprived of that right'.[45] This was contentious because, in protecting the franchise of those women who had won the right to vote in the colonies, the amendment bound the new Commonwealth Parliament. Those who supported the motion emphasised the former aspect of preserving the right to vote for women who had already won it at the State level. As George Turner affirmed, 'Mr Holder wants to have this amendment passed in order that the Parliament when declaring the uniform franchise shall not be able to deprive any woman, who can now vote, of that right.'[46] If that were done and the franchise made uniform, then arguably it would necessitate female suffrage. This point was not lost on astute supporters like George Reid from New South Wales, who interjected: 'It will compel female suffrage'.[47] Opponents like Barton did not want to bind the new federal parliament: 'It ties the hands of the Federal Parliament entirely. I cannot understand many of our friends, who profess to trust the people we are constituting, and who now cannot trust them in this matter.'[48] Kingston, however, was quick to point out that in other matters, such as the relative numbers of the two houses of parliament, Barton had not been prepared to trust the people.[49]

Some who supported female suffrage, like the trade unionist William Trenwith from Victoria, nevertheless opposed the amendment on strategic grounds. Trenwith was confident that the extension of the female franchise would be adopted by the new Commonwealth but did not want to require this through a specific constitutional clause. O'Connor supported this view, arguing that 'If the supporters of woman suffrage have faith in it, why should not they have faith in the gradual education of the people throughout the colonies till they secure the final adoption of this principle?', to which Dr Quick responded 'where is the harm in putting in a security?'[50]

In the continuing debate, opponents conjured up potential dangers. For example, the conservative Simon Fraser objected: 'Under this amendment, if South Australia put on the roll of the Northern Territory 10,000 Chinamen who might reside in the country, we should be compelled to put them on the roll of the Commonwealth, and I do not think the Commonwealth should be bound in this way'.[51] Nevertheless, Holder's revised amendment was carried eighteen votes to fifteen.

Barton and others were most unhappy with the clause, and the convention returned to it on April 22. Barton explained that some members who voted for the provision had not sufficiently considered its application to the suffrage 'after the date of the establishment of the Commonwealth'. Whereas Fraser had used the racist example of adding '10,000 Chinamen', Barton instanced giving females of eighteen or nineteen years of age, or 'a certain undesirable class', the right to vote which could not then be touched by the law of the Commonwealth.[52]

Defending his earlier amendment, Holder tried to clarify what was intended; namely, to leave with the State parliaments the right to freely alter the franchise up until the point when the new federal parliament established its own franchise:

> I want the States to have their rights with regard to the franchise unimpaired up to the day when the federal franchise is indicated, and that whatever the franchise shall be at that date it shall be preserved, and so that no person having a right up to that date shall have it taken from him, and that this

> shall apply not only to South Australia but also to other colonies who may widen their franchise before a federal franchise is provided.[53]

Holder was quite prepared to leave it up to the States for the interim period either to extend or to curtail the franchise as they saw fit. In order to ensure this State discretion, either to extend or restrict the franchise, the convention agreed to his subsequent amendment and added the words 'whilst the qualification continues'.[54]

However, the matter did not end there, because the actual wording of the clause permitted a broader reading and potentially had two far-reaching consequences. The first was, as some of its supporters suggested earlier, that if the Commonwealth were to adopt a uniform franchise, which was intended, all women would have to be enfranchised. The second consequence was that the States might manipulate the Commonwealth franchise by changing their own franchise in unacceptable ways.

Hence Barton brought the final Melbourne convention in 1898 back to consider this contentious clause. He explained that the section had not received as full a discussion as it might have in Adelaide, and that 'a great deal of harm might be done by the unlimited effect of the provision as in the Bill'.[55] The problem, as he put it succinctly, was as follows:

> By the effect of the clause, as passed in Adelaide, any state might alter from time to time its suffrage for its House of Assembly, and, having altered it, notwithstanding the existence of the Commonwealth, the person who acquired under that alteration a right to vote for the House of Assembly in that particular state might vote – although the extension of the suffrage gave it not only to women, but, perhaps, to such a class as the young persons of sixteen years of age who are now agitating in some places for a vote – notwithstanding the different suffrages of other states, at elections for either House of the Commonwealth.[56]

Barton claimed they had made a mistake in Adelaide: 'it is not a rational provision to allow it to be in the hands of any state, not merely to alter its own suffrage for its own internal Legislature, but to alter it in such a way that it might affect the composition of the two Houses of the Commonwealth Parliament, and the character of its legislation'.[57]

With more far-fetched examples, Barton illustrated how this might affect the Commonwealth's uniform franchise. If one State enfranchised sixteen-year-olds they would have to be given the right to vote across Australia. Alternatively, the Commonwealth franchise would be left 'not uniform, but rugged and uneven; because it would be deprived of making the suffrage uniform, unless it acted in a manner acceptable to that one state'.[58] George Turner, a Victorian and a supporter of the Adelaide clause, said that Barton was going too far in conjuring up unlikely instances that were never intended at Adelaide. O'Connor, as usual, supported Barton, arguing that 'the clause as it stands goes far beyond anything that [Mr Holder] asked for, even in the course of the debate'.[59]

But Isaacs and others insisted that once the Commonwealth had passed its franchise Act the ability of the States to affect the Commonwealth franchise by manipulating their own franchise would cease. Although perhaps the most likely practical outcome, this was not guaranteed by the wording of section 41. Nevertheless, it seemed to be sufficient assurance for the majority. The debate on the clause petered out with no further vote being taken.

Surprisingly, in all of this debate, Aboriginal people were not mentioned. Opponents referred to the possibility that groups of people – such as Chinamen, women of eighteen or nineteen, and youths of sixteen – might vote, as examples of aberrations the section might allow. The omission of any mention of Aborigines is puzzling in view of the alarmist picture that the opponents of the clause were intent on painting. This is in contrast to the extensive discussion and, by some, denigration of Aboriginal people when the first Commonwealth Franchise Bill was debated a few years later. That section 41 would apply to Aboriginal people who enjoyed the franchise in a State was clear in the 1902 parliamentary debates and in the *Commonwealth Franchise Act*, which allowed a section 41 exemption to the general exclusion of Aborigines. That Aborigines were covered by the section 41 guarantee was acknowledged at the Adelaide convention in the exchange between Barton, O'Connor, Deakin and Cockburn quoted earlier. In that exchange, O'Connor assured Cockburn that the 'amendment you have carried already preserves their votes'. Cockburn referred to 100 or 200 Aborigines who, he knew, had the right to vote in South Australia. He wanted to ensure that their right to vote was not jeopardised by the clause excluding Aborigines from the census.[60]

Thus, although section 41 was designed to ensure the franchise of women rather than Aborigines, it might have been significant in guaranteeing the right to vote for those Aborigines entitled to vote in the States. Such obvious constitutional entitlement was recognised by the first *Commonwealth Franchise Act* of 1902, which exempted such Aborigines from the general exclusion from the franchise of 'aboriginal natives of Australia'. Sadly, this limited constitutional right was trumped by subsequent administrative action in which Aborigines from South Australia, who were on electoral rolls in that State and had been entered on the Commonwealth rolls, were struck off.[61] Belatedly, in a 1983 case concerning the right to vote at a forthcoming Commonwealth election of people on State rolls who had missed the deadline for the Commonwealth rolls, the High Court ruled that section 41 applied only to people on State rolls at the time of the first *Commonwealth Franchise Act*.[62] This interpretation, while not supported by the plain meaning or textual history of the clause, finally laid to rest this enigmatic section.

Empty Subjecthood

Unfortunately, the Constitution otherwise contains no positive mention of citizenship or statement of basic rights and privileges to which an aggrieved person might appeal. Aboriginal people and other excluded groups such as the Chinese had no constitutional recourse against discrimination or denial of basic rights on the part of either the States or the Commonwealth government. The Constitution was framed in this way for two reasons: one was to avoid republican overtones that the term 'citizen' as opposed to 'subject' might have; the other was so as not to erode the States' power over citizenship, according to which States could discriminate against classes of people.

Positive definition of citizenship was quite deliberately omitted from the Constitution for two reasons. The negative reason was quite shameful – to enable governments to manipulate the construction of citizenship so as to exclude various categories of people. The colonies, most notably Queensland and Western Australia, were already doing this and would toughen their exclusionary regimes as States in the decades after federation. The Commonwealth would follow suit and exclude 'aboriginal natives' from 1902 until the 1960s. The positive reason, if it can be called positive, was a deep respect for parliamentary responsible government. Citizenship rights and entitlements would not be constitutionalised but left for democratically elected parliaments and governments of both the Commonwealth and the States to determine.

Even the term 'citizen' was deliberately omitted from the final draft of the Australian Constitution after having been included in the earlier draft. The 1891 draft Constitution bill had borrowed directly from the American Constitution in including a guarantee of a citizen's privileges and immunities. A State was barred from making or enforcing 'any law abridging any privilege or immunity of citizens of other States', and could not 'deny to any person . . . the equal protection of the laws'.[63] This was essentially a paraphrase of the US Constitution's Article 4 and 14th Amendment.

In the 1897–98 Convention, however, the mood swung back in favour of the term 'subject' rather than 'citizen'. As Quick and Garran comment, it had been thought that, in a federal Commonwealth like the one being created, 'there should be a full-bloomed national citizenship above and beyond and immeasurably superior to State citizenship'. But such a 'full-bloomed national citizenship' did not eventuate: 'These contentions, apparently logical, were not sustained. Membership of the federal Commonwealth may, as a legal relation, be deduced from the Constitution, but it is not expressed there'.[64] The American-style positive guarantee of a citizen's privileges and immunities in the 1891 draft was replaced by a safeguard for subjects of the Queen:

> A subject of the Queen, resident in any State, shall not be subject in any other State to any disability or discrimination which would not be equally applicable to him if he were a subject of the Queen resident in such other State.[65]

Part of the unease with the term 'citizen' was based on concerns about the dual sites of citizenship in a federation. Delegates were unclear whether the clause referred to citizens of the States or citizens of the Commonwealth. Charles Kingston, the South Australian Premier, argued that the Constitution should define a concept of 'federal citizenship' and that the States should be prevented from legislating in such a way as to deprive citizens of the Commonwealth of privileges that Commonwealth citizenship conferred. But the prevailing view opposed this. O'Connor argued that 'Any declaration of the rights of the citizens, and any interference with the local rights of the states . . . would be very mischievous.' O'Connor, who was among the majority of delegates opposed to the delineation of positive citizenship rights, asked rhetorically: 'If we do not give any definite rights, what is the use of placing in the Constitution a provision which will be a fruitful source of litigation?'[66]

The central concern of those opposed to the use of the word 'citizen' in the Constitution was that it would lead to an erosion of State power over citizenship. Early in the debates, Sir John Forrest, the bluff West Australian Premier, signalled his concern for preserving his State's right both to exclude Asian and African people from obtaining mining licences and to prohibit 'even undesirable British subjects from entering the colony'. In a subsequent exchange, Forrest challenged that the citizenship clause, then clause 110, might serve to prevent New South Wales from legislating to stop a Victorian 'Chinaman' from crossing its borders, on the grounds that this would interfere with the rights of the person gained through clause 110. To this the New South Wales

Premier, George Reid, retorted: 'Surely we would have the right to abridge his rights'.[67]

To ensure that the States retained this 'right' to abridge the rights of certain categories of people, the word 'citizen' was removed from clause 110 and replaced by 'subject of the Queen'. The Constitution was never invested with any additional core citizenship values. The right of the States to determine their own citizenship criteria, subject to the specific powers given to the Commonwealth, would continue. Australian citizenship would be determined not by constitutional or legislative pronouncement, but by piecemeal legislation and incremental administrative practice at both the Commonwealth and State level. The status of British subject might have been treasured by generations of Australians who considered themselves 'independent Australian Britons',[68] and lauded by Sir Robert Menzies as late as the 1960s, but such status did nothing for Aborigines.

The definition of 'British subject' had been clearly established, as far back as Calvin's case (1608), as any person born inside the dominions of the King or Queen of Great Britain whose parents did not belong to certain classes of people such as foreign diplomats or prisoners of war. This was reaffirmed by British legislation in 1914.[69] Australia's *Nationality Act 1920*, which superseded earlier federal legislation, adopted the Imperial Code of 1914 and defined 'natural-born British subjects' to be 'any person born within His Majesty's dominions and allegiance'. Such definition included many people, Indians and Hong Kong Chinese for example, who were denied citizenship rights in Australia.

There had been some debate in the early nineteenth century between colonial officials and the British Colonial Office as to whether Aborigines were British subjects. However, 'At Federation there was no doubt of their [Aborigines'] status as subjects of the Queen and some were on the rolls of Victoria and South Australia'.[70] Between 1901 and 1961, when the Commonwealth Parliament's Select Committee on Voting Rights of Aborigines issued its report, Aboriginal Australians were 'all, without question, natural-born subjects of the Queen, permanently resident within the limits of the Commonwealth of Australia'.[71]

But the total lack of basic citizenship rights afforded by one's status as a British subject was nicely summarised by Geoffrey Sawer in 1961 for the Select Committee:

> Every aboriginal native of Australia born in Australia after 1829 . . . became a British subject by birth; his race was irrelevant, and there were no other circumstances capable of qualifying the allegiance . . . [But being] a British

> subject is by itself worth little; it is the foundation on which further conditions of disqualification or qualification are built, such as being a member of a particular race or meeting residential requirements.[72]

Retaining subjecthood in the Commonwealth Constitution and deliberately excluding any positive notion of citizenship or statement of core citizenship values allowed for the systematic discrimination against Aborigines and others by State and Commonwealth governments.

Even when in 1948 the Australian citizen became a formal legal entity, following the passage of the *Nationality and Citizenship Act*, little was changed. In June 1949, five months after the Act came into operation, the Attorney-General's Department advised the Immigration Department to respond to an inquiry about the citizenship status of Aborigines and 'half-castes' in the following terms:

> Aborigines or half-caste aborigines are . . . Australian citizens.
>
> It is pointed out, however, that the *Nationality and Citizenship Act* does not itself purport to alter the effect of existing legislation upon the rights and duties of individuals, and the position of aborigines in relation to such legislation has not been altered solely by reason of the provisions of that Act.[73]

Being British subjects in the new Australian nation was indeed 'worth little' to Aborigines for the first half-century of federation. For them such subjecthood was 'the foundation on which further conditions of disqualification' would be built through legislative and administrative action. This is examined in the next chapter. Sadly, the adoption of Australian citizenship in 1948 made little difference to the rights and duties of individuals that were enshrined in existing legislation, and which were not changed. And, as the Attorney-General's advice affirmed in 1949, Aborigines, although now enjoying the empty shell of Australian citizenship, continued to be excluded by such legislation.

To conclude, the Constitution itself did not cause Aborigines to be excluded from citizenship. As we have shown, the two references to Aborigines in the Constitution alone did not have this effect. But, at the same time, the decision of the founders not to provide any positive statement of the meanings of Australian citizenship did impact on Aborigines. For the ultimate determination of who was and was not a citizen lay not in a reading of the Constitution, but in the hands of a range of legislators and administrators at both the State and federal level. For several generations until the 1960s, presumably supported by the active or tacit consent of the Australian people whom they represented, Commonwealth and State parliaments, governments and bureaucracies systematically excluded Aboriginal people from basic citizenship rights and entitlements. They, rather than the Constitution, were to blame.

Table 3 Formal restrictions affecting Aborigines on key citizenship criteria, 1901

	Statutory bar on voting	*Able to be removed to reserves*	*Employment formally regulated*
Victoria	No	Yes	Yes
Queensland	Yes	Yes	Yes
Western Australia	Yes	Implied	Yes
New South Wales	No	No relevant legislation	No relevant legislation
South Australia and the Northern Territory	No	No relevant legislation	No relevant legislation
Tasmania	No	No relevant legislation	No relevant legislation

CHAPTER 4

The Commonwealth Defines the Australian Citizen

(in association with Tom Clarke)

The exclusion of Aborigines from citizenship was by no means a constitutionally ordained necessity, but rather a deliberate product of Commonwealth and State government legislation and administration. The exclusionary category of 'aboriginal native' was central to the institutional definition and development of Australian citizenship, and was created by the legislature, defended to a certain extent by the judiciary, and most importantly, developed, nurtured and administered by the bureaucracy for over sixty years. Far from being a product of a rigid constitution, conceived and endorsed by nineteenth-century colonial racists, the long exclusion of Aboriginal Australians from Australian citizenship was implemented and routinely administered by Australian governments and bureaucracy until well into the second half of the twentieth century.

This chapter covers virtually the first half-century of Australian government, from the establishment of the Commonwealth in 1901 to the 1948 *Nationality and Citizenship Act*, which recognised Australian citizenship in law for the first time. For purposes of exposition, the period is divided roughly into two halves, separated by a brief transitional period in the early to mid-1920s. The first period covers the early decades of federation, 1901 to 1920, when the Commonwealth's legislative and administrative regime, or regimes, were set in place and the first attempts made to define 'aboriginal native'. The transitional phase, from 1920 to 1926, was typified by confusion and compromise as the Commonwealth came to terms with the implications of its citizenship activity and modified its approach under both domestic and international political pressures. The period following this administrative shake-up until the late 1940s saw substantial changes to the social security, electoral and nationality laws and a shift in the administrative focus. This period was dominated by pressures for consolidation and problems of delineating more precisely the boundaries of the now clearly defined 'aboriginal native'. It was also the period in which the Commonwealth first came under sustained domestic and international pressure because of its discriminatory treatment in denying 'aboriginal natives', and most persistently Australian Aborigines, basic citizenship rights.

1901 to 1920: Constituting the Body of Citizens

Legislative Provision

The establishment of the Commonwealth government in 1901, empowered to act in specific areas relating to citizenship, was quickly translated into legislative regimes embodying a range of exclusionary practices. Perhaps the best known was the infamous dictation test required by the *Immigration Restriction Act 1901*, which was deftly administered to screen-out non-white immigrants and prevent them from entering Australia. Dealing with non-white people who were already in Australia was more difficult and engaged the efforts of generations of legislators and bureaucrats. The legislative regime of the early Commonwealth, which defined basic citizenship rights and entitlements, was dominated by the exclusion of 'aboriginal natives'. It was through the definition and development of this exclusionary category – which applied to Aboriginal Australians and peoples from Asia, Africa and the Pacific Islands – that the boundaries and meaning of Australian citizenship would be worked out.

The term 'aboriginal native' was the most commonly employed racial category in Commonwealth legislation and administrative language. As we have seen in earlier chapters, the term had wide currency in nineteenth-century colonial practice and had been picked up in section 127 of the Constitution. It was prominent in the areas of electoral franchise, naturalisation and pensions. The *Commonwealth Franchise Act 1902*, which was later incorporated in the *Commonwealth Electoral Act 1918*, excluded any 'aboriginal native of Australia Asia Africa or the Islands of the Pacific except New Zealand' from the franchise. The *Naturalization Act 1903* excluded any 'aboriginal native of Asia, Africa, or the Islands of the Pacific, excepting New Zealand' from becoming naturalised. Australian Aborigines did not need to appear in this exclusionary clause, since they were British subjects by birth and had nothing to gain from naturalisation. The *Invalid and Old-Age Pensions Act 1908* denied pensions to otherwise qualified 'Asiatics (except those born in Australia), or aboriginal natives of Australia, Africa, the Islands of the Pacific, or New Zealand'. The *Maternity Allowance Act 1912* barred the allowance to 'women who are Asiatics, or are aboriginal natives of Australia, Papua, or the islands of the Pacific'.[1]

Not all legislative clauses employing the term 'aboriginal native' did so in an exclusionary or punitive manner. In the area of employment, the *Sugar Bounty Act 1905* and the *Bounties Act 1907* exempted 'aboriginal natives' of Australia from an otherwise racially discriminatory bounty system.[2] A protective, although demeaning, provision of the *Emigration Act 1910* prohibited the emigration, without a permit, of:

(a) any child who is under contract to perform theatrical, operatic, or other work outside the Commonwealth;
(b) any child of European race or extraction unless in the care or charge of some adult person of European race or extraction; and
(c) any aboriginal native.[3]

While the term 'aboriginal native' was the principal exclusionary category employed, on more minor occasions other racial descriptions such as 'white' and 'European descent' were used. 'White labour' clauses were routinely used to restrict financial incentives provided by the Commonwealth: for example in the *Excise Tariff Act 1902*, the *Sugar Bounty Act 1903* and *Sugar Bounty Act 1905*, as well as the *Bounties Act 1907*. In addition to domestic financial benefits for white labour, the Commonwealth also passed the *Customs Tariff (South African Preference) Act 1906*, which extended reduced tariffs to South African sugar 'produced solely by white labour' as opposed to sugar 'produced wholly or partly by black labour'.[4] Finally, the *Defence Act 1903*, when amended in 1909 to add to the purely voluntary peacetime standing army a regime of compulsory peacetime military training, exempted those 'not substantially of European origin or descent' from combat training. The following year, the same persons were exempted from possible war-time conscription for combat service.[5]

While the legislative regime of the early Commonwealth was defining basic citizenship rights and entitlements, considerations of 'blood' and 'race' dominated. The main definitional category was that of 'aboriginal native', a phrase that was used to refer not only to Australia's indigenous inhabitants, but to people from Asia, Africa and the Pacific Islands. It was through the definition and development of this category that the boundaries and meaning of Australian citizenship would be worked out, and the exclusion of Aboriginal Australians would be ensured.

Administrative Definition

So what was an 'aboriginal native'? One might think that such a category is self-evident, but it took a considerable period of time before an administrative consensus on the meaning of the term emerged. There were two questions that concerned the bureaucracy: when did a person cease or begin to be an 'aboriginal native'?; and what was it that made such a person an 'aboriginal native' as opposed to merely an Aboriginal, a native, or something else? The first was a question of boundaries; the second was one of definition or meaning. It is important to appreciate Australian usage and the manner in which its peculiarities were taken up and embellished by official practice.

In late twentieth-century dialogue, the terms 'aboriginal' and 'native' tend to be used interchangeably, although the latter is usually reserved for flora and fauna. Nineteenth-century British usage was quite different and early twentieth-century Australian usage was idiosyncratic in ways that were significant for the administrative definition of this key category.

The British traditionally steered clear of using the words 'aborigine' and 'aboriginal' when referring to indigenous inhabitants under their control.[6] The Select Committee on Aboriginal Tribes (1835–1837), set up to investigate the appalling conditions of indigenous inhabitants under British dominion, had settled on the term 'aborigines' to describe such persons, but this generally had not extended to legal and administrative practice. Usage varied between countries: while the British continued to refer to 'their' indigenous populations as 'natives', Americans and Canadians employed the term 'Indians', the French and Latin countries used '*indigènes*', and the Germans and Germanic countries utilised '*eingeborenen*'.[7] The term 'aborigines' only became common in the Imperial era, when 'the problem of the contact between civilized and uncivilized races [was] considered as distinct from its relation to any one civilized state, and as a matter of common interest to all civilized states'.[8] 'Aborigines' and 'aboriginal' were useful generic terms for the European powers to employ when discussing each other's indigenous inhabitants.

Australian usage at the turn of the last century, however, was quite different. The two terms 'aboriginal' and 'native', when used individually, meant quite different things. One was used to refer to race, often described in terms of 'blood'; the other to place of birth. With a keen ear for local usage, the visiting Anthony Trollope noted in his *Australia* that:

> It will be as well to call the race by the name officially given to it. The government styles them 'aboriginals' . . . the word native is almost universally applied to white colonists born in Australia.[9]

Thus the Australian Natives' Association was not, as one might expect, an association for Aboriginal Australians, but a body formed by and for white Australians born in Australia. The term 'native', it seems, was imbued with the idea of nativity, of birth in a particular place.

'Aboriginal', on the other hand, had a related meaning but in early Australian usage was given a different slant. It meant being the *original inhabitant or descendant thereof*. 'Aboriginal native' was a composite term meaning a descendant of the original race of a particular region who was also born in that place. Thus an 'aboriginal native of Australia' was a black indigenous person whereas a 'native' referred to an Australian-born white person.

Until the *Muramats* High Court case in 1923, there was no authoritative judicial definition of 'aboriginal native' in Commonwealth administrative law and practice. Instead the bureaucracy relied on the opinions of the Attorneys- and Solicitors-General to interpret this key legislative term. These opinions were couched in specific rather than general terms, and interpreted 'aboriginal native' in the context of the particular section of the Act in question. As a result, 'aboriginal native' was not defined uniformly, but instead developed different meanings in a series of largely parallel regimes which defined particular citizenship rights and benefits. Each regime employed its own definition of 'aboriginal native' and, although these tended to coalesce around a central core meaning, the finer points occasionally diverged and changed over time.

The Commonwealth Franchise Act 1902

The 1902 *Commonwealth Franchise Act* is justly famous for enfranchising women. In so doing the Commonwealth adopted the best practice of several of the States and set the national standard which all the other States soon adopted; it was also a leader internationally in enfranchising women. The *Commonwealth Franchise Act* gave 'all persons not under twenty-one years of age whether male or female married or unmarried' who had lived in Australia for six months, were natural born or naturalised subjects of the King, and whose names were on the electoral roll, the right to vote for Senate and House of Representative elections.[10]

Well, not quite all persons: section 4 of the Act excluded persons of 'unsound mind', 'attainted of treason, or . . . convicted . . . for any offence punishable . . . by imprisonment for one year or longer'. Furthermore, in an amendment carried against the government, section 4 also excluded Aboriginal natives in the following way:

> No aboriginal native of Australia Asia Africa or the Islands of the Pacific except New Zealand shall be entitled to have his name placed on an Electoral Roll unless so entitled under section forty-one of the Constitution.

The New Zealand exception was to facilitate entry of that country into the new federation because Maoris already had voting rights. The section 41 exception was supposed to ensure that Australian Aborigines who had the State franchise, such as Aborigines in South Australia, were also entitled to the Commonwealth franchise. This provision was rendered meaningless, however, by the subsequent action of Commonwealth electoral officials, who took to striking such Aborigines off the Commonwealth roll.[11]

Despite this partial section 41 exemption, which administrative practice soon jettisoned anyway, the 1902 *Commonwealth Franchise Act* effectively barred Australian Aborigines from the rights of citizenship. Subsequent legislation on citizenship rights and benefits routinely copied the *Commonwealth Franchise Act* in excluding 'aboriginal natives', so the carrying of the exclusionary amendment for the *Commonwealth Franchise Act* was an historical turning point that deserves special attention.

The Commonwealth Franchise Bill was brought to parliament by Senator O'Connor, government leader in the Senate, eminent founding father and member of the three-man constitution drafting committee in the 1897–98 Federation Convention, and one of the three original appointees to the High Court the following year. The bill did not exclude Aborigines. That was done by way of an amendment, initially (but at first try unsuccessfully) brought forward by Senator Matheson of Western Australia after some heated exchanges in the Senate. In support of his amendment Matheson argued: 'Nobody can for an instant maintain that the framers of the Constitution regarded it as in the least degree possible that a vote would be given in any State or in the Commonwealth to aboriginal natives'. Matheson claimed that the framers of the Constitution never contemplated giving the vote to Aboriginal people; he even doubted whether the framers were aware that Aborigines had the vote in any State. This was patently false, but Matheson was driven primarily by racial prejudice as evidenced in the following passage which passed muster as parliamentary language of the day:

> Surely it is absolutely repugnant to the greater number of the people of the Commonwealth that an aboriginal man, or aboriginal lubra or gin – a horrible, degraded, dirty creature – should have the same rights, simply by virtue of being 21 years of age, that we have, after some debate today, decided to give to our wives and daughters. To me it is as repugnant and atrocious a legislative proposal as any one could suggest.[12]

Matheson linked the disfranchisement of Aborigines with the enfranchisement of women – as if the inclusion of 'our wives and daughters' made the exclusion of Aborigines, and especially Aboriginal women, more imperative. Western Australia had just enfranchised women but continued to disfranchise Aborigines. Other senators supporting Matheson contrasted the worthlessness and degredation of Chinese people, who were also to be excluded from the franchise, with the virtue of white women who were being included. Strong support came from Queensland senators with Senator Stewart railing against Aborigines as 'these opium-eating blacks, these ignorant aboriginals, these people who do not care two straws about the government of the country so long as they can get their daily tucker and their allowance of opium'.[13]

Richard O'Connor's defence of the government's original inclusionary bill and his statements about the Constitution and the status of Aboriginal people did not carry the day. They are worth quoting at some length, however, because they were the best view of the issue, both constitutionally and morally. Had O'Connor prevailed, and the government's franchise bill been adopted at this early stage, Australia's Aboriginal people might have been saved from sixty years of deprivation of basic citizenship rights, the consequences of which are still clearly visible. Richard O'Connor said:

> In New South Wales, Victoria, South Australia, and Tasmania an aboriginal has the same right to vote as has any other inhabitant . . . This is the policy in four States out of the six. In the remaining States of Western Australia and Queensland, where the largest number of what are generally described as wild blacks exist, the right to vote is given to an aboriginal, provided that he is the owner of property to the value of £100. Why was that right given? Every one was aware at the time that there were numbers of these aboriginals who, perhaps, would not understand very much about political questions. But I think it occurred to those who were framing these laws in the States, that it would be a monstrous thing, an unheard of piece of savagery on our part, to treat the aboriginals, whose land we were occupying, in such a manner as to deprive them absolutely of any right to vote in their own country, simply on the ground of their colour, and because they were aboriginals . . .
>
> Although the aboriginals in New South Wales, Victoria, Tasmania, and South Australia, had the right to vote through all these years, when they were more numerous and more savage, now under the Commonwealth, with the liberal views we are supposed to entertain and to bring into the legislative field, we are asked to take away from the sons of those people for ever the right to vote. Why are we to do that? . . .
>
> We shall have a class of aboriginals who will be entitled to be put on the roll, and entitled to vote under the existing laws, and those very men will have to tell their sons who are becoming more civilized, and perhaps as civilized, and as worthy of the franchise as the white men among whom they

are living – 'Although your people owned this territory for centuries before the white man came here, although you are his equal in intelligence, it has been prescribed by the Commonwealth that you shall not have the right to vote at all.' I say it would be a monstrous and a savage application of this principle of a white Australia. I do not believe this committee will consent to go back upon what has been the policy of Australia ever since the white man came here.[14]

O'Connor was defeated. When the Senate voted on Matheson's motion to insert the exclusionary clause that later became law, O'Connor managed to maintain the vote for Australian Aborigines.[15] But an amendment moved by Henry Higgins in the House of Representatives extended the exclusion of other 'aboriginal natives' to any 'aboriginal native of Australia', and was ultimately endorsed by both houses.[16] Thus the *Commonwealth Franchise Act*, which according to its title aimed to provide a 'Uniform Federal Franchise', ended up disfranchising Aboriginal people. In so doing it adopted the worst State practice for the new Commonwealth, a practice that saw most Aborigines disfranchised for sixty years.

The *Commonwealth Franchise Act*, rather than the Constitution, set the legislative paradigm, with the exclusionary category 'aboriginal native' being enshrined throughout subsequent naturalisation and pension legislation. In this way Australian Aboriginal people were lumped together with other alien 'aboriginal natives' and denied the benefits of citizenship.

The deprivation for Aboriginal people was horrendous, but in addition the enforcement of such an exclusionary policy institutionalised callous injustice at the heart of Australia's citizenship administration. For example, in 1938 a representation was made by the Eastern Suburbs District Council of the Returned Servicemen's Association of New South Wales through the local member, Mr E.J. Harrison, that the *Maternity Allowance Act* be amended to give Aboriginal mothers whose husbands were ex-members of the AIF the maternity allowance. The response was handled routinely but at the highest level with the Commissioner of Maternity Allowances advising the Minister that:

the present policy is governed by legislation and it is considered that action to amend the law in the direction requested would not be desirable. If the law were so amended it would be difficult to withstand requests for a similar concession to all other aboriginal mothers who are at present debarred under the Act. Moreover, the granting of the request would, it is thought, soon be followed by demands for similar concessions to aborigines under the Invalid and Old-age Pensions Act.[17]

Once put in place, the exclusionary regime developed an administrative logic of its own in which the category of 'aboriginal native' was developed by generations of ministers and bureaucrats. Decisions were made in quasi-common law style, by defining and refining definitional categories and otherwise proceeding on a case-by-case basis, which provided precedents for a body of administrative practices. Much of this developed around the category of 'half-caste' or people of mixed Aboriginal-white parentage.

'Half-castes' and 'Preponderating blood'

Because 'aboriginal native' was an exclusionary category, defining its boundaries was an important issue. How were people of 'mixed race', and in particular those with one Aboriginal and one white parent, so-called 'half-castes', to be classified? Alfred Deakin, the first Attorney-General, made an early ruling 'that half-castes are not "aboriginal natives"' and so were not affected by section 127 of the Constitution. According to Deakin:

> Section 127 of the Constitution makes a particular exception that in reckoning the numbers of the people of the Commonwealth or a State, 'aboriginal natives shall not be counted'. The rule as to the construction of such exceptions, where, as in this case, they are not remedial, is that they should be construed strictly.
>
> I am of opinion that half-castes are not 'aboriginal natives' within the meaning of this section, and should be included in reckoning the population.[18]

In September 1905 Robert Garran, the Secretary of the Attorney-General's Department, agreed with this view in interpreting the *Commonwealth Franchise Act 1902.* Garran advised 'that half-castes are not disqualified [from voting], but that all persons in whom the aboriginal blood preponderates are disqualified'. This arcane notion of 'preponderating blood' was clarified in a handwritten comment initialled 'R.R.G.' (Garran's usual initial mark) interpreting 'blood' as 'ancestry'. Isaac Isaacs, the then Attorney-General, minuted his opinion, stating 'I think this is reasonable and should be followed'.[19]

Aboriginality

Defining Aboriginality quickly became an issue in determining the status of 'aboriginal natives' of Asia, Africa and the Pacific. In 1904 Garran was asked by the Department of Home Affairs to give an opinion on the nationality of children born of Asian parents in Australia for purposes of establishing their right to vote. He replied that 'Persons born in the British Dominions are British subjects –

whatever the nationality of their parents'.[20] Thus, he implied that the term 'native' was related to a person's place of birth, regardless of the parents' racial and native status.

Two months later, however, the Department of External Affairs came up with a much looser racial interpretation for the *Naturalization Act.* The case concerned the application for naturalisation of Joseph Bakhash, who was of 'Syrian' racial parentage but born in New York. His application was rejected on the grounds that:

> As the applicant, although of Asiatic race is not a native of Asia he is not in strictness debarred from applying for naturalization. As, however, the intention of Parliament apparently was to refuse the privilege of naturalization to persons of Asiatic descent, it is submitted whether advantage should be taken in this and similar cases of the provisions of section 7 to withhold the issue of a certificate.[21]

According to this broader view, which invoked a racist intention of Parliament, a person of Asian descent could be refused naturalisation although not technically an 'aboriginal native of Asia'.

Coincidently, two days later, Higgins, then Attorney-General, confirmed Garran's stricter interpretation in a different case involving the term 'aboriginal native' in the context of the *Naturalization Act.* Mr R.A. Saleeby, born in Syria, had contended that 'aboriginal' meant literally the first inhabitants of a place. In applying for naturalisation, Saleeby claimed that as a descendant of the Crusaders he was not an Aboriginal of Asia. He argued:

> (1) That the modern Syrian has no relation whatsoever to the ancient Aboriginal Syrians.
> (2) That the Syrian language is not spoken by the present nation, although they are called Syrians.
> (3) That the lineal line of my ancestors in particular dates back from the Crusaders, as the name of the family bears this contention out, being the literal Arabic translation of 'Crusaders'.
> (4) That the modern Syrians are admitted to be of the white or Caucasian races of the world and no coloured stigma has ever been attributed to our people in any era.[22]

Mr Saleeby's proposed interpretation of the word 'aboriginal' caused considerable consternation in the Department of External Affairs, which baulked at narrowing the definition of Aboriginal and having to sort out ancient migrations of people. Atlee Hunt, Secretary of the Department, wrote anxiously to the Minister:

> Considering that there are very few peoples whose migration to the locality where they now live cannot be traced either historically or by irresistible inference from language and customs, to narrow the meaning of the word

> 'aboriginal' as Mr Saleeby appears to suggest would, in my opinion, render it practically of no effect.[23]

Attorney-General Higgins agreed with the practical position in providing formal advice:

> In my opinion the words 'aboriginal native' of Asia etc. in the *Naturalization Act* mean 'a native belonging to a native race' of Asia etc. The word 'aboriginal' is meant, in the context, to contrast such natives of Asia etc., as are born in the home or present habitat of their race, and such natives as are not so born. It was meant to be a practical modern distinction, not a distinction depending on knowledge of the obscure beginnings of history.[24]

Saleeby was deemed an 'aboriginal native of Asia' and this basic definition eventually won general acceptance in interpreting the franchise, but not until many years later. The issue was whether the term 'aboriginal native' meant non-European persons in general – as the Department of External Affairs ruled in rejecting the application for naturalisation of Joseph Bakhash – or whether it referred to a particular class of persons, namely those of a particular race (Aboriginal) born in a particular place (native). The latter view, as evidenced in the majority of the rulings cited above, was dominant. It was clearly enunciated by Garran, Secretary of the Attorney-General's Department, in November 1912, after a decade of administrative practice:

> Strictly speaking there is no race disqualification in the *Franchise Act.* Aboriginal natives of Australia, Asia, Africa, and the Islands of the Pacific (except New Zealand) are disqualified from having their names placed on an Electoral Roll, but *to be an aboriginal native of a place a person must be born in that place.* The effect is that persons of Asiatic race [for example] born in Australia are not disqualified.[25]

Not all discrimination against naturalised persons was racial, however, with one's place of birth being significant in certain instances. For example, the *Commonwealth Electoral (War-Time) Act 1917* disfranchised all persons (even if naturalised) born in enemy territory for the duration of the war and for six months afterwards. Of the countries of the British empire, only Canada had enacted similar legislation, and very quickly after the war it had become a source of some embarrassment. Naturalisation in Australia made an alien a naturalised 'British subject',[26] but such persons were still subject to the strictures of Commonwealth citizenship law. Naturalisation could not affect one's racial status nor one's place of birth.

Variegated Regimes

There was no core instrument or definition of Australian citizenship, but rather a series of Acts that granted particular rights, such as the franchise or naturalisation, or benefits, such as the maternity allowance or invalid and old-age pensions. Each Act was administered separately with the consequent development of discrete regimes. Uniformity of definition, if not practice, was largely achieved within each regime across the whole of Australia, but these regimes were far from being logically compatible with one another.

All people entering Australia were first screened under the *Immigration Restriction Act.* Having passed through this, the immigrants, as well as Australian Aborigines, were subject to two further tests for citizenship: first, and most important, if they fell within the 'aboriginal native' category they were barred from exercising specific rights or from receiving designated benefits; and second, other disadvantages followed if they were not of 'European' or 'white' racial origin. Qualifying for one regime did not guarantee entitlement in all the others. Thus, successful naturalisation, for example, did not automatically entitle a person to access to the franchise, or to pensions.

Nationality did not equal citizenship. Indeed, as Garran noted in October 1904: 'the law of a [British] possession need not confer the same rights upon a naturalized person as upon a natural-born subject, or even confer the same rights upon all naturalized persons'.[27] Patrick McMahon Glynn, when Attorney-General, supported this principle, arguing in October 1909 that:

> it appears to me reasonable to require that [for example] the national status should have existed for a certain period before the naturalized person is qualified for certain high offices [such as Federal parliamentarians: five years] and for certain other privileges of citizenship [such as pensions: three years].[28]

The Impact of Geography

Geography played a key role in determining one's citizenship prospects. The franchise and naturalisation Acts excluded all non-European 'aboriginal natives' except those of New Zealand. The invalid and old-age pensions were denied to all 'aboriginal natives' and 'Asiatics', whereas the maternity allowance Act did not deny Africans and New Zealanders, but excluded Papuans as well as other 'aboriginal natives' and Asiatics. Only Australian Aborigines were affected by all of these exclusions as well as by census and emigration restrictions, although they alone benefited from 'white' bounty exemptions.[29]

Inevitably there were problems with the exact meaning and boundaries of such words as 'Asia', 'Africa', 'the Islands of the Pacific' and the like. In March 1905, for purposes of the *Naturalization Act*, Garran determined that Jules Peno, an 'aboriginal native' of the Cape Verde Islands, some 320 miles off the coast of Africa in the Atlantic Ocean, was not an 'aboriginal native of Africa'. On the same day, he decided that Johannes Bine, an 'aboriginal native' of Timor, was similarly not an 'aboriginal native' of Asia or the islands of the Pacific. Garran's reasoning was based on information given to him that 'Timor lies to the east of "Wallace's line", and . . . is considered by scientists never to have been connected with Asia, but from geological, ethnological and zoological affinities rather to belong to Australia'.[30]

Geography could be very cruel. In April 1905 Garran rejected the application of Christoa Gomez, from Goa, a Portugese colony on the coast of India, on the grounds that he was an 'aboriginal native' of Asia.[31] In July 1910 Garran advised that Java should be considered as part of Asia.[32] In 1916 he advised that a certificate of naturalisation had been improperly granted to a Turk in 1911. It had been assumed by the department that the place of birth given by the man was in geographical Europe, whereas it had been discovered years later that the city in question lay in fact in the Asian part of Turkey. Thus the original certificate had been granted improperly, and therefore did 'not hold good'.[33]

Racial Categories

Successful avoidance of the 'aboriginal native' categories did not ensure that one avoided other racial classes that were occasionally employed. Terms such as 'Asiatic', 'white' and 'European origin' were held to be substantially different from 'aboriginal native', and could be used as a basis for restricting eligibility for certain benefits. The exclusion of 'Asiatics' from the maternity allowance was a case in point. Garran was asked by Treasury to advise on two cases where:

(1) The mother was born in Spain. Her parents were born in Asia and were of Asiatic descent.
(2) The mother was born in Australia. Her father was a Chinese and her mother a European.

In responding, Garran applied the criterion of racial origin in the first case and the by now well-established exemption of 'half-castes' to the second:

> In my opinion 'Asiatics' in this section means 'of Asiatic race'. I therefore think that a woman of wholly Asiatic blood is disqualified, wherever she may have been born.
>
> In the case of mixed descent, I think that a woman should be considered as an Asiatic or not, according as the Asiatic descent does or does not predominate; and that in the case of a woman of the half-blood (i.e. one of whose parents only was Asiatic) she should, as the Act is a beneficial one, be considered as *not* being an Asiatic.[34]

On this reasoning the first woman should be denied the allowance, but the second granted it. Garran reiterated this view in 1922: that 'race' meant 'belonging to a particular ethnical stock', so that, although 'Australian-born Chinese are natural-born British subjects, they still belong to the Asiatic ethnical stock'.[35]

Opinion was divided over the meanings of 'white labour' and 'European descent'. Deakin, in an opinion on the 'white labour' clause of the *Excise Tariff Act 1902*, argued in April 1902 that:

> Aboriginal labour cannot be considered white labour . . . As to persons of mixed race, quadroons may reasonably be considered as white labour; persons in whom the blood of a coloured race predominates should not. Half-castes are on the border line; but in view of the affirmative and restrictive language of the provision, I think that half-castes should be excluded.[36]

This was contrary to the line he had taken only seven months earlier in ruling that 'half-castes' were not covered by the 'aboriginal natives' exclusion in section 127 of the Constitution. But having qualified as de facto whites for the census, they did not satisfy as 'white labour' for the *Excise Tariff Act.* In contrast to this, Garran argued in September 1905, in the context of the *Immigration Restriction Act 1901,* that 'European descent' had 'reference to race and not to nationality', and that 'the test should be the preponderating blood – and that in cases of the half-blood the person charged is entitled to the benefit'.[37] Garran applied the same principles to the 'white labour' clause of the *Post and Telegraph Act 1901.* This phrase, he confirmed in November 1921, included all 'half-castes' regardless of race.[38]

Citizenship Status

To summarise the situation for the period 1901 to 1920, formal Commonwealth citizenship entitlements and restrictions separated 'white' Europeans from 'black' non-Europeans (see table 4).

This strict dichotomy only held for the first generation of persons. For the second and subsequent generations, everyone was 'native' or

Table 4 The citizenship status of first generation persons up to 1920

White	Automatic full citizenship	Natural-born (including 'half-castes') British subjects
	Acquired citizenship	Naturalised aliens[39]
Black	Automatic non-citizens	Aliens ('full blood') Australian Aborigines ('full blood') British subjects ('full blood')

Table 5 The citizenship status of second and subsequent generation persons up to 1920

Automatic full citizenship[40]	Natural-born (all, including 'half-castes')
Automatic non-citizens	Australian Aborigines ('full blood')

'natural born' and, with the notable exception of Aboriginal Australians, generally entitled to most Commonwealth citizenship rights and benefits. However, racial background could still be used for some relatively minor racial discrimination. The consequence was that only Australian Aborigines remained trapped on the wrong side of the citizenship divide, as starkly illustrated in table 5.

By the end of the period under discussion the generally accepted definition of an 'aboriginal native' was a person born in a particular place, of a racial group found in that same place prior to the arrival of Europeans. Persons of non-Australian 'aboriginal' blood born in Australia were deemed not to be 'aboriginal natives'. The test of one's 'aboriginality' would be that of 'predominating blood'. A person in whom no blood predominated, a 'half-caste', was on the whole regarded as European.

1920–1926: Pressures for Change

During the period 1920 to 1926, the regimes of citizenship that had developed during the two previous decades went through a period of considerable transformation. Many were modified, but the centrality of the 'aboriginal native' category as the principal definitional term for citizenship remained. The term itself finally received judicial interpretation by the High Court, in the *Muramats* case. The changes were caused by two interrelated sets of factors. The first was international pressure against racial discrimination, particularly against Indians who had a special claim as British subjects and whose grievances were taken up by British Imperial authorities. The second cause of dissatisfaction involved increased internal concern over the blatant inconsistencies in citizenship rights and benefits across various legislative regimes.

The only new legislation employing the term 'aboriginal native' passed during this period was the *Passports Act 1920.* This required all persons leaving Australia, with certain exceptions, to obtain a valid passport and visa. The list of people exempted from this requirement, however, included: seafarers; naval personnel; persons leaving for New Zealand, Papua, and Norfolk Island; deportees; and 'any aboriginal native of Asia, or of any island in the East Indies, or in the Indian or Pacific Oceans, leaving the Commonwealth'.[41] The effect of this was to make it less difficult for such persons to leave Australia than for other persons. It appears that this was, in effect, a surreptitious encouragement for these people to leave.

As early as 1916 there appears to have been some bureaucratic disquiet over the continuing racial disqualifications in the franchise legislation. During the drafting stages of the *Commonwealth Electoral Act 1918,* the Law Department queried the necessity for the offending provision, now in subsection 39(5), which incorporated the racial disqualifications contained in the 1902 *Commonwealth Franchise Act.*[42] Later, the Crown Solicitor's office also questioned the retention of racial disqualifications in the Act: 'Clause 39: I would suggest that the necessity for continuing subsection 5 be considered. The provision looks to me to be somewhat dangerous and ought to be unnecessary if a complete rational system is laid down.'[43] There is unfortunately no explicit statement as to what the 'complete rational system' might have been, but it is not unreasonable to assume that it referred to either a complete abandonment of the racial disqualification, or more likely, to a comprehensive linking of the franchise to the acquisition of nationality. In a prescient comment, the Minister foreshadowed the government's dilemma in allowing Indians full citizenship rights under the Bill: 'Natives of India? To admit would affect other Asiatics'.[44] It would take some time and substantial Imperial pressure before Australia stopped discrimination against Indians.

Naturalisation

Meanwhile, in 1920 the Commonwealth dropped its exclusion of 'aboriginal natives' of Asia, Africa and Islands in the Pacific in passing a new *Nationality Act*, which replaced the *Naturalization Act*. The changes brought about by the new Act, which derived from the Imperial *British Nationality and Status of Aliens Act 1914*, had in fact been under consideration by the Commonwealth since as early as 1904.[45] The countries of the Empire had agreed to make their naturalisation laws uniform and applicable across all countries, with British law providing the basis for uniform nationality laws throughout the Empire. Persons naturalised under this law would be deemed 'British subjects'. Each colonial legislature could pass its own complementary naturalisation laws, but they were not supposed to be more restrictive than the British law.

Following the British example, the Australian legislation contained no exclusions from naturalisation of 'aboriginal natives'. Theoretically, all those persons who had been denied naturalisation under the previous Act on grounds of their status as 'aboriginal natives' could, if they satisfied the other criteria, apply for, and perhaps receive, Australian nationality. Of course, the Commonwealth retained the power to ensure that such persons did not enter Australia in the first place through its migration policies, and the new Act contained the same absolute ministerial discretion in allowing naturalisation as had the previous one.[46]

The new *Nationality Act*, however, was largely formal window dressing. As well as removing the exclusionary bar of 'aboriginal native', it seemed to entitle all naturalised persons to full citizenship rights, powers and privileges:

> A person to whom a certificate of naturalization is granted by the Governor-General shall, subject to the provisions of this or any other Act, be entitled to all political and other rights, powers and privileges, and be subject to all obligations duties and liabilities to which a natural-born British subject is entitled or subject, and, as from the date of his naturalization, have to all intents and purposes the status of a natural-born British subject.

An additional paragraph, however, made abundantly clear that such was not the case.

> Provided that where, by any provision of the Constitution or of any Act or State Constitution or Act, a distinction is made between the rights, powers or privileges of natural-born British subjects and those of persons naturalized in the Commonwealth or in a State, the rights, powers and privileges conferred by this section shall, for the purposes of that provision, be only those (if any) to which persons so naturalized are therein expressed to be entitled.[47]

Thus naturalisation had no effect on the franchise rights of 'aboriginal natives', as Garran summarised on 3 June 1921:

I am of opinion that such a person would not be entitled to be enrolled or to vote under the *Commonwealth Electoral Act 1918–1919.* By s.11 of the *Nationality Act 1920* that person is upon the grant of the certificate of naturalisation 'entitled to all political and other rights, powers, and privileges to which a natural-born British subject is entitled'; but a natural-born British subject who is an aboriginal native . . . is *not* entitled to be enrolled or to vote under the *Commonwealth Electoral Act 1918–1919* and in my opinion, therefore, a naturalised British subject who is an aboriginal native . . . is similarly *not* entitled.[48]

So, despite a more liberal regime for naturalisation, the racially divided citizenship regimes remained fully in operation.

In addition to the fact that naturalisation meant very little, its granting was also highly discretionary. This was evidenced in the case of Pedro Bautista, a Filipino and therefore of American nationality, who applied for naturalisation under the new Act. The Department of Home and Territories advised the Minister in early 1922 that:

There is nothing in the present Act to make [the] applicant ineligible, but it is the practice of the Department not to naturalize natives of Asia, Africa or the Islands of the Pacific. The Minister has power to accept any applicant.
I recommend that Bautista's application be proceeded with.

Three days later the reply was that the 'Minister is unable to authorize'.[49] Later that same month, the reverse decision was made regarding a Turk, who had previously been denied naturalisation under the old Act. The department advised the Minister that: 'All other late enemy aliens are being naturalized by the Department . . . Turks should be brought into line with other European people and permitted to become naturalized'. The Minister agreed on this occasion.[50] Consequently, naturalisation started being granted regularly to Syrians and Assyrians.

A year later, the much more controversial issue of naturalisation of Chinese people came up. Unlike previously, the Department's advice was far more negative because of fears of opening the floodgates to Asians:

I do not think that the Department should make a precedent for the naturalization of Chinese. There are about 20,000 Chinese in Australia, and if a precedent be created for the naturalization of such aliens, the Department would find it very difficult to discriminate between those who should be naturalized and those who should not . . . Owing to the operation of the *Immigration Restriction Act* and the White Australia policy generally, the Chinese residents of Australia know exactly where they stand, and are more or less reconciled to the present state of affairs . . . [In addition] if we permit the naturalization of Chinese, we cannot very well refuse Japanese and other aboriginal natives of Asia and the islands of the Pacific.

The Minister agreed, stating in June 1923 that 'I cannot agree to the naturalization of Chinese'.[51]

Meanwhile, internal queries were being raised within the Commonwealth bureaucracy regarding the logic of allowing some persons to be naturalised but not enfranchised.[52] This came to a head in 1922 in the case of David Mack (Daoud Barakah), a Syrian who had been naturalised but whose subsequent application for the franchise had been refused on the ground of his being an 'aboriginal native' of Asia. An internal memorandum from the Home and Territories Department of October 1922 noted: 'It seems an anomaly that persons . . . who are deemed eligible and desirable to be made naturalized British Subjects, should be debarred from the use of one of the principal privileges of naturalization'.[53] Another internal paper expressed similar concern in asking:

> When Parliament passed the *Nationality Act 1920*, which removed racial grounds as a disqualification from applying for naturalisation, should it not have reviewed the racial disqualifications imposed by the *Electoral Act*, in cases where certificates of naturalisation were granted?[54]

Cabinet sat on the problem from October 1922 to February 1924, when it was decided that this issue could only be dealt with in conjunction with the related issue of natural-born British subjects who were also 'aboriginal natives' (such as Indians), who were similarly denied the franchise. This decision was deferred indefinitely on 2 May 1924.[55]

Thus, despite first appearances, restrictions on the basis of race and place of birth continued to apply for many basic citizenship rights. The citizenship status of first generation persons in the period 1920 to 1925 is summarised in table 6.

Table 6 The citizenship status of first generation persons from 1920 to 1925

White	Automatic full citizenship	Natural-born (including 'half-castes') British subjects
	Acquired citizenship (with most rights)	Naturalised aliens (including 'half-castes')
Black	Acquired citizenship (with no rights)	Naturalised aliens ('full blood')
	Automatic non-citizens	Australian Aborigines ('full blood') British subjects ('full blood')

Table 7 The citizenship status of second generation persons from 1920 to 1925

Automatic full citizenship	Natural-born (all, including 'half-castes')
Automatic non-citizens	Australian Aborigines ('full blood')

The second generation situation was as before with Australian Aborigines remaining trapped in the non-citizen category as shown in table 7.

Accommodating India

It seems unlikely that the clearing up of this anomalous situation would have occurred as quickly as it did, had it not been for international, and the resulting domestic, political embarrassment. Although often overlooked, international treaties began to impact on Commonwealth–State relations far earlier than the 1982 *Koowarta* and 1983 *Franklin Dam* High Court cases. In the 1920s and 1930s, the Commonwealth quite self-consciously moved to present an image of Australia to the international community that was not merely a clone of Great Britain on the other side of the world. Australia was represented at Versailles and was actively involved in the League of Nations. It also played a major role in the Imperial Conferences, in many ways the forerunners to the current Commonwealth Heads of Government Meetings. At these Conferences the Commonwealth was finally pressured into changing its electoral and pensions Acts to remove discrimination against Indians.

The 1917 and 1918 Imperial War Conferences passed resolutions calling upon the members of the British Empire to address the discriminatory position of British Indians in many of these countries. Accordingly, in March 1918, a Cabinet sub-committee recommended that:

> The Commonwealth Electoral Act, 1918, Section 39, Sub-section (5), be amended to entitle Indians, subject to the other provisions of the Act, to have their names placed on the Roll for the Senate and House of Representatives . . .
>
> The Invalid and Old-Age Pensions Act, No. 17 of 1908, Section 16, 1C, be amended to permit, subject to the other provisions of the Act, Indians to be entitled to receive Invalid and Old-Age Pensions.

Cabinet accepted the latter but not the former on 18 March 1918.[56] Watt, the then acting Prime Minister, responded in April 1919 to pressure from the Secretary of State for the Colonies, arguing that in terms of the pensions, 'legislative proposals will be submitted as soon as possible to place Indians on an equality with other British subjects'.[57] However by 1921, with another Imperial Conference pending, legislation had been drafted and approved, but 'Owing ... to pressure of time ... it was decided to allow the matter to await a more favorable opportunity'.[58]

At the 1921 Imperial Conference, this situation was discussed at far greater length. This conference, at which Australia was represented by Prime Minister Hughes, passed the following resolution:

> The Conference, while reaffirming the Resolution of the Imperial War Conference of 1918, that each community of the British Commonwealth should enjoy complete control of the composition of its own population by means of restriction on immigration from any of the other communities, recognizes that there is an incongruity between the position of India as an equal member of the British Empire and the existence of disabilities upon British Indians lawfully domiciled in some other parts of the Empire. The Conference accordingly is of the opinion that in the interests of the solidarity of the British Commonwealth, it is desirable that the rights of such Indians to citizenship should be recognized.[59]

It must be stressed that Australia was never the major player in this debate, which largely revolved around the position of Indians in Africa, particularly South Africa. Indeed, South Africa never accepted this resolution.[60]

In Australia, concern was being voiced about the inconsistencies that resulted from a patchwork of interrelated State and Commonwealth regimes which, in differing degrees, discriminated against Indians. The Chief Electoral Officer pointed out in February 1922:

> (a) that in four States [NSW, Vic, Tas, SA] British subjects being natives of India are entitled to the same political rights as other British subjects in so far as State elections are concerned;
> (b) that some of these persons are entitled to Commonwealth political rights and others are not so entitled [under section 41 of the Constitution];
> (c) that in two States [Qld and WA] they are not entitled either to State or Commonwealth political rights;
> (d) that when they remove from a State in which they have no State political rights to one in which there is no bar to their exercising such rights, they can, in due course, become State electors, but although they may have resided in the first mentioned State prior to the coming into operation of the *Franchise Act 1902*, cannot become Commonwealth electors;
> (e) that if they have acquired both State and Commonwealth electoral rights in one State and then become residents of another in which the law precludes them from being enrolled as State electors their Commonwealth rights disappear.[61]

The Commonwealth was fully aware of the level of discrimination suffered by 'coloured' people in general in Australia, having gone as far as to draw up a paper entitled 'Disabilities of Aliens and Coloured Persons within the Commonwealth and its Territories' in 1920.[62] This showed that, while most discrimination was conducted at State level, there was considerable room for Commonwealth improvement. Indeed Prime Minister Hughes, in a widely circulated public letter of 1 July 1922 to the prominent visiting Indian politician Srinivasa Sastri, committed his government to supporting the extension of the franchise and pensions to Indians resident in Australia.[63]

By the 1923 Conference, however, nothing had been done. Australia was now represented by Prime Minister Bruce (with Garran as secretary). Of particular concern was discrimination at State level, such as the tough measures against Asians found in Queensland and Western Australia. Bruce affirmed the continuance of the Commonwealth's immigration policy, claiming that it was not a policy founded on feelings of race or colour, but was founded on 'economic considerations'. Nonetheless he promised to see what action should be taken to alleviate the citizenship situation of Indians in Australia.[64] Although an Imperial problem, responsibility for the removal of discrimination against Indians remained with individual countries.

In the end, as often seems to be the case in Australian history, it was not politicians or bureaucrats who forced a resolution of the issue, but the judiciary and public opinion.

Judicial Resolution on Mitta Bullosh

In September 1924 a Melbourne Police Magistrate ruled that Mitta Bullosh, an Indian, and therefore an 'aboriginal native of Asia', was entitled to the Commonwealth franchise under section 41 of the Constitution. The Magistrate interpreted section 41 to mean that all persons who secured the vote at State level, which Mitta Bullosh had done, had the right to the franchise at the Commonwealth level. While there had been, and continues to be, much disagreement about the meaning of section 41, the implications of this case concerned many at the Commonwealth level. Constitutional questions aside, the decision raised the spectre of having, as the Chief Electoral Officer put it, 'to enrol aboriginal natives of Australia, Asia, Africa or the Pacific Islands, who secure State enrolment and are otherwise qualified for Commonwealth enrolment'. This would lead to a 'somewhat important extension of the franchise'.[65] The Commonwealth immediately sought an *order nisi* and sought leave to appeal to the High Court.

On 2 December 1924 Cabinet considered the appeal. The Attorney-General's Department argued that an appeal was necessary 'as an authoritative interpretation under the existing law is necessary for Departmental purposes . . . [but if] it is proposed in the near future to alter the existing law, the question as to whether or not the appeal should be made should be further considered'.[66] Latham had sent a strongly worded letter to the Prime Minister a week earlier in which he wrote:

> I appeal to you to consider the political aspects of this matter in view of the public statements made by Mr Hughes to Sastri and by yourself. I urge that it is a grave political error, from both an Australian and an Imperial point of view, to proceed with the attempt to upset the magistrate's decision.[67]

Considerable public attention was given to this case in the media.[68] Provoked by foreign reports, the Secretary of State for the Colonies inquired what the Commonwealth was going to do about it.[69] Moved by such pressures and uncertain of the High Court's likely ruling on section 41,[70] Cabinet decided not to proceed with the appeal but to deal with the anomalies in citizenship laws that had given rise to the case.[71]

A Minimal Response

The answer was as simple as it was limited. The Commonwealth would act to clear up the international embarrassment caused by the Indian debacle, and at the same time ensure that those other people, the 'aboriginal natives' who had been naturalised but denied the franchise and pensions, could get their citizenship rights as well. Accordingly, Cabinet approved in principle, on 4 March 1925, a bill to enfranchise Indians and entitle them to invalid and old-age pensions. In August Cabinet further decided to enfranchise naturalised Asiatics, but would not yet grant them the invalid and old-age pensions.[72]

The changes in legislation were the bare minimum that the Commonwealth could do to defuse the situation. The main beneficiaries were naturalised non-Europeans and British Indians, the two most troublesome groups. However, those who were not naturalised – for example British 'aboriginal natives' who were not Indians, as well as Aboriginal Australians (including Papuans and Torres Strait Islanders) – continued to be excluded from the rights of citizenship. All these categories of persons were still subject to the 'aboriginal native' citizenship exclusions that remained in other Commonwealth and State legislation. If one was not born in the British Empire and

Table 8 The citizenship status of first generation persons from 1926 to World War II

Automatic full citizenship	Natural-born (including 'half-castes') British subjects (white)
Acquired citizenship (with most rights)	Naturalised aliens British Indians
Automatic non-citizens	Alien 'aboriginal natives' ('full blood') Australian Aborigines ('full blood') British subject 'aboriginal natives' ('full blood' non-Indian)

Table 9 The citizenship status of second generation persons from 1926 to World War II

Automatic full citizenship	Natural-born (all, including 'half-castes')
Automatic non-citizens	Australian Aborigines ('full blood')

was lucky enough to get through the immigration cordon, then naturalisation provided access to most formal citizenship rights previously screened by the 'aboriginal native' category in the pre-1920 *Naturalization Act.* If one was born in the Empire, racial background still provided the key to citizenship rights, with the exception of British Indians. After this change, the schema of citizenship status was as shown in tables 8 and 9.

Muramats *case*

In addition to the changes in the legislative regime that excluded 'aboriginal natives' from citizenship, the actual term itself came in for further refinement during the period 1920–1926. The question of 'half-castes' had been dealt with in the context of section 25 of the Constitution in a manner that, had it been followed in subsequent years, could have changed a number of unfortunate cases. Garran wrote on 7 March 1921 that 'persons of the half-blood cannot, I think be regarded as persons of any race'.[73] The double criterion of 'aboriginal native' in the context of the franchise was modified in 1923, in line with Higgins' 1904 opinion, to ensure that for a person to be an 'aboriginal native', not only had he or she to be of the specific racial group and born in a specific area, but the race itself had to be native to that area. Thus it was held by Garran in 1923 that a man born in Syria, which was deemed to be part of Asia, would only be an 'aboriginal native' if he was a descendant of ethnic Syrians.[74]

The 1904 Higgins view was given further solidity in 1923 when he, now Justice Higgins of the High Court, handed down the key judgment in the *Muramats* case.[75] In this case Jiro Muramats, who had been born in Japan of Japanese parents, claimed Commonwealth enrolment under section 41 of the Constitution. He had been naturalised in Victoria in 1899, and had therefore been deemed to be naturalised across the whole of Australia under the Commonwealth's *Naturalization Act.* Having moved to Western Australia in 1900, he had in May 1922 successfully got his name placed on the electoral roll for the West Australian Legislative Assembly, despite that State's disfranchisement of any 'aboriginal native of Australia, Asia, Africa, or the Islands of the Pacific, or a person of the half-blood'.[76] He then moved to get his name placed on the Commonwealth electoral roll in September 1922, but this was rejected both by the State Commonwealth Electoral Officer, and later on appeal by a Police Magistrate. Muramats appealed to the High Court, which handed down its judgment in September 1923. He lost because of a technicality in the West Australian Act, which provided that even if an 'aboriginal native' somehow got on the electoral roll such a person was debarred from actually exercising the power to vote. On this ground alone Muramats could not claim enrolment under section 41, as it only protected those who gained the right to vote at State elections.[77]

More importantly for us here, Higgins went on to discuss at some length the meaning of the words 'aboriginal native of Asia'. Muramats had submitted that he was not a descendant of the literal first inhabitants of Japan (the Ainu) but was a descendant of later colonists. The West Australian courts had apparently allowed this claim, deciding 'that it was not proved that Mr Muramats was an aboriginal native of any country'.[78] Higgins broadened the category on the grounds that it was 'not sufficient for him even to show that his race is not "aboriginal" to Japan; he must show that it is not aboriginal to Asia or the Islands of the Pacific'.[79] Higgins ruled that the word 'aboriginal'

> means 'aboriginal' in the vernacular meaning of the word . . . [meaning those] who are of the stock that inhabited the land at the time that Europeans came to it. It may be, as some assert, that there was a race peopling Australia before those whom we call 'the Australian aborigines', and that the Tasmanian blacks were the remnant of that race, driven from Australia; it may be that before the present Japanese came to Japan there was a previous race called 'Ainus', and again before them pit-dwellers; but such a fact would not prevent the present Australian black people from being the aborigines of Australia from the point of view of white settlers or of Australian laws, or prevent the present Japanese from being the aborigines of Japan . . . [80]

This became the key definition of 'aboriginal' for the Commonwealth, with Justice Higgins legalising his own opinion of some nineteen years earlier.

Australian 'aboriginal natives'

It was around 1925 that the Commonwealth first came under serious pressure to consider the citizenship position of Australian Aborigines and other Aborigines under Commonwealth jurisdiction, such as those in Papua and New Guinea. New Guinea, a protectorate granted after the dissolution of the German empire following World War I, was on the cusp of British and Australian laws regarding the nationality and rights of 'natives'. In advice given in February 1925, Garran noted that it was perfectly possible for a native woman who had married an alien, in this case a Chinese man, to be, for the purposes of nationality, an alien by reason of her marriage. But at the same time she could be deemed a native, under Territorial Ordinances, because of her 'aboriginal native' origin and her living habits.[81]

Meanwhile, in response to pressure from the Aborigines Progressive Association, the bureaucratic position regarding Australian Aborigines was simply stated:

> Aboriginal natives of Australia are not entitled to be enrolled under the Commonwealth Electoral Act, or to vote at Commonwealth elections. The question of whether this disqualification should be continued, or whether it should be removed is one that touches a matter of Government policy.[82]

Thus by 1926 the Commonwealth had successfully modified its 'aboriginal native' citizenship exclusions to defuse domestic and international political pressure, while at the same time maintaining the rationale behind them. The category of the 'aboriginal native' remained embedded in most citizenship legislation and continued to be the key defining feature of the administration's view of Australian citizenship. For the first time possession of Australian nationality became partially linked with the acquisition of some citizenship rights, but this was a concession to political necessity rather than an indication of a sea-change in thinking.

1926–1948: Consolidation and Occasional Confusion

Following this period of relative turmoil in the area of national formal citizenship, the subsequent couple of decades were ones of relative certainty and consolidation. The attention of administrators turned to refining further the meaning of 'aboriginal native', and to defining the 'blood' boundary separating Europeans and 'aboriginal natives'.

In the late 1930s and early 1940s a new raft of legislation dealing with passports and social security was passed. This augmented and later replaced much of the existing structure but did not change the key boundary marker to Australian citizenship, the category of 'aboriginal native'. This was despite increasing pressure within the Australian polity for changes to the citizenship status of Aborigines in general, and Australian Aborigines in particular. The period culminated with the passage of the *Nationality and Citizenship Act 1948* and with changes to the *Commonwealth Electoral Act* in 1949, although these changes were minimal rather than sweeping in nature.

Refining the Boundary: Aboriginality Revisited

Despite earlier efforts at administrative and judicial definition, the meaning of 'aboriginal' in 'aboriginal native' remained unclear. Nativity, meaning where a person was born, could be checked against birth records, but Aboriginality was more opaque and remained a serious administrative problem for the bureaucracy. In keeping with contemporary thought, and in contrast to current practice, Aboriginality was seen quite literally as a question of 'blood', rather than identity. Taking a different tack from that followed in America and South Africa, the Commonwealth bureaucracy, led by Garran, strongly resisted moves to construct a complex caste system.

The boundary between 'half-caste' and 'full blood' was hard to draw. When the Minister of Home Affairs wrote to Attorney-General Latham in 1929, questioning the status of 'half-castes', Garran rather than Latham handled the response. Garran reiterated Deakin's 1901 advice and summarised his own advice of 30 September 1905, arguing that 'half-castes' were not disqualified under section 4 of the *Commonwealth Franchise Act 1902* (now section 39(5) of the *Commonwealth Electoral Act 1918–1925*), but that all persons in whom the 'aboriginal blood' preponderates were disqualified. Garran did not support the Attorney-General's suggestion regarding the preparation of a scale corresponding to American terms such as 'mulatto' and 'quadroon'. Instead, he favoured the principle that a person with a greater than one-half proportion of 'white blood' was entitled to vote, while a person with a less proportion of 'white blood' was not.[83]

Thus, instead of a complex division between 'full bloods', 'half-castes', 'quarter-castes' and so on, as was suggested by politicians and was in popular use, a pragmatic system based on a relatively simple 'full blood', 'half-caste', 'European' division was maintained by the Commonwealth, with 'half-castes' assumed to be 'European' for administrative purposes. This, as we have seen and shall discuss in the next chapter, was not consistent with the practices in State jurisdictions. But even the Commonwealth's comparatively simple idea – avoiding as it did such things as 'mulatto', 'quadroon', 'octoroon' and the like – could produce much confusion.

Mixing Aboriginality

Defining an Aboriginal in terms of 'preponderating blood' may have been clear enough for people of mixed Aboriginal-white parentage, but it raised uncertainties for those of mixed Aboriginal parentage. This issue arose in the case of a Thursday Islander, whose father was a naturalised South Sea Islander from Lifu (Loyalty Islands) and whose mother was a Murray Islander (then under the Imperial Government). Was the son an 'aboriginal native' or a 'half-caste'? The Chief Electoral Officer commented that this 'raises some novel questions which may be affected by [section 39(5) of the *Commonwealth Electoral Act*] ... upon which the Electoral administration has not previously had occasion to seek advice'.[84] The Assistant Secretary of the Attorney-General's Department replied that the proffering of the father's naturalisation certificate should be sufficient. A 'half-caste' 'should not be regarded as an aboriginal within the meaning of section 39'.[85] Moreover, the Attorney-General's official pointed out:

> Descendants of South Sea Islanders or Asiatics born in Australia are natural born British subjects. I do not think that, in view of their country of birth they can be regarded as 'aboriginal natives of Asia or the Islands of the Pacific'. They are accordingly not disqualified from enrolment merely on the ground of race.[86]

Thus, this Thursday Islander was entitled to be enrolled to vote on two counts: first, he was strictly a 'half-caste' and therefore not an 'aboriginal native'; and second, he was born in Australia so again could not be an 'aboriginal native' of the Islands of the Pacific.

Two years later, however, a similar situation produced the opposite result. The Broome Electoral Office in Western Australia asked for advice on the enrolment of Maunga Katie, a woman whose mother was a 'full blood' Australian Aboriginal, and whose 'reputed' unnaturalised father was from the Philippines. The question of her potential status as a 'half-caste' obviously concerned the Broome office, which expressed concern over the 'large number of half-castes in Broome'. Initially the Kalgoorlie Divisional Officer suggested, following the opinions given by the Attorney-General's Department on 27 April 1904 and 14 June 1906,[87] that 'Descendants of South Sea Islanders or Asiatics born in Australia are native born British Subjects'. Accordingly,

Maunga Katie was not disqualified from enrolment.[88] This was also consistent with the Thursday Island example. This advice caused considerable distress in Broome with the local electoral office warning:

> your decision will have a far reaching effect ... The applicant is an aboriginal half-caste illegitimate of doubtful male parentage ... There is a large number of half-castes resident in Broome and District, from whom claims may be anticipated if this claim is accepted, because it will be assumed that the only qualification necessary to secure enrolment, is to state that the father is an Asiatic and the claimant born in Australia. (It would be an optimist who would claim to state, with any degree of certainty, the male parentage of any of the progeny of the Broome gins). If accepted I am of the opinion that objections will be lodged under Section 39(5) of the Act.[89]

The Chief Electoral Officer was sufficiently concerned to refer this case to the Solicitor-General, raising specifically the issue of the mother's Aboriginality which so worried Broome officials:

> The descendant of a South Sea Islander or Asiatic (the father) born in Australia is a natural born British Subject and is apparently not disqualified from enrolment merely on racial grounds unless the fact that the mother is a full blooded aboriginal affects the question.

The practice of the Broome office, it seems, had been to deny enrolment to those with Aboriginal mothers: 'It has evidently been the practice to refuse enrolment to persons of this class and any change now is regarded as important'.[90] The acting Solicitor-General, Knowles, replied:

> Although the matter is doubtful, I think that sub-section (5) of section 39 would apply in this case and disentitle her to enrolment under the Electoral Act.
>
> I think that, if it is desired to exclude from enrolment all persons who are the half-caste offspring of aboriginal natives of Australia, section 39(5) should be amended accordingly. In this connexion I would refer to section 18 of the Electoral Act of Western Australia [which excludes half-castes] ... Such an amendment would remove any doubts which might arise from a claim to enrolment made by any person of half-blood, e.g. – a person whose mother was an aboriginal native and whose father was a British subject.[91]

While the last comment indicates that Knowles was aware of the Thursday Island case, he did not seem to support the general principle it enunciated. He contradicted Garran's 1921 ruling that 'half-castes' could not be regarded as belonging to any particular race, and that they therefore could not be covered by any racial exclusions.[92] Had Knowles followed either of these precedents, Maunga Katie would have been exempted from the 'aboriginal native' franchise exclusion on the basis that she was a 'half-caste'. Taken together, these rules deemed a 'half-caste' to be equivalent to a 'European', regardless of the parents' racial backgrounds. The result of Knowles' ruling was that while Maunga Katie was 'half-caste Filipino' *and* 'half-caste Australian Aboriginal', she could not be a 'half-caste' herself, because she contained no European 'blood'.

Despite the alleged difficulties confronting the Broome Electoral Office in determining the fathers of children born to Aboriginal women, there was a tendency to favour patrilineality in determining 'half-caste' status. For example, in 1934 the Divisional Returning Officer for Wide Bay in Queensland ruled the following 'half-castes' to be entitled to enrol and vote at the Commonwealth level:

> (1) All half-caste aboriginal males over 21 years (Married or Single) who have European fathers.
> (2) All half-caste females over 21 years of age (Unmarried) who have European fathers.
> (3) All half-caste aboriginal females over 21 years of age (with European fathers) who have married half-caste aboriginal males, also with European fathers.[93]

On the other hand, and this appears to have been a factor in denying 'half-caste' status and the right to vote to Maunga Katie, the Aboriginality of women seemed to be 'transmissible' and to 'preponderate' for female descendants: 'Half-caste aboriginal females (with European fathers) who have married fullblood aboriginals are not entitled to enrolment'.[94] The fact that such 'half-caste' Aboriginal females were married to 'full blood' Aborigines was probably also significant since that might have suggested they were living within the Aboriginal rather than the white community.

On Being Aboriginal and Non-Aboriginal at the Same Time

As had been the case in 1925 in New Guinea, instances where an individual was deemed to be an 'aboriginal native' for the purposes of one law but not for another arose on a number of occasions during this period. Most States and the Northern Territory, as we shall see in the next chapter, had laws or ordinances governing the activities and rights of Aborigines. These contained definitions of Aboriginality that varied markedly on some points. The main point of difference was whether 'half-castes' were 'aboriginal' or not. In many of the States, 'protection' legislation deemed a large percentage of 'half-castes' to be 'aboriginal'.

This led to incongruous situations. 'Half-castes' in South Australia, for instance, were deemed to be subject to the *National Registration Act*

1939 and required to register for compulsory military conscription. 'Full bloods', meanwhile, were not.[95] Yet, under State law, 'half-castes' were often classed with 'full blood' Aborigines and had their rights severely restricted. The Commonwealth was prepared to live with such disparities across the various jurisdictions. As Knowles put it: 'The fact that some law of a State treats half-castes as aboriginals . . . does not affect the interpretation of the Commonwealth Constitution nor does it affect the interpretation of a Commonwealth Act'.[96]

Furthermore, inconsistency could occur within parts of the Commonwealth's own jurisdiction. The Commonwealth Returning Officer for the Northern Territory was presented with a confusing administrative problem arising out of a conflict between the Northern Territory *Aboriginals Ordinance* and the *Commonwealth Electoral Act* and associated regulations. The familiar question concerned the 'aboriginal' status of 'half-castes'. The dual status of the person concerned arose as follows:

> An Ordinance, No. 5 of 1927, amends the Aboriginal Ordinance in such a way that a male half-caste whose age exceeds 21 years and who, in the opinion of the Chief Protector, is incapable of managing his own affairs and is declared by the Chief Protector to be subject to that Ordinance, is included in the definition of 'aboriginal'. This provision has been put into effect as regards one half-caste who is enrolled for the subdivision of Darwin. I am taking it that this, however, does not affect his right to enrolment, since he is not an aboriginal native of Australia in the sense of being a person in whom the aboriginal blood preponderates.

The question was whether such declared 'aboriginality' would affect the person's right to Commonwealth electoral enrolment: 'I shall be pleased if the Law Officers will be asked to advise as to whether the opinion [of Garran and Isaacs on the "preponderance of blood" definition of Aboriginality] . . . is affected by [the] Ordinance'.[97] Garran, then Solicitor-General, replied in July 1928:

> The advice quoted in the above memorandum is on the interpretation of section 127 of the Constitution. The meaning of words in the Constitution cannot be affected by Ordinance. I accordingly advise that Ordinance No. 5 of 1927 does not affect the advice previously given as to the meaning of the words 'aboriginal natives'.[98]

Effectively then, a person could be both Aboriginal and not Aboriginal at the same time under different legal regimes of the same government.[99]

A similarly rigorous interpretation of 'aboriginal native' status was applied in a 1938 case concerning payment of the maternity allowance to Torres Strait Islanders. Such people were clearly 'aboriginal natives' of the Torres Strait, but did that also mean they were 'aboriginal natives' of Australia or Papua who were specifically excluded under the Act? The Queensland Premier was keen to get a 'favourable consideration' from the Commonwealth government.[100] However, the Assistant Crown Solicitor ruled that 'the Torres Straits Islands are a part of Australia and the native women of these islands are aboriginal natives of Australia'. They were thus denied the maternity allowance.[101]

As late as 1940, 'aboriginal native' voting rights remained contentious for 'British born Malays' living on Thursday Island. The Attorney-General, Hughes, ruled that:

> The birthplace of the persons in question is not stated, but if they were born in a territory or island which was, before the arrival of Europeans, mainly peopled by Malays, then, although they may be natural-born British subjects, they are aboriginal natives of Asia or the Islands of the Pacific, and hence ineligible for enrolment unless they come within one of the exceptions contained in paragraphs (a) and (c).[102]

This was correct if the persons were Malays born in Malaya, but dubious if they were born in Australia or in an Australian territory. Thus, after forty years, the boundaries of the term 'aboriginal native' were still not entirely settled as administrative categories. For something as vital for citizenship as the franchise, this was a significant deficiency. Clarity was only achieved when the term 'aboriginal native' was removed from the Commonwealth franchise legislation in 1962.

A Perennial Problem: Indians and Naturalised 'aboriginal natives'

While the international embarrassment regarding the position of Indians had been largely resolved at the Commonwealth level by 1926, it remained an issue of some irritation between the Commonwealth and the States throughout the 1930s. The States, in particular Queensland and Western Australia, maintained a raft of discriminatory legislation governing issues ranging from the franchise through mining permit rights and specific industry protection. The Commonwealth continued to receive communications from the Indian government reminding it of its international commitments and the incongruity between these commitments and the situation in the States.[103]

It had been assumed that when the Commonwealth altered its franchise laws to accommodate Indians, the States would do the same. At least this was the view of the Chief Electoral Officer in 1922, who commented that should the Commonwealth remove its restrictions against Indians, then 'it seems to be not improbable that the States of Western Australia and Queensland . . . would be disposed to bring their legislation into line with that of the Commonwealth and the other States'.[104]

Despite numerous promises given by State politicians to Indian delegates, it took until 1930 for Queensland to remove its franchise discrimination against Indians, and until 1934 for Western Australia to do so. A firm commitment had been given by West Australian Premier Collier in 1930 to address the issue, but he had lost office shortly afterwards.[105] As the Commonwealth had done in its legislative amendments of 1925 and 1926, Western Australia and Queensland made only the bare minimum alteration necessary to defuse the situation. Rather than rewriting the discriminatory clauses in their franchise legislation, they specifically exempted British Indians from the operation of these clauses, and they steadfastly refused throughout the late 1930s to alter their mining and industry restrictions.[106]

In addition to the on-going problem of discrimination against Indians, the very minimalist nature of the 1926 reforms returned to haunt the Commonwealth in the late 1930s. Two principal arms of social support, the invalid and old-age pensions, continued to be denied to 'aboriginal natives' who had been naturalised. Even though they possessed the franchise, and some could receive the maternity allowance, 'aboriginal natives' were precluded from other pensions. In 1939 this situation was reviewed after persistent petitioning by Syrians, Lebanese and Armenians, who had been allowed through the migration screen and had been accepted for naturalisation. Such people were treated differently from 'the distinctly coloured races, such as Chinese and Japanese', who were refused naturalisation in the event that they had successfully negotiated discriminatory immigration policies.[107] The Minister for Social Services was told that a change in pensions policy was inadvisable because:

> (a) It would be a clean break away from a policy which has been adhered to for many years notwithstanding strong representations.
> (b) The granting of naturalization rights would automatically confer pension rights (subject to any period qualification that may be imposed).
> (c) It would extend to Asiatics a privilege which is withheld from aboriginal natives.
>
> ... There are no doubt many deserving cases amongst these people, but it is quite likely that there are also deserving cases amongst those Asiatics who are not admitted to naturalization ... [108]

The Minister then advised Prime Minister Menzies that 'it would be extremely dangerous to reopen the pension legislation for any reason other than one of the greatest urgency, and this hardly comes under that category'.[109] Menzies agreed, so the Syrians, Lebanese and Armenians continued to be denied pension rights.

Legislation: Lots of It, But Little Change

The bulk of the relevant legislation passed during the 1940s dealt with pensions and social security benefits. These benefits were funded by the enhanced revenue base gained by the Commonwealth after it monopolised income tax in 1942. The new legislation dealing with citizenship continued to use 'aboriginal native' as an exclusionary category, but increasingly the category was narrowed to 'aboriginal natives of Australia'. This occurred despite the fact that all Australian 'aboriginals and halfbloods' were required to pay income tax to the Commonwealth upon earning sufficient income.[110] The narrowing of the exclusionary category effectively removed the remaining source of international embarrassment regarding the classification of non-Europeans as 'aboriginal natives', a classification that had been used as the basis for denying certain rights under Australian legislation.

Legislation during this period can be seen as building on existing regimes of citizenship rather than radically changing them. Thus the *Child Endowment Act 1941* prohibited payment of the endowment in respect of an 'aboriginal native of Australia' who was nomadic or dependent on Commonwealth or State support. Meanwhile, the *Widows' Pensions Act 1942* denied this pension to any 'aboriginal native of Africa, the Islands of the Pacific or New Zealand' and, of course, to any 'aboriginal native of Australia'.[111] The *Unemployment and Sickness Benefits Act 1944* stated that an:

> aboriginal native of Australia shall not be qualified to receive unemployment benefit or sickness benefit unless the Director-General is satisfied, by reason of the character, standard of intelligence and development of the aboriginal native, that it is reasonable that the aboriginal native should receive benefit.[112]

On the other hand, the *Invalid and Old-Age Pensions (Reciprocity with New Zealand) Act 1943* allowed for invalid and old-age pensions to be paid to persons from New Zealand, including Maoris, as if they were white Australian nationals.[113] All these pensions Acts were combined in 1947 under the *Social Services Consolidation Act*, which precluded most Australian Aborigines from receiving invalid and old-age pensions, widow's pensions, maternity allowances, the child endowment, and unemployment and sickness benefits.[114]

By 1947, the racial exclusion in the field of social services had been narrowed to Australian Aborigines. While no doubt this would have been welcomed by those other 'aboriginal natives' previously excluded, the Commonwealth excluded its own Aboriginal population from the enhanced welfare state benefits.

The Final Battleground: The 'aboriginal native' of Australia

While the Commonwealth spent some energy in the late 1930s hosing down the spot fires generated by the naturalised 'aboriginal natives' and Indian questions, the most significant category of 'aboriginal native', that of the Australian Aboriginal, also began to generate significant heat. The Commonwealth had rejected any move to assume national control of Aboriginal affairs, in keeping with the majority opinion of the 1929 *Royal Commission on the Constitution.*[115] More spectacularly, a petition signed by 1814 Australian Aborigines called upon the King:

> To prevent the extinction of the Aboriginal Race and better conditions for all and grant us power to propose a member of parliament in the person of our own Blood, or White man known to have studied our needs and to be in Sympathy with our Race to represent us in the Federal Parliament.[116]

The petition, organised by the Australian Aborigines League, was presented to the Prime Minister. Not surprisingly, the Commonwealth was reluctant to present this embarrassing petition to the King. Nevertheless, the Commonwealth bureaucracy, as a matter of course, generated reports analysing the contents of the petition and the demographic characteristics of the leading petitioners, in terms of race, 'intelligence' and character.[117] This was combined with the legal considerations of Solicitor-General Knowles on the question of Aboriginal representation in the Commonwealth Parliament.[118] McEwen, the Minister for the Interior, recommended that Cabinet take no action on the petition, and this was agreed to.[119]

The prodigious output of A.P. Elkin, Professor of Anthropology at the University of Sydney, Reverend J.H. Sexton, President of the Aborigines' Friends' Association, and others did much to raise public and official awareness of the position of Australian Aborigines.[120] These activists for Aboriginal rights had some significant impact in the successful campaign throughout the 1940s to encourage the Commonwealth to modify its existing franchise law. The campaign resulted ultimately in the passage of the 1949 *Commonwealth Electoral Act,* which enfranchised, at Commonwealth level, all Aboriginal Australians in States that gave them the franchise. In addition, the Commonwealth enfranchised Aborigines who had served in the military.[121] This, however, left most Aborigines in Western Australia, Queensland and the Northern Territory disfranchised. The Menzies government had moved swiftly in 1940 to ensure the franchise to all adult soldiers, Aboriginal and non-Aboriginal, who were serving or had served overseas in World War II. The *Commonwealth Electoral (War-Time) Act 1940,* however, was worded in such a manner so as to terminate six months after the completion of the conflict.[122] The Commonwealth had moved in 1941 to enfranchise in perpetuity any adult Aboriginal who had served outside Australia as a member of the defence force in either World War I or II, and who had not been discharged on account of their own misconduct. However, it had shelved this proposal for the duration of the war.[123]

In summary, by the end of World War II, most 'aboriginal natives' born outside Australia had improved their access to social welfare benefits, but were still excluded from open entry under the immigration policy and remained unlikely to gain the ultimate citizenship right of the franchise because of the discretionary application of naturalisation laws. The majority of Aboriginal Australians did not improve their lot, being eligible for social services only if deemed not to be Aboriginal, and remaining largely disfranchised under the 1949 *Commonwealth Electoral Act.*

The Chimera of Citizenship: The 1948 Nationality and Citizenship Act

In 1948 the Commonwealth created the Australian 'citizen' as a legal entity. The *Nationality and Citizenship Act,* prompted by Canadian and Imperial legislation, was carefully worded so as to limit the possible effect of allowing greater rights to 'British subjects' who were also 'coloured persons'.[124] Thus the Australian Act, while symbolically very important, actually changed very little by way of actual citizenship rights. This was because of the distinct separation between the acquisition of Australian 'nationality', now termed 'citizenship', and the restrictions on personal rights that existed at Commonwealth and State levels.

This bifurcation of citizenship rights and law was confirmed in June 1949, five months after the Act came into operation, when the Attorney-General's Department advised the Immigration Department to reply in the following manner to a letter inquiring into the citizenship position of Australian Aborigines and 'half-castes':

> Aborigines or half-caste aborigines are . . . Australian citizens. It is pointed out, however, that the *Nationality and Citizenship Act* does not itself purport to alter the effect of existing legislation upon the rights and duties of individuals, and the position of aborigines in relation to such legislation has not been altered solely by reason of the provisions of that Act.[125]

In other words, despite changing appearances, the Act changed little or nothing at all for 'aboriginal natives', except perhaps by giving them a rhetorical and political weapon to use in striving for full citizenship rights and benefits.

There are many issues that arise from the potent mixture of race, racism, and the rhetoric and reality of Australian 'citizenship', but two only are flagged here.

First and most important, the entire exclusionary edifice erected around 'aboriginal native' was a conscious legislative and administrative creation that was developed and refined for the first half-century of Australian nationhood. At any point, the Commonwealth could have given full citizenship to all or some 'aboriginal natives', at least at the national level. It was not constitutionally bound to act in the manner it did. The fact that it chose to exclude Aboriginal Australians was not simply a result of colonial ignorance and bigotry, although both of those qualities could well be ascribed to some of the participants in the story. The exclusion of 'aboriginal natives' went to the heart of the very idea of those qualities thought by the administration to make up an Australian 'citizen'. These qualities were negative. That is, the Australian citizen was thought to be simply a 'natural-born or naturalised' person *who was not an 'aboriginal native'*. It was the 'aboriginal native', in other words, who was the key boundary marker to Australian citizenship.

Second, this story emphasises the importance of the bureaucracy as the principal arm by which the boundaries of Australian citizenship were defined and policed. Despite the intentions of the original legislators and pleas from the likes of Higgins for simplicity, the interpretation of the term 'aboriginal native' by the administering authorities became increasingly complex. Ad hoc decisions, such as Deakin's 'half-caste' ruling, took on the mantle of holy writ in administrative circles. The key concern shown by major bureaucratic players throughout the period was for clarity and certainty of the exclusionary principles, rather than for the justice or rectitude of the exclusionary policy. Pressure for change, be it political or judicial, was uniformly greeted by an incremental and minimal response.

CHAPTER 5

The States Confine the Aboriginal Non-citizen

> A licence to employ aboriginals shall not entitle the holder thereof to employ under that licence any male half-caste of any age whatsoever, notwithstanding that that half-caste is an aboriginal within the meaning of the word 'aboriginal' in section three of the *Aboriginals Ordinance* . . .
>
> *Northern Territory Regulation, 1930*[1]

While the new Commonwealth parliament had been defining the Australian citizen, the States and Territories retained and exercised the power to determine the citizenship rights of 'aboriginal natives'. In this chapter we provide an overview of the citizenship status of Australian Aborigines in the various State and Territory jurisdictions between the years 1901 and 1948, after which the Australian citizen became a legal entity. Our central argument is that the States became increasingly more authoritarian in their dealings with Aborigines, reaching a low point in the 1930s. This contributes to one main theme of the book by challenging the view that the various Australian parliaments began their dealings with Aborigines in hostility and moved progressively to adopt more liberal positions. It further illustrates a second main theme, that under Australia's federal Constitution the States are as significant as the Commonwealth in determining citizenship rights and entitlements.

Our focus in this chapter will largely be on the extraordinary amount of legislation passed in the various State and Territory jurisdictions in the first four decades of this century. In their own ways, but often borrowing from each other, the States in these years presented a relatively uniform position on the way in which Aboriginal affairs would best be administered. Legislation in all but one State gave administrators wide-ranging powers to control the movement, marriage and employment of Aborigines. Central to the use of broad legislation was the belief that Aborigines needed to be placed under heavily regulated government control in each State. What had been done in the previous century by force would now be done by law.[2]

This is not to suggest that all the restrictive laws were uniformly enforced. Indeed, there is evidence that many of the restrictive provisions that we will be considering were far from evenly policed.[3] But our attention here, and in this book generally, is not on the way rules were enforced, nor is it on the ways Aboriginal people managed to lead dignified lives in the face of undignified 'protection' regimes. Rather, our attention is on governmental and administrative thinking and practices dealing with Aboriginal affairs.

Nowhere was the search for government control more ludicrously exhibited than in the various governmental attempts to define who was Aboriginal. In the face of a growing population of people of mixed European and Aboriginal ancestry, the States maintained their determination to set out in legislation who was and who was not Aboriginal, and thus who was and was not under their control. As we shall see, this led to some absurd results. In some jurisdictions Aborigines who fulfilled certain criteria would be deemed not to be Aborigines for the purposes of one piece of legislation, yet they would remain Aborigines under other laws. It did not occur to the legislators that individuals should be left to choose whether or not to identify themselves as Aboriginal. Rather, this was considered to be a governmental obligation.

Victoria

In chapter 1 we examined the legislation covering Victorian Aborigines until 1910, when an amendment to the 1886 legislation enabled the Board for the Protection of the Aborigines to govern the lives of 'half-castes'. This power was continued in 1915, when the Victorian Parliament passed the *Aborigines Act 1915* (Vic), an Act which also was consistent with the main provisions of earlier legislation in its definition of 'aboriginals', its delegation of administrative functions to the Board for the Protection of Aborigines, and in the scope of regulatory power given to the Executive.[4] Although the Board in 1910 had relented slightly from its draconian policy of 1886, it was still determined to remove 'half-castes' from its care wherever possible. A new regulation gazetted in 1916 placed a duty on station managers to 'discourage any further introduction of half-castes'. A further regulation provided that:

> All quadroon, octoroon, and half-caste lads on the Board's stations and reserves of or above the age of eighteen (18) years shall leave same on a notification from the Board, and shall not again be allowed upon a station or reserve, except for a brief visit to relatives, at the discretion of Managers of stations.[5]

In 1921 the Board ordered the local guardian of the Framlingham reserve to remove 'fairer' residents on the basis that 'The Board is limited by the Act and Regulations to assisting fullbloods and (full) half-castes only'.[6] The notion that people could be '(full) half-castes' was certainly novel.

In 1928 the Victorian parliament consolidated its legislation. The short *Aborigines Act 1928* (Vic) continued the narrow definition of 'Aboriginal' first put in place in 1886. Included in the definition were: any 'female half-caste' who had married an Aboriginal prior to 1887; every Aboriginal child unable to earn his or her own income; any 'half-caste' who held a licence to reside with Aborigines; and any 'half-caste' who had reached thirty-four years of age by 1887 and who habitually associated and lived with 'an aboriginal'. This last ground for inclusion in the definition of Aboriginal could only have been satisfied by Aborigines who were at least seventy-five years old when the 1928 legislation was passed. By 1948, when the legislation was still in force, 'half-castes' who habitually associated with Aborigines but who did not hold licences would need to have been at least ninety-five years old to have been officially termed Aborigines, a factor that testified more to the parliament's neglect of Aboriginal affairs than it did to the lifespan of Victorian Aborigines. The executive retained the enormous scope for regulatory power that it had possessed the previous century. The Governor-in-Council had the following powers: to order where individual Aborigines would reside; to prescribe the terms on which contracts of employment with Aborigines could be made; to provide for the care, custody and education of children of Aborigines; and to prescribe the conditions on which 'half-castes' could receive State assistance.[7] Meanwhile, Aborigines were not permitted to be sold or given alcohol.[8]

Draconian disciplinary regulations remained in force in Victoria from 1900 to 1948, one of which empowered reserve managers to fine Aborigines for 'any breach of good behaviour'. Some Victorian disciplinary regulations were considered by the Crown Solicitor in 1946 to be unenforceable for being beyond the regulatory powers granted by the governing Act. However, despite his call for their revocation, they remained in force, presumably for their deterrent value.[9]

While the Board for the Protection of the Aborigines remained the administrative body in charge of Victorian Aboriginal affairs, its members were meeting less and less frequently. Control over Aboriginal affairs vested in practice in the Under Secretary and a clerk. In 1917 the Board decided that its policy would be to close all but one station and gather all the Aborigines living on reserves at the Lake Tyers station in Gippsland.[10] Failure to move would result in the cessation of assistance from the Board. This was the sole policy objective that the Board could be said to have been pursuing around this time. In 1912 there had been around 73 residents at Lake Tyers. By 1923 there were 230 residents, and in 1945, 270 Aborigines lived at Lake Tyers. However, not all Aborigines moved. A number of residents at Coranderrk, Framlingham and Lake Condah defied the Board's policy and remained on those reserves.[11]

Those Aborigines at Lake Tyers were clearly subject to a different system of justice than that which applied to other Victorians. This was clearly spelt out in 1927 by a Police Magistrate, who argued that cases from Lake Tyers ought not to be tried at the local court because it would give outsiders the wrong impression of what happened there. The public, he argued, 'was inclined to sympathise with the natives'.[12]

According to a regulation first gazetted in 1871, and which reappeared in each new set of regulations passed in the period under consideration, the employment of Aborigines was to be directly overseen by the Board. Where employment was to last for more than three months, Aborigines had either to have their contracts approved by the Board, or they needed to hold special certificates that enabled them to pursue their own work agreements.[13] However, the extent to which the Board actually regulated Aboriginal employment is questionable, a point reinforced by the fact that the Board took out advertisements in 1937 stressing that its permission was required before Aborigines could be employed. According to Diane Barwick the use of work certificates was abandoned in the 1880s, and while the evidence for such a broad proposition is sketchy, there is certainly evidence that many Aborigines did work without the Board's approval. Clearer still is the fact that Aboriginal employees, whether or not their employment was approved by the Board, did not receive award wages.[14]

Any hopes the Board had of regulating Aboriginal employment were well beyond its administrative capacity, for in 1937 even the issuing of licences to 'half-castes' to reside at Lake Tyers ceased because of the clerical work involved, technically making 'half-castes' at Lake Tyers immune from disciplinary regulations.[15] In November 1942 a deputation from a number of organisations interested in Aboriginal welfare called for a reconstitution of the Board and the appointment of people who could devote more time to its duties. Eight and a half months later the Board met again, and turned its attention to the topic of meeting more regularly. The next meeting was four months later.[16]

The citizenship status of Aborigines in the late 1940s at Lake Tyers, the only Victorian station, can be surveyed by considering some of the disciplinary rules in force there. Phillip Pepper and Tess De Araugo, in their book *The Kurnai of Gippsland*, outline some of these rules: residents needed permission to leave the reserve; the manager could and did fine people for speaking back in their own defence; and residents could only speak to white visitors in front of the manager or sub-manager. It was little wonder the station earned the name the 'Prison Farm'.[17]

Queensland

We saw in chapter 2 that Queensland was the second State to establish an Aborigines protection regime. The *Aboriginals Protection and Restriction of the Sale of Opium Acts 1897–1901* (Qld) remained the principal Queensland legislation until 1934, when an amending Act brought in some significant changes.[18] Of course it was not only Aboriginal legislation as such that affected Queensland Aborigines and Torres Strait Islanders. Other Queensland legislation, for instance, prevented people who could not read and write English from holding certain jobs.[19]

From 1934 the word 'Aboriginal' referred to: an Aboriginal inhabitant or resident of Queensland; a 'half-caste' living as husband or wife of an Aboriginal; a 'half-caste' habitually associating with an Aboriginal; a 'half-caste who in the opinion of the Minister has not sufficient intelligence to manage his own affairs'; and a 'half-caste' child under twenty-one years of age. 'Half-caste' was redefined as: the offspring of one Aboriginal or two 'half-castes'; a person with one Aboriginal or two 'half-caste' grandparents who lives as or associates with Aboriginals or who in the opinion of the Chief Protector is in need of control; and a person 'of aboriginal or Pacific Island extraction' who lives or associates with Aboriginals or who in the opinion of the Chief Protector is in need of control.[20]

The definition of 'Aboriginal' was thus broadened significantly, and led to some Aborigines being brought under Aboriginal legislation for the first time.[21] Equally, the definition increased the discretionary power with which an administrator might term someone 'Aboriginal'. Once a person was deemed to be Aboriginal there was little chance that the bureaucracy would permit a reversion. One could apply for an exemption, but only on certain limited criteria, as we discussed in chapter 2. A person could not lose their Aboriginality in the way that they could lose their nationality. This was a view endorsed by the

Queensland Supreme Court, which ruled that an Aboriginal woman who had married a Malay man still continued to be Aboriginal. One Judge commented that:

> There is a difference between race and nationality. This is a question of race. A man or woman can no more change their race than a leopard can change its spots.[22]

The intention behind the 1934 legislation had been simply to give the Chief Protector the power to bring a person of Aboriginal or Islander 'extraction' under his Department's jurisdiction if that person was deemed to be 'in need of control or protection', irrespective of whether that person had a 'preponderance' of black or white blood. There was some concern that the word 'extraction' might refer only to offspring of Aborigines and Islanders and not descendants. But the prevailing view was that the wording of the legislation had achieved its purpose.[23]

From 1919 Aborigines not living on reserves were required to contribute up to five per cent of their wage to an Aboriginal Provident Fund, which made funds available to other Aborigines. This was in addition both to the amounts they were forced to save, and to the taxation they were obliged to pay. The fund was one of many trust accounts held by the government on behalf of Aborigines, and this control of Aboriginal money, in the opinion of at least one historian, helps to explain why the Queensland government was so reluctant to surrender its control of Aboriginal affairs to the Commonwealth.[24]

In the early decades of the twentieth century the administration of Aboriginal affairs became progressively more restrictive in Queensland, a change motivated largely by the fear of an increasing 'half-caste' population. Official figures listed a jump in this population from 3869 in 1929 to 6461 in 1938, although 'quadroons' were included in official calculations from 1934.[25] From 1934 the employment of male 'half-castes' needed to be documented in the way the employment of other Aborigines had since 1897. Furthermore, Aborigines in lawful employment were no longer immune from being sent to reserves, and could be forced to undergo medical treatment. Another new clause exemplified the broader powers to which Aborigines were now subject:

> If the Minister is of the opinion that any aboriginal or half-caste is uncontrollable he may, by writing under his hand, order such aboriginal or half-caste, as the case may be, to be kept in some institution, and either for such time as he shall think fit or until he shall direct that such aboriginal or half-caste shall be released.[26]

A further provision held that 'no testamentary instrument or deed of gift or transfer of any land or other property' could be executed by an

Aboriginal except if it had been approved and witnessed by an authorised protector.[27] The ranks of district protectors continued to be filled largely by police officers, a fact that concerned the British Anti-Slavery and Aborigines Protection Society. The Society commented that 'it must be difficult for the Australian aborigines to look for protection to those whom (for obvious reasons) many of them have cause to fear'.[28]

The fact that Queensland Aborigines and Islanders did not all lead uniform lifestyles presented difficulties for the administrators, who sought to implement consistent policies. As a result, Queensland administrators, particularly in the 1930s, became obsessed with classifying Aborigines in order that they could more easily be governed. In 1935 the Chief Protector, J.W. Bleakley, argued that there were three types of 'half-caste': the 'inferior type', which included people of Asiatic and Islander ethnicity; the 'superior types', who had a 'preponderance of European blood'; and the children of this latter group. Bleakley further summarised Queensland's Aboriginal policy in six points:

> (a) Check breeding of half-castes . . .
> (b) Encourage marriage amongst their own race.
> (c) Segregate aboriginals and lower types of Crossbreeds in Settlements and Missions or control them in supervised employment.
> (d) Grant exemption to superior types of Crossbreeds found after careful inquiry to be able to look after themselves.
> (e) . . . place light coloured children in European environment for ultimate absorption into the white community . . .
> (f) Raise the standard of living of the aboriginal communities . . . [29]

Two years later, Bleakley revised his categorisations. He now divided Aborigines into four groups: the 'primitive nomads'; those 'still living a precarious existence on their own country, but whose lands have been selected'; the 'detribalized'; and the 'crossbreed'. The latter group were again divided into four categories, this time: those with a 'preponderance of aboriginal blood'; those with Islander or Malay backgrounds; those with European or 'higher Asiatic' ethnicity; and those with a 'preponderance of European blood'.[30]

The legislation governing Queensland Aborigines was changed in 1939, when some of the Commonwealth's administrative terminology made an appearance. According to the *Aboriginals Preservation and Protection Act 1939* (Qld) the term 'aboriginals' applied to: a person with a 'preponderance' of Aboriginal native blood; any 'half-blood' declared to be in need of protection; any 'half-blood' living as husband or wife of an Aboriginal or who habitually associated with Aboriginals; and any child on an Aboriginal reserve whose mother was Aboriginal. Torres Strait Islanders were not deemed to be Aborigines unless they were residing on Aboriginal reserves. The term 'half-blood' was itself defined to refer to a person who had one Aboriginal parent and one parent with 'no strain of the blood of an aboriginal'. It also referred to a person with 'more than twenty-five per cent of aboriginal blood but who has not a preponderance of such blood'. The Queensland Act was now administered by a Director of Native Affairs, to whom a number of 'protectors of aboriginals' were responsible.[31] According to the Director of Native Affairs, the purpose behind the new legislation was to uplift the 'civilised half-castes' by conferring upon them 'freedom and full citizen rights where their circumstances and associations qualified them for such privilege'.[32]

Heather Wearne has argued that whereas the 1897 legislation was born of guilt, the 1939 legislation was born of concern to preserve white community standards.[33] This, as we shall see, was a significant and common theme throughout the State and Territory administrations in the 1930s.

Throughout the 1930s and 1940s Aboriginal Queenslanders had their lives regulated even more comprehensively than they had been in the previous century. No Aboriginal could be employed without the permission of a protector. No marriage between an Aboriginal and a non-Aboriginal could be celebrated without the authority of the Director of Native Affairs or a specially empowered protector. And the Director of Native Affairs could order the removal of an Aboriginal to a reserve. Meanwhile, the Executive retained broad discretionary power to regulate the 'discipline and good order' of reserves, and to provide for the care, custody and education of Aboriginal children.[34]

From 1939 concurrent legislation in Queensland governed the lives of Torres Strait Islanders. Although Islanders were considered by the federal bureaucracy to be 'aboriginal natives',[35] the Queensland government passed specific legislation for them. The *Torres Strait Islanders Act 1939* (Qld) enabled the establishment of Island courts and an elected Island Council, but in large part duplicated the regulatory provisions in the Aboriginal Act. One minor exception provided that Torres Strait Islanders could only be forced to move to reserves if the Island court had first recommended their removal.[36] Very minor amendments to both Acts were passed in 1946, but both remained in force in Queensland until 1965.[37]

Regulations passed as late as 1945 continued Queensland's patronising and almost complete control over Aborigines. In particular, Aborigines on reserves continued to be subject virtually to the whims of protectors and superintendents, who could order Aborigines to 'observe habits of orderliness and cleanliness' to their satisfaction, who could prevent the 'playing of any game', and who could open any mail to or from Aborigines. The restrictions were characterised by one regulation which provided that: 'Every aboriginal who disobeys an order of the protector or superintendent to cease dancing and/or other native practices shall be guilty of an offence'.[38]

As at 1948 Queensland continued to formally deny Aborigines the right to vote. The controlling legislation in 1915 had provided that: 'No aboriginal native of Australia, Asia, Africa, or the Islands of the Pacific shall be qualified to be enrolled upon any electoral roll'.[39] This was amended in 1930 to also prevent any 'aboriginal native of the islands in Torres Strait' or the children of such a person from voting. Further, 'half-castes' supervised under the existing protection legislation were barred from voting. At the same time a 'native' of British India or Syria was now able to vote in Queensland.[40] Bleakley, the Chief Protector, was one administrator who was concerned that his State's franchise laws were not consistent with the situation federally, where 'half-castes' in whom Aboriginal blood did not 'preponderate' could vote. In 1934 he wrote to the Home Department, unsuccessfully urging the Commonwealth authorities to follow Queensland's lead and exclude from the franchise all 'half-castes' who were subject to Aboriginal protection Acts. He considered that 'the major portion of the half-castes subject to the control of this Department have no desire to exercise the franchise and in most cases could not intelligently do so if given the privilege'.[41]

The strictness of the 'preponderating blood' rule did, however, belie the reality of implementation. For example, in 1934 the Acting Chief Electoral Officer for the Commonwealth wrote that:

> generally no action is taken to enforce the compulsory enrolment and voting provisions of the law in respect of half-caste aboriginals who do not possess intelligence of a sufficiently high standard as to produce a desire to secure enrolment or to record an intelligent vote.

The detail as to who decided what a sufficient degree of intelligence amounted to, and on what criteria such intelligence was judged, was not communicated. It was clear, however, that for a 'half-caste' to vote, he or she would have to do plenty of persuading, a point reinforced by the Acting Chief Electoral Officer's comment that the names of only ten 'half-castes' appeared on the federal roll for the subdivision in which the Cherbourg station was located.[42]

Western Australia

West Australian Aborigines continued to have their lives regulated in much the same way as Aboriginal Queenslanders. Walter Roth's

Royal Commission report in 1904 led to the passage of new legislation in 1905.[43] The *Aborigines Act 1905* (WA) continued the existence of the Aborigines Department, which was responsible for regulating the use of Aboriginal reserves and for overseeing the custody and education of Aboriginal children. The Act also created the position of Chief Protector of Aborigines, who automatically became the legal guardian of all Aboriginal and 'half-caste' children. The term Aboriginal was defined as it was in Queensland legislation, and the power to remove Aborigines to reserves was now legislatively expressed.[44] Aboriginal employment continued to be heavily regulated, and, as was the case in Queensland, Aborigines in Western Australia were subject to an extraordinary amount of discretionary power. Aborigines could have their property taken from their control, they could be removed from towns, and they could be told that they could not stay in certain areas. Aboriginal women required the Chief Protector's permission to marry non-Aboriginal men, and at night they could not go near 'any creek or inlet used by the boats of pearlers or other sea boats'.[45] The fact that Aborigines stood as non-citizens in Western Australia was evidenced by their subservient legal standing. Aborigines had no right to vote, and could be arrested without warrant for any breach of the *Aborigines Act*. Further, Aborigines were still prohibited from drinking alcohol, and they could not 'loiter' about licensed premises.[46]

From 1911 the State assumed even greater power over Aboriginal children. Following legislation passed in that year, the Chief Protector remained the legal guardian over all Aboriginal and 'half-caste' children, but this was now 'to the exclusion of the rights of the mother of an illegitimate half-caste child'. A new clause gave the governing authority of Aboriginal institutions all the powers over Aboriginal and 'half-caste' children that State institutions had over wards of the State.[47]

Just as in Queensland, white people in Western Australia were becoming increasingly fearful about the growing 'half-caste' population. The ability of administrators to control this population was temporarily stalled in the late 1920s by a court ruling that the offspring of two 'half-castes' was not a 'half-caste' under the Act.[48]

A change in terminology was the most significant result of a 1936 amending Act, according to which the governing legislation was now called the *Native Administration Act 1905–1936* (WA). The words 'Aboriginal' and 'Aborigine' were replaced with 'native'. A 'native' was defined as: a person of the 'full blood descended from the original inhabitants of Australia'; and any person of less than 'full blood' who is descended from the original inhabitants of Australia. The desire of administrators to classify Aborigines became as manifest in Western

Australia in the 1930s as it was in Queensland. Excluded from the definition were: a 'quadroon' under twenty-one years of age who neither associates with or lives like natives; a 'quadroon' over twenty-one unless ordered by a magistrate to be classed as a 'native'; and 'a person of less than quadroon blood' who was born before the end of 1936. A 'quadroon' was defined as a person of 'one-fourth of the original full blood'.[49]

The Chief Protector of Aborigines was now replaced by a Commissioner of Native Affairs. The terminology might have been less patronising, but the position retained all the power of its predecessor, and more. The Act was partly the result of another West Australian Royal Commission, headed this time by H.D. Moseley, which had been established following national and international embarrassment at the State's treatment of Aborigines. Moseley's view was that the destiny of Aborigines lay in their ultimate absorption with the people of the Commonwealth. This view led to the establishment of an increasingly restrictive regime, all the more so when one considers that only Moseley's more regressive recommendations were implemented.[50]

After 1936 the legal guardianship over Aboriginal children, which had vested in the Chief Protector, now vested in the Commissioner 'notwithstanding that the child has a parent or other relative living', and the Commissioner could force 'natives' to undergo medical procedures. Their refusal to do so was an offence, which rendered them liable to imprisonment for up to six months.[51] Whereas previously the marriage of a female Aboriginal to a non-Aboriginal needed special approval, now no 'marriage of a native' could take place without the approval of the Commissioner. The proscriptions against inter-racial sexual relations were more clearly enunciated than ever before, the words 'sexual intercourse' appearing for the first time in legislation.[52]

Meanwhile, the executive retained its strong power. It had an express power now not only to send Aborigines to reserves, but also to hospitals and institutions. It could also now establish courts 'of native affairs' to deal with cases where Aborigines committed offences against other Aborigines. Where tribal custom was the reason for an offence, this could be taken as a mitigating factor for sentencing purposes. But from these courts there was no appeal. The government's view of tribal customs was clearly set out in one provision, according to which the Minister could give all such instructions 'to minimise or stamp out the practice' when the 'tribal practice of the natives' seemed injurious.[53]

Consistent with other States' practices, certificates of exemption, or 'dog licences' as Aborigines called them, were able to be granted to West Australian Aborigines. Administrators issued 276 certificates of exemption, and revoked 75, in the years between 1937 and 1944.[54]

A seemingly minor amendment to the *Native Administration Act* in 1941 spoke volumes for the view held by the West Australian government as to the citizenship rights of Aborigines. In a move to prevent the spread of leprosy, the government legislated to prevent any Aboriginal living north of the twentieth parallel – which roughly crosses Port Hedland – to come south of it. The only permissible exceptions to this were when an Aboriginal needed specialist medical attention, when legal proceedings required an Aboriginal's attendance, or when an Aboriginal's employer held a special permit to take the Aboriginal to the south.[55]

Without doubt the piece of State legislation that set out most clearly the citizenship status of Aborigines was Western Australia's *Natives (Citizenship Rights) Act 1944* (WA). This extraordinary Act enabled an Aboriginal to apply for a Certificate of Citizenship, which, if granted, meant that the Aboriginal would 'be deemed to be no longer a native or aborigine and shall have all the rights, privileges and immunities and shall be subject to the duties and liabilities of a natural born or naturalised subject of His Majesty'.[56] An application for a Certificate of Citizenship was made by submitting a statutory declaration to a Magistrate, accompanied by two written references from 'reputable citizens' as evidence of the 'good character and industrious habits' of the applicant. Applicants had to attest that for the two years prior to the date of the application they had 'dissolved tribal and native association except with respect to lineal descendants or native relations of the first degree'. They also had to show that they had served in the Naval, Military or Air Force and had received or were entitled to receive an honourable discharge, or otherwise show that they were 'a fit and proper person to obtain a Certificate of Citizenship'.[57]

The criteria on which a Magistrate then decided whether to grant a Certificate of Citizenship, which like exemption certificates were referred to by Aborigines as dog tags,[58] provides an illuminating statement of what it meant to be a citizen in Western Australia in 1944 and beyond. The Magistrate had to be satisfied that:

(a) for the two years immediately prior the applicant has adopted the manner and habits of civilised life;
(b) the full rights of citizenship are desirable for and likely to be conducive to the welfare of the applicant;
(c) the applicant is able to speak and understand the English language;
(d) the applicant is not suffering from active leprosy, syphilis, granuloma or yaws;
(e) the applicant is of industrious habits and is of good behaviour and reputation;
(f) the applicant is reasonably capable of managing his own affairs.[59]

Successful applicants could lose their citizenship 'rights' by not adopting the manner and habits of civilised life, by being twice convicted of an offence under the *Native Administration Act*, or by contracting any of the above diseases.[60] That an individual's citizenship could be lost through the contraction of a disease showed just how precarious the basis was on which some Aborigines were granted citizenship.

Upon being granted a Certificate of Citizenship, an Aboriginal ceased to be 'a native or aborigine'. A photograph of the holder was required to be affixed to the Certificate 'in the manner of a passport'.[61] The passport analogy was indeed apt, for that was what the Certificate was. It enabled the holder, who had been born in Australia, to travel freely within the country.

At the time when the *Natives (Citizenship Rights) Act 1944* (WA) was passed, the following people were prevented from voting for either house of the West Australian parliament: any 'aboriginal native of Australia, Asia (except British India), Africa, or the Islands of the Pacific (except New Zealand), or a person of the half-blood'.[62] This prevention remained, with the exception that Aborigines who held Certificates of Citizenship were no longer 'aboriginal natives', and could therefore vote.

The notion that Aborigines could gain and lose citizenship status in the ways specified made a mockery of the 'rights' terminology. Aborigines, according to the West Australian government, clearly did not have citizenship rights. The most they had was an ability to be exempted from the citizenship exclusion that otherwise affected all Aborigines.

Moreover, one's exemption from State exclusionary regimes did not necessarily exempt one from federal disadvantages. The 1961 federal Select Committee on the Voting Rights of Aborigines was told that:

> The grant of a State Certificate of Citizenship, with the effect of giving full civil rights under the law of the State, does not, and was not intended to, trench in any way upon the status of an aboriginal as an Australian citizen by virtue of the Commonwealth *Nationality and Citizenship Act*, or upon any rights or duties arising under any other law of the Commonwealth. State law could not have such an effect.[63]

Thus, for example, in the years to 1948 even a West Australian Aboriginal who held a Certificate of Citizenship had no right to the federal vote.

New South Wales

Aborigines in New South Wales were less numerous than in most other States, and were also less regulated. The *Liquor Act 1898* (NSW) forbade the holders of liquor licences from supplying 'any aboriginal native of Australia' with alcohol. Interestingly, the phrase 'aboriginal native' in this context was ruled in 1903 not to refer to 'half-castes', a Judge ruling that: 'if there is any trace of white blood in a man he cannot be called an aboriginal native'.[64]

Two years later, the New South Wales parliament responded by amending the liquor Act and by providing a definition of 'aboriginal native'. The phrase now referred to 'full blooded' Aborigines and people with 'an admixture of aboriginal blood' who received rations or aid from the Aborigines Protection Board or who resided on Aboriginal reserves. Again the phrase was tested in Court, this time when a man, described by some as Aboriginal and by some as 'coloured', was supplied with alcohol. It was not clear that the man was a 'full blooded' Aboriginal, the Judge commenting that it was 'rare to find pure blooded aboriginals' in New South Wales. However, the Aboriginal in question gave evidence that he had been given a blanket at the 'Aborigine Home'. This was taken to be a reference to the Aborigines Protection Board, which in turn then brought the man under the legislative definition of 'aboriginal native'.[65]

The first piece of New South Wales protection legislation, the *Aborigines Protection Act 1909* (NSW), gave legislative basis to the New South Wales Board for the Protection of Aborigines, and largely mirrored the existing Victorian legislation that we considered in chapter 1. It defined an Aboriginal to be 'any full-blooded aboriginal native of Australia, and any person apparently having an admixture of aboriginal blood who applies for or is in receipt of rations or aid from the board or is residing on a reserve'. The Act did not specifically enable Aborigines to be moved to reserves, but they could be prevented from camping in or around towns or reserves. The Act also conferred broad regulatory power on the executive.[66]

Liquor remained doubly barred to Aborigines in New South Wales by virtue of the *Aborigines Protection Act* and the *Liquor Act*. An amendment in 1946 removed the latter prohibition, although the prohibition curiously remained in the *Aborigines Protection Act* until 1963.[67]

The New South Wales Board for the Protection of Aborigines was certainly less preoccupied with removing 'half-castes' from its care than was its Victorian counterpart, although the New South Wales Board did at one stage consult with the Victorian Board about the removal of 'half-caste' children from reserves. C.D. Rowley attributes this difference in policy to the numbers involved in the respective States, in that Victoria's relatively small 'half-caste' population led administrators there to believe that they could completely isolate 'half-castes' from 'Aborigines'.[68]

Although Aborigines in New South Wales were not specifically prevented from voting, they and anyone else in receipt of charitable aid could not vote.[69] The impact that living on a reserve could have for an Aboriginal's voting rights was profound, and in New South Wales there is evidence that Aborigines who initially exercised the federal vote subsequently had it taken away.

A significant number of Aborigines, both male and female, living in the Riverina area of southern New South Wales voted in the 1903 federal election.[70] As the correspondence from one divisional returning officer in 1904 indicates, these Aborigines subsequently lost the vote at both State and federal levels. In one letter, the officer referred to a group of Aborigines living on a mission, who were on the federal roll and who had been on the State roll. The divisional officer reported that: 'these electors have been struck off the State Electoral Roll by a recent State Revision Court on the grounds that they are in receipt of continuous State aid – they are therefore not entitled to be on the Commonwealth Roll.'[71]

Soon after, the same divisional returning officer became even more rigorous and peremptory. He forwarded to the Commonwealth Electoral Office a list of the names of Aboriginal women who resided at Cumeragunja mission station, and wrote the following:

> These [women] are in the receipt of continuous State aid and in consequence are not entitled to a vote – they have not yet been struck off the State rolls but will be at the next revision court . . . Under the Commonwealth Act Aboriginals are not entitled to vote except under clause 41 of the Constitution. Am I justified in striking them off the Commonwealth rolls before they are struck off the State rolls . . . Should an election be held and they are allowed to vote it might lead to complications afterwards.[72]

The bureaucrat's concerns about 'complications afterwards' were sufficient for him to seek to remove the franchise from this group of Aboriginal women. The Commonwealth Electoral Office's stance was that such people were entitled to vote at the Commonwealth level until their names were removed from the State rolls.[73]

Clearly, Aborigines in New South Wales, Victoria, South Australia and Tasmania who held the Commonwealth vote did so tenuously. As we discussed in the previous chapter, it was soon the practice that only Aborigines already on the State rolls in 1902 could qualify for the section 41 exemption and exercise the Commonwealth vote. Further, once a person was removed from a State roll, section 41 provided no protection, and he or she would be removed from the federal roll. By 1922 it was estimated that only 175 'aboriginal natives' in New South Wales were enrolled federally by virtue of section 41.[74]

The New South Wales Board's power over Aboriginal children was increased enormously from 1915. One new section set out that if an Aboriginal child did not go to the person to whom the board apprenticed the child, then the child could be removed to a home or institution. Any absconding from these places, the new section spelt out, rendered a child liable to be labelled 'neglected', and he or she could then be dealt with under the *Neglected Children and Juvenile Offenders Act 1905* (NSW). A further amendment in 1915 left no doubt about the Board's authority to remove children, and simply gave the Board the power to 'remove such child to such control and care as it thinks best'.[75] Under the Board's dispersal policy, over 1500 Aboriginal children were separated from their families between 1912 and 1938.[76]

It was not until 1918 that the Board gained a specific power to confine Aborigines on reserves, by which time Aborigines were defined to be 'any full-blooded or half-caste aboriginal who is a native of New South Wales'.[77] As was the case in Victoria, the New South Wales Board had little enthusiasm for its task. Bain Attwood and others argue that this is perhaps partly explainable by the contradictory nature of the Board's work. For while it sought to implement its policy of dispersing Aborigines, the Board also at some level realised that it had a duty to care for Aborigines.[78]

Our chief concern in this chapter is to document the ways in which the States increasingly used legislation as a means of controlling Aborigines, but it would be wrong to view this period as devoid of Aboriginal resistance to the protection regimes. The formation of the Australian Aboriginal Progressive Association in 1924 signalled the beginning of organised Aboriginal resistance to the protection regime. Parliament and the press were lobbied on issues ranging from the sexual violence suffered by Aboriginal women and girls to Aboriginal education, and the Association caused some alteration to the child removal policy.[79] The Association's principal platform, which it outlined in a letter to Prime Minister Bruce, was that:

> As it is the proud boast of Australians that every person born beneath the Southern Cross is born free irrespective of origin, colour, race, creed, religion or any other modern impediment, We, the representatives of the original Australian people, in conference assembled demand that we shall be accorded the same full rights and privileges of citizenship as are enjoyed by all other sections of the community.[80]

The government's predictable response was that the principle enunciated could not be challenged, but that in 'practical affairs' the Australian Aboriginal was not entitled to be placed on the level suggested.[81]

Further amendments to the Aborigines' legislation in New South Wales came in 1936, from when an Aboriginal was deemed to be 'any full-blooded or half-caste aboriginal who is a native of Australia and who is temporarily or permanently resident in New South Wales'. One of the Act's principal sections widened the scope for the removal of Aborigines to reserves by enabling a Magistrate to order such removal if the Board considered the person to be living in 'insanitary or undesirable conditions'.[82] As with the situation in Western Australia, Aborigines in New South Wales could lose their freedoms purely because they lived in poverty.

Amendments to the legislation in 1936 were, in effect, an admission that the dispersal policy had failed, and it was around this time that the policy of assimilation could be said to have taken hold in New South Wales. In the mid-1930s the Board for the Protection of Aborigines decided that all Aborigines, not just children, needed to be trained to mix with the white population. To this end, reserves were expanded from which Aborigines would not leave until they could effectively assimilate. In the late 1930s New South Wales had seventy-one Aboriginal reserves.[83]

In addition to the increased power to remove Aborigines to reserves, from 1936 the Board could direct employers to pay Aborigines' wages to an official rather than to the worker, and could order an Aboriginal to undergo medical treatment. This latter provision was justified by the widespread infection of Aborigines with gonococcal ophthalmia. One member of the Aborigines Protection Board argued that the measure was urgent 'because the health of our own people is very seriously threatened'. Where an offence was alleged to have been committed against the legislation, it was now presumed that the person concerned was Aboriginal, and the power to determine Aboriginality in legal proceedings was given to a range of judicial officers.[84]

From the mid- to late 1930s an increasing proportion of Aborigines in New South Wales were deemed to come under the 'Dog Act', and were moved to reserves. Thus, Aboriginal protection laws in New South Wales, as elsewhere, became increasingly more restrictive throughout the 1930s.[85] The realisation that Aborigines were not going to die out was catching hold in all parts of Australia, motivating the nationwide shift from dispersal to assimilationist policies.

Two significant Aboriginal groups gained prominence in the 1930s for their attempts to counter the increasingly restrictive nature of the administrative regimes. The Australian Aboriginal League, headed by William Cooper, was formed in 1934 and had links in both Victoria and New South Wales. In 1933 in Melbourne, Cooper prepared a petition to King George V, calling for federal control of Aboriginal affairs and for an Aboriginal member of federal parliament.[86] By 1938 the petition had attracted 1814 signatures from Queensland, Western Australia, South Australia, New South Wales and the Northern Territory. The petitioners argued that it was a term of the commission under which white people had come to Australia that the original occupants and their heirs would be adequately cared for. The petitioners maintained that this term of commission had been breached through the expropriation of Aboriginal lands and the denial of legal status to Aborigines. Unsurprisingly, the Commonwealth government decided that no good purpose would be achieved by submitting the petition to the King.[87]

In a letter to the Prime Minister in 1937, the League again sought direct Aboriginal representation in parliament, noting that the Maoris in New Zealand had four members for an area the size of Victoria. The League wanted to safeguard the rights of Aborigines from the zealous administrative officers, who in large 'interpret their responsibilities to the aborigines in much the same way as a gaol governor does his criminal population'.[88]

The federal government viewed the League's request for direct representation with sufficient gravity to obtain the opinion of the Solicitor-General. He argued that while the Commonwealth parliament could not provide for direct Aboriginal representation in Australia as a whole, it could, by virtue of section 122 of the Constitution, permit Aborigines in the Northern Territory to elect an Aboriginal member for the Territory.[89]

In 1938 Cooper masterminded the Aboriginal Day of Mourning, to coincide with Australia's '150th anniversary'. The Australian Aboriginal League petitioned parliament for the freedom to irrigate land, initially around the Cumeragunja reserve.[90] In the meantime, the Aborigines' Progressive Association (replacing the Australian Aboriginal Progressive Association) demanded civil rights for Aborigines and the demise of the Protection Board. Two of the organisation's leaders, John Patten and William Ferguson, detailed the organisation's political agenda in the publication *Aborigines Claim Citizen Rights!*. The call for citizen rights was justified not by pointing to the existence of inalienable human rights, but by the argument that many Aborigines were sufficiently civilised to be entitled to full citizen rights.[91] The Day of Mourning in 1938, and the Cumeragunja walk-off the year later, in protest at the refusal of the Board to permit the irrigation plan, remain the starkest images of 1930s Aboriginal protest.

This activity coincided with the completion of a report on New South Wales Aborigines by the Public Service Board, which led to the adoption of assimilation as the new Aboriginal affairs policy in New South

Wales. By this stage, there were over 5000 Aborigines on reserves in New South Wales.[92]

In 1940 the Board for the Protection of Aborigines was replaced by the Aborigines Welfare Board. Three years later the Board was required to have two Aboriginal members, one 'full-blooded' Aboriginal and the other either 'full-blooded' or having an 'admixture' of Aboriginal blood, both of whom would be elected by Aborigines. This development notwithstanding, the Aborigines Welfare Board was given even wider powers than its predecessor in order to gradually implement its new policy. The power of the Board to remove Aborigines to reserves was increased by a clause that enabled the Board to remove any Aboriginal who 'should in the opinion of the board be placed under control'.[93]

Aboriginal children could be removed from their families under general legislation regarding neglected children. In 1939 the new *Child Welfare Act* provided that Aboriginal and non-Aboriginal children could now be removed from their families for being 'uncontrollable' as well as for being neglected. Peter Read argues that as many Aboriginal children were removed under this new legislation as had been under the *Aborigines Protection Act.*[94]

At the same time, the Board's power over Aboriginal children was extended in the 1940s by a rather circuitous route. The Board had power to send 'wards' to homes or bind them as apprentices, and the 1940 legislation defined 'ward' to be any child admitted to the control of the Board. A child could be admitted to the control of the Board by application of a parent or guardian, or by a Court's decision that the child was neglected or uncontrollable. Any ward absconding from 'proper custody' was guilty of an offence.[95] This power was extended in 1943 when the power to have a child admitted to the control of the Board was given to the Board itself. Thus the Board could now make a child a ward by giving itself control over that child. The Board could now freely determine the custody arrangements of any Aboriginal child.[96]

South Australia

South Australia's first protection legislation, the *Aborigines Act 1911* (SA), closely followed the Queensland legislation in its definition of who was Aboriginal, and in its granting of broad discretionary powers to administrators. Just as in Queensland, a Chief Protector could 'cause any aboriginal or half-caste' to be moved to a reserve, could act as a trustee of any Aboriginal's property, and could order medical inspections and procedures to be performed on Aborigines.[97] Other provisions enabled protectors to move any Aboriginal camp or proposed camp, and, as usual, the executive held broad regulatory power, including the power to direct that Aborigines not loiter in certain proclaimed places. In contrast to the position in most other States, the employers of South Australian Aborigines were not required to hold permits, but Protectors did have power to inspect any Aboriginal's work environment. An Aboriginal in lawful employment could not be ordered to reside on a reserve.[98]

A Royal Commission set up after the enactment of the 1911 legislation advocated two courses of action which many States had already adopted: greater government regulation of Aborigines, and the separation of 'full-bloods' from 'half-castes'. The latter group, the Royal Commission recommended, should be removed from their communities and become self-supporting.[99]

Consistent with developments in other States, broad-ranging regulations were gazetted in South Australia that severely curtailed the lives of Aborigines. The freedom with which the South Australian executive was gazetting restrictive regulations was momentarily halted when two lay Justices of the Peace ruled that regulations made in May 1917 were so broad-ranging as to be beyond the scope permitted by the 1911 Act. The particular regulation that gave rise to the court hearing was one according to which an Aboriginal man had been forbidden to reside at the Point Pearce Aboriginal Institution. He had occupied a cottage there with his family and had been employed there when work was available. He argued that the regulation, which enabled administrators to remove Aborigines from Aboriginal institutions, was broader than the Act permitted, and that it was so unreasonable and oppressive that the power to make it could not have been intended by parliament. On appeal from the Justices of the Peace, the South Australian Supreme Court disagreed, a Judge ruling that the Act itself so curtailed the rights of Aborigines that the regulation in question had to be viewed as being of a nature intended by parliament.[100]

Peggy Brock argues that by the 1930s the South Australian government policy towards Aborigines began to change from a policy of segregation to one of assimilation. The new guiding philosophy was that assimilation would ensure both that Aborigines' blood would disappear, as would their customs and way of life.[101]

In new legislation in 1934, Aborigines were defined to be: an Aboriginal native; a 'half-caste' living as the husband or wife of an Aboriginal native; a 'half-caste' who habitually resided with an Aboriginal native; and a 'half-caste' child under eighteen years of age. In the absence of evidence as to a person's lineage, the presumption was that they were covered by the Act. In legal proceedings, the determination of a person's Aboriginality was left to the opinion of a range of judicial officers. In 1939 the definition of 'Aboriginal' was changed so that the word now referred to any person 'of the full blood' or 'of less than full blood' who was descended from the original inhabitants of Australia.[102]

The desire of bureaucrats to classify Aborigines into castes caused headaches for the judiciary in South Australia. According to the *Licensing Act* it was an offence for any 'aboriginal native of Australia, or any half-caste of that race' to consume alcohol. In 1925 an Aboriginal man argued that he had been wrongly convicted of being a 'half-caste' found drinking liquor, since all the evidence pointed to him being a 'full-blood'. After some deliberation, the South Australian Supreme Court affirmed his conviction.[103]

Three years later a publican, charged with supplying alcohol to a 'half-caste', sought a similar defence. The man who received the alcohol gave evidence that his mother was a 'half-caste', but that his mother's mother was black, as was his father. The Magistrate hearing the case simply crossed out 'half-caste' on the charge sheet and wrote in 'Aboriginal', and then convicted the publican. On appeal, the Supreme Court affirmed the conviction.[104]

From 1934 the Aboriginals Department was the administrative body governing the lives of South Australian Aborigines. A Chief Protector, appointed by the executive, was responsible for the administration of the Department and had power to remove to reserves those Aborigines not lawfully employed. The Chief Protector could also act as trustee over Aborigines' property, and could order the medical treatment of any Aboriginal or 'half-caste'.[105] Local protectors, meanwhile, could move Aborigines who had camped or were 'about to camp' away from townships, and they and police officers could inspect the employment conditions of any Aboriginal.[106] The South Australian executive retained broad discretionary regulatory power, and had express power to declare areas into which Aborigines were not permitted to go.[107]

A further change took place in 1939, when a new Aborigines Protection Board, two of whose seven members were required to be women, took over the administration of Aboriginal affairs. The Board now managed and regulated all Aboriginal reserves, and had the power to move Aborigines, other than those legally employed, to or from reserves. The Board could also act as trustee over the property of Aborigines, and could exempt any Aboriginal from the operations of the Act by declaring that an 'aborigine shall cease to be an aborigine for the purposes of this Act'.[108] Once a person was exempted he or she could not continue to associate with Aborigines for fear of breaching provisions that made it illegal for Aborigines to associate with non-Aborigines.[109]

Aborigines in South Australia, as in Victoria and New South Wales, were not specifically prohibited from voting at State level, and through section 41 of the Constitution had a means by which they could vote federally. But Pat Stretton and Christine Finnimore have shown that, despite the existence of section 41, seventeen South Australian Aborigines at Point McLeay, some of whom had probably been on the Commonwealth electoral roll since 1902, lost the Commonwealth vote between 1922 and 1946. Bureaucratic practice simply prevailed over legal rights.[110]

The most striking aspect of the South Australian legislation was the power it gave administrators over Aboriginal children. From 1934 the Chief Protector was the legal guardian of all Aboriginal children, and the Aboriginals Department oversaw their custody, maintenance and education. As had been the case since 1923, the Chief Protector had power, with the approval of the Children's Welfare and Public Relief Board, to institutionalise any Aboriginal child, following which the child would be treated as though he or she were neglected.[111] From 1939 these powers vested in the Aborigines Protection Board, and a new section required all Aboriginal children in Aboriginal institutions between fourteen and sixteen years of age to attend school. If they did not 'attend at a school on every occasion when the school is open for instruction', their parents were guilty of an offence.[112]

Northern Territory

Just prior to the removal of the Northern Territory from South Australian control, the South Australian legislature passed the *Northern Territory Aboriginals Act 1910* (SA), the first piece of Northern Territory protection legislation. This Act was very similar to the 1911 legislation passed to govern South Australian Aborigines. The definition of 'Aboriginal' and the restrictions imposed on Aborigines' movement and their ability to control property were similar in both Acts, each of which was administered by a Chief Protector.[113] But, in contrast to the position in South Australia, the employers of Aborigines in the Northern Territory needed to hold special licences. Another difference saw Aboriginal women in the Northern Territory require express permission to marry non-Aboriginal men. Somewhat curiously, given that the situation in the Northern Territory was, if anything, more restrictive than it was in South Australia, the power to force Aborigines to undergo medical treatment was absent in the Northern Territory legislation.[114]

From 1911 the Northern Territory ceased to be governed by the laws of South Australia and came under Commonwealth jurisdiction. It is worth looking in some detail at the way Northern Territory Aborigines were treated in the period under consideration, because the 1967 referendum, following which the Commonwealth gained the constitutional power to make laws for all Aborigines, is commonly seen as being the point at which Aborigines became Australian citizens. The belief that 1967 was the citizenship year for Aborigines is largely based on the fact that this extension of power to the Commonwealth coincided with a number of positive developments in the administration of Aboriginal affairs. But would Australian Aborigines have been better served if the Commonwealth had been granted this power earlier? By looking at the Commonwealth's governance of Aborigines in the Northern Territory in the years 1911 to 1948 we can attempt to answer this question.

In 1911 the new Chief Protector of Northern Territory Aborigines, Baldwin Spencer, was asked to report on Aborigines in the Northern Territory. He advocated the establishment of reserves and the non-interference with Aboriginal custom where it did not impact on white people. However, in the major centres, Darwin and Alice Springs, Spencer supported policies aimed more at protecting white people than Aborigines.[115] Regulations were passed in that year governing the employment of Aborigines.[116]

Without exception, the administration of Aboriginal affairs in the Northern Territory was every bit as oppressive as it was in Queensland and Western Australia. The Commonwealth's first Northern Territory Ordinance governing Aborigines was passed in 1911, and it incorporated and supplemented the 1910 South Australian Act. The Ordinance continued the restrictions on Aborigines' citizenship rights as before. In addition, the Chief Protector was empowered to undertake the 'care, custody, or control' of any Aboriginal or 'half-caste', and could direct a police officer to take an Aboriginal or 'half-caste' into custody. The Northern Territory Administrator had power to declare a place to be a 'prohibited area', into which Aborigines could not go. Regulations were also made governing the manner in which employers could apply for licences to employ Aborigines.[117]

In 1918 the Commonwealth government repealed the existing Aboriginal legislation in the Northern Territory and made its first full statement of how Aboriginal affairs would be regulated. The *Aboriginals Ordinance 1918* (NT) stands as the Commonwealth's first comprehensive piece of Aboriginal affairs legislation, and warrants detailed consideration for this reason.

An 'Aboriginal' was defined as being any of the following people: an 'aboriginal native' of Australia or the islands adjacent thereto; a 'half-caste' living as the spouse of an Aboriginal; a 'half-caste' who habitually lived or associated with 'aboriginal natives'; a 'half-caste' male under eighteen years; and 'a female half-caste not legally married to a person who is substantially of European origin or descent'. The term 'half-caste' referred to any person with one Aboriginal or 'half-caste' parent. The division between 'half-caste' men and women, according to which 'half-caste' men were only deemed to be Aboriginal if they lived or associated with Aborigines, was fudged a little nine years later, when an amendment extended the definition of Aboriginal so that it applied to 'half-caste' men who were deemed to be incapable of managing their own affairs.[118]

The Northern Territory's Chief Protector of Aborigines was vested with all the powers held by Chief Protectors in other jurisdictions. He had the power to provide for the custody and education of Aboriginal children, over whom he was the legal guardian, and he could force Aborigines not 'lawfully employed' to reside on reserves.[119] Meanwhile, the employment regime continued as before. Potential employers of Aborigines, who could not be 'Asiatic' men, had first to apply for annual licences, following which they had to enter written contracts if the worker was to be employed in a town. The nature of most employment situations was revealed by the language of one provision, which sought to protect Aborigines from ill-treatment. It maintained that it was an offence if an Aboriginal was not being treated properly 'by any person having the custody or control of the aboriginal (whether employer or otherwise)'.[120] Employment was synonymous with custody or control.

Consistent with legislation in other jurisdictions, the 1918 Ordinance evidenced an administrative preoccupation with miscegenation. Female Aborigines could not marry non-Aborigines without special permission, and it was an offence for a non-Aboriginal to have 'carnal knowledge' of a female Aboriginal.[121] Of course, the fact that sex between white men and Aboriginal women was an offence did not mean that convictions necessarily followed. Ann McGrath writes of a policeman, who was also a protector, who was charged with the 'ill-use' of Aboriginal women. These charges were dismissed in 1919 because the Judge claimed that all fifteen Aboriginal witnesses were liars.[122]

Local protectors in the Northern Territory also exercised large amounts of power over Aborigines. They had power to move an Aboriginal camp or 'proposed camp', they could authorise the removal of Aborigines from one district to another, or between reserves and institutions, and they could arrest without warrant any person suspected of committing an offence against the Ordinance. This was an extraordinary power, considering that the breach of an employment agreement was an offence against the Ordinance.[123] Other restrictions saw Aborigines prevented from entering hotels and any other areas declared to be 'prohibited'. In addition, the Northern Territory Administrator held broad regulatory power. He could order that Aboriginal children be detained in schools or institutions, and could regulate for the maintenance of 'discipline and good order' upon a reserve.[124]

Regulations made the following year clarified the nature of Aboriginal employment in startling terms. Aborigines living on employers' properties, or on reserves within certain town districts, could not be 'at large' in towns one hour after sunset without written permission. Those who were 'at large' faced one month's imprisonment.[125] Regulations like these support the contention that it was not Aborigines who were sought to be protected by the protection regime.

Ten years later this situation still more or less prevailed, and the argument that Aborigines were aliens in their own land was strengthened by new regulations that enabled Aborigines to go into prohibited areas only after being issued with a permit.[126] As in Western Australia a little later, Aborigines virtually required passports to go to some parts of their own country.

In 1929 J.W. Bleakley, the Queensland Chief Protector of Aborigines from 1913 to 1940, reported on the condition of Aborigines in the Northern Territory. Bleakley, as Peter Read has argued, was torn between the desire to protect Aborigines and the desire to control them.[127] This was clearest in his quite convoluted proposals with regard to 'half-castes'. He sought to 'check as far as possible the breeding of half-castes', but the methods by which he proposed to do this indicated clearly that he saw the sexual exploitation of Aboriginal women by single white men as being the reason for the growing 'half-caste' population. Bleakley proposed the stricter enforcement of laws designed to protect female Aborigines, and sought to encourage the increased immigration of white women to the Territory. Bleakley further proposed that all illegitimate 'half-castes' under sixteen years of age who were not being satisfactorily educated be placed in Aboriginal industrial homes, and that education be made compulsory for all 'half-castes' up to the age of sixteen. Meanwhile, he proposed that those Aborigines 'with [a] preponderance of white blood' be sent to European institutions at an early age.[128]

In other ruminations on Aboriginal policy, Bleakley considered the proposal that a self-governing Aboriginal State be established, but then dismissed the idea on the grounds that it would 'thrust upon [Aborigines] a social machine they cannot understand'. He wrote that it would be 'a great stride in citizenship for one generation' if young Aborigines could be trained to appreciate settled family life, develop the desire for self-dependence, and learn something of the spirit of social service.[129]

The reality of relations between white people and Aborigines in the Northern Territory was never more evident than in the aftermath of the murder of five Japanese crew members at Caledon Bay in the early 1930s and the murder of a police officer in 1933 on Woodah Island. All of the murders had allegedly been committed by Aborigines. After missionaries had acted as go-betweens, five Aborigines, including a man named Tuckiar, agreed to come to Darwin to face trial, in what they thought was to be a peace mission. Three of these men were convicted of killing the Japanese crew members and were sentenced to twenty years' imprisonment, while Tuckiar was convicted of murdering the policeman and sentenced to death. The evidence used to convict Tuckiar, who spoke no English, included two statements he had made to Aboriginal witnesses, which the Court took to be contradictory. Tuckiar's statement to the first Aboriginal witness suggested that Tuckiar had murdered the policeman. His statement to the second witness indicated that Tuckiar had acted more in self-defence. Both stories made reference to the dead policeman taking away one or more of Tuckiar's wives, the second story indicating that the policeman had had sex with one of Tuckiar's wives. Commentators at the time, and since, have accepted that Tuckiar's statements, both of which were interpreted by different people, may well have been complementary rather than contradictory. Nevertheless, Tuckiar's counsel put it to him that one of his statements had to be wrong. At this stage, Tuckiar withdrew the second story, a fact which Tuckiar's counsel communicated to the Judge in chambers. In charging the jury, the Judge all but told them which story they should believe, saying that the first of Tuckiar's statements was highly probable and that the other was an obvious fabrication. He added that the jury could draw any inference it liked from Tuckiar's failure to give evidence.

As the famous anthropologist A.P. Elkin argued, the fact that Tuckiar, through an interpreter and then through his counsel, withdrew the self-defence version did not indicate he did not believe it. He had been kept for weeks in jail in Darwin, and then told that one of his statements was a lie. His only choice was to withdraw one of the 'contradictory' statements so that the trial could end and he could receive the freedom he believed he would then enjoy. Further, as C.D. Rowley argues, the death sentence received by Tuckiar could only be explained by the fact that a white man had been the victim of the crime. Only a short time before the same Judge had ordered the imprisonment of the men who had killed the Japanese crew members.

Tuckiar was subsequently acquitted by the High Court, which ruled that the trial Judge had erred in a number of fundamental respects. Included among these errors were his comments on Tuckiar's failure to give evidence, and his charge to the jury, during which he had said that a verdict of not guilty would denigrate the deceased policeman.

So concerned had the trial Judge been to clear the policeman's name that he admitted evidence as to his character, a matter irrelevant to the trial. So Tuckiar was cleared by the High Court and allowed to go home. But he never made it home, and it is commonly understood that he was murdered en route.[130]

The fact that Tuckiar seems in the end to have been the victim of a revenge killing makes the legal rights, which the High Court declared him to have, seem somewhat fantastic. Important as it was, the Court's decision clearly meant little in practice to a person like Tuckiar.

As we have seen, the caste divide was as strongly enforced in the Northern Territory as it was elsewhere. Ann McGrath points out that the 'half-caste' policies were at their most destructive with regard to children.[131] The bizarre complexity that resulted from the attempt to divide 'half-castes' from 'Aborigines' was most clearly apparent in 1930, when the Government Resident gazetted the 'Apprentices (Half-Castes) Regulations'. These regulations excluded from the definition of 'half-caste under twenty-one' any person 'in whom aboriginal native blood predominates', although a further regulation belied this rigid distinction. Remembering that the overriding legislation, the *Aboriginals Ordinance 1918–1928* (NT), had an expansive definition of 'aboriginal', the following regulation sought to exclude male 'half-castes' from the legislation governing the employment of other Aborigines. It is worth repeating in full:

> A licence to employ aboriginals shall not entitle the holder thereof to employ under that licence any male half-caste of any age whatsoever, notwithstanding that that half-caste is an aboriginal within the meaning of the word 'aboriginal' in section three of the *Aboriginals Ordinance 1918–1928.*

This regulation was so ridiculous as almost to be humorous, but the profoundly disturbing belief in the need to regulate the level of interaction between 'castes' saw a further regulation empower the Chief Protector to stipulate that where six or more 'aboriginal natives' were to be employed on a station, one 'half-caste' between sixteen and twenty-one years of age had also to be employed. Where twelve or more 'aboriginal natives' were employed, he could order that two 'half-castes' be required to be employed. And so on.[132] From 1936 a person could be deemed not to be a 'half-caste', and from 1943 a person could be deemed not to be Aboriginal. Around 500 'half-castes' and other Aborigines had been exempted from the operations of the Ordinance by the early 1950s.[133]

Throughout the 1930s the restrictions on Aborigines became, if anything, even greater than they previously had been. Aborigines were specifically excluded from the benefits of workers compensation. An

Aboriginal or 'half-caste' caught drinking or in charge of liquor was guilty of an offence, and Aborigines staying on reserves in certain towns, or on employers' properties, continued not to be allowed in towns after dark without special permission.[134] Meanwhile, government spending on Aborigines in the Northern Territory continued to be low. Indeed, the Commonwealth's poor record in the administration of Aboriginal affairs in the Northern Territory is highlighted by the level of its spending. Andrew Markus has calculated that in the years 1935 to 1936 the Victorian administration, which was anything but generous, spent more on an Aboriginal population of under 1000 than the Commonwealth did on a population of over 15,000.[135]

During the 1937 conference of State and Commonwealth Aboriginal Authorities, when the policy of assimilation is generally thought to have become the guiding philosophy in Australia, Cecil Cook, the Northern Territory's Chief Protector, outlined the policy that the Commonwealth had been pursuing in the Territory. Cook revealed the Commonwealth to have followed a policy analogous to that of Queensland. Under Commonwealth policy, he said, Aborigines, as opposed to 'half-castes', had been divided into three categories: the 'wild, uncivilized blacks', who had been left on reserves; the 'semi-civilized', who lived near white settlements; and the 'detribalized', who it was proposed would be trained and educated so that 'they can make a living without competing with the whites'. With regard to 'half-castes', Cook argued that the 'policy of the Commonwealth is to do everything possible to convert the half-caste into a white citizen'.[136]

Cook argued at the 1937 conference that delegates needed to consider what policy should now be pursued. He gave three options: they could do nothing; they could 'develop an enlightened elaborate system of protection which will produce an aboriginal population that is likely to swamp the white'; or they could adopt the policy under which Aborigines would be absorbed into the white population. He favoured the latter, commenting that 'unless the black population is speedily absorbed into the white, the process will soon be reversed, and in fifty years, or a little later, the white population of the Northern Territory will be absorbed into the black'.[137]

John McEwen, the Commonwealth Minister for the Interior, issued his now famous Aboriginal policy in 1939. The 'final objective' of the Commonwealth government with regard to Aborigines was to be the 'raising of their status so as to entitle them by right and by qualification to the ordinary rights of citizenship'. McEwen indulged in the now familiar practice of classifying Aborigines. He pointed to four classes of Aborigines: the 'fully detribalized'; the 'semi-detribalized'; the 'aboriginals in their native state'; and the 'half-castes'. This latter group was then divided into two: those 'born in wedlock of half-caste parents and those born of an aboriginal mother and a non-aboriginal father'. His view was that the 'near-white children' should be trained apart from the 'general half-caste children', which meant their removal from their families.[138]

In 1939, consistent with contemporary moves in Queensland and Western Australia, the Northern Territory's Chief Protector became the Director of Native Affairs. The creation of the Native Affairs Branch would, according to McEwen, enable the Aboriginal administration to be separated from the Northern Territory health service.[139] The following year legislation was passed to oversee the establishment of Courts for Native Matters. These courts were established to deal with disputes between 'natives', who were defined in similar fashion to 'aboriginals' in previous legislation. The courts had power to order the corporal punishment of Aboriginal children, and the Minister had broad regulatory power over: marriage and divorce; the jurisdiction and powers of the Courts for Native Matters to determine civil and criminal matters; the establishment of gaols on reserves; and the rights of 'natives' to real and personal property.[140] The fact that serious legal procedures, such as the hearing of criminal charges, were able to be altered by regulation speaks volumes for the Commonwealth's view of Aborigines' legal rights.

In 1945 the Native Affairs Branch requested V.C. Carrington to investigate the condition of Aborigines in the Northern Territory. He reported on poor sanitary conditions, the inappropriate labelling of some Aborigines as 'dependants' of workers, when they were in fact workers themselves who were entitled to wages, and he concluded that the position of Aborigines was not all that far removed from slavery.[141]

The electoral position of Aborigines in the Northern Territory was identical to their position federally. In 1922 the Commonwealth legislated to provide representation for the Northern Territory in the Commonwealth parliament, and put in place the same voting restrictions as existed in the *Commonwealth Electoral Act.* In the 'Northern Territory Electoral Regulations', gazetted in 1922, the vote was specifically denied to every 'aboriginal native of Australia' except those permitted to vote under section 41 of the Constitution.[142]

The maze of legislation that affected Aborigines often overlapped, creating headaches for those charged with the smooth running of the bureaucracy. One such headache was caused for Robert Garran, the Commonwealth Solicitor-General, in 1928. As mentioned earlier, a 1927 Ordinance extended the definition of 'aboriginal' in the Northern Territory to include any male 'half-caste' deemed incapable of administering his own affairs. Did this mean, however, that a male 'half-caste' who came within this new category could not vote at either the Territory or Commonwealth level? The Returning Officer for the Northern Territory took the view that a 'half-caste' man who was now included in the 'aboriginal' definition was nevertheless still entitled to vote, 'since he is not an aboriginal native of Australia in the sense of being a person in whom the aboriginal blood preponderates'. Garran agreed that a person could both be 'aboriginal' for the purposes of protection legislation, yet not be an 'aboriginal native' in other respects.[143]

This right of 'half-castes' to vote caused some concern in the Northern Territory. The Administrator commented in 1933 that it would be beneficial to the Territory if 'half-castes' were not extended the 'privilege' of being enrolled as electors. This comment was revealing in itself, showing the Northern Territory Administrator to be unaware that 'half-castes' in whom Aboriginal blood did not 'preponderate' were theoretically entitled to vote in the Territory. The Administrator's main concern was that it would only be a matter of time before the 'half-castes' and Chinese would themselves be able to choose the member for the Territory in the House of Representatives.[144] Needless to say, the possibility referred to earlier that the Commonwealth government might legislate to allow Aborigines in the Northern Territory to directly elect Aboriginal representatives was not one pursued by the Commonwealth.

It was not just the franchise legislation that caused administrative problems in the Northern Territory. A 1931 Ordinance stated that no 'aboriginal native of Australia' was entitled to workers compensation. But the Ordinance did not define 'aboriginal native'. Was a 'half-caste' entitled to workers compensation? The Secretary of the Commonwealth Attorney-General's Department took the view that, although the *Aboriginals Ordinance* included half-castes in the term 'aboriginal', the definition had 'no general application' to other legislation. Thus 'half-castes', presumably on the preponderating blood test, were entitled to workers compensation.[145]

Tasmania

In all but one jurisdiction in Australia during the period 1900 to 1948, severely restrictive Aboriginal legislation was enacted under the guise of protecting Aborigines. The one exception was Tasmania, where the official position was that the State had no Aborigines. The *Licensing Act 1908* (Tas) and the *Cape Barren Island Reserve Act 1912* (Tas) did at least acknowledge the existence of Tasmanian 'half-castes', although not on the Tasmanian mainland. The former Act banned the supply of alcohol to any 'half-caste', a term defined to mean a resident of Cape Barren Island. The latter Act, meanwhile, and its replacement Act in 1945, entitled some Tasmanian Aborigines to remain on Cape Barren Island as lessees, although they were given far from secure interests in the land. Both Cape Barren Island Acts prohibited alcohol on the island, and gave administrators a blanket power to remove people from the island who were not lessees.[146] Tasmania never enacted protection legislation as such, for officials believed that there was no-one to protect. Meanwhile, Aborigines in the Australian Capital Territory were governed by New South Wales protection legislation until 1954.

The most uniform aspect of all the State and Territory Aboriginal protection regimes was that they all became increasingly regressive from the time of their establishment until the 1930s, when it became apparent that Aborigines were not going to die out. It was at this point that the assimilation policy, although not officially endorsed until the 1950s, began to be put into practice. As already mentioned, the point commonly taken to mark the beginning of the assimilation policy is the 1937 conference of State and Commonwealth Aboriginal authorities. That conference adopted the following resolution:

> That this Conference believes that the destiny of the natives of aboriginal origin, but not of the full blood, lies in their ultimate absorption by the people of the Commonwealth and it therefore recommends that all efforts be directed to that end.[147]

Other resolutions called for 'children of mixed aboriginal blood' to be educated to white standards, with a view to them taking their place in the white community, and for the control of Aboriginal affairs to be retained by the States but for there to be uniformity of legislation. To this end, the conference delegates expressed their preference for the definition of 'native' contained in the prevailing West Australian legislation.[148] The reason for the adoption of the 'absorption' policy was put succinctly by the West Australian Commissioner of Native Affairs, A.O. Neville. He asked rhetorically:

> The different States are creating institutions for the welfare of the native race, and, as the result of this policy, the native population is increasing. What is to be the limit? Are we going to have a population of 1,000,000 blacks in the

Table 10 Official Aboriginal population estimate, 1947

Vic.	*Qld*	*WA*	*NSW*	*SA*	*NT*	*Tas.*	*ACT*	*Aust.*
1277	16,311	24,912	11,560	4296	15,147	214	100	73,817

Source: F. Lancaster Jones, *The Structure and Growth of Australia's Aboriginal Population*, 1970.

Commonwealth, or are we going to merge them into our white community and eventually forget that there ever were any aborigines in Australia?[149]

This was entirely the same reasoning that the Commonwealth adopted in John McEwen's statement two years later.

Table 11 Governance of Aboriginal affairs, 1948

	Definition of Aboriginal	*Governing body*
Victoria	Aboriginal natives and small number of 'half-castes'	Board for the Protection of Aborigines
Queensland	Aboriginal natives and 'half-bloods' habitually associating with them	Director of Native Affairs
Western Australia	Anyone descended from the original inhabitants of Australia (now called 'natives') except for some 'quadroons'	Commissioner of Native Affairs
New South Wales	'Full-blooded' or 'half-caste' Aboriginal natives	Aborigines Welfare Board
South Australia	Anyone descended from the original inhabitants of Australia	Aborigines Protection Board
Northern Territory	Aboriginal natives, most female 'half-castes', and some male 'half-castes'	Director of Native Affairs
Tasmania	No relevant legislation	No relevant legislation

Table 12 Formal restrictions affecting Aborigines on key citizenship criteria, 1948

	Statutory bar on voting	*Able to be removed to reserves*	*Employment formally regulated*
Victoria	No	Yes	In theory
Queensland	Yes	Yes	Yes
Western Australia	Yes	Yes	Yes
New South Wales	No	Yes	No
South Australia	No	Yes	No
Northern Territory	Yes	Yes	Yes
Tasmania	No	No	No

Towards Commonwealth Control

From the 1930s Aborigines were increasingly active in their calls for the Commonwealth to take control of Aboriginal affairs, an issue that State parliamentarians and other prominent citizens had been discussing on and off since federation.[150] In 1933 the National Missionary Council of Australia, in a move later supported by the Aborigines' Friends' Association and the Association for the Protection of Native Races, lobbied the federal government to assume control over Aboriginal affairs and to set up an advisory board containing representatives from all States to help in the formulation of Aboriginal policies.[151] Four years later the delegates at the 1937 conference, although resolving that Aboriginal affairs would remain within the control of the States, agreed that the Commonwealth should give increased resources to the States to assist them in their dealings with Aborigines. The argument supporting this was that the States, by maintaining Aborigines, were saving the Commonwealth from spending money on them through invalid and old-age pensions (for which Aborigines generally were ineligible). In addition, the people of the nation were supporting Aborigines in the Northern Territory, and they should therefore help in the support of Aborigines elsewhere. Further, in view of the role played by central governments in other countries, the Commonwealth, it was argued, should bear a considerable part of the cost for supporting Aborigines. Behind all of this was the fear that the failure to increase services to Aborigines would bring discredit on Australia, something for which the Commonwealth would, in the end, bear responsibility.[152]

The arguments against Commonwealth control had been summarised by J.W. Bleakley eight months earlier, in response to a call by the Bishop of Carpentaria for Commonwealth control. Bleakley acknowledged that other nations looked upon the welfare of Aborigines as a national affair, and that centralised control would lead to uniform laws and more secure finance. However, he argued that transport and communication problems would hinder control being centred in Canberra, that State police services had been efficient and inexpensive in carrying out 'protection and supervision', and that all States were not faced with the same problems.[153]

Two concerted efforts were made in the early 1940s in a bid to have the Commonwealth empowered to make laws for Aborigines. Following a constitutional convention in late 1942, the States were requested to pass legislation giving the Commonwealth power to make laws in a number of areas relating to post-war reconstruction. The last of these proposals, which had little to do with post-war reconstruction, would have enabled the Commonwealth to make laws on Aboriginal affairs. That all the States could not agree on the powers to be given to the Commonwealth did not surprise many people, one parliamentarian commenting that anyone who hoped that six State Premiers could get six State parliaments to agree to give exactly the same powers would be qualified for life membership of an optimists' society.[154]

That left a constitutional amendment, via a nationwide referendum, as the only feasible method by which the Commonwealth could get the powers it sought. A referendum was held in 1944, in which the Commonwealth sought to be granted power over fourteen areas for a period of five years. The extension for five years was sought despite the Commonwealth receiving legal advice that a constitutional alteration could not be made for a limited period. The last of the proposals was that the Commonwealth be empowered to make laws for Aborigines. The Commonwealth needed this power, one member argued, because unless Aborigines were properly cared for, Australia 'would be subjected to the criticism levelled at Hitler and his followers when they oppress the minority populations under their domination'.[155]

The Aboriginal amendment had not been included in an October 1942 draft of the Constitution Alteration (War Aims and Reconstruction) Bill. But the following month, after representations from A.P. Elkin, among others, the form of the bill that was circulated at the Constitutional Convention would have given the Commonwealth the power to make laws for 'the protection of the aboriginal natives of Australia'.[156] In the form that it was finally put to the people, the Constitution Alteration (Post-War Reconstruction and Democratic Rights) 1944 Proposed Law sought to give the Commonwealth, through a new clause 60A of the Constitution, the power to make laws for 'the people of the aboriginal race'.[157]

The referendum was defeated by an overall margin of 54 to 46 per cent. But the result gave no real indication of people's thoughts about Aboriginal affairs. The Aboriginal head of power was only one of the fourteen proposals that were put en masse. The choice was between accepting all the extensions of power to the Commonwealth, or rejecting them. Thus the failure of the referendum, as some commentators have argued, probably revealed more about people's objection to the continuation of government control than it did about their thoughts on Aboriginal policy.[158] Indeed, had the Aboriginal power proposal been central to the referendum, the Commonwealth would have sought an amendment to section 51(26) of the Constitution, rather than just tack the proposal onto the end of a new list of Commonwealth powers.

Even so, several strong arguments were made against the proposal that the Commonwealth be empowered to make laws for Aborigines.

One argument was that it was ridiculous for the power to be handed to the Commonwealth for only five years.[159] More important, however, were the observations of several federal parliamentarians about the situation of Northern Territory Aborigines. They argued that the Commonwealth's control over Aborigines in the Northern Territory was as bad if not worse than the States' treatment of Aborigines. Given this, one member stated, it was difficult to understand why it was necessary during wartime to give the Commonwealth the power to legislate for all the country's Aborigines.[160]

That the Commonwealth's administration of Aboriginal affairs in the Northern Territory was every bit as restrictive as any other State's, if not more so, made the proposal something about which few had reason to be optimistic. It is remarkable, then, that in the space of only two decades the success of such a proposal would be seen as the moment at which all Aborigines became Australian citizens.

CHAPTER 6

The Slow Path to Civil Rights

> The rights and disabilities of Australian citizens . . . are not to be found in the Nationality and Citizenship Act. Those rights and disabilities are to be found in the general law of Australia which is made up of the common law and Federal and State statutory laws . . .
>
> Being born in Australia . . . the aborigine is an Australian citizen. But to ascertain what rights Australian citizens, including aborigines, have and to what disabilities they are subject, it is necessary to look to the general law.
>
> *Commonwealth Attorney-General Garfield Barwick, 1959*[1]

As the above advice of Attorney-General Garfield Barwick made clear, the 1948 citizenship legislation gave no new citizenship rights to Aborigines. The legislation theoretically made Aborigines Australian citizens, but they were citizens who had no right to vote in Western Australia, Queensland, the Northern Territory or federally, and their access to social security was extremely limited. Even if the new legislation had given new rights to Aborigines, Australia's federal system of government still rendered a person's citizenship status dependent upon the rights accorded to him or her at State level. Barwick himself at one stage made reference to there being 'nine different "citizenships" in Australia'.[2] The power to determine a person's citizenship status did not rest with the Commonwealth alone.

So when political support was given to the idea that Aborigines should in a meaningful sense become Australian citizens, this in practice required changes on a number of fronts. Most particularly, federal and State legislation affecting citizenship rights needed to be changed. At varying rates these changes largely occurred in the 1950s and 1960s, although the vestiges of some State regimes remained visible as late as the 1980s. However, the changes were accompanied by a policy of assimilation that for some Aborigines was more detrimental than their exclusion from citizenship, particularly for those Aboriginal children who were forcibly removed from their parents. That story has been told, and is being told, elsewhere. Our aim here is not to detail these horrendous practices but to concentrate on the repeal of Commonwealth and State restrictions that barred Aborigines from any meaningful status as citizens.

Commonwealth Moves to Formal Inclusion

In 1948, when Aborigines along with all other Australians technically became 'Australian citizens', the Commonwealth was still restricting the access of Aborigines to two principal rights of citizenship: the federal franchise and social security.

Franchise

Prior to 1949 the only Aborigines who had a right to the Commonwealth vote were those who were so entitled by section 41 of the Constitution, or those Aborigines who were not labelled as such by the Commonwealth's 'preponderating blood' definition of Aboriginality. During World War II Aborigines in the defence force were enfranchised, along with other previously ineligible army personnel, but this right lasted only until six months after the end of the war.[3] This was changed in 1949, when the Commonwealth franchise was extended to Aborigines who were in, or had served in, the defence force. A year earlier the Government had intended not to enfranchise Aborigines who had been discharged from the army due to their own misconduct. But this rider was dropped after A.P. Elkin, among others, argued that the clause would make moral standards a qualification for the enfranchisement of Aborigines, whereas such standards did not apply to the enfranchisement of others.[4]

A more significant change to the franchise legislation in 1949 was the extension of the Commonwealth vote to those Aborigines entitled to vote at the State level.[5] We have seen how a broad reading of section 41 of the Constitution would have made this legislative provision unnecessary, but such a reading did not hold sway. Section 41, when bureaucrats paid heed to it, was deemed only to protect the vote of those Aborigines actually on State rolls prior to the first Commonwealth franchise legislation in 1902. During the 1940s the Chief Electoral Officer had been suggesting that the Commonwealth, like Western Australia, create a 'certificate of citizenship'. He suggested that Commonwealth certificates of citizenship, which would enable the holders to exercise the federal franchise, might be granted to Aborigines who had served in the army or who possessed the following attributes: a surname, literacy, employment, and good behaviour. His proposal found favour with the secretary of the Department of the Interior, but was not adopted.[6] Instead, an Aboriginal's eligibility for the federal vote was tied to his or her eligibility for the State vote.

This remained the case from 1949 until 1962, with legislation in 1961 restating that:

> An aboriginal native of Australia is not entitled to enrolment . . . unless he –
> (a) is entitled under the law of the State in which he resides to be enrolled as an elector of that State . . . or
> (b) is or has been a member of the Defence Force.[7]

This meant that formal restrictions prevented Aborigines in Queensland, the Northern Territory and Western Australia from exercising the federal franchise, unless they had served in the defence force. In addition to the defence force exemption, West Australian Aborigines who held certificates of citizenship could vote federally (since they had the State vote), as could Northern Territory Aborigines who had not been declared wards under Territory legislation. In April 1961 there were only seventy-two people officially classed as Aborigines in the Northern Territory so entitled to vote.[8]

Two recurrent themes operated to restrict further the limited franchise enjoyed by Aborigines: confusion surrounding inconsistent State and Commonwealth practices, and bureaucratic indifference to the enrolment of Aborigines. Confusion surrounded the eligibility of some 'half-castes' to exercise the federal franchise. Even though eligibility for the federal franchise was now linked to State franchise eligibility, the Commonwealth position in 1961 remained that a 'half-caste (or any person in whom the aboriginal blood does not preponderate) is NOT an aboriginal native for Commonwealth purposes, and he is therefore entitled to the same Commonwealth enrolment and voting rights and privileges as any other Australian citizen, irrespective of any State law'.[9] This caused confusion in a State like Queensland, where 'half-castes' who were 'controlled' by State legislation were denied the State vote. The Commonwealth Electoral Officer for Queensland was of the opinion that there were about four or five hundred Aborigines at the Cherbourg settlement, for instance, who were entitled to enrol for the Commonwealth but who, as 'controlled half-castes', were denied the State vote.[10] Confusion also surrounded the eligibility of Torres Strait

Islanders to vote federally. Although now treated separately to Aborigines by Queensland law, Islanders in the 1960s continued to be classed as 'aboriginal natives' for federal purposes.[11]

The unceasing bureaucratic efforts to negotiate these inconsistencies were rendered somewhat superfluous by the remarkable indifference of electoral officers to the enrolment of eligible Aborigines. As late as September 1961, the Chief Electoral Officer was advising State and Territory counterparts that the 'policy of this Branch in relation to aborigines, is not to solicit enrolment from persons who are quite incapable of understanding the law and not to enforce the compulsory enrolment or compulsory voting provisions in such cases'.[12] The Commonwealth Electoral Officer in South Australia, in virtual disregard of eligibility criteria, thus took no action to enrol Aborigines who were 'primitive, illiterate, nomadic, periodically nomadic, or associated only loosely or periodically with missions, or with government agencies for native welfare'.[13]

In April 1961 the House of Representatives set up a Select Committee to examine the extension of the franchise to Aborigines. The Committee held public meetings in all mainland States and Territories, and took evidence from 327 witnesses. Despite giving support to some bureaucratic myths – such as that the Commonwealth disfranchisement of Aborigines had been based on lifestyle characteristics rather than on racial grounds – the Committee did manage to counter other powerful myths. Much of the weight of the Committee's argument about extending the franchise to Aborigines was based on the realisation that Aborigines were not dying out and were 'a permanent part of the Australian community'.[14]

The Committee found that roughly 30,000 adult Aborigines were denied the federal vote in Australia. This figure consisted of 26,000 'full-blood' Aborigines and Torres Strait Islanders and 4000 West Australian and Queensland people who were of 'preponderantly aboriginal descent'. These figures did not, of course, include those Aborigines who were unaware that they theoretically had federal rights on the basis that they were not of 'preponderantly aboriginal descent'. Such Aborigines, who were often included in State definitions of Aboriginality, were regularly unaware of their federal rights.[15]

Indeed, one of the most disturbing findings of the Committee concerned the lack of administrative action that had been taken to inform eligible Aborigines of their right to vote. The Committee found that 'thousands' of Queensland and West Australian Aborigines who were eligible for the federal vote under the preponderating blood rule had not been informed of their rights. Other Aborigines knew that ex-service personnel could vote but thought that such people first needed State exemptions. The Committee found that many members of the Torres Strait Islands Regiment were unaware of their right to vote. Only 57 out of 659 members were enrolled in a local division. Even in those States where restrictions had not been in place for decades, there was often little knowledge about the rights of Aborigines to vote. For instance, at one Aboriginal Station in New South Wales, only five out of fifty Aborigines had enrolled. Further, the Committee found that the compulsory enrolment requirements that theoretically applied to Aborigines in New South Wales and Victoria were not being enforced. The administrators of the franchise had chosen not to observe the letter of the law, and the Committee recommended that 'early action be taken by the Commonwealth Electoral Office to inform [eligible Aborigines] of their entitlement to be enrolled and to vote'.[16]

All of this severely implicated the administrators of the franchise, in particular the Commonwealth Electoral Office, in the disfranchisement of Aborigines. Given the extraordinarily complex web of rules and practices that governed federal franchise eligibility, the failure of the Electoral Office to make reasonable efforts to inform eligible Aborigines of their right to vote casts a permanent shadow over the Office's operations. For even when particular Aborigines did have rights to vote, a virtual conspiracy of silence emanated from the bureaucracy.

The Select Committee examined several possibilities for the enfranchisement of Aborigines. Among these was the proposal that Aboriginal electorates be established in the States and Territories, or even that one nationwide Aboriginal electorate be established, as had occurred for the Maoris in New Zealand. However, section 29 of the Constitution proved a bar to most of these propositions. The one possibility that did not strike constitutional barriers – that a separate Aboriginal electorate be established in the Northern Territory – was not taken further.[17]

Regularly confronting the Committee were opinions of people such as Cornelius O'Leary, the Director of Native Affairs for Queensland. Referring to a group of Aborigines from Edward River mission, O'Leary testified:

> Let me put it this way: We white people have a background of more than 1961 years; these people at Edward River have a background of 25 years of civilization. When we talk about the rights to full citizenship of people like that we are talking about people who would not know the meaning of the term 'full citizenship'. I say that anyone who would advocate the right to vote for these people does not know his subject and does not appreciate the value of the vote to the citizen of the Australian community.[18]

According to O'Leary, Queensland's Aboriginal population could be divided as follows: 10,284 'controlled' Aborigines; 1080 'non-controlled' Aborigines; 7920 'controlled' 'Half Bloods'; 19,700 'non-controlled' 'Half Bloods'; and 7250 Torres Strait Islanders. It was the 1080 'non-controlled full-blood aboriginals', of whom 600 were old enough to be prospective voters, who O'Leary saw to be relevant to the Committee's work. These people, in O'Leary's words, were 'ordinary citizens of the State, but without the right to vote or drink'.[19] This belief that people could be citizens without rights resonated clearly with the federal citizenship legislation. It seems that O'Leary recognised that it would be embarrassing not to call Aborigines citizens, so instead he used the term and rendered it meaningless.

In its overall findings, the Committee rejected positions such as O'Leary's, along with the proposal that the right to vote be linked to various standards of living – such as literacy, fitness to consume alcohol, or the possession of a bank balance – on the basis that these criteria did not apply to other voters. Instead, it recommended that 'the right to vote at Commonwealth elections be accorded to all aboriginal and Torres Strait Islander subjects of the Queen, of voting age, permanently residing within the limits of the Commonwealth'. It recommended that Aboriginal enrolment, for the time being, be voluntary, but that voting be compulsory once enrolment had occurred.[20]

The extension of the franchise was seen by many to be a further step in the direction of assimilation. The chairman of the Committee reported to parliament that the Committee hoped the report 'will be a large step forward in the assimilation and integration of the aboriginal people in the Commonwealth of Australia'. Paul Hasluck, the Minister for Territories, saw the enfranchisement of Aborigines as 'one step further towards the ideal of one people in one continent'.[21]

Another factor pressuring the Commonwealth for a change in policy was international embarrassment. A confidential letter in January 1962 from the Department of External Affairs and the Department of Territories to Australian diplomatic posts overseas recorded a rise in international interest in Aborigines over the past year, a level of interest which 'could rapidly increase much further'. In order for Australian diplomats to set Australia's record straight, they were advised that:

> A frequent error of critics is reference to 'withholding of citizenship' from the Aborigines. Australian Aborigines are Australian citizens by virtue of the *Nationality and Citizenship Act.* The [special] rights and disadvantages which some of them have under State and Territory statutes do not derogate from their status as Australian citizens . . .

Despite this well-worn rhetoric, the letter evidenced a concern about Australia's standing abroad. Reference was made to the fact that in the future:

> political agitators in Asia, Africa and Latin America are likely to indulge . . . in emotional criticism of other countries' domestic policies, especially where these appear to involve discrimination by white people against coloured people. (In May, 1961, a member of Ghana's mission to the United Nations hinted confidentially to the Head of our Mission at the possible inclusion of the Aboriginal question on the General Assembly's agenda.)[22]

Later in 1962, all adult Aborigines were enfranchised. In a typical procedure, the discriminatory provision in the *Commonwealth Electoral Act* was simply repealed.[23] The Commonwealth parliament's enfranchisement of Aborigines was, as Kim Beazley Snr pointed out, the first time an Australian parliament had specifically acted to enfranchise Aborigines without restriction, since none of the State jurisdictions that then permitted Aboriginal voting had ever had to remove legislative obstacles.[24]

While the enfranchisement of Aborigines was largely endorsed by senior bureaucrats and politicians, the precise timing of it had an air of ignobility. In advising Prime Minister Menzies to accept most of the recommendations put forward by the Select Committee, the Minister for the Interior pointed out that 'since there is likely to be a redistribution before the 1964 Election, it would be opportune to extend the franchise at this time so that any differences in electoral results could not be attributed entirely to exercise of the franchise by aborigines, but would in part be attributed to changes in boundaries'.[25] The Minister was clearly concerned about the political backlash that might follow if Aboriginal voters were seen to influence the outcome of an election.

Aboriginal enrolment throughout Australia was made voluntary, in contrast to the Select Committee's recommendation that this be the case only for Aborigines in some States. This uniform measure had the effect of changing the franchise rights of Aborigines in States such as Victoria. Enrolment there changed from being compulsory to being voluntary.[26]

Social Security

According to the *Social Services Consolidation Act 1947* (Cwlth), an 'aboriginal native of Australia' was only entitled to receive any of a range of government benefits if he or she was exempt from the provisions of the Aboriginal protection legislation in force in his or her State or Territory. This applied to old-age and invalid pensions, widows' pensions, and the maternity allowance. In States without provision for exemption from protection regimes, namely Victoria and Tasmania, these benefits were only payable where the Director-General was satisfied that 'by reason of the character and of the standard of intelligence and social development of the native, it is desirable that a pension should be granted'. The policy followed for these States was that benefits would only be paid 'where the native's standard of living is such that he would be granted a certificate of exemption if residing in a State in which such exemption is provided for'. Unemployment and sickness benefits were payable to Aborigines only according to the Director-General's discretion as to their degree of 'social development'. The child endowment, meanwhile, was not payable in respect of a 'nomadic' child or one who was dependent on the Commonwealth or State for support. Those Aborigines able to slip through this very tight exclusionary cordon still had to confront the reality that these benefits were able to be directed to institutions rather than to individuals.[27]

Meanwhile, the payment of other benefits to Aborigines, such as the war widows' pension under the *Repatriation Act* (Cwlth), involved a level of administrative complexity that almost defied comprehension. Administrative ink was spilled on the question of whether the war widows' pension was payable to: an Aboriginal widow of a non-Aboriginal soldier; the Aboriginal widow of an Aboriginal soldier; and an Aboriginal widow where the marriage was not a registered one. The answer, ultimately, was affirmative to the first two questions, and negative to the last one, subject to some uncertainty about whether tribal law marriages, although not registered, were nonetheless valid common law marriages which therefore brought them under the Act.[28]

The general linkage of social security eligibility to State exemption regimes gave the Commonwealth a convenient excuse when it was criticised for not broadening its eligibility criteria. William McMahon, the Minister for Social Services and later Prime Minister, replied to one inquirer in 1955 that the cabinet had decided that:

> except in Commonwealth Territories, the care of unexempt aboriginal natives is a State responsibility, and there should be no departure from the existing law and policy, under which the widening of the field of eligibility is dependent upon any action by the States themselves to widen the conditions for exemption from State control laws.

McMahon defended this policy by referring to section 51(26) of the Constitution, which he dubiously interpreted as reserving for the States 'the power to make laws affecting aborigines'.[29] On this analysis the Commonwealth would have had no power to make any laws that affected Aborigines, rather than simply no constitutional power to pass laws solely concerning Aborigines. Indeed an entirely contradictory proposition to McMahon's was put by P. Brazil of the Attorney-General's Department the following year. Brazil argued that section 51(26) enabled the Commonwealth to make laws that applied 'indiscriminately to all Australians irrespective of race, including aborigines', and he suggested that an Act, such as the *Social Services Act*, that contained 'special provisions according discriminative treatment to aborigines' might in fact contravene section 51(26) because of its discriminatory provisions.[30]

Although the social security legislation purported to link eligibility for benefits to one's exemption from State protection regimes, the gaining of a State exemption did not correspond to a right to social security. This fact was brought home in 1958 to a group of Aborigines in Western Australia. Twenty-four Aborigines, who resided at one West Australian mission and who all held certificates exempting them from the State Aboriginal protection legislation, submitted claims for social security. The Department of Social Services rejected twenty-one of the claims, on the basis that the Act 'does not make it mandatory to grant a pension to an exempt native'. In this case 'only three of the claimants were sufficiently advanced to receive pensions'. Thus these twenty-one claimants, who had managed to become exempt from oppressive State protection legislation, were not entitled to one of the key rights of Australian citizenship, on the basis that they were not 'sufficiently advanced' Aborigines.[31] A similar rejection for social security benefits was given to a group of applicants from Fantome Island, off the coast of Queensland, all of whom had obtained State exemption certificates.[32]

In 1959 the range of exclusionary provisions that had limited the right of Aborigines to receive social security benefits were, with the exception of the child endowment, repealed and replaced by one provision that was more in keeping with departmental practice:

> An aboriginal native of Australia who follows a mode of life that is, in the opinion of the Director-General, nomadic or primitive is not entitled to a pension, allowance, endowment or benefit under this Act.[33]

In announcing the 1959 changes, the Minister for Social Services said:

> An additional £1,000,000 will be paid towards the welfare of Australia's aborigines as evidence of the Commonwealth Government's intention to give them equality with other Australians in the field of social services. Unless they are nomadic or primitive, aborigines will in future qualify for age, invalid and widows' pensions, and maternity allowances, on the same basis as other members of the community.

The changes were expected to benefit around 4000 Aborigines, who would now obtain the old-age, invalid and widows' pensions, and about 1200 Aboriginal mothers, who would now receive the maternity allowance.[34]

Until 1959 Aborigines had been largely denied social security on the basis that they were not part of the Australian polity. Even after 1959 those who were 'nomadic or primitive' were still denied access to one of the fundamental rights of citizenship. Moreover, those Aborigines who could now receive pensions, particularly those living on government settlements, had hardly been given a ticket to freedom. The Department of Social Services intended that for Aborigines on settlements, the pension would be paid to their institution, from which a percentage would be put into the individual Aboriginal's trust account. This could then be drawn upon 'under supervision by the Superintendents of the Settlements where such supervision is considered necessary'.[35]

The citizenship legislation passed 11 years earlier clearly had had no impact on the right of Aborigines to receive social security. Only in 1966 was the last exclusionary provision removed from social security legislation.[36]

States and Territories Move to Formal Inclusion, 1948–1967

In 1948, in addition to federal restrictions, Aborigines in Western Australia, Queensland and the Northern Territory were still being denied the right to vote, the right to move freely, and the right to work. Some Aborigines in these jurisdictions could move freely, and some could work. But, as we saw earlier, the most that Aborigines could do was seek exemption from the restrictions that otherwise affected all Aborigines. In this section we chart the paths that the States and Territories took to granting Aborigines citizenship rights in the period leading up to the 1967 referendum.

Western Australia

In the last chapter we saw that the West Australian government legislated in 1944 to permit some Aborigines to be granted Certificates of Citizenship. The holder of such a certificate was 'deemed to be no longer a native or aborigine' and therefore ceased to be subject to the restrictions suffered by other Aborigines. This 1944 legislation was amended in 1950 so that the children of certificate holders could have their names placed on certificates until they reached twenty-one years of age. Then, from 1951, the power to grant certificates was given to various local boards, which consisted of a Magistrate and a ministerially appointed 'district representative', who was generally a local politician.[37]

A further change in 1951 resulted in the removal of the double-speak clause, according to which an Aboriginal who was granted a certificate was 'deemed to be no longer a native or aborigine'. This left certificate holders to be classed simply as having 'all the rights, privileges and immunities and . . . subject to the duties and liabilities of a natural born or naturalised subject of His Majesty'.[38] This was a dubious classification, as we shall see shortly. The removal of the double-speak clause necessitated other legislative amendments, since a certificate holder would once again now be classed as 'a native or aborigine', and was thus once again subject to all the provisions that applied to other Aborigines. So, the West Australian electoral legislation was changed in the same year to specifically enfranchise those Aborigines who held Certificates of Citizenship.[39]

With amendments in 1958 the West Australian government removed several of the criteria that had previously been essential to the granting of State 'citizenship': the dissolution of tribal associations, the adoption of the habits of 'civilised life', and the non-existence of certain diseases.[40] But in order to be classed as citizens of the State, West Australian Aborigines still had to hold Certificates of Citizenship.

Those who did hold Certificates of Citizenship, however, were still rarely told of the rights at State and Commonwealth level to which they were now entitled. In 1961 the Commonwealth Electoral Officer for Western Australia told the Select Committee on Voting Rights of Aborigines that although 1500 to 1600 Aborigines had gone to the trouble of obtaining Certificates of Citizenship, less than 1000 of them were enrolled to vote at Commonwealth level. One electoral officer reported, after conducting his own investigations, that only 54 out of 230 eligible Aborigines in one electorate were on the Commonwealth roll. Committee member Kim Beazley Snr later surmised, in a rhetorical question to the Chief Electoral Officer of the Commonwealth, that 'I think it would be true to say that [Western Australia] in granting citizenship rights is not particularly enthusiastic about the person granted the rights enrolling on the State or Commonwealth roll?'.[41]

For those West Australian Aborigines who did not hold citizenship or exemption certificates, the principal Act that in 1948 governed their lives was the *Native Administration Act 1905–1947* (WA), which we considered in the last chapter. Slowly, changes began to occur. In 1954 a small group of Aborigines – those who had served for at least six months in the defence force in Australia, or who had served in it for any period of time in New Guinea or outside Australia – were exempted from the operations of the Act.[42] Later in 1954 a number of changes were made to the principal Act, which was now called the *Native Welfare Act 1905–1954* (WA). The administrative department responsible for implementing the Act was renamed the Department of Native Welfare, which was headed by the Commissioner of Native Welfare. The Commissioner now had a specific power to determine who was to have custody of 'native' children.[43] At the same time, many of the more regressive powers previously embodied in Aboriginal legislation were removed. These included the powers: to remove Aborigines to reserves; to compel medical treatment; to remove Aboriginal camps; to order Aborigines out of town; to declare areas into which Aborigines could not go; and to regulate Aboriginal marriages. Also, from 1954 formal permits were no longer required for the employment of Aborigines, and the executive no longer retained specific power to regulate the wages of Aborigines. Furthermore, the special Aboriginal courts were now abolished. Yet these changes were largely superficial, hiding the wide discretionary powers over Aboriginal movement and property that remained vested in the executive.[44] Indeed, this would become a feature of the dismantling of many of the State and Territory protection regimes. Overtly oppressive provisions would be replaced by ones simply allowing wide discretionary power. This was a simple way to save face at home and abroad, while changing little.

We have already pointed to several instances where inconsistencies between State and federal laws and practices produced absurd results. Perhaps the clearest statement about the manifestly unclear relationship between laws and practices in the various Australian jurisdictions was made in 1959 by Attorney-General Garfield Barwick, in response to a letter from a Mr Sandy McDonald. In 1959 McDonald wrote to Paul Hasluck, the Minister for Territories, saying that he was regarded as a citizen in the Northern Territory, but that when he crossed the border into Western Australia he was regarded as an Aboriginal. Hasluck sought Barwick's opinion, commenting that while McDonald could obtain a passport and could thus be recognised as an Australian citizen in every foreign country, the passport would apparently have no meaning for him in Western Australia. Barwick's opinion was that:

> Mr McDonald is an Australian citizen wherever he may be in Australia and this citizenship is not lost on his passing from one State or Territory to another. But this does not mean that he is necessarily entitled to all the rights enjoyable by a non-aboriginal Australian citizen throughout Australia.

In an earlier draft of his opinion, Barwick had been more expansive:

> I think . . . there could be nine different 'citizenships' in Australia. A person who is an 'Australian citizen' by virtue of the [Nationality and Citizenship] Act . . . has this status, and the rights that attach to it, wherever he may be in Australia; it is a national status. A person who, whether an 'Australian citizen' or not, has a local citizenship conferred upon him by the laws of a State or Territory, [and] has that citizenship, and the rights that attach to it, only in the State or Territory concerned.[45]

McDonald was thus an Australian citizen who was not entitled to the rights held by non-Aboriginal Australian citizens. He had no right to vote at State level and was liable to have his life regulated in ways that white West Australians could not.

The electoral position of West Australian Aborigines corresponded directly with their status under protection legislation. As late as 1961 a person could not enrol or vote for the Legislative Assembly or Legislative Council if he or she was 'a native according to the interpretation of that expression in [the native welfare legislation] and is not the holder of a Certificate of Citizenship'. Changes to the *Native Welfare Act* (WA) in 1960 mirrored the 1951 amendments to the State citizenship legislation, with the removal of the clause that deemed certain Aborigines to 'be no longer a native'. The legislation now simply provided that the term 'native' covered 'any person of the full blood descended from the original inhabitants of Australia', and 'any person of less than full blood . . . except a quadroon or person of less than quadroon blood'. The proviso mentioned earlier now specified that Aboriginal soldiers who had served outside Australia, or who had served for at least six months within Australia, and who had received or were entitled to receive an honourable discharge, were entitled to 'all the rights, privileges and immunities . . . of a natural born or naturalised subject of Her Majesty'.[46]

The removal of the double-speak clause was brought about by a desire of West Australian politicians to cease deeming Aborigines not to be Aborigines.[47] But the solution of leaving an exempt Aboriginal to be classed as a 'subject of Her Majesty' was highly ambiguous, because all Aborigines were theoretically entitled to this status, albeit one that entailed no substantive rights. In an opinion given to the Select Committee on the Voting Rights of Aborigines, Kenneth Bailey argued that the favoured terminology was 'not very apt because of course under the law of the Commonwealth an Australian aboriginal *is* a natural-born subject of Her Majesty, and the terms of the proviso rather imply the contrary'.[48] The use of this terminology in the State citizenship legislation from 1951 did not lead to any legal complications, however, because holders of citizenship certificates had a statutory right to vote. But its use in the *Native Welfare Act* caused ambiguity. It was unclear now, for instance, whether an Aboriginal who had served sufficient time in the army, who the 1960 legislation deemed to have the rights of a natural-born subject, could vote in West Australian elections without taking out a Certificate of Citizenship.

In evidence before the Select Committee, the Chief Electoral Officer for Western Australia took the simple way out of this dilemma, saying that to vote in Western Australia, an Aboriginal 'must get his certificate of citizenship even if he is a member of the Forces'. This led the committee to conclude that the West Australian Electoral Act was being 'incorrectly administered'.[49]

This confusion was only resolved in 1962, following the Commonwealth franchise amendments, when West Australian Aborigines were given the right to vote at State level.[50] But the right to vote in Western Australia did not on its own equate with citizenship. The Minister for Native Welfare, who supported the enfranchisement of Aborigines, hastened to tell parliament in 1962 that:

> I cannot, of course, say at the moment when I would be prepared to recommend full citizenship . . . When I myself feel the time is ripe to grant full citizenship, I can assure members I will not hesitate to recommend to the Government that that step be taken . . . [51]

So, despite the fact that West Australian Aborigines now had a right to vote at State and Commonwealth levels, they were far from being in possession of full citizenship rights. For instance, Aboriginal men could legally be whipped for breaches of the criminal code until 1963.[52] And the passage through parliament of the consolidating *Native Welfare Act 1963* (WA), which was largely consistent with previous West Australian protection legislation, confirmed that Aborigines were far from having 'full citizenship rights'. This Act provided wide discretionary powers to administrators in their management of Aboriginal reserves, in their management of Aboriginal property, and in their dealings generally with Aborigines. A first offence against the Act carried a fine of up to fifty pounds or imprisonment for up to six months. The Minister even had power to extend the operation of the Act to Aborigines who did not come within the definition of 'native'.[53]

Queensland

The most significant piece of Queensland legislation that affected Aborigines between 1948 and 1967 was the *Aborigines' and Torres Strait Islanders' Affairs Act 1965* (Qld). This Act replaced both the *Torres Strait Islanders Acts 1939 to 1946* (Qld) and the *Aboriginals Preservation and Protection Acts 1939 to 1946* (Qld). This new legislation put in place yet another scheme by which the term 'Aborigine' would be defined. Now the term referred to the following people: a 'full-blood descendant of the indigenous inhabitants of the Commonwealth'; a person with 'a preponderance of the blood of an Aborigine'; a 'part-Aborigine' living as the spouse of an Aborigine; and a resident of an Aboriginal reserve who had some 'Aboriginal blood'. A 'part-Aborigine' was defined to be: a person who had one 'full-blood' parent and one parent with no Aboriginal 'blood'; and a person 'both of whose parents have a strain of the blood of the indigenous inhabitants of the Commonwealth' and who themselves have 'more than twenty-five per centum of such blood but who has not a preponderance of such blood'. An 'Islander' was: a 'full-blood descendant of the indigenous inhabitants of the Torres Strait Islands'; someone of less than 'full-blood' who habitually associated with Islanders; and a descendant who lived as the spouse of an Islander or who lived on an Aboriginal or Islander reserve.[54]

To further complicate the Act there were two additional categories into which Aborigines and Islanders could be placed: 'assisted Aborigines' and 'assisted Islanders'. These were people who lived on reserves at the commencement of the Act, or who had at least 'a strain' of Aboriginal or Island 'blood' and who were deemed to 'be in need of care'. A document known as a 'certificate of entitlement' proved that an Aboriginal or Islander was 'assisted' and therefore subject to the Act.[55]

This 1965 legislation created the new position of Director of Aboriginal and Island Affairs, who, subject to ministerial guidance, had responsibility for the implementation of the Act. The Director had power to order 'assisted Aborigines' and 'assisted Islanders' to reside on reserves, and was required to draw up certificates naming all the residents of reserves. The Director could also grant aid to any Aboriginal or Islander.[56]

District Officers, no longer called Protectors, retained extensive power over those Aborigines and Islanders who were deemed to be 'assisted'. In particular, a District Officer could undertake and maintain the management of any property of an 'assisted' person, if the Officer was 'satisfied that the best interests' of the person warranted it. This enabled the Officer to retain, sell, or otherwise dispose of such property.[57] Further, regulations gazetted in 1966 set out that alcohol, although permitted to Aborigines elsewhere, was not permitted on reserves.[58]

As usual, the executive retained strong power in the 1965 Queensland legislation. The Governor in Council had power to appoint managers of reserves and to govern the operation of Aboriginal and Island

Courts. In addition, the executive's regulatory power extended to thirty-eight headings, and included the power to regulate for: the discipline and good order of reserves; the employment of assisted Aborigines and Islanders; and the care of the children of assisted Aborigines and Islanders.[59]

The records of Aboriginal Courts, which operated to enforce extraordinarily intrusive regulations, display the lack of freedom of Aborigines on reserves. One entry in a court record book went as follows:

> 22 February, 1962. Committing an act subversive to the good order and discipline of the Settlement, viz., that on the 21st February, 1962, at Cherbourg Settlement you were required to produce a sample of faeces to the Hygiene Officer, Mr. J.H.P., and failed to do so. And further that you wilfully destroyed the bottle provided for that purpose. Plea: guilty. Convicted and sentenced to 14 days imprisonment.[60]

Queensland was the last Australian jurisdiction to enfranchise Aborigines. From 1959 'aboriginal natives' of Asia and Africa were permitted to vote, but until 1965 Queensland law prohibited any 'aboriginal native of Australia or the Islands of the Pacific' from voting. A further clause disfranchised any 'aboriginal native of the islands in Torres Strait' and the offspring of two such people. The exclusion extended to any 'half-caste' as defined in the protection legislation who was subject to 'the control and general supervision of the Protector of Aboriginals'.[61] The wording of these exclusions meant that the only Aborigines who could exercise the franchise were those 'half-castes' who were not covered by the protection legislation, for although 'full-blood' Aborigines could be exempted from the protection regime, this would not give them a right to vote under the electoral legislation. Further, there was no provision for any Torres Strait Islanders to be given the State franchise. The Queensland franchise was not even given to Aboriginal or Islander members of the defence force.[62] In 1961 the right to vote in Queensland was held by only 19,700 'non-controlled half-bloods', out of an official Aboriginal population of 46,234.[63]

At this time the view was still being expressed by Queensland Cabinet members that, contrary to talk of racial discrimination, 'a person, who by virtue of the fact that he is unable to take his place in the community . . . surely forfeits his right to exercise voting privileges'.[64] For leading Queensland politicians, the notion of 'citizenship' was the opposite of 'protection'. One could not both be protected and be a citizen. This was most clearly stated by H.W. Noble, the author of the above comments, who was Minister for Health and Home Affairs. He argued that: 'To grant full citizenship rights to every Queensland aboriginal and then compel that aboriginal to apply for protection . . . is contrary to everything that is implied by the word protection.'[65]

A parliamentary committee in 1964 strongly recommended that Aborigines be enfranchised.[66] Only in 1965 were the formal obstacles to Aboriginal enfranchisement removed.[67]

That the granting of the State franchise did not equate with full citizenship, particularly for Aborigines on reserves, was spelt out in regulations gazetted in 1966 under the *Aborigines' and Torres Strait Islanders' Affairs Act 1965* (Qld). The following was among the 110 new regulations:

> When any assisted Aborigine on a Reserve or community –
> (a) Commits an offence against discipline; or
> (b) Without lawful permission or excuse leaves or *escapes* or attempts to leave or *escape* from such Reserve or community; or
> (c) Is guilty of any immoral act or immoral conduct . . .
> the Aboriginal Court or Visiting Justice may . . . order in writing his detention in a dormitory.

A person committed 'an offence against discipline' if he or she was 'idle, careless or negligent at work', or behaved 'in an offensive, threatening, insolent, insulting, disorderly, obscene or indecent manner'.[68] Aboriginal residents of government reserves in Queensland may now theoretically have had the vote, but the regulations governing their conduct treated them as prisoners and children, rather than as citizens.

Northern Territory

As we saw in the last chapter, the power of Northern Territory administrators in the late 1940s over the lives of Aborigines was as great as anywhere else in Australia. Aborigines could not vote, they were able to be forced to reside on reserves, their employment was regulated, and they could not enter certain 'prohibited' areas of the Territory.[69]

The power of the Director of Native Affairs in the Northern Territory was tested in 1951, when Fred Waters, also known as Fred Nadpur, argued in the High Court that he had illegally been detained on an Aboriginal reserve against his will. Waters was said to have played a leading part in a 'protest strike' at Bagot Aboriginal reserve in Darwin on 12 February 1951. That day Waters was taken into custody in Darwin and was removed to Haast Bluff Aboriginal reserve according to an order signed by the Director of Native Affairs. The Acting Secretary of the North Australia Workers' Union argued that the Director told him that Waters had been sent to Haast Bluff 'for creating a nuisance and organizing yesterday's protest'. Waters made two arguments: that the

Aboriginals Ordinance did not authorise his removal; and that his removal had been an abuse of power. Justice Fullagar, however, found against Waters. He found that the Ordinance, which 'gives very wide powers indeed to the Director', did authorise the action. He repeated himself in further finding that although the 'powers given by the Ordinance are extremely wide ... I consider it impossible on the material before me that ... they were either misunderstood or abused.'[70]

At around the same time that Waters had been arrested, several incidents in Alice Springs led Aborigines there to agitate for change. In December 1950 a man was arrested for being 'an unexempt half-caste found to be drinking intoxicating liquor'. He claimed to be exempt but his name did not appear on a list of exempted persons held by Alice Springs police. The action against the man failed when he managed to prove his exemption.[71]

The following month two women were charged with the same offence. They pleaded guilty, whereupon one Justice of the Peace imposed a penalty of seven days' imprisonment. An appeal against the severity of the punishment was lodged, but while bail was being arranged for the hearing of the appeal, the police brought another charge against the women. This time they were charged with being 'unexempted half-castes upon a prohibited area', and bail was refused.[72]

Police in Alice Springs then began breaking an unofficial policy – according to which they had ignored the presence of 'part-Aborigines' in town areas of Alice Springs – and began asking Aborigines at social functions in the prohibited area either to show evidence of their exemption or to produce a permit that allowed them to be there. Police arrested Aborigines who failed to comply. The prohibited area covered the residences of many Aborigines, and in February 1951, following some intense lobbying, the Director of Native Affairs issued a general permit that permitted 'part-Aborigines' to be in the prohibited area. Town meetings ensued and led to the creation of an organisation known as the 'Australian Halfcaste Progressive Association', which called on the Prime Minister to exclude 'people of mixed blood' from the *Aboriginals Ordinance* and to grant them 'full Citizenship Rights'.[73]

In September 1951 representatives from the Commonwealth and all States, except Victoria and Tasmania, met in Canberra for a 'Conference on Native Welfare'. Conference delegates decided that the 'Commonwealth and States, having assimilation as the objective of native welfare measures, desire to see all persons born in Australia enjoying full citizenship'. It was acknowledged that different definitions of 'native' and 'aboriginal' in State and Commonwealth legislation created 'anomalies', and that the system whereby certain people were exempted from these categories was no longer appropriate. Instead, conference delegates decided that 'our view is that those persons to whom the special legislation applies are wards of the State who, for the time being, stand in need of guardianship and who should automatically cease to be wards when they are able to assume the full citizenship to which they are entitled'. The aim was thus to have legislation changed so that instead of defining the terms 'native' or 'aboriginal', the legislation would only apply to people in need of guardianship.[74]

Following this conference, the Commonwealth decided to overhaul its legislation in the Northern Territory. Instead of attempting to define the terms 'native' and 'aboriginal' the Commonwealth opted for the racially neutral category of 'ward'. Paul Hasluck, the Minister for Territories, addressed the inaugural meeting of the Native Welfare Council, saying that the change in terminology in the Northern Territory legislation was intended to give effect to the recommendations of the 1951 conference regarding citizenship. He continued:

> Under the old system it was assumed that every native came under restrictive legislation unless he applied for and was granted exemption from it. Under the new system it is assumed that every British subject has citizenship as a birthright and that the enjoyment of the right is only withheld because a person stands in need of special care and assistance.[75]

In 1953 the *Aboriginals Ordinance* was amended so that the definition of 'Aboriginal' was changed to refer only to an 'aboriginal native' or person who lived like an 'aboriginal native'. This and another new provision had the effect of making 'half-caste' Aborigines exempt from the definition of Aboriginal unless the Director deemed them to be Aboriginal.[76] In October 1953, following an announcement by the Northern Territory Administrator, it was reported that from 1 October 1953, 'all part aborigine citizens of the Territory were automatically exempted from the provisions of the *Aboriginal Ordinance*'.[77]

Also in 1953, the new approach foreshadowed by Hasluck, under which people lost citizenship rights on the basis of personal characteristics rather than race, was put into Territory legislation by the *Welfare Ordinance 1953* (NT). This ordinance, which did not come into operation until 1957, repealed all the previous Aboriginal Ordinances, and referred throughout to 'wards' rather than Aborigines. The four ostensibly racially neutral criteria on which people could be deemed to be wards consisted of: their manner of living; their ability to manage their own affairs; their standard of behaviour; and their 'personal associations'.[78]

But this approach was anything but racially neutral, as was shown by one section of the *Welfare Ordinance*, which deemed any 'person' who was governed by Aboriginal protection legislation in Queensland, Western Australia or South Australia to be a ward upon entering the Northern Territory.[79] In 1961, 99.5 per cent of Northern Territory Aborigines had had their 'birthright' removed because of personal characteristics. Out of an official population of around 17,000, there were only 89 Aborigines who were not declared to be wards. These figures did not apply to people 'of part aboriginal descent', as such people were 'not regarded as ... aboriginal in practice in the Northern Territory'.[80]

The Director of Welfare exercised enormous power over wards, and could order a ward be taken into custody or removed to a reserve or institution. A ward could not marry a non-ward without the permission of the Director, nor could a male non-ward live with a female ward unless they were married. The *Police and Police Offences Ordinance* (NT), just to be sure, made it an offence for a non-ward, other than a relation, to live with a ward. From 1957 a ward could not even sell a painting without the permission of the Director or his or her institution.[81] Wards were also prohibited from consuming or being in possession of alcohol.[82]

In addition, the employment of wards was regulated, and anyone found employing a ward without a licence was subject to a one hundred pound fine or six months imprisonment. Further, a ward's wages could be directed to go to a third person.[83] The formal employment licensing system ended in 1960, from which time employers only had to give notice to the Director when they employed wards. The 1960 amendments to the *Wards' Employment Ordinance* ensured that the Director retained the power to forbid people from employing wards, although this power was rarely exercised, if at all. It has been calculated that wards employed as pastoral workers under the *Wards' Employment Ordinance* received roughly one-fifth of white wages. All of this suggests that the Ordinance, which was finally repealed in 1971, served more to ensure a regular supply of cheap labour than it did to protect wards from oppressive employment practices.[84]

The power of the Director of Welfare to prevent the marriage of a ward received high publicity during the debacle surrounding the marriage of Mick Daly, a white drover, and Gladys Namagu, a West Australian Aboriginal who was viewed to be a ward. After travelling together on a droving trip in 1959, Mick was charged with cohabitation, and, despite numerous requests by the couple, they were not allowed to marry. Daly went so far as to contact authorities in Western Australia to see whether they could marry in that jurisdiction. In August 1959, after advocates for the couple had sought the involvement of the Secretary-General of the United Nations, the Director gave three grounds for his refusal of permission: that Gladys had changed her mind too often; that she was tribally married to someone else; and that Daly was not a fit and proper person. The couple disputed all of these assertions. One of the couple's advocates, a member of the Territory Legislative Council who was appropriately named Mr Ward, moved an amendment to the welfare legislation that would enable an appeal to a Magistrate against the Director's decision on marriage. In December the bill containing the amendment was gazetted, and shortly after Ward sought to overturn the Director's decision regarding Gladys, on the ground that she was not a ward. The Director did not contest the appeal, stating that he did not have sufficient evidence to prove that Gladys was a ward. On 1 January 1960 Mick and Gladys married.[85] What this case, and the publicity it received, revealed was that even mainstream Australia was shocked by the power that administrators had over the lives of Aborigines. Certainly the case would not have received the publicity it did had Daly not been white. But even so, the inability of someone to decide who they would marry was quite genuinely confronting to many.

Ten years after its first meeting, the Native Welfare Conference of 1961, attended by representatives of Commonwealth and State governments, sought to explain the general lack of Aboriginal civil rights. It referred to oppressive legislation as 'temporary measures not based on colour but intended to meet [the need of Aborigines] for special care and assistance to protect them from any ill effects of sudden change'. It was this kind of statement that led C.D. Rowley to conclude that the Native Welfare Conference was becoming in part an exercise in public relations.[86]

However, slowly international and domestic embarrassment was forcing changes. A new Northern Territory Ordinance in 1964 once again changed the terminology by which Aborigines were categorised. Rather than 'wards', the *Social Welfare Ordinance 1964* (NT) gave the Director of Social Welfare power over 'persons who in the opinion of the Director are socially or economically in need of assistance'. The Director had power to 'exercise a general care' over such people and to supervise and regulate the use of reserves.[87] As was occurring in other jurisdictions, the governing Northern Territory legislation was changed to make its language less offensive.

By ceasing to class Aborigines en masse as 'wards', certain general prohibitions that applied to wards – such as the ban on alcohol – no longer automatically applied to Aborigines.[88] However, the wide discretionary powers that still existed in the welfare legislation meant there had been no sharp break with past policy.

The Northern Territory electoral regulations, which by 1947 governed the elections of the Territory Legislative Council and the Territory representative to the House of Representatives, had to be amended often to keep up with changes in terminology. In 1947 the only Aborigines in the Territory who could vote were those who were so entitled by section 41 of the Constitution. This entitlement meant very little to Aborigines in the Northern Territory, since it only applied to people who had been enrolled as voters in States prior to 1902 and who continued to be enrolled as voters in States. From 1949 Aborigines could vote only if they were deemed under the *Aboriginals Ordinance* not to be Aboriginal, or if they were or had been a member of the defence force.[89] In 1957 Aborigines could only vote if they were not defined as 'wards' by the *Welfare Ordinance*, or if they had been members of the defence force. This exclusion of Aborigines from the vote in the Northern Territory was spelt out again as late as 1961. While wards could not vote, the *Welfare Ordinance* made something of a hypothetical and confusing statement in declaring that people who could vote could not be declared wards. Finally, in 1962, the restrictions against Aboriginal voters were removed.[90]

After the 1962 changes, officers of the Commonwealth Electoral Office took to telling Aborigines in the Northern Territory about their rights to vote. But even then, according to the Minister for the Interior, the officers 'cautioned them that they should not enrol unless they understand fully what is involved'.[91]

Other Jurisdictions

We have seen, then, the developments in the three jurisdictions with the largest Aboriginal populations in the period between the creation of the Australian citizen and the 1967 referendum. A brief summary of the developments in the other States follows.

In Victoria the *Aborigines Act 1928* (Vic) remained the prime piece of Aboriginal legislation until 1957. In that year, retired Magistrate Charles McLean conducted an inquiry into the operation of the 1928 Act. McLean's main recommendations concerned administration, although he also commented on the exploitation of Aboriginal workers in Victoria and the 'misapprehension which exists as to the citizen-rights of aborigines'. On this last issue he pointed out that Victorian Aborigines had the same right and obligation to vote at State and federal elections as had other citizens, something that was clearly not understood by many people. Similarly, he explained the entitlement of Aborigines to social security. McLean recommended that several laws be amended: he sought the repeal of the provisions in the *Licensing Act* and the *Aborigines Act* that prohibited Aborigines from being supplied with alcohol, and also recommended the repeal of one section in the

Police Offences Act that rendered non-Aborigines to be idle and disorderly and subject to one year's imprisonment if they were found 'wandering in company with any of the aboriginal natives of Victoria'. All of these recommendations were based on McLean's view that the best way forward was 'to implement an effective system of assimilation'.[92]

The *Aborigines Act 1957* (Vic) adopted most of McLean's recommendations. The statutory provisions he criticised were repealed, while the Board for the Protection of Aborigines was replaced by the Aborigines Welfare Board, whose ten members were appointed by the executive. The new Board's role was 'to promote the moral intellectual and physical welfare of aborigines . . . with a view to their assimilation into the general community'. Any person of 'aboriginal descent' was able to come within the Act's operation. In order to fulfil its role, the Board was required to have among its members a specialist in each of the following fields: education, housing, health, and anthropology or sociology. Two members were required to be Aborigines. The Board could allocate money and rations to Aborigines, and was responsible for managing and regulating the use of Aboriginal reserves. The Executive Officer of the Board was now termed the Superintendent of Aborigines Welfare. The executive, as always, retained strong discretionary power, and had the specific power to prescribe the condition of employment of Aborigines in areas not subject to industrial awards.[93]

Ten years later the Victorian parliament passed the *Aboriginal Affairs Act 1967* (Vic). This Act abolished the Aborigines Welfare Board and replaced it with a Ministry of Aboriginal Affairs and an Aboriginal Affairs Advisory Council. The Council, whose members were to include three Aborigines as well as experts in the fields of public health, education, housing and social welfare, was intended to consult with Aboriginal groups and advise the Minister on Aboriginal affairs. The Minister was empowered to assist Aborigines in a range of matters, such as the provision of suitable housing, and the executive retained power to govern the development and management of Aboriginal reserves. The 1967 Act defined an Aboriginal as 'any person who is descended from an aboriginal native of Australia'.[94]

In New South Wales the administration of Aboriginal affairs in 1967 had changed only marginally from the position, outlined in the last chapter, that had existed in 1948. During this time the governing Act had been amended only once, in 1963, when several of the more offensive and prohibitive sections were repealed. Aborigines could no longer be ordered to go to reserves; the Aborigines Welfare Board could no longer order employers to pay Aborigines' wages to others; the Board could no longer order Aborigines to undergo medical procedures; the power to order Aborigines to move their camps was now repealed; and it was no longer a crime for non-Aborigines to wander with Aborigines. The ban on Aborigines consuming alcohol had been removed from the *Liquor Act* in 1946, yet the same ban was only removed from the *Aborigines Protection Act* in 1963. In other respects, the situation in New South Wales remained as it had been in 1948.[95]

In contrast to some other States, there existed few legal mechanisms by which Aborigines in New South Wales could be excluded from citizenship rights. But this lack of legal machinery did not prevent the existence of social forms of exclusion. Country towns in New South Wales, in particular, manifested a system of 'petty apartheid' during the 1950s and 1960s according to which Aborigines were excluded from certain public spaces. This informal system, of course, applied whether or not one was officially 'Aboriginal'. Perhaps this was one reason why many Aborigines refused to surrender their dignity by applying for exemption certificates. Only 1500 applications for exemption were made between 1943 and 1964 from a population of 14,000. No doubt another reason for the relatively low number of applications was the fact that those who did become exempt were subject to a thinly disguised surveillance scheme operated by the District Welfare Officers.[96]

Although Aborigines were eligible to vote in New South Wales, regardless of their status under protection legislation, relatively low numbers of Aborigines actually enrolled. For instance, only 487 out of 1042 eligible Aborigines on government stations in New South Wales were enrolled to vote in 1961. In response to a question by the Select Committee on Voting Rights of Aborigines as to what action would be taken to enrol the other 555 eligible Aborigines, the Commonwealth Electoral Officer for New South Wales replied: 'Actually, the policy has been not to take any action at all.'[97] Thus the low enrolment of eligible Aborigines is largely explainable by the lack of action taken to inform them of their right, even if the low figures do also manifest some degree of reluctance on the part of Aborigines to involve themselves in a citizenship regime from which, at least in social terms, they were still largely excluded.

New South Wales protection legislation applied in the Australian Capital Territory until the enactment of the *Aborigines Welfare Ordinance 1954* (ACT). This Ordinance defined 'aboriginal' to mean 'a person who is a full-blooded or half-caste aboriginal native of Australia', and gave broad powers to the responsible Minister. These included the power to manage and regulate reserves, to make regulations 'for the care and custody of aborigines', and generally to 'exercise a general supervision and care over all aborigines'. Aborigines living in 'insanitary or undesirable conditions', together with those Aborigines who the Minister determined 'should be placed under control', could be ordered by a Court to reside on reserves. Aborigines from other States who came within these broad criteria could be ordered to return to their home States. The Ordinance forbade the sale of alcohol to Aborigines, and enabled the wages of an Aboriginal to be paid to a third person. Aborigines could be exempted from the operations of the Ordinance and, in a vain bid to achieve some uniformity between the various jurisdictions, Aborigines exempted from the operations of other Territory or State protection regimes were automatically exempt from 'corresponding' provisions in the ACT Ordinance.[98] One can only imagine the amount of paperwork that such an Aboriginal would need to have carried, and that consequently would have been generated, for this kind of automatic exemption to have been put into practice. Eleven years after its enactment, the Ordinance was repealed.[99] Jurors in the Territory, meanwhile, had to be male and 'of European race or extraction' until 1967.[100]

The eligibility of Aborigines to vote in the Australian Capital Territory was manifestly unclear, and this lack of clarity alone, doubtless, served to disfranchise Aborigines. The *Advisory Council Ordinance 1936–1938* (ACT), which governed elections to the ACT Advisory Council, sought to apply the provisions of the *Commonwealth Electoral Act* 'in relation to elections under this Ordinance' as they applied to the election of members of the Senate. However, Aborigines did not appear on a list of people in the Ordinance who were barred from voting. This list would seem to have been superfluous had Commonwealth eligibility criteria applied.[101]

Further confusion was caused by the 'Australian Capital Territory Electoral Regulations', passed in 1949, which governed the election of an ACT representative to the Commonwealth House of Representatives. Again, the regulations linked voting eligibility to the *Commonwealth Electoral Act*, but they then went on to specify that certain people were excluded from the vote, including any 'aboriginal native of Asia, Africa or the Islands of the Pacific (except New Zealand)'. The inference here was that an 'aboriginal native of Australia' could vote.[102] In terms of voting for the House of Representatives, the Commonwealth Act that excluded most Australian Aborigines (and most Aborigines in the ACT) from voting clearly took precedence over the regulations that suggested otherwise. But matters were confused almost beyond comprehension in the 1950s by amendments to the *Advisory Council Ordinance*, according to which voting eligibility for the Council was linked to voting eligibility under the 'Australian Capital Territory Electoral Regulations'.[103] Thus a person could vote for the Territory Council if he or she was eligible under the regulations to vote for the ACT member of the House of Representatives. These regulations, as we have argued, suggested that Australian Aborigines could vote. Further, it was far from clear in this case that the *Commonwealth Electoral Act* took precedence over the regulations, since the Act did not specifically bar Australian Aborigines from voting for the Territory Council.

By 1962 the position had been clarified only by the removal of all Commonwealth restrictions on Aboriginal voters.[104] It is, however, unclear, and probably unlikely, that any ACT Aborigines did exercise the franchise by means of these apparent loopholes. Indeed, the fact that the loopholes survived for so long indicates that they had not been presenting electoral officers with any substantial or practical problems.

Until the South Australian parliament passed the *Aboriginal Affairs Act 1962* (SA), Aborigines in that State remained subject to the 1934–1939 legislation outlined in chapter 5. And, indeed, many of the provisions of the 1962 Act mirrored the earlier legislation. Aborigines continued to be defined as people descended from the original inhabitants of Australia – although a distinction was now drawn between 'Aboriginal', meaning 'full blood', and 'of Aboriginal blood', meaning 'less than full blood'. Members of the former group could be forced to undergo medical procedures, and while their employment was not formally regulated, administrators had the power to inspect employment conditions. Meanwhile, the executive retained broad regulatory power over all Aborigines.[105] There were some significant differences, however, which contrasted the 1962 legislation with earlier South Australian legislation. In particular, there was no longer a specific power under which Aborigines could be forced to reside on reserves.

Restrictions on the supply of alcohol to Aborigines were removed by the South Australian executive in early 1965.[106] Further, from 1966 an Aboriginal Lands Trust was constituted to which land could be transferred, and from which financial and other assistance to Aborigines could be provided. All members of the Trust were required to be Aborigines. In addition, from 1967, Aboriginal Reserve Councils gained legislative recognition, which enabled some Aboriginal autonomy in the governing of reserves.[107]

Responsibility for the implementation of the South Australian legislation was now divided between an Aboriginal Affairs Board, and the Minister and Department of Aboriginal Affairs. The Minister was responsible for apportioning Aboriginal affairs money; for managing and regulating Aboriginal reserves; and for providing 'in cases of need' for the maintenance and education of Aboriginal children. The Aboriginal Affairs Board, meanwhile, was responsible for advising the Minister on Aboriginal affairs, and had the curious responsibility of maintaining a 'Register of Aborigines'. The Board was required to maintain the register of names accurately, and it could 'from time to time remove therefrom the names of those persons who, in its opinion, are capable of accepting the full responsibilities of citizenship'.[108] Reminiscent of the justification for the 1886 Victorian legislation considered in chapter 1, this provision enabled the South Australian Aboriginal Affairs Board to cease providing relief to those Aborigines it deemed worthy of accepting the 'full responsibilities of citizenship'. Here was a clear statement, then, that despite changes in the legislative position of South Australian Aborigines since 1948, citizenship was by no means their right. It was something to be earned.

In Tasmania, the only Aborigines who were directly regulated by legislation were the residents of Cape Barren Island. In addition to being the sole subjects of specific Acts, the Tasmanian licensing law until 1958 made it a crime to supply the residents of Cape Barren Island with alcohol.[109]

The 1967 Referendum

As we saw in chapter 5, calls for Commonwealth involvement in Aboriginal affairs date back at least to the 1930s. The 1944 'post-war reconstruction' referendum failed in its bid to empower the Commonwealth to pass special laws for Aborigines. But the failure of this referendum indicated little about the will of the people on this issue, since the proposal was only one of fourteen suggested constitutional amendments.

Throughout the 1940s Aboriginal groups continued to lobby for the Commonwealth to be given the power to legislate for Aborigines. For instance, Kim Beazley Snr, after an approach from Pastor Doug Nicholls, wrote to Prime Minister Chifley in 1949, urging him to consider holding a referendum to amend section 51(26) of the Constitution.[110]

All the while the momentum to repeal section 127, which excluded Aborigines from the census, was gradually becoming irresistible. A Joint Parliamentary Committee on Constitutional Review recommended in 1958 and 1959 that section 127 be repealed, although the Committee interpreted the historical context giving rise to the existence of section 127 somewhat benignly. It commented that at federation the available means of communication made it almost impossible to obtain an accurate count of Aborigines, and reported that 'section 127 is liable to be misconstrued abroad'. The Committee did not have time to formulate

Table 13 Official Aboriginal population estimate, 1966

Vic.	*Qld*	*WA*	*NSW*	*SA*	*NT*	*Tas.*	*ACT*	*Aust.*
1790	19,003	18,439	13,613	5505	21,119	55	96	79,620

Source: F. Lancaster Jones, *The Structure and Growth of Australia's Aboriginal Population*, 1970.

Table 14 State and Territory Governance of Aboriginal Affairs, 1967

	Definition of Aboriginal	*Governing body*
Victoria	Any descendant of an 'aboriginal native'	Ministry of Aboriginal Affairs and Aboriginal Affairs Advisory Council
Queensland	Person of 'full-blood' or 'preponderance' of Aboriginal blood; 'part-Aborigine' living as spouse of an Aborigine; resident of reserve who has some 'Aboriginal blood'	Director of Aboriginal and Island Affairs
Western Australia	A 'native' was 'any person of the full blood' or of 'less than full blood' descended from the original inhabitants of Australia, except a person of 'one-fourth' or less of the original 'full blood'	Commissioner of Native Welfare
New South Wales	'Full-blooded' or 'half-caste' Aboriginal natives	Aborigines Welfare Board
South Australia	Distinction between Aboriginal ('full blood') and person 'of Aboriginal blood' (less than 'full blood')	Department of Aboriginal Affairs and Aboriginal Affairs Board
Northern Territory	Many Aborigines now deemed to be persons 'in need of assistance'	Director of Social Welfare
Australian Capital Territory	Legislation repealed	N/A
Tasmania	N/A	N/A

Table 15 Formal restrictions affecting Aborigines on key citizenship criteria, 1967.

	Statutory bar on voting	*Able to be removed to reserves*	*Employment formally regulated*
Victoria	No	No	No
Queensland	No	Yes	No
Western Australia	No	No	No
New South Wales	No	No	No
South Australia	No	No	No
Northern Territory	No	No	No
Australian Capital Territory	No	No	No
Tasmania	No	No	No

recommendations regarding amendments to section 51(26), but clearly saw merit in such a course of action.[111]

On several occasions after 1959, Arthur Calwell, the Labor Opposition leader, moved motions recommending that the Committee's proposals be put to referendum.[112] From the early 1960s onwards, politicians were, with greater force and in greater numbers, calling for a referendum to amend section 51(26) and to delete section 127.[113]

In understanding why the 1967 referendum took on the mantle of citizenship maker, it is useful to consider the comments of Kim Beazley Snr, who was one of the first politicians to voice support for the changes that ultimately came about. As well as supporting the deletion of section 127, Beazley argued that in order for Aborigines to be 'fully Australian citizens', their constitutional position had to show that they were subject to State and federal law in the same way as 'other citizens'. He argued: 'The truth is that they are not citizens in the same sense as are other Australians while [section 51(26)] exists.' In addition, Beazley noted that the Commonwealth could confer full citizenship rights on Aborigines in the Northern Territory, but that these rights could be lost when the person entered Western Australia or Queensland, and he argued that the 'Commonwealth is powerless to insist that citizenship rights have Australia-wide force'. Beazley acknowledged that the deletion of the reference to Aborigines in section 51(26) could not affect the State franchise, but he argued that other features of citizenship, such as the right of free movement, might be positively affected as a result. The removal of the phrase 'other than the aboriginal race in any State' would be the 'removal of a barrier to effective Commonwealth power to confer a meaningful nationality and citizenship on the people of the aboriginal race'.[114]

One constitutional obstacle referred to in parliamentary discussions about the deletion of section 127 was section 25, which still prevents 'persons of any race' from being counted in a State that does not give them the vote. In time section 25 would become dead-letter. But in Queensland, for instance, it provided an additional bar to the counting of that State's Aboriginal population until 1965, the year in which Queensland's Aborigines were given the State franchise.[115]

The tortuous path to the 1967 referendum involved a number of false starts. On 14 May 1964 Arthur Calwell presented a bill to the House of Representatives that was identical to the ultimately successful one.[116] But Calwell's desire to amend section 51(26) was not shared by the government. In November 1965 Prime Minister Menzies presented a bill that had the sole purpose of repealing section 127. His bill did not seek to amend section 51(26) because in his view the reference to Aborigines in that section was not discriminatory. Menzies even went so far as to say that: 'In truth, the contrary is the fact. The words are a protection against discrimination by the Commonwealth Parliament in respect of Aborigines.' Menzies ended his comments with: 'I repeat that the best protection for Aborigines is to treat them, for all purposes, as Australian citizens.'[117] Menzies' bill was passed but the proposal never went to referendum.

A new bill was put to parliament in March 1966, according to which the wording in section 51(26) would be changed to enable the Commonwealth to make laws for 'the advancement of the Aboriginal natives of the Commonwealth of Australia'. The bill, which was not passed, had also contained a new section 117A, which would have prohibited racial discrimination.[118]

Finally, in March 1967, the Constitution Alteration (Aboriginals) Bill 1967 was presented by Prime Minister Harold Holt. It proposed simply to repeal section 127 and strike the words 'other than the aboriginal race in any State' from section 51(26). Holt argued against the inclusion of a constitutional guarantee against racial discrimination, on the grounds that such a guarantee could provide a fertile source for attack on legislation that earlier might not have been considered discriminatory.[119]

The referendum that accepted Holt's proposals was held on 27 May 1967 and was passed in all States by an overall majority of 90.77 per cent of voters. The States that recorded votes over 90 per cent in favour were those with the smallest Aboriginal populations, with Victoria the highest 'yes' vote at 94.68 per cent. Western Australia, on the other hand, recorded the lowest 'yes' vote at 80.95 per cent.[120]

The official 'yes' case, which received across-party support, encouraged the amendment of section 51(26) in order to remove words from the Constitution that 'many people think are discriminatory against the Aboriginal people'. The proposal was not viewed at the time as one that would transfer power over Aboriginal affairs to the Commonwealth, a point lost sometimes on subsequent commentators. The 'yes' case stressed that the Commonwealth's object would be 'to co-operate with the States to ensure that together we act in the best interests of the Aboriginal people'.[121]

Meanwhile, the argument in support of repealing section 127 was straightforward in the official 'yes' case: 'Our personal sense of justice, our commonsense, and our international reputation in a world in which racial issues are being highlighted every day, require that we get rid of this out-moded provision.'[122] Concerns about international reputation, to be sure, had long convinced politicians of the need to amend the Constitution's references to Aborigines.[123]

In many ways, the successful referendum was the result of a groundswell in public opinion that Aboriginal groups had sought for decades. The most prominent group in the lead-up to the referendum was the Federal Council for the Advancement of Aborigines and Torres Strait Islanders (FCAATSI). Their work gained the support of all major parties and ultimately the media, which argued that the constitutional amendments were needed in order that Aborigines be treated equally, as fellow Australians.[124]

One of the most poignant moments in the campaign occurred in 1965, when a delegation from FCAATSI met with Prime Minister Menzies. After the meeting, Menzies offered drinks. He asked Oodgeroo Noonuccal (then Kath Walker) whether she would like a whiskey or some other alcoholic beverage. She told Menzies that if he had done that in Queensland he would have been gaoled. Menzies paused, then said that he was 'the boss around here' and poured her a drink.[125]

After the Referendum

The Commonwealth

In the years after the 1967 referendum the Commonwealth was slow to respond to its new power to legislate for Aborigines. During this time the last vestiges of the old regime – such as the requirement that permits be issued for some Aborigines wishing to leave the country – were still being dismantled.[126] Legislation passed in 1973 enabled the transfer of State Aboriginal affairs responsibilities to the Commonwealth.[127] In 1980 the Commonwealth legislated to establish the Aboriginal Development Commission, whose function was to attract sufficient capital funds to assist Aborigines, among other things, to acquire land, housing and to engage in business.[128] Then, in 1983, the Commonwealth amended its electoral law to make it compulsory for Aborigines and Islanders to enrol and vote in elections.[129] These few Acts, and the fact that Aborigines were now required to be included in census statistics, hardly enable the 1967 referendum to be viewed as a citizenship maker.

In 1982 the Department of Aboriginal Affairs addressed the argument that the Commonwealth had not done as much as had been expected of it since the referendum. The Department noted that the referendum had created the expectation of significant Commonwealth involvement in Aboriginal affairs, but that 'the responsibility of each State to provide services for its Aboriginal citizens as citizens remains'. Clyde Holding, the Minister for Aboriginal Affairs, echoed these views in 1986, commenting that 'Aborigines are citizens of the States like everybody else. They are entitled to look to the States to provide them with those basic services that State governments normally provide to their citizens.'[130]

The States

After 1967 the States continued, and in some cases began, to dismantle their regimes. South Australia in 1968 removed the legislative provision that required a register of Aborigines to be kept. Legislation in 1962 had required the register to contain the names of all Aborigines except those deemed to be 'capable of accepting the full responsibilities of citizenship'. Another amendment in 1968 removed the provision according to which Aborigines with contagious diseases could be forced to undergo medical procedures.[131] In the same year the parliament removed the possibility that Aborigines could be publicly whipped for wilfully making false statements in evidence while not on oath. Three years later, Aboriginal murderers were no longer able to be executed at the scene of the crime.[132] Responsibility for Aboriginal affairs in South Australia passed to the Department for Community Welfare from 1972. The executive, however, retained the power to set aside lands as Aboriginal reserves, yet these lands were not to be placed under Aboriginal control.[133]

Developments in Western Australia were as slow as anywhere. In the *Liquor Act 1970* (WA) it remained an offence for any 'native' to receive or possess liquor in certain proclaimed areas. This provision was repealed in 1972, although the prohibition had effectively been removed region by region between 1964 in the south-west and 1971 in the north-west. Indicative of Western Australia's slowness to abandon its discriminatory regime was the fact that the infamous *Natives (Citizenship Rights) Act* was only repealed in 1971.[134]

The next major piece of West Australian legislation was the *Aboriginal Affairs Planning Authority Act 1972* (WA), which repealed the *Native Welfare Act.* According to the new legislation, a 'person of Aboriginal descent' was a person living in Western Australia who was 'wholly or partly descended from the original inhabitants of Australia who claims to be an Aboriginal and who is accepted as such'. One part of the Act dealing with Aboriginal estates and property, however, applied to 'a person of Aboriginal descent only if he is also of the full blood descended from the original inhabitants of Australia or more than one-fourth of the full blood'. The Act established an Aboriginal Affairs Planning Authority, whose role it would be to consult with Aborigines and 'to promote the economic, social and cultural advancement of persons of Aboriginal descent in Western Australia, and to that end to apportion, apply or distribute the moneys available to it'. The Act, which was to be administered by a Commissioner for Aboriginal Planning, also established an Aboriginal Advisory Council and an Aboriginal Lands Trust, to be made up of such Aboriginal people as the Minister chose. The Trust was empowered to control and manage land placed under its control by the executive. Another body created by the Act was the Aboriginal Affairs Co-ordinating Committee, which was to bring representatives from several government departments to co-ordinate those persons and bodies providing 'service and assistance' to Aborigines. Miscellaneous provisions in this Act empowered the Department for Community Welfare to address a court when an Aboriginal was charged with any crime. Further, guilty pleas from Aborigines regarding serious crimes were not to be taken at face value where it seemed that the person was not capable of understanding the nature of the plea.[135] An amendment to this legislation in 1973 enabled the Commonwealth to assume the functions contained in the State Act, where intergovernmental arrangements had been made.[136]

A limited degree of self-determination in Western Australia was made possible by the *Aboriginal Communities Act 1979* (WA), which enabled some Aboriginal communities to pass their own by-laws. However, the executive retained the power to declare that the Act no longer applied to a particular community.[137]

In New South Wales, in line with other States, the responsibility for Aboriginal affairs passed in 1969 from the Aborigines Welfare Board to a governmental corporation under the name 'The Minister, Aborigines Act, 1969'. Aborigines were now defined to be any 'descendant of an aboriginal native of Australia'. At the same time an Aborigines Advisory Council, nine of whose ten members were required to be Aborigines, was established to report to the minister as required. Six of the nine Aboriginal members were to be elected. Under this legislation Aboriginal reserves, except for those leased to Aborigines, were deemed to be public places for the purposes of police offences.[138]

Amendments in 1973 required all members of the Aborigines Advisory Council to be Aborigines. At this time an Aboriginal Lands Trust was created, consisting of the Council members, which had the power to sell and acquire land. These provisions were repealed in 1983 with the enactment of New South Wales' first land rights legislation, which we will consider in the next chapter.[139]

Minor changes occurred in the administration of Aboriginal affairs in Victoria in the years after 1967. The number of Aboriginal representatives on the Aboriginal Affairs Advisory Council went up from three out of thirteen to six in 1968, and these representatives were now to be elected.[140]

In 1974 Victoria legislated to repeal the *Aboriginal Affairs Act 1967* (Vic), and to transfer the power and goods formerly belonging to the Aboriginal Affairs Minister to the Housing Commission. This legislation also authorised the transfer of rights and possessions formerly vested in the Aboriginal Affairs Minister to the federal government.[141]

New legislation in Queensland in 1971 overhauled the regulation of Aboriginal affairs. Two Acts, the *Aborigines Act 1971* (Qld) and the *Torres Strait Islanders Act 1971* (Qld), made some changes to the previous regime, and were administered by the Director of Aboriginal and Island Affairs. An 'Aborigine' was now defined as a person who was descended from an indigenous inhabitant of the Commonwealth of Australia other than the Torres Strait Islands, and an 'Islander' was a descendant of an indigenous inhabitant of the Torres Strait Islands. The categories of 'assisted Aborigine' and 'assisted Islander' were withdrawn. The Acts required a judge to visit reserves once every three months, and gave broad powers of inspection to the Director and delegates. Aborigines and Islanders wishing to reside on reserves had to apply to an Aboriginal Council or an Island Council, or where these did not exist, to the Director. The Minister had power to authorise mining on reserves, and police had all the powers in relation to reserves that they had elsewhere in the State. District officers retained the power to manage the property of Aborigines and Islanders when the individuals requested them to do so. A further provision stipulated that female Aborigines were not compellable witnesses in criminal proceedings against men with whom they were cohabiting. Traditional marriages were now recognised for the purposes of disposing of the assets of deceased Aborigines. As in the past, the executive retained wide regulatory power over: the establishment and function of Aboriginal and Island courts; the 'development, assimilation, integration, education, training and preservation' of Aborigines and Islanders; the peace, order and 'proper discipline' of reserves; the establishment of police and gaols on reserves; and the inspection of reserves.[142] From 1975 the name of the administering body became the Director of Aboriginal and Islanders Advancement.[143]

Amendments to the governing legislation in 1979 established an Aboriginal and Islander Commission, which consisted of Aborigines and Islanders and such other people chosen by the Minister. The Commission's role was to make policy suggestions. This legislation also provided for appeals to be made from Aboriginal and Island Courts.[144]

Queensland Aborigines living on reserves had to deal not only with oppressive Acts, but also with reserve regulations, or by-laws, that were as intrusive as one could possibly imagine. Garth Nettheim has noted the following regulations that were in force on some Queensland reserves during the late 1970s:

> A householder shall wash and drain his garbage bin after it has been emptied by the collector. If necessary disinfection of the bin by the householder may be directed by an authorised person.
> A person shall not use any electrical goods, other than a hot water jug, electric radio, iron or razor, unless permission is first obtained from an authorised officer.
> Parents shall bring up their children with love and care and shall teach them good behaviour and conduct and shall ensure their compliance with these By-laws.[145]

In theory reserve by-laws could be made by Aboriginal Councils, although Nettheim suggests that a standard set of by-laws was produced by the Department which Councils then adopted.[146] If that was so, then regulations like the ones above, which probably contravened the Commonwealth *Racial Discrimination Act 1975*, are testimony to the extraordinary faith held by administrators in the power of legislation. Parents, according to the law, were to love their children.

The oppressive 1971 legislation remained in force until 1984, although the Commonwealth intervened in 1978 with legislation that sought to give Aborigines and Islanders on reserves greater control over their own affairs. The Commonwealth legislation provided for the establishment of Aboriginal and Island Councils on reserves that did not have such representative bodies.[147]

A break with past Queensland policy seemed to come in 1984, with the enactment of new legislation that appeared to promote self-determination for Aborigines and Islanders. Local Aboriginal and Island Councils would now be elected to govern 'trust areas', being those areas 'granted in trust' or set aside as Aboriginal and Islander reserves by the executive. The Councils had power to make by-laws concerning the peace, order, discipline, 'moral safety', housing and welfare of their areas' inhabitants. The Councils could appoint 'Aboriginal police' or 'Island police', and Aboriginal and Island Courts consisting of indigenous justices could be established under the legislation to hear complaints about breaches of by-laws and other matters. Legislation passed the following year enabled the Councils to grant leases over land within their areas. However, the extent to which the 1984 legislation represented a move towards self-determination was circumvented by the ultimate power that rested with the executive. The executive had the 'absolute discretion' to dissolve an Aboriginal or Island Council, and a Council's budget had no force until the Minister approved it. Moreover, in its usual breadth of regulatory power, the executive had power over: the composition of the Councils; the qualification of candidates for membership of Councils; the franchise for elections of Councils; the composition of Aboriginal and Island police forces; the jurisdiction of Aboriginal and Island Courts; and it retained power to regulate 'the development, assimilation and integration' of Aborigines and Islanders.[148]

In the Northern Territory a number of Ordinances and – from 1978 – Acts began to dismantle the 'welfare' regime that had so regulated the lives of Territory Aborigines. The criminal code was amended in 1968 so that Aborigines convicted of murder could receive a 'just and proper' penalty in lieu of a death sentence. The *Liquor Act 1978* (NT) enabled local groups to ask the Liquor Commission to ban alcohol within specified areas to all but permit-holders. At the same time, recognition began to be given to traditional forms of Aboriginal family associations for administrative purposes.[149]

Two key themes emerge from the overview in this chapter about the gradual attainment by Aborigines of formal citizenship. Most important, in terms of popular misconceptions, is that the 1967 referendum provided no legal watershed in the citizenship status of Aborigines. Its passage was certainly contemporaneous with the removal of many of the regimes that excluded Aborigines from citizenship. But the referendum took place after all voting restrictions against Aborigines had been removed, and at a time when most jurisdictions had begun to dismantle their restrictive regimes. That is not to deny, however, that the referendum was of clear symbolic importance. The fact that an overwhelming majority of Australians supported, in effect, the argument that the States had failed their obligation to Aborigines should not be forgotten. Aboriginal groups worked tirelessly for the 'yes' vote, and their success did give an immeasurable impetus to contemporary Aboriginal political action.

The second theme to emerge is a recurrent one throughout this book: the citizenship status of Aborigines has been decided at two levels of government. To use Garfield Barwick's phrase quoted at the beginning of this chapter, there have in effect been 'nine different "citizenships" in Australia'. In the various jurisdictions, and in varying degrees, the existence of oppressive laws, and the harsh exercise of wide discretionary powers, have operated to deny Aborigines citizenship throughout Australia.

But gradually, from the 1950s to the 1980s, the various federal, State and Territory regimes that had operated to deny Aborigines basic citizenship rights were wound down. Correspondingly, the classification of Aborigines received less emphasis, with the term 'Aboriginal' coming uniformly to be interpreted as a descendant of the 'original inhabitants of Australia' (Western Australia), or a descendant of 'an indigenous inhabitant of Australia' (Queensland). The emphasis now was on ignoring any differences between Aborigines and non-Aborigines, and on using the idea of equal citizenship as a means of facilitating the assimilation of Aborigines into white society. The achievement of formal citizenship was thus a victory for Aborigines that carried with it a threat to the concept of an indigenous identity. As full citizens, Aborigines would now have to struggle against the assimilationist effect that citizenship entailed. From the 1970s onwards the search by Aborigines for the legal recognition of their indigenous rights – primarily their rights to land and self-determination – saw their status as citizens used against them. Citizens, they were told, should all share equal rights. The achievement of formal citizenship was, of course, a positive development for Aborigines, but it brought with it new challenges as Aborigines sought legal recognition of their indigenous rights.

CHAPTER 7

From Civil to Indigenous Rights

> There have been two great themes to our struggle: citizenship rights, the right to be treated the same as other Australians, to receive the same benefits, to be provided with the same level of services; and indigenous rights, the collective rights that are owed to us as distinct peoples and as the original occupiers of this land.[1]
>
> *Lois O'Donoghue, chairperson of the Aboriginal and Torres Strait Islander Commission, 1996*

Since the late 1960s there has been little improvement in the life situations and health of Aborigines. Incarceration rates remain much higher for Aborigines than for non-Aborigines, and poverty affects a much higher percentage of Aborigines than non-Aborigines.

But politically, the period since the late 1960s has witnessed some significant changes in the conception of Aboriginal rights. Indeed the concept of 'Aboriginal rights' itself has gained currency in the last quarter century, a fact brought about by the concerted political action of Aborigines. From the 1960s the formal Commonwealth and State restrictions that denied Aborigines any meaningful status as Australian citizens were slowly abandoned. These legislative changes at both levels coincided roughly with the timing of the 1967 referendum, a fact that probably explains why the referendum is accorded the status of citizenship maker.

Legal changes in the period since Aborigines were accorded formal citizenship status have resulted now in the acknowledgment that Aborigines possess certain rights that do not pertain to other Australians. Over the last twenty-five years, changes have occurred that have started to challenge the idea that it is enough for Aborigines to be given formal equality with non-Aboriginal Australians. Initially, these changes came about through legislation, but more recently they have been the result of an expansionist judiciary.

In this final chapter we address three key stages in the development, since the late 1960s, of Aboriginal citizenship and indigenous rights: the prohibition on racial discrimination; the legal recognition of land rights; and the facilitation of Aboriginal self-determination. Our argument is that only recently has legal recognition been given to the view that Aborigines have certain indigenous rights over and above their rights as Australian citizens. The securing of enhanced rights for Aborigines has been gradual and highly contentious, and has been partly the result of Aboriginal political protest, partly the result of changing public attitudes, and partly due to key institutional changes, such as the 1992 *Mabo* decision that recognised native title. A number of key Aboriginal protests that took on symbolic dimensions for both Aboriginal and non-Aboriginal Australians acted as precursors to legislative and judicial changes.

Aboriginal Protests

Two Aboriginal protests in country Australia in the 1960s were particularly symbolic. In 1963 the Yirrkala people in Arnhem Land sent a bark petition to the House of Representatives protesting at the permission given to the mining company Nabalco to mine 390 square kilometres of their land. This protest resulted in a parliamentary inquiry, which made a groundbreaking recommendation that compensation was owed to the Yirrkala people. However, a subsequent land rights case, to be considered later, was decided against three Yirrkala representatives, who had claimed native title to the land that was now subject to a mining lease. Then, in 1966, following an Arbitration Commission decision to delay the payment of equal wages to Aboriginal pastoral workers until 1968, 200 Gurindji people staged the best known of the resultant strikes by walking off the Wave Hill pastoral station in the Northern Territory. This fight for wage justice soon became one for Aboriginal ownership of the land, when the strikers set up a new camp on their traditional land and sought the transfer of part of the Wave Hill lease. As Richard Broome notes, both of these disputes became significant symbols in the struggles for Aboriginal land rights.[2]

Meanwhile, urban Aborigines were raising people's awareness of the discrimination suffered by them. Charles Perkins's freedom rides in 1965 were one of the two most enduring symbols of these protests.

Perkins, borrowing an idea from the United States civil rights movement, took around twenty Aborigines and white sympathisers on a bus-ride through towns in north-western New South Wales, highlighting the existence of segregationist practices.[3]

The other enduring symbol of Aboriginal protest from this time was the establishment, on Australia Day 1972, of the Aboriginal Embassy. Protesting at the refusal of the McMahon government to recognise Aboriginal land rights, a group of Aborigines proclaimed a beach umbrella and some plastic sheeting they had set up on the lawns of Parliament House in Canberra to be the Aboriginal Embassy. The Embassy, soon reinforced by the presence of a number of tents, was a poignant moment in the history of race relations in Australia, and it gathered wide and favourable publicity. The government's farcical attempts to disband the Embassy added to the support it had already received. A new ordinance needed to be gazetted in order for the government to remove the Embassy, and this was later ruled to have been improperly gazetted. Police no sooner removed the tents and protestors, than the Embassy was again set up. Opposition leader Gough Whitlam made a visit to the Embassy, promising support for Aboriginal land rights. One significant, though intangible, legacy of the Embassy was its promotion of the idea of a united and national Aboriginal movement.[4]

Other significant protests of the 1970s tended inevitably to involve the mining of Aboriginal land. One such protest occurred in 1979 and 1980 in Noonkanbah, Western Australia, when Charles Court's government ignored Aboriginal protests and gave its full assistance to enable the Amax Corporation to drill for oil on a sacred site. Police accompanied over fifty trucks, issued with special licence plates, as the mining equipment was brought to Noonkanbah. Local Aboriginal protestors were assisted by trade union bans, while the dispute was given intense media coverage.[5]

While it is impossible to specify the direct results of each of these protests, and while each protest had its own specific focus, their overall significance was their ability to be read as a commentary on one central issue: that formal citizenship for Aborigines had not put an end to injustice. As Aborigines continued their search for justice these protests would become important symbols both to them and to those parliaments and courts that took to re-evaluating their past practices.

The first tentative step taken by the Australian state to respond to this commentary was the outlawing of racial discrimination.

Racial Discrimination Legislation

On 21 November 1973 federal Attorney-General Lionel Murphy introduced the first racial discrimination bill into federal parliament. After three failed attempts the bill was passed in 1975 as the *Racial Discrimination Act* (Cwlth). The Act defined as Aboriginal 'a person who is a descendant of an indigenous inhabitant of Australia'. Torres Strait Islanders were excluded from the definition, but were specifically covered by certain provisions. The Act prohibited the doing of:

> any act involving a distinction, exclusion, restriction or preference based on race, colour, descent or national or ethnic origin which has the purpose or effect of nullifying or impairing the recognition, enjoyment or exercise, on an equal footing, of any human right or fundamental freedom in the political, economic, social, cultural or any other field of public life.[6]

The Act was a legislative response to the adoption by the United Nations in 1965 of the *International Convention on the Elimination of all forms of Racial Discrimination,* to which Australia had become a signatory in October 1966 and which Australia ratified in September 1975. Signatories to the convention undertook to guarantee the right of everyone, regardless of race, to the enjoyment of certain rights, including: the right to equal treatment before the law; the freedom to participate in elections; freedom of movement; the freedom to leave and return to one's country; to own property; to work; to housing; to public health; to education; to participation in cultural activities; and the right of access to any place intended to be used by the general public, including hotels.[7]

While the *Racial Discrimination Act* clearly sought to prevent discrimination against people of many disparate backgrounds, it was discrimination against Aborigines that motivated the legislation's supporters. As such, it amounted to the first serious attempt by the Commonwealth government to do more for Aborigines than simply remove the restrictions that had prevented their attainment of ordinary citizenship rights.

In introducing the original bill, Murphy said:

> Perhaps the most blatant example of racial discrimination in Australia is that which affects Aboriginals . . . There are still remnants of legislative provisions of the paternalistic type based implicitly on the alleged superiority of the white race in which it is assumed that Aboriginals are unable to manage their own personal affairs and property. Discrimination affects Aborigines so far as it concerns the administration of the criminal law and the enjoyment of civil, political, social and economic rights . . . It is clear that past wrongs must be put right so far as the Aboriginal population is concerned and that special measures must be provided.[8]

The Act specifically outlawed racial discrimination in the provision of access to certain places, to accommodation, and in the provision of goods and services. One section of the Act applied only to Aborigines and Torres Strait Islanders, and sought to override State and Territory legislation that allowed government delegates to manage their property. Specific legislation, the *Aboriginal and Torres Strait Islanders (Queensland Discriminatory Laws) Act 1975* (Cwlth), clarified this even further, by effectively invalidating Queensland legislation that allowed the property of Aborigines and Islanders to be controlled without their consent, and that restricted their entry onto reserves.[9]

The passage of the *Racial Discrimination Act*, although derided by one historian as 'virtually useless' for its lack of criminal sanctions,[10] represented a small victory for Aborigines, and it marked a progression in the thinking about the citizenship rights of Aborigines. Moreover, as we shall discuss later, the Act was to take on added significance following the High Court's recognition of native title in 1992. The *Racial Discrimination Act* gave no special rights as such to Aborigines, but it did display an acceptance of the view that the mere removal of the exclusionary legislative edifice was not sufficient to ensure and promote equality and fairness. The law for over a century had been central to the denial of citizenship rights to Aborigines, but the slow deletion of exclusionary provisions had hardly amounted to proclamations that Aborigines now enjoyed full civil and political rights. The deletion of exclusions, it was now recognised, was not enough. The law now had a role to play in changing attitudes. As Murphy said, 'special measures' were needed.

Limited though they were, the special measures contained in the Act still drew strong criticism. Opposition to the Act centred on three key issues: its constitutionality, its challenge to the principle of free speech, and its challenge to the rule of law. The government relied on its external affairs power, section 51(29) of the Constitution, to pass the Act. The adoption of the International Convention that provided the basis for the Act was clearly a foreign affairs issue, but the enactment into domestic law of many of the Convention's articles was less clearly an exercise of the foreign affairs power. In the *Koowarta* case in 1982, however, the High Court accepted that the *Racial Discrimination Act* was a valid exercise of this power.[11]

The concern that the Act jeopardised the rule of law centred on the manner in which complaints were to be investigated. The possibility that complainants would remain anonymous led some to argue that the Act put in place 'Star Chamber' investigative methods, and the mere existence of an Act of this nature raised concerns for the freedom of speech.[12] The response to these last two criticisms was most eloquently put, in a different context, by Hal Wootten, in evidence before the Senate Standing Committee on Constitutional and Legal Affairs in 1972:

> It would be the height of hypocrisy for white Australians now to say to Aborigines that from here on the race must be on equal terms, without

> taking into account the 180 years start which white Australians have given themselves. This is particularly unfair when one considers how much power, prestige, affluence and education in the white community has been built on the exploitation of land from which whites ousted blacks.[13]

When it became clear that jurisprudential concerns would not defeat the bill, its opponents reverted to the now familiar practice of questioning the level of Aboriginality of agitators. Individuals like Charles Perkins, who claimed that Australia was still a racist country, were subjected to highly defamatory attacks in parliament. Another parliamentary line of attack saw an oblique and unfavourable comparison made between Jews and Aborigines, the former being 'one of the most intelligent, best educated and most creative people in the world despite all that has been done against them'. This prompted the response: 'Do you mean by that that discrimination is good for people?'[14] Despite all this, the legislation, in amended form, ultimately won bipartisan support when the principle was accepted that legislation of this sort had a role to play in changing attitudes.[15]

Most States passed more or less complementary anti-discrimination legislation between the late 1960s and early 1990s. South Australia's *Prohibition of Discrimination Act 1966* was the first such piece of legislation, imposing fines of up to $200 on people who refused to provide services or accommodation, or who sacked an employee, 'by reason only of his race or country of origin or the colour of his skin'.[16]

The New South Wales *Anti-Discrimination Act 1977* similarly outlawed racial discrimination, along with other forms of discrimination, but, in the manner of most anti-discrimination legislation, provided a process of conciliation in the event of a breach. The constitutionality of this Act was tested in the High Court in the *Viskauskas* case in 1983, where it was held that the New South Wales legislation was inconsistent with the federal discrimination legislation. Both pieces of legislation similarly outlawed racial discrimination, but each provided different complaint processes following the report of a breach.[17] This problem was soon resolved by the Commonwealth through a peculiar amending Act that disentitled a person to make a complaint under the Commonwealth Act after lodging a complaint under State discrimination legislation.[18] In 1989 New South Wales amended its anti-discrimination legislation by making it an offence to incite racial hatred.[19]

Victoria and Western Australia legislated in 1984 to outlaw racial discrimination in the provision of accommodation, goods and services, and in employment.[20] It was not until 1991 that Queensland outlawed racial and other forms of discrimination, and the following year the Northern Territory did likewise. Tasmania only outlawed sex discrimination, but not racial discrimination, in 1994.[21]

The passage of Commonwealth and State discrimination legislation represented a significant step forward in the history of race relations in Australia. The passage of these laws amounted to official recognition that the gradual removal of restrictive laws was not sufficient for Aborigines to be included in Australian citizenship in any meaningful sense. The next step would be the acknowledgment that Aborigines had certain rights that were not available to non-Aboriginal people. But this was a principle that was not officially recognised until 1992.

Land Rights

Land rights, in both a symbolic and substantive sense, represent the most fundamental challenge that has ever faced Australia's legal system. In a symbolic sense, the granting of land rights by courts and parliaments gives judicial and legislative recognition to the view that, contrary to contemporary white opinion, Aborigines did have ownership rights to their land in 1788, of which the 'settlement' of Australia wrongly deprived them. In a substantive sense, the granting or acknowledgment of land rights challenges contemporary thinking about the rights of Aborigines as citizens. For with the legal recognition of native title, Aborigines, for the first time, have been recognised by the law to possess certain rights that cannot be possessed by non-Aborigines.

Northern Territory Legislation

Of all jurisdictions, the Northern Territory has been the leader in the granting of land rights to Aborigines. However, it was not until the election of the reformist Whitlam government in 1972 that land rights in the Northern Territory extended beyond pure tokenism. Northern Territory legislation in 1969 enabled leases over unleased land in Aboriginal reserves to be given to adult Aborigines or co-operatives that benefited Aborigines.[22] But the right of Aborigines to use land was inevitably subject to the rights of miners. In the *Mining Ordinance 1970* (NT) the Administrator, who was responsible for granting exploration licences, was required, when considering applications over Aboriginal reserves, only to consider the 'interests, well-being and employment of aboriginals in the vicinity'.[23]

In February 1973 Edward Woodward was appointed by the Whitlam government to conduct a Commission of inquiry into the means by which Aboriginal land rights, particularly in the Northern Territory, might be recognised or established. Woodward's 1974 report was itself a landmark in the history of land rights in Australia. One of Woodward's operating principles was that:

> white settlers and their descendants have gradually taken over the occupation of most of the fertile or otherwise useful parts of the country. In doing so, they have shown scant regard for any rights in the land, legal or moral, of the Aboriginal people.[24]

Although confining his attention to the Northern Territory, Woodward recognised that his recommendations would set a precedent for action elsewhere. He recommended that Aboriginal reserves be returned to Aborigines and, although not recommending that town land be automatically transferred to Aborigines, Woodward urged Aboriginal groups to press for the purchase of town land.

To implement his proposals, Woodward recommended the passage of an Aboriginal Land (Northern Territory) Act. Woodward's proposed legislation vested freehold title over Aboriginal reserves in Aboriginal groups. In addition, the proposed legislation established a mechanism by which land that was neither a reserve nor in a town could be claimed by Aborigines. Woodward recommended the establishment of an Aboriginal Land Commission to which applications would be made for the granting of land. On receipt of a favourable Commission finding, the Minister and the trustees of a new body, the Aboriginal Land Fund, could then authorise the acquisition of the land, which would later be proclaimed as Aboriginal land. Aboriginal land would be held by certain Land Trusts on trust for the benefit of Aborigines. Interestingly, the proposed legislation gave the Commonwealth executive the power to declare that mining could be conducted on Aboriginal land if it was in the 'national interest', however, such a declaration would be invalid if either house of parliament passed a contrary resolution within twenty-one days.[25]

Commonwealth legislation in 1974 saw one of Woodward's recommendations come to fruition, with the establishment of an Aboriginal Land Fund Commission. The Commission was empowered to make grants to Aboriginal corporations and trusts for the purpose of purchasing land, and also had power to grant some interests in land.[26] However, the Whitlam government was dismissed from office before its Aboriginal Land Rights Bill, which closely followed Woodward's recommendations, could be passed.[27]

Although the dismissal of the Whitlam government threatened the possibility of land rights legislation, Woodward's recommendations were implemented, in slightly weaker form, with the passage of the *Aboriginal Land Rights (Northern Territory) Act 1976*. This Act provided for the transfer to Aboriginal groups of a number of specified parcels of former reserve land. The Act also established a mechanism by which Aborigines could claim other land by showing a traditional attachment to it. While the Act, by and large, only enabled reserve and unalienated

Crown land to be transferred to Aborigines, it was still a major achievement, and was far ahead of developments in most of the States. Under the Act, Aboriginal people were immediately granted freehold over 258,000 square kilometres of land which had been reserve land.[28]

The *Aboriginal Land Ordinance 1978* (NT) supplemented the Commonwealth legislation by forbidding unauthorised entry onto Aboriginal land. An Aboriginal person, defined to be a member of the Aboriginal race of Australia, could enter or remain on Aboriginal land if entitled by Aboriginal tradition to do so. The relevant Land Councils were empowered to issue permits for people to enter Aboriginal land, and could recommend to the Territory Administrator that lands be declared open and not covered by the permit system. Members of the federal and Northern Territory parliaments were able to go onto Aboriginal land without permits, and government employees could be issued with permits by the Minister.[29] The following year police were given greater power to stop unauthorised people entering Aboriginal land.[30] By June 1989, when a further legislative grant of land had been made, Aborigines, who numbered just under one-quarter of the Territory population, held freehold title to around one-third of the land in the Northern Territory.[31] This significant figure is, however, easily overstated as much of the land is arid.

State Land Rights Legislation

Since 1966 Australian State parliaments have shown only a very limited desire to recognise Aboriginal rights to land. South Australia's *Aboriginal Lands Trust Act 1966* was the first piece of land rights legislation passed by any Australian parliament. This Act established a trust, comprised of Aboriginal members, to which the executive could transfer crown lands, or lands reserved for Aborigines. The lands transferred would be free of all encumbrances, with the notable exception that minerals were reserved for the crown.[32] Later South Australian legislation enabled around 180,000 square kilometres of land to be vested, again subject to mining rights, in the Anangu Pitjantjatjaraku and Maralinga Tjarutja peoples. The High Court held that legislation vesting land in the Anangu Pitjantjatjaraku people was racially discriminatory under the Commonwealth discrimination legislation, but also found that the transferral was valid on the basis that it was a 'special measure' under the discrimination legislation. By June 1989 South Australian Aborigines held just under one-fifth of the land in the State, much of which is desert.[33]

In 1970 the Victorian parliament passed the *Aboriginal Lands Act 1970* (Vic). This created the Framlingham Aboriginal Trust and the Lake Tyers

Aboriginal Trust and authorised the land at Framlingham and Lake Tyers to be vested in Aborigines. This followed years of protest by Aboriginal groups, culminating in 1963 in a protest march to parliament by forty Lake Tyers residents who petitioned to keep their reserve.[34] Many years later, in a changed political environment, the Victorian government took an unusual step in its bid to legislate for land rights. Faced with a hostile upper house, the Cain Labor government requested the Commonwealth to legislate the vesting of land at Lake Condah and Framlingham, exclusive of minerals, in local Aboriginal communities. The federal government took the extraordinary step of distancing itself from any acknowledgment of an Aboriginal legal right to the land – stating that it did 'not acknowledge the matters acknowledged by the Government of Victoria' – but with this qualification passed the legislation.[35] Other Victorian Acts enabled the vesting of small parts of land to Aboriginal groups and co-operatives, but by the middle of 1989 Aboriginal Victorians, who represented one-third of one per cent of the population, held under one per cent of Victorian land.[36]

Western Australia has been the slowest State to recognise Aboriginal rights to land. The *Aboriginal Affairs Planning Authority Act 1972* (WA) established an Aboriginal Lands Trust, which was empowered to control and manage land placed under its control by the executive. The limited extent to which this led to the recognition of land rights was spelt out in the *Mining Act 1978* (WA), where lands reserved for Aborigines under the 1972 Act were able to be mined following the written consent of the Minister.[37]

During the 1980s the few promising developments that occurred were soon quashed. A 1983 Aboriginal Land Inquiry conducted by Paul Seaman recommended, among other things, that Aborigines have the power to refuse mining on their lands. Seaman's report was rejected by the government within weeks of its tabling. Then, in 1985 an Aboriginal land bill was defeated in the upper house. Following this the government instituted a program for granting 99-year leases to Aboriginal communities over Aboriginal land. By the middle of 1989 Aboriginal people held around 12 per cent of West Australian land, most of it as leasehold.[38]

In the ACT a 1977 ordinance enabled land in the Jervis Bay area to be leased to an Aboriginal housing company. One unusual and somewhat punitive requirement expressed in the ordinance, however, required the company to keep all land leased to it 'clean, tidy and free from debris, dry herbage, rubbish, carcases of animals, and other unsightly or offensive matter'.[39] Commonwealth legislation in 1986 enabled land around Jervis Bay in the ACT to become legally 'Aboriginal land'. Adjoining land could also become Aboriginal land upon a ministerial declaration, although either house of parliament had the power to override such a declaration. The right to any minerals, as usual, remained with the Commonwealth.[40]

New South Wales legislation in 1973 had established an Aboriginal Lands Trust, that comprised the members of the Aborigines Advisory Council. The trust had the power to sell and acquire land.[41] Ten years later, New South Wales passed its first land rights legislation, which transferred title over former trust land to the New South Wales Aboriginal Land Council and other local Aboriginal land councils. These councils could also now make claims for 'claimable Crown lands', a term defined to mean lands not lawfully used or occupied and not likely to be needed for an essential public purpose. Claims were made to the Crown Lands Minister, and once land was vested in a land council it could not be sold. Local land councils could only lease land vested in them under certain conditions. The Act also gave 7.5 per cent of the State's land tax revenue for fifteen years to the New South Wales Aboriginal Land Council, with which it would be able to purchase land.[42] Changes to the New South Wales legislation in 1990 disempowered regional land councils to purchase land. This had the effect of centralising power over land rights with the New South Wales Aboriginal Land Council at the expense of regional councils.[43]

Almost on a par with Western Australia, Queensland has been slow to recognise Aboriginal and Islander rights to land. Testimony to Queensland's general approach was the legislative authority given to a bauxite mining agreement over land at Aurukun in 1975. Earlier, the Director of Aboriginal and Islanders Advancement had entered an agreement for bauxite to be mined on the Aurukun reserve, with a small percentage of profits to be paid to him 'on behalf of Aborigines' generally. The agreement was followed by a franchise agreement between the State and mining companies, which then received the force of law following the passage of the special legislation. Aboriginal residents at Aurukun subsequently took legal action against the Director for breach of trust over his decision to enter the agreement, but this failed when the Privy Council decided that the *Aborigines Act* had authorised his actions.[44]

In 1978 the Queensland and Commonwealth governments played out a legislative battle over the management of Aboriginal reserves. Commonwealth legislation in 1978 enabled residents of Queensland reserves to request self-management from the Commonwealth. In response, the Queensland government shortly after legislated to create the 'shires' of Mornington and Aurukun, making these former 'reserves' no longer susceptible to the Commonwealth legislation. This manoeuvre by the Queensland government may, however, have been unnecessary since residents of other Queensland reserves, to whom the Commonwealth legislation still in theory applied, had little success in attempting to gain self-management from Canberra.[45]

The 1978 Queensland legislation provided for the incorporation of the Mornington and Aurukun Aboriginal councils, to whom shire land would be leased. This legislation also restricted the entry of non-Aborigines onto land in the shires. But the very limited extent to which this move was a recognition by the State of Aboriginal rights to land was exemplified by the exemptions contained in this legislation. Rights of access to the shires for the search for minerals were largely unaffected, and the shires, with the exception of residential or work premises, were deemed to be public places. This gave police an enormous surveillance potential. Amendments three years later enabled an individual within the shires to be placed under a 'prohibition order', which would forbid the person to possess or consume alcohol within the shire, and which would empower police to search the person and his or her premises at any time for liquor. The breach of a prohibition order rendered a person liable to a $200 fine or fourteen days imprisonment.[46]

Rather than pass specific legislation to grant Aborigines title to reserve lands, as was happening in other States, the Queensland Bjelke-Petersen government decided in 1982 that Aboriginal and Islander groups would only be able to receive 'deeds of grant in trust' over reserve land.[47] Legislation in 1985 then enabled Aborigines and Islanders to apply for perpetual leases over land once deeds of grant in trust had been issued to community councils. In October 1985 title deeds were handed over for all inhabited islands in Torres Strait, with the exception of Murray Island – over which the *Mabo* action had been instituted. A year later six Aboriginal communities received their title deeds, the day before a State election. In 1989 Aborigines and Islanders, who comprised 2.4 per cent of the Queensland population, held 1.9 per cent of its land, nearly all of it in leasehold.[48]

The Goss Labor government in Queensland passed legislation in 1991 that gave Aborigines and Islanders a somewhat more generous framework through which to seek recognition of their land rights. The preambles to the legislation acknowledged that many Aboriginal people (not Islanders) had been 'dispossessed and dispersed' after European settlement and that land was of spiritual, social, historic, cultural and economic importance to Aboriginal and Torres Strait Islander people. The complex legislation authorised the automatic transferral of Aboriginal and Islander reserve land, and land in Aurukun and Mornington Island shires, along with other specified land, to trustees for the benefit of Aborigines and Islanders. In addition, groups of Aborigines and Islanders wishing to be granted certain 'claimable land' had to show a traditional or customary affiliation, an historical association, or the 'economic or cultural viability' of the land claimed, although this last criterion was not a sufficient ground for claiming certain lands. Claims would be made to a Land Tribunal, which had power only to make recommendations to the Minister. Only if the Minister agreed with the Tribunal's recommendation would a grant of land ultimately be made. Then, even if the Minister did grant land, the Crown's right to minerals was reserved, and minerals legislation remained in force over much Aboriginal and Islander land 'as if that land were not Aboriginal land' and 'as if that land were not Torres Strait Islander land'.[49]

All of these parliamentary initiatives represented limited and somewhat token attempts to recognise Aboriginal rights to land. Indeed, the inability of legislatures to articulate a broadly defined right of Aborigines to the land from which they were dispossessed will surely be looked upon as one of the less noble facets of Australian parliamentary democracy. This inability led to a unique period in Australian history, when the leadership on Aboriginal rights was taken over by the judiciary. Parliaments had been able to repeal their exclusionary regimes, but had been reluctant to do significantly more. Only with the *Mabo* High Court decision in 1992 would Aborigines be legally recognised to have certain rights not available to others.

The Judiciary Takes the Running

The development of the common law on land rights has been extremely slow in Australia when compared with developments in other countries like the United States and Canada.

Milirrpum v. Nabalco, or the Gove land rights case, was the first significant land rights case in Australia. Decided in 1971, the action was instigated against a mining company and the Commonwealth government by a group of Aborigines who claimed the possession and enjoyment of areas of Arnhem land in the Gove peninsula. Mineral leases had been granted over the area by the Commonwealth government to the mining company Nabalco. In the Supreme Court of the Northern Territory, Mr Justice Blackburn decided that the 'communal native title' claimed did not form part of the law in Australia. The judge found that although the Aboriginal claimants did make ritual and economic use of the areas claimed, and indeed had established a recognisable system of law, this did not give them any proprietary interest in the land. They did not have a legal right to the land.[50] The argument that there was such a thing as native title was a novel one in an Australian court, and that was reason enough for the judge to find that native title was not a concept recognised by Australian law.

In 1992, the *Mabo* land rights case was the most radical piece of judicial law-making in Australian history. Ten years earlier, the three Meriam plaintiffs – who lived on the Murray Islands (Mer, Dauar and Waier) in Torres Strait – brought an action against the Queensland and Commonwealth governments, claiming that the crown's sovereignty over the islands was subject to the land rights of the Meriam people based upon local custom and traditional native title. On 3 June 1992 six out of seven High Court judges decided that the Meriam people were entitled to the possession, occupation, use and enjoyment of the lands of the Murray Islands.[51]

The *Mabo* judgment was, and remains, immensely significant, but the qualifications that limit its generally applicability to other potential land claims need to be stressed. All of the judges who decided in favour of the Meriam people also decided that a valid exercise of sovereign power inconsistent with the right to enjoy native title would extinguish native title. In other words, the Queensland and Commonwealth governments had sovereignty over the Murray Islands, and they could, subject to other Acts of parliament, override the existence of native title.

This factor severely limited the effect of the case. Immediately after the case was decided, prominent politicians took part in an astonishing hysteria by saying that people's suburban properties were not safe from native title rights.[52] This was clearly nonsense. Native title existed, the High Court argued, only where there had not been any overriding governmental action. Native title continued to exist in the Murray Islands only because there had been no valid governmental action to extinguish it.

The legal reasoning concerning native title becomes somewhat more complex when consideration is given to the operation of the 1975 *Racial Discrimination Act* (Cwlth). In 1985, after the *Mabo* case had been initiated, the Queensland government ingloriously passed the *Queensland Coast Islands Declaratory Act*, which sought to railroad the litigation and override any native title that might exist on islands off the Queensland coast, including the Murray Islands. The High Court, however, decided that this Act was inconsistent with section 10 of the Commonwealth *Racial Discrimination Act*, in that it discriminated against Aborigines and Islanders in their enjoyment of property rights.[53] As a result of this finding, any governmental action that might have extinguished native title but that was done after the *Racial Discrimination Act* came into force, had the potential to be invalid on the basis that it was racially discriminatory. This was an uncertainty to which Commonwealth and State legislatures would soon apply Machiavellian manoeuvres, which we shall describe shortly.

The radical aspect of the High Court's *Mabo* decision was that it recognised native title as a legal interest. In making the decision the

High Court recognised that Aboriginal people had a legal relationship to the land before the arrival of Europeans. In all other Australian land rights decisions this had been rejected. But the case represented a window of opportunity only for people who could show a long-standing association with land that had never been the subject of valid governmental appropriation.

The High Court's recognition of native title led to debate about whether the court was overplaying its role as law-maker. Since Europeans first came to Australia, English and Australian courts had routinely refused to recognise native title as a legal interest in land. Then, in 1992, the High Court suddenly changed tack. This left the court open to the charge that it was merely responding to current sympathies and was not doing what it should, namely to interpret and apply the law. The High Court's most radical decision saw it subjected to sustained criticism.

One line of criticism levelled at the High Court was that the court was acting fundamentally undemocratically. This view was put by people like Hugh Morgan, the Chief Executive of Western Mining. He argued that the High Court had divided the country by reaching a 'major indeed revolutionary constitutional change without any deference to the role of Parliament or the authority of the people'.[54] His point was that for the High Court to say that the law now recognised native title, after effectively denying it for 100 years, was not an exercise in interpreting and applying the law. Rather, it was an exercise in creating the law, something which should be left to parliaments.

The contrary argument, supported by most members of the High Court, was that the law is a fluid, changing thing. The common law, the argument runs, is an evolutionary collection of principles that changes and develops to meet new situations and circumstances.

Some of the judges in *Mabo* reflected upon their freedom to overturn existing law. Justices Deane and Gaudron were the most transparent in their willingness to break with the past. They argued that:

> If this were any ordinary case, the Court would not be justified in reopening the validity of fundamental propositions which have been endorsed by long-established authority and which have been accepted as a basis of the real property law of the country for more than one hundred and fifty years.

Yet, they concluded, this was no ordinary case. The dispossession of Aborigines of most of their traditional lands constituted 'the darkest aspect of the history of this nation', and they argued that the 'nation as a whole must remain diminished unless and until there is an acknowledgment of, and retreat from, those past injustices'. Under these circumstances, Deane and Gaudron argued, the court was under a duty to re-examine the law.[55] Thus, for them, the extent of the wrong forced their reappraisal of the law.

Justice Brennan was the other majority judge to directly confront this issue. He argued that the High Court was 'not free to adopt rules that accord with contemporary notions of justice and human rights if their adoption would fracture the skeleton of principle which gives the body of our law its shape and internal consistency'. Nevertheless, he did find that Australian law

> can be modified to bring it into conformity with contemporary notions of justice and human rights . . . [and that] no case can command unquestioning adherence if the rule it expresses seriously offends the values of justice and human rights (especially equality before the law) which are aspirations of the contemporary Australian legal system.[56]

In some ways the particularity of the dispute over the law-making role of the High Court was rendered moot when legislation was passed in 1993 complementing the decision and setting out how native title claims were to proceed. But the criticism levelled at the High Court will surely be revisited should the court extend its reasoning to other areas of once-settled law, such as the question of who held sovereignty in Australia in 1788.

Parliamentary Responses

The next significant moment in the history of land rights came with the Keating government's legislative response, the *Native Title Act 1993* (Cwlth). Though legislation of this sort could theoretically have been passed at anytime, the Keating government used the *Mabo* decision as a reason for passing the Act. The *Mabo* decision, Prime Minister Keating argued, presented the nation with the opportunity to negotiate a new relationship between indigenous and other Australians. Keating adopted the words of some of the High Court judges, who said that Aboriginal people, after European settlement, had suffered 'a conflagration of oppression and conflict which was, over the following century, to spread across the continent to dispossess, degrade and devastate [them]'. To deny these basic facts, Keating argued, would be to deny history, 'and no self-respecting democracy can deny its history'.[57]

The *Native Title Act* set up the National Native Title Tribunal, which was given power only to make non-binding determinations. These determinations would then be lodged at the Federal Court and, subject to a review process, could ultimately take effect as orders of that court. The legislation also sought to validate some governmental actions that were considered in jeopardy following the High Court decision.[58] It was feared that governmental actions that seemed to extinguish native title may have been invalid on the basis that they contravened the constitutional requirement, contained in section 51(31), that just terms be paid for acquired property. Further, such purported extinguishment after 1975 potentially contravened the *Racial Discrimination Act.*

To get around these problems the Commonwealth legislated to provide an entitlement to 'just terms' where past Commonwealth actions contravened this constitutional requirement. Further, the Commonwealth legislation suspended the operation of the *Racial Discrimination Act* in its validation of past acts.[59] To be sure, this was the most controversial and least understood aspect of the Commonwealth legislation. The fear that generated this extraordinary exemption was that any governmental action after 1975 that purported to extinguish native title could have been invalid on the basis that it was racially discriminatory. The government justified the suspension of the discrimination legislation on the basis that it was part of an overall package that sought to secure the position of native title holders.[60]

The question of whether the legal recognition of land rights ought to be seen as a special measure to compensate for past injustices, or merely the long-delayed recognition of legal rights, was not answered with the passage of the *Native Title Act.* The Act's preamble, referred to by Keating in his second-reading speech, positioned the Act as 'a special measure for the advancement and protection of Aboriginal peoples and Torres Strait Islanders' under the International Convention on the Elimination of all Forms of Racial Discrimination and the *Racial Discrimination Act.*[61] It was unnecessary to position the Act in this way as an exercise of the foreign affairs power, a point reinforced by the High Court's subsequent decision that the Act was a valid exercise of the races power, section 51(26) of the Constitution. But it shows that the legislation may fairly be interpreted as a special measure, in the language of affirmative action, just as it may be seen simply as the overdue recognition of pre-existing indigenous rights.

At State level, meanwhile, parliaments were legislating to negotiate the uncertainty generated by the *Mabo* decision. The *Native Title Act* contained a provision that enabled States to validate past acts in certain ways that would also make them immune from the operation of the *Racial Discrimination Act.*[62] Victoria passed legislation in 1993 that sought to confirm titles to land granted after the *Racial Discrimination Act* came into force, and this legislation established a mechanism by which claims for compensation could be made where such a grant interfered with the enjoyment by Aborigines of 'customary title'. This legislation was, however, replaced a year later in order to bring Victoria's validation of past acts in line with the mechanisms for doing so set out in the Commonwealth legislation.[63]

Queensland legislated in 1993 and 1994 to complement the federal Act by establishing a Queensland Native Title Tribunal to determine native title and compensation applications, and this legislation simultaneously validated past State actions whose status was uncertain.[64] Similarly, New South Wales legislated in 1994 to validate past Acts and to establish a mechanism by which claims for native title determinations could be made. The Land and Environment Court, or a warden's court in the case of mining-related claims, were empowered to make determinations as to the existence of native title. Tasmania, the Northern Territory and the Australian Capital Territory also passed short Acts that complied with the Commonwealth's mechanism for validating past Acts. South Australia, meanwhile, chose to amend existing legislation, as well as pass a new *Native Title (South Australia) Act 1994*, in a response that was consistent with the Commonwealth legislation.[65]

Western Australia's *Land (Titles and Traditional Usage) Act 1993*, however, fundamentally challenged the Commonwealth legislation. Rather than seeking to validate past Acts in the manner set out in the Commonwealth legislation, the West Australian parliament sought to extinguish native title and replace it with certain statutory rights.[66] The legality of this course of action was challenged in the High Court, which applied its 1988 ruling in reasoning that the West Australian legislation was contrary to the Commonwealth's *Racial Discrimination Act*. Further, the Court held that the *Native Title Act 1993* (Cwlth) was a valid exercise of the Commonwealth's power in section 51(26) of the Constitution to make laws for the people of any race.[67] Western Australia subsequently enacted legislation that validated past State actions in a manner consistent with the federal legislation.[68]

Western Australia's attempt to go it alone put it at one extreme of the States' responses to the Commonwealth legislation. But the most that other States did was follow the Commonwealth's lead. The view of most State leaders was clearly that the Commonwealth should retain the lead in the field of Aboriginal affairs. Indeed, the responses of State parliaments to the *Mabo* decision and the Commonwealth legislation have been consistent with other State activities, or inactivities, in Aboriginal affairs since 1967. Such has been the extent of State government inactivity on Aboriginal affairs in recent decades that one could be forgiven for thinking that the 1967 referendum had stripped the States of their powers over Aboriginal affairs, rather than simply made these powers concurrent with the Commonwealth.

Perhaps unsurprisingly, given its recent development, the law regarding native title remains decidedly unclear. It took until October 1996 for the Dunghutti people of New South Wales to be party to the first mainland native title agreement to be resolved by the National Native Title Tribunal.[69] Aside from this, there have been few native title claims established as a result of the *Native Title Act* (Cwlth), and it remains to be seen whether the Act will yield any tangible benefits to Aboriginal people. Moreover, uncertainty still exists as to the manner in which native title is able to be extinguished. It is clear that grants of freehold interests in land nullify native title rights, but the granting of leases is more problematic. Grants of leasehold that provide rights of exclusive possession were considered in *Mabo* to extinguish native title. In 1995 the President of the National Native Title Tribunal held that native title was extinguished by the grant of a lease that did not contain any reservation in favour of indigenous people.[70] However, in December 1996 the High Court in the *Wik* case held that the granting of a pastoral lease did not necessarily extinguish a native title right over the same land.[71] This seemingly commonsense decision has sparked another bout of hysteria from conservative politicans, who have called on the federal government to limit the common law and statutory native title rights of indigenous Australians.

The recognition of native title, both judicial and legislative, finally and authoritatively undermines the historical fiction that Australia was a land belonging to no-one (*terra nullius*) when Europeans arrived. Further, we might now say that the recognition of Aborigines' relationship with the land goes some way towards an official acknowledgment that special provisions need to be made to enable Aborigines to take their place within the Australian polity. The judicial and legislative acknowledgment that native title is part of Australian law is evidence of a shift in the state's thinking which now accepts that justice requires more than for Aborigines to be treated as white citizens. The belated recognition that Aborigines possess certain indigenous rights is the significant development of the 1990s, and it remains to be seen how indigenous rights will be further recognised and developed.

One possible restriction to the further development of indigenous rights is their collective nature, which tends to make indigenous rights stand uneasily with western notions of individual rights. Native title is essentially a collective right that is not enforceable by individuals.

Australian developments in this field are very recent, and so far there has been little opposition to the concept of collective rights. But as Will Kymlicka argues, the notion of group rights or collective rights disturbs many people. What rights can a group possess that are not ultimately reducible to the rights of individuals? And how might collective rights interfere with individual rights?[72]

It remains to be seen how collective rights will impact upon other people's individual rights. It is unclear, for instance, what the High Court would decide should an Aboriginal member of a group in possession of native title take action against the group for some limited title to land. Presumably the Court would find for the group on the basis that the right to self-preservation, the foundational right given to groups capable of having rights, is premised upon the ability to possess land.[73] But such a view at present is purely speculative.

Self-determination

In the earlier chapters we noted two recurring themes in the administration of Aboriginal affairs: that exclusionary regimes have denied Aborigines the rights of citizenship, and that as a consequence administrators have been empowered to police the boundaries of citizenship. By their ability to enforce these regimes, administrators have exercised enormous power over Aborigines. While the removal of restrictive laws and the granting of new rights to land are important developments, clearly the next important step is for powers that could prejudice Aborigines in their exercise to be handed over to Aborigines.

This point was clearly made by Commissioner Elliott Johnston in his unprecedented report on Aboriginal deaths in custody in 1991. Johnston wound up the Royal Commission, which investigated ninety-nine deaths in custody and which examined many papers prepared specifically for it on social and historical contexts. The Commission made 339 recommendations in five voluminous reports, but Johnston commented that there was one central theme to his report:

> that substantial change in the situation of Aboriginal people in Australia will not occur unless government and non-Aboriginal society accept the necessity for Aboriginal people to be empowered to identify, effect and direct the changes which are required. The process of empowerment is at the same time the process of self-determination.[74]

At its logical extreme self-determination equates, probably, with nationhood, and only a few commentators have advocated the establishment of a separate Aboriginal nation or nations. The question then remains, if self-determination does not equate with absolute power and control, what does it mean? Johnston argued that confusion surrounded the meaning of 'self-determination' because the concept was an evolving one. He nevertheless isolated some factors common to most contemporary usages of the word as it related to Aborigines and Torres Strait Islanders: that Aboriginal people have control over the decision-making processes and over the ultimate decisions concerning a variety of matters, including political status and economic, social and cultural development; and that an economic base be provided with which Aborigines may control the future of their communities.[75]

The most concerted governmental attempt to put the principle of self-determination into practice has been the establishment of the Aboriginal and Torres Strait Islander Commission (ATSIC). In 1973 the Whitlam government had established the National Aboriginal Consultative Committee, which drew over 28,000 Aboriginal voters to its election in December 1973 and which was seen as something of a representative and powerful organisation, despite its purely advisory status.[76] But ATSIC, which began to function in 1990, represented the first occasion when Aborigines were given more than advisory power in the administration of Commonwealth programs designed to benefit them.[77]

ATSIC has existed as something of an amalgam body, being at once the peak elected Aboriginal representative body, and yet existing virtually as a parliamentary department, responsible to parliament for the expenditure of vast amounts of money. This dual role has beleaguered ATSIC since its formation. It has existed as the first democratically elected national representative body for Aborigines, and yet has operated to shield government from criticism by Aborigines by simultaneously being partly responsible for the administration of Aboriginal affairs finances. Most of ATSIC's budget has been devoted to two programs. Community Development Employment Projects, which account for around a quarter of Aboriginal employment, involve Aboriginal workers giving ATSIC control of their unemployment benefits while ATSIC then funds their communities to pay wages for work on community projects. The other major ATSIC program, Community Housing and Infrastructure, provides housing, water supplies, roads and sewerage to under-resourced communities.[78]

The competing nature of ATSIC's responsibilities is reflected in the manner in which ATSIC Commissioners have been appointed. The principles of self-determination and representative democracy have been reflected in the requirements that Regional Councils be elected by Aborigines and Torres Strait Islanders. These Councils, grouped into zones, then elect Commissioners to represent them. At the same time, however, the principle of ministerial responsibility justified the requirements that the ATSIC Chairperson and two of the other nineteen Commissioners, as well as the Chief Executive Officer, be appointed by the Minister for Aboriginal Affairs. Further, ATSIC's accounting responsibilities have identified it more clearly as a government department than an instrument of Aboriginal representative democracy.[79]

These limitations and contradictions were highlighted in 1991 by Johnston in the Royal Commission into Aboriginal deaths in custody. He saw a number of key limitations confronting ATSIC. First, ATSIC was only one of the bodies responsible for administering large budgets for the benefit of Aborigines. Other government departments not committed to the principle of self-determination were responsible for spending large budgets on Aboriginal affairs, thus limiting the capacity with which ATSIC could operate as an instrument of self-determination. Second, Johnston pointed out that ATSIC staff were Commonwealth public servants who were responsible to the Chief Executive Officer, who in turn was appointed by the Minister. While most of the Commissioners were elected, their staff were ultimately responsible to the Minister for Aboriginal Affairs, whose priorities could be different to those of the Commissioners. Johnston recommended that consideration be given to ATSIC employing staff outside the public service.

For Johnston, an important part of the establishment of ATSIC would be the role played by Regional Councils. While in theory Regional Councillors would have the power to formulate their own plans and assist and advise federal, state and local government bodies on their implementation, the early indications were that Regional Councillors would not have much input into the economic programs to be administered by ATSIC. Regional Councils were responsible for drawing up annual budgets, but these had to be approved by ATSIC.[80]

A 1993 amendment to the ATSIC Act stressed the government's desire for ATSIC to be an instrument of self-determination, with a preamble inserted according to which the objective of overcoming the disadvantages suffered by indigenous Australians was to be furthered 'in a manner that is consistent with the aims of self-management and self-sufficiency for Aboriginal persons and Torres Strait Islanders'.[81] The establishment in 1995 of the Indigenous Land Corporation and the Aboriginal and Torres Strait Islander Land Fund gave some substance to the promise that increased autonomy would be made possible for Aborigines and Islanders.[82]

Further, the goal of self-determination has been notably advanced for Torres Strait Islanders by the creation of the Torres Strait Regional Authority, which exists within the ATSIC structure. The Authority took over from ATSIC staff in the middle of 1994 and elections for it are held in line with local government elections in Queensland. While there is no talk at present of the Authority taking over the place of all other government authorities operating in Torres Strait, it has sought greater devolution to it of funding administered by the Queensland and Commonwealth governments. The establishment of the Authority is viewed as one step on the way to greater regional autonomy. One possibility is that the Authority or some successor body would move outside the ATSIC structure and adopt a residential constituency rather than representing the interests only of Aborigines and Islanders. This could result in greater regional autonomy and power being devolved over a wider range of government services.[83]

Things do not look so positive for mainland Aborigines. One significant problem caused by the creation of a special Aboriginal body like ATSIC is that other vital service providers, such as State governments, have been given an excuse to give less priority to Aboriginal affairs. According to Lois O'Donoghue, a former Chairperson of ATSIC, this is the great current issue in indigenous affairs: 'the lack of accountability of State and Territory governments to their indigenous citizens'. The problem with having special funds made available for Aborigines is that direct government responsibility for basic services, such as education, housing and health services, is allowed to disappear. In this way ATSIC provides a convenient excuse for State governments to retreat. With ATSIC overseeing the application of funds to provide basic services to Aboriginal communities, State governments become once-removed from an obligation to provide disadvantaged Aboriginal communities with the basic services they would be obliged to provide for non-Aboriginal citizens.[84]

This is one of the costs of the principle of self-determination, that it provides a ready excuse for governments wishing to curtail their spending on Aborigines. The other significant cost is the perceived threat that self-determination presents to the principle of ministerial (fiscal) responsibility. The defeat of the Keating government in 1996 led to some heated and often patronising discussion about the future of ATSIC, some commentators revealing a deep distrust of the ability of Aborigines to handle money. Anecdotes concerning rorting by ATSIC-funded groups have been used to support broader arguments about ATSIC's structure being inappropriate for the management of public funds. At the same time as addressing and investigating instances of rorting, ATSIC leaders have responded to this line of argument by asking why similar outrage has not visited other, more costly, instances of mismanagement of public funds.[85]

More recent governmental concerns about ATSIC sank to new depths when the government expressed the view that an elected ATSIC Chairperson, as opposed to one chosen by the government, might embarrass the nation when dealing with foreign dignitaries.[86] The expression of this view was followed by an enormous cut to ATSIC's budget in 1996, which has made its long-term future uncertain.

ATSIC's future was cast further into doubt when Pauline Hanson, an independent member of the House of Representatives, called for its abolition in her first speech to parliament. Hanson placed this call in the context of her views regarding 'the privileges Aboriginals enjoy over other Australians'.[87] The Howard government's refusal to reject outright Hanson's views led to the staging of a degenerative race debate that was only somewhat quelled by an all-party parliamentary motion which, among other things, reaffirmed the country's commitment to the process of reconciliation with Aboriginal and Islander people.[88] If these unedifying developments have revealed anything, it is that ministerial responsibility seems destined to prevail over self-determination in the administration of Aboriginal affairs.

Towards the Future

Possibilities for the future enhancement of Aboriginal citizenship and indigenous rights rest in three key areas: the development of the common law on indigenous rights; the possibility of a negotiated treaty; and constitutional reform.

Common Law

The common law in relation to land rights will inevitably develop further, as claimants test the boundaries to native title rights. In addition, further common law developments may force a reassessment of the decision on sovereignty that Paul Coe received from the High Court in 1979. Coe attempted to challenge the British Crown's, and therefore the Commonwealth's, claim to sovereignty over Australia. His action failed on something of a legal technicality, but the majority judges nonetheless found that the legality of the annexation of the east coast of Australia in 1770, and the subsequent adoption of the whole of Australia as a dominion of the British crown, was beyond question. Chief Justice Gibbs outlined Coe's argument:

> it is intended to claim that there is an aboriginal nation which has sovereignty over its own people, notwithstanding that they remain citizens of the Commonwealth; in other words, it is sought to treat the aboriginal people of Australia as a domestic dependent nation, to use the expression which Marshall CJ applied [in 1831] to the Cherokee Nation of Indians.

But the Marshall judgment was not applicable in Australia, according to Gibbs, because Aborigines did not, unlike the Cherokee Nation, form a distinct political society separated from others. Aborigines, he continued, 'have no legislative, executive or judicial organs by which sovereignty might be exercised ... The contention that there is in

Australia an aboriginal nation exercising sovereignty, even of a limited kind, is quite impossible in law to maintain.' Justice Jacobs took a different tack, and argued that the British Crown's, and then the Commonwealth's, claims to sovereignty were not able to be challenged in a court exercising jurisdiction under that sovereignty. Justice Murphy, on the other hand, foreshadowed the *Mabo* judgment by finding that Coe was entitled to argue that the sovereignty acquired by the British Crown did not extinguish Aboriginal 'ownership rights', and that he was entitled to argue that Aborigines retained certain proprietary rights.[89]

The judges in *Mabo* gave no encouragement that the principles stated in *Coe* would in future be overturned. None of the judges argued that the crown's sovereignty over Australia could be challenged in a domestic court. As Chief Justice Mason, in a more recent case, said:

> *Mabo* . . . is entirely at odds with the notion that sovereignty adverse to the Crown resides in the Aboriginal people of Australia. The decision is equally at odds with the notion that there resides in the Aboriginal people a limited kind of sovereignty embraced in the notion that they are 'a domestic dependent nation'.[90]

However, Frank Brennan points to the possibility that the notion of sovereignty itself might be developed further so that some limited kind of sovereignty might be seen to exist in Aboriginal communities. This developing notion of sovereignty has begun to see sovereignty defined as something which 'derives from the people' rather than as something claimed by nations.[91]

Given that the *Mabo* decision has radically altered the once-settled principle that Aborigines did not have legal interests in the land prior to the arrival of Europeans, it is likely in the long-term future that some qualification will be built onto the rigid stance taken by the High Court on the question of sovereignty. While the High Court has given no support as yet to such a change, neither was there support for the recognition of native title until the *Mabo* decision. Indeed, common sense dictates that as the High Court has now recognised that Aborigines had land rights before 1788, surely it must also recognise that Aborigines exercised sovereignty at this time. As Henry Reynolds has recently argued, the High Court in *Mabo* released one pinioned arm of Australian law by acknowledging that Aborigines had rights to land before the arrival of Europeans. And while the other pinioned arm, representing sovereignty, seems as firmly secured as ever, 'in the long run the situation will prove unstable'.[92]

Aside from these possible common law developments, there are two essentially constitutional issues that may also cause further attention to be given to Aboriginal citizenship and indigenous rights. These possibilities are that a treaty may be signed to give the process of reconciliation between black and white Australia some surer footing, and that the Constitution may be amended to cater better for the rights of Aborigines.

Treaty

From the late 1970s the calls for a treaty have gained mixed support. Various politicians, most notably Prime Minister Bob Hawke, have lent their support to the idea of a treaty. But the difficulties of Aboriginal views being fairly represented in a treaty so long after their dispossession, not to mention the existence of a strong lobby group that fears that a treaty may lead to new rights for Aborigines, have so far conspired to defeat the idea.[93] The prime argument in support of a treaty is that it would, in a more negotiated and dignified way than the *Mabo* decision, overturn the legacy of years of state-endorsed dispossession. In the words of Galarrwuy Yunupingu, Chairman of the Northern Land Council, a treaty 'will wipe out injustice and redress the wrongs of today, which can be traced to the wrongs of the past'. Others have claimed that a treaty would recognise the sovereign status of Aborigines.[94] Suggestions for the form a treaty would take have ranged from the simple signing of a compact of understanding, to the use of section 105A of the Constitution to adopt a formal treaty.[95] Governmental support for a treaty was at its strongest in 1988 when Prime Minister Bob Hawke endorsed the idea in front of 10,000 Aborigines at the Barunga festival. At the same time, Hawke was presented with the Barunga Statement, a list of Aboriginal claims that sought, among other things, the negotiation of a treaty 'recognising our prior ownership, continued occupation and sovereignty and affirming our human rights and freedoms'.[96]

Opposition to a treaty have come from a variety of corners. Some Aborigines have raised concerns about the benefits to be achieved by an agreement between Aborigines and the federal government, parties of such unequal bargaining powers. Another concern has been that a treaty might simply serve to legitimise Aboriginal dispossession.[97] Interestingly, some prominent white commentators have opposed the signing of a treaty on the basis that the status of Aborigines as Australian citizens would be challenged.

In 1988 Opposition Leader John Howard, later to become Prime Minister, wrote that 'It is an absurd proposition that a nation should make a treaty with some of its own citizens. It also denies the fact that Aboriginal people have full citizenship rights now.' Hugh Morgan, meanwhile, has argued that 'A treaty with the Aboriginal people will immediately put Aborigines, however defined, outside the orbit of Australian citizenship, and the issue of passports, and all other appurtenances of citizenship will one by one be brought into question.'[98] The irony of someone in Morgan's position being concerned about the citizenship status of Aborigines would be lost on no-one, but his and Howard's position is that indigenous rights are not consistent with citizenship rights.[99] The possibility that the status of Aborigines as citizens might preclude the recognition, by a treaty, of their indigenous rights would be a cruel irony. But this is just one view. Another view is that citizenship is merely a stepping stone to the recognition of indigenous rights, rather than a reason for their denial.

One of the tasks of the Council for Aboriginal Reconciliation, which was established in 1991 to 'promote a process of reconciliation' between Aborigines and Islanders and the wider Australian community, is to consult these groups to establish whether reconciliation would be advanced by a formal document or documents of reconciliation.[100] Their determination is awaited.

Constitutional Change

If the Constitution, as we argued in chapter 3, was not responsible for denying citizenship to Aborigines, is it the wrong place to turn to now in seeking to further enhance Aboriginal citizenship?

One response to this is to argue that the current constitutional position of Aborigines is analogous to the process by which Aborigines gained formal citizenship. Just as the restrictive legislative and administrative regimes were removed, so the Constitution's references to Aborigines were simply removed. There is no positive mention of Aborigines in the Constitution, an absence that has motivated some people to look for alternatives.

Two propositions for constitutional change are currently gathering momentum. One is that a new preamble to the Constitution be adopted that would operate as a formal acknowledgment of Aboriginal dispossession. One suggestion put forward by ATSIC is as follows:

> Whereas the territory of Australia has long been occupied by Aboriginal peoples and Torres Strait Islanders whose ancestors inhabited Australia and maintained traditional titles to the land for thousands of years before British settlement;
> And whereas many Aboriginal peoples and Torres Strait Islanders suffered dispossession and dispersal upon exclusion from their traditional lands by the authority of the Crown;

> And whereas Aboriginal peoples and Torres Strait Islanders, whose traditional laws, customs and ways of life have evolved over thousands of years, have a distinct cultural status as indigenous peoples . . . [101]

A new preamble would operate to set the historical record straight about Aboriginal dispossession, and might even serve in some capacity as an official apology for this dispossession. Few attempts have ever been made by representatives of the Australian state to apologise to Aborigines for past injustices, and most of these attempts have occurred only in recent years. In 1975 the Senate adopted a motion of Senator Neville Bonner, the first Aboriginal Senator, officially recognising that 'the indigenous people of Australia, now known as Aborigines and Torres Strait Islanders, were in possession of this entire nation prior to the 1788 First Fleet landing at Botany Bay'. That this seemingly simple statement of fact took Bonner months of negotiation before its adoption shows how unlikely it was that there would be any accompanying motion expressing regret or apology.[102] Thirteen years later, both houses of federal parliament passed a resolution that acknowledged Aboriginal occupation of Australia prior to 1788 and that supported the process of reconciliation. This resolution added to the mythology surrounding the 1967 referendum by affirming that 'Aborigines and Torres Strait Islanders were denied full citizenship rights of the Commonwealth of Australia prior to the 1967 Referendum'.[103] Then, in 1992, Prime Minister Keating made a significant symbolic apology in Australia's launch of the International Year of the World's Indigenous People. In a rare Prime Ministerial display, Keating acknowledged that:

> We took the traditional lands and smashed the traditional way of life.
> We brought the diseases, the alcohol.
> We committed the murders.
> We took the children from their mothers.
> We practised discrimination and exclusion.
> It was our ignorance and our prejudice.[104]

Aside from this, the closest thing there has been to a state-endorsed apology for Aboriginal dispossession has been the preamble to the *Council for Aboriginal Reconciliation Act 1991* (Cwlth), which acknowledged that Aborigines and Islanders inhabited Australia before British settlement and that many indigenous people were dispossessed of their lands. A comparable act of symbolism came in the preamble to the *Native Title Act 1993* (Cwlth), which went further by adding that the dispossession suffered by Aborigines and Islanders had occurred largely without compensation and that, as a group, Aborigines and Islanders were 'the most disadvantaged in Australian society'. A similar preamble was added to the ATSIC Act in 1993.[105]

Another symbolic concession to historical reality has been the establishment in 1995 of the National Inquiry into the Separation of Aboriginal and Torres Strait Islander Children from their Families. It has been the task of this inquiry, led by former High Court Judge Sir Ronald Wilson, to investigate the fate of the stolen generations of Aboriginal children who were taken from their parents.

A new constitutional preamble, while of limited legal significance, would draw these symbolic acts together and give them prominence in the nation's most important document.

A more substantive proposal for constitutional reform is the adoption of a bill of rights. A bill of rights could consist of a small number of new sections in the Constitution that set out the rights and duties of citizenship. As we discussed in chapter 3, the only real citizenship clause contained in the Australian Constitution is section 117. This says that 'A subject of the Queen, resident in any State, shall not be subject in any other State to any disability or discrimination which would not be equally applicable to him if he were a subject of the Queen resident in such other State'. This clause has not provided any substantive protection against discrimination, largely because States have rarely discriminated against individuals on the basis of their residency in other States.

As with a treaty, the concept of a constitutional bill of rights has received mixed support over the years, and any discussion of it must countenance the difficulty that would be faced in having it approved in referendum. Should a constitutional bill of rights ever be adopted by Australia, the rights therein could not be so easily suspended as have those contained in racial discrimination legislation.

The political rights of Aborigines have received far greater attention and enhancement over the past thirty years than in any previous period. The prohibition on racial discrimination, the legal recognition of indigenous rights – particularly native title to land – and moves towards self-determination have given a currency and meaning to the phrase 'indigenous rights' that was unthinkable and unpalatable to all Australian governments in the early 1960s. But these victories at present have been more theoretical than practical: successful native title claims remain a remote possibility for the vast majority of mainland Aborigines, and the limited moves that have been made towards self-determination have now been placed in jeopardy by a Commonwealth government that places a higher priority on maintaining direct responsibility for moneys spent on Aboriginal affairs. Thus the slow recognition of indigenous rights has not translated into material improvements in the life situations of most Aborigines.

As we approach the new millennium it is decidedly unclear whether Aboriginal rights will be further expanded. The continued evolution of the common law regarding indigenous rights, the viability of native title legislation, the possibility of constitutional change, and the future of self-determination (and in particular the Aboriginal and Torres Strait Islander Commission) will all be decided in the short-term future. It has been said that relations between Aboriginal and non-Aboriginal Australians will be the thing most remembered about Australian history in the centuries to come. It remains to be seen whether Australia's shameful treatment of Aborigines will enter its fourth century and second millennium.

Notes

Introduction

1 T.H. Marshall, 'Citizenship and Social Class' [1950], in T.H. Marshall and Tom Bottomore, *Citizenship and Social Class*, 1992, pp. 8, 10.
2 See, for example, Tim Rowse, 'Diversity in Indigenous Citizenship', *Communal/Plural*, vol. 2, 1993, pp. 47–63; Terry Widders and Greg Noble, 'On the Dreaming Track to the Republic: Indigenous People and the Ambivalence of Citizenship', *Communal/Plural*, vol. 2, 1993, pp. 95–112; Jeremy Beckett, 'Aboriginality, Citizenship and Nation State', *Social Analysis*, No. 24, 1988, pp. 3–18.
3 For recent developments in the study of citizenship see Will Kymlicka and Wayne Norman, 'Return of the Citizen: A Survey of Recent Work on Citizenship Theory', *Ethics*, vol. 104, 1994, pp. 352–381. See also the following publications of Bryan S. Turner: *Citizenship and Capitalism: The Debate over Reformism*, 1986; 'Outline of a Theory of Citizenship', *Sociology*, vol. 24, 1990, pp. 189–217; 'Rights and Communities: Prolegomenon to a Sociology of Rights', *Australian and New Zealand Journal of Sociology*, vol. 31, 1995, pp. 1–8.
4 Faith Bandler, *Turning the Tide: A Personal History of the Federal Council for the Advancement of Aborigines and Torres Strait Islanders*, 1989; Roberta B. Sykes, *Black Majority*, 1989; Kevin J. Gilbert, *Because a White Man'll Never Do It*, 1973; Charles Perkins, *A Bastard Like Me*, 1975.
5 Sally Morgan, *My Place*, 1987; Margaret Tucker, *If Everyone Cared: Autobiography of Margaret Tucker M.B.E.*, 1977; Ruby Langford, *Don't Take Your Love to Town*, 1988; Ruby Langford Ginibi, *Real Deadly*, 1992; Wayne King, *Black Hours*, 1996.
6 For written contributions see Jackie Huggins, 'Response', in Susan Janson and Stuart Macintyre (eds), *Through White Eyes*, 1990; Jackie Huggins and Thom Blake, 'Protection or Persecution? Gender Relations in the Era of Racial Segregation', in Kay Saunders and Raymond Evans (eds), *Gender Relations in Australia: Domination and Negotiation*, 1992; Maykutenner (Vicki Matson-Green), 'Tasmania: 2', in Ann McGrath (ed.), *Contested Ground: Australian Aborigines under the British Crown*, 1995.
7 *Commonwealth Parliamentary Debates*, Senate, vol. 9, 10 April 1902, pp. 11584–6.

1 The Citizenship Divide in Colonial Victoria

1 Statement of the Board for the Protection of the Aborigines (hereafter the Board), 7 May 1884, VPRS 10265, Unit 266, Victorian Public Record Office (hereafter VPRO).

2 See Brian Galligan, *A Federal Republic: Australia's Constitutional System of Government*, 1995.

3 Throughout this chapter we use the term 'Aborigines' rather than 'Kooris' to refer to the Aboriginal inhabitants of Victoria. We do this on the understanding that 'Koori' has only been used in this broad context over the last thirty or so years. Our discussions and research have found that the present convention is that 'Koori' is used to refer to Victorian Aborigines only when discussing the period from the 1960s onwards. See Richard Broome, 'Why Use Koori?', *La Trobe Library Journal*, vol. 11, 1989, p. 5; Broome, 'Victoria', in Ann McGrath (ed.), *Contested Ground: Australian Aborigines under the British Crown*, 1995, p. 155.

4 C.D. Rowley, *Outcasts in White Australia*, 1972, p. 5; P. Marcard, 'Early Victoria and the Aborigines', *Melbourne Historical Journal*, vol. 4, 1964, p. 23; R.L. Wettenhall, 'Administrative Boards in Nineteenth Century Australia', *Public Administration*, vol. 22, 1963, p. 259; Henry Reynolds, *Aborigines and Settlers: The Australian Experience 1788–1939*, 1972, p. 160.

5 N.G. Butlin, *Our Original Aggression: Aboriginal Populations of Southeastern Australia 1788–1850*, 1983, p. 144. Diane Barwick, 'Changes in the Aboriginal Population of Victoria, 1863-1966', in D.J. Mulvaney and J. Golson (eds), *Aboriginal Man and Environment in Australia*, 1971, p. 288.

6 'Report of the Select Committee of the Legislative Council on the Aborigines', *Votes and Proceedings of the Legislative Council*, 1858–9, p. iii.

7 'Third Report of the Central Board Appointed to Watch over the Interests of the Aborigines in the Colony of Victoria', *Victorian Parliamentary Papers* (hereafter *VPP*), Legislative Assembly (all references to the *VPP* from hereon give the volume numbers relevant to the papers presented to the Legislative Assembly), 1864, vol. 3, p. 13; 'Royal Commission on the Aborigines', *VPP*, 1877–8, vol. 3, p. vii; *Victorian Year-Book, 1902*, 1903, p. 30. The official number of Aborigines in 1911, including both those of 'pure blood' and 'half-castes', was 643: *Victorian Year-Book, 1915–16*, 1916, p. 239.

8 The speaker is Mr J.M. Fowler (Perth), *Commonwealth Parliamentary Debates* (hereafter *CPD*), Representatives, vol. 9, 24 April 1902, p. 11979.

9 *CPD*, Senate, vol. 10, 29 May 1902, p. 13002. See also the comments of Senator Barrett (Victoria) at p. 13004.

10 *An Act to Establish a Constitution in and for the Colony of Victoria 1855* (Vic); *Adult Suffrage Act 1908* (Vic).

11 The 1855 Constitution had a limited property qualification that would have prevented anyone in receipt of charitable relief from voting. From 1865 the exclusion was made explicit: *An Act to Establish a Constitution in and for the Colony of Victoria 1855* (Vic), section 12; *Electoral Act 1865* (Vic), section 20; *Constitution Act Amendment Act 1890* (Vic), section 142; *Electoral Act 1910* (Vic), section 13(a).

12 Diane Barwick, A Little More than Kin: Regional Affiliation and Group Identity among Aboriginal Migrants in Melbourne, PhD Thesis, Australian National University 1963, p. 183. Unfortunately, there are no detailed studies of this area.

13 *Victorian Parliamentary Debates* (hereafter *VPD*), Assembly, vol. 78, 22 October 1895, p. 2712.

14 *CPD*, Representatives, vol. 9, 24 April 1902, p. 11978.

15 We searched the Victorian electoral roll prepared prior to the 1899 Federal Referendum to see whether any of 60 Aboriginal men were enrolled. Many of the men on our list were 'half-caste' and, given the policy implemented after 1886, would not have been in receipt of charitable aid. Therefore, they were eligible to be enrolled. We found that 34 of the names did not appear on the roll, and that 26 names did. But of the 26, only two of the names were likely to refer to Aboriginal men on our list (the other 24 were most likely, given their occupations and places of residence, to have been other Victorians with the same names as the Aborigines on our list). It is worth noting the difficulty inherent in this research. The most well-known Aborigines of the time, and the ones whose names appear in extant documentation, generally resided on stations. They were, therefore, among the Aborigines who were most unlikely to be enrolled.

16 *Compulsory Voting (Assembly Elections) Act 1926* (Vic), section 3.
17 *Commonwealth Franchise Act 1902*, section 4. Pat Stretton and Christine Finnimore, 'Black Fellow Citizens: Aborigines and the Commonwealth Franchise', *Australian Historical Studies*, vol. 25, 1993.
18 The estimation was that 100 'aboriginal natives of Australia, Asia, Africa and Islands of the Pacific' had enrolled in Victoria by virtue of section 41: memorandum provided at the request of the Chief Electoral Officer, 3 April 1922, A406/62, item E1945/1, part 1, Australian Archives (hereafter AA), Canberra.
19 For information regarding the governance of Victorian Aborigines prior to 1860, see: Philip Felton, 'Victoria: Lands Reserved for the Benefit of Aborigines 1835–1971', in Nicolas Peterson (ed.), *Aboriginal Land Rights: A Handbook*, 1981, pp. 169–73; Rowley, *Outcasts in White Australia*, p. 85; Peter Corris, *Aborigines and Europeans in Western Victoria*, 1968; M.F. Christie, *Aborigines in Colonial Victoria 1835–86*, 1979; Barwick, 'Changes in the Aboriginal Population', pp. 288–9; Broome, 'Victoria'; Edmund J.B. Foxcroft, *Australian Native Policy: Its History especially in Victoria*, 1941.
20 Kathryn Cronin, *Colonial Casualties: Chinese in Early Victoria*, 1982, p. 82; *Wines Beer and Spirit Sale Statute 1864* (Vic), section 51.
21 'Report of the Select Committee of the Legislative Council on the Aborigines', p. v.
22 Charles McLean, 'Report upon the Operation of the Aborigines Act 1928 and the Regulations and Orders made Thereunder', *VPP*, 1956–58, vol. 2, p. 4.
23 'First Report of the Central Board', *VPP*, 1861–62, vol. 3, p. 11.
24 *An Act to Provide for the Protection and Management of the Aboriginal Natives of Victoria 1869* (Vic), sections 2, 3, 8.
25 McLean, 'Report upon the Operation of the Aborigines Act', p. 4. In 1895 two out of the eight Board members were members of parliament: 'Thirty-first Report of the Board', *VPP*, 1895–96, vol. 4, p. 2. In 1910, four of the nine members were parliamentarians: 'Forty-sixth Report of the Board', *VPP*, 1910, vol. 2, p. 2. For comments on the composition of the Board in its early years, see Marcard, 'Early Victoria and the Aborigines', pp. 25–8.
26 On the importance of the Secretary to the Board's decision-making, see Myrna Deverall, 'Records of the Administration of Aborigines in Victoria, c. 1860–1968', *Aboriginal History*, vol. 2, 1978, p. 110.
27 McLean, 'Report upon the Operation of the Aborigines Act', p. 4; 'Royal Commission on the Aborigines', pp. vii–xi. For material written about Aboriginal stations in Victoria, in addition to the material contained in note 19, see: Diane Barwick, 'Coranderrk and Cumeroogunga: Pioneers and Policy', in T. Scarlett Epstein and David H. Penny (eds), *Opportunity and Response: Case Studies in Economic Development*, 1972; Jan Critchett, A History of Framlingham and Lake Condah Aboriginal Stations, 1860–1918, MA thesis, Melbourne University 1980; Critchett, *Our Land Till We Die: A History of the Framlingham Aborigines*, 1980; Keith Cole, *The Lake Condah Aboriginal Mission*, 1984; Cole, *The Aborigines of Victoria*, 1982; Marcard, 'Early Victoria and the Aborigines'; Aldo Massola, *Aboriginal Mission Stations in Victoria: Yelta, Ebenezer, Ramahyuck, Lake Condah*, 1970.
28 *Victorian Government Gazette*, 1878, p. 1163.
29 'Regulations and Orders Made Under the Act to Provide for the Protection and Management of the Aboriginal Natives of Victoria', *Victorian Government Gazette*, 1871, pp. 338–9.
30 *Victorian Government Gazette*, 1880, p. 1912, regulation 2. See also M.F. Christie, 'Aboriginal Literacy and Power: An Historical Case Study', *Australian Journal of Adult and Community Education*, vol. 30, 1990, pp. 117–21.
31 *Aborigines Protection Act 1886* (Vic). The term quoted is used in a letter from the Vice-Chairman of the Board to the Chief Secretary, 14 July 1891, B329/2, item 5, AA, Melbourne.
32 *Aborigines Protection Act 1886* (Vic), sections 4, 6, 8.
33 *VPD*, Assembly, vol. 53, 15 December 1886, pp. 2912–13.
34 *An Act to Provide for the Protection and Management of the Aboriginal Natives of Victoria* 1869 (Vic), section 8. See also *VPD*, Assembly, vol. 53, 15 December 1886, p. 2913.

35 Letter from Captain Page to the Chief Secretary of Victoria, 8 June 1881, B329/2, item 3, AA, Melbourne.
36 Christie, *Aborigines in Colonial Victoria*, p. 194. The policy was formally reaffirmed in March 1884: *Argus*, 6 March 1884, p. 9; 'Twentieth Report of the Board', *VPP*, 1884, vol. 4, p. 4.
37 'Royal Commission on the Aborigines', p. xii; 'Seventeenth Report of the Board', *VPP*, 1881, vol. 3, p. 4. See also: Christie, *Aborigines in Colonial Victoria*, pp. 192–7; Bain Attwood, *The Making of the Aborigines*, 1989, chapter 4; Critchett, 'A History of Framlingham', pp. 128, 132–5; Barwick, 'Coranderrk and Cumeroogunga', pp. 35–7; Patricia Marcard, 'The Aborigines in Victoria, 1858 to 1884: Attitudes and Policies', BA(Hons) Thesis, Melbourne University 1963, pp. 56–64.
38 Statement of the Board, 7 May 1884, VPRS 10265, Unit 266, VPRO (their emphasis).
39 *Age*, 11 January 1888, quoted in Andrew Markus, *From the Barrel of a Gun. The Oppression of the Aborigines, 1860–1900*, 1974, pp. 65–6.
40 See Attwood, *The Making of the Aborigines*, pp. 96–7.
41 Christie, *Aborigines in Colonial Victoria*, pp. 182–95. The report following the Coranderrk inquiry is contained in *VPP*, 1882–83, vol. 2.
42 *Argus*, 28 May 1884, p. 5.
43 Christie, *Aborigines in Colonial Victoria*; Corris, *Aborigines and Europeans in Western Victoria*; Critchett, *Our Land Till We Die*; Critchett, 'A History of Framlingham'; Barwick, 'Equity for Aborigines? The Framlingham Case', in Patrick N. Troy (ed.), *A Just Society? Essays on Equity in Australia*, 1981, pp. 180–90; Linda Wilkinson, 'Fractured Families, Squatting and Poverty: the Impact of the 1886 "Half-Caste" Act on the Framlingham Aboriginal Community', in Ian Duncanson and Diane Kirkby (eds), *Law and History in Australia. Vol. II*, 1986; Phillip Pepper and Tess De Araugo, *The Kurnai of Gippsland. What did Happen to the Aborigines of Victoria*, 1985, pp. 207–12; Attwood, *The Making of the Aborigines*, chapter 4 (the remark appears at p. 101). For Attwood's general comments on the Act's implementation see pp. 55–6, 100–3, 121. For other general comments on the Act's implementation see: Barwick, 'A Little More Than Kin'; Barwick, 'Changes in the Aboriginal Population of Victoria'; Barwick, 'Coranderrk and Cumeroogunga'; Broome, 'Victoria', pp. 139–41.
44 Statement of the Board, 7 May 1884, VPRS 10265, Unit 266, VPRO. This document also appears in: the Board's minutes of meeting, 13 May 1884, B314, item 3, AA, Melbourne; and in the 'Twentieth Report of the Board', *VPP*, 1884, vol. 4, pp. 4–5.
45 'Twenty-third Report of the Board', *VPP*, 1887, vol. 2, pp. 3–4; minutes of Board meeting, 3 March 1887, B314, item 4, AA, Melbourne; *Argus*, 5 March 1887, p. 5.
46 The admission came in an undated memorandum entitled 'Aboriginals Bill', which contains the Board's clause-by-clause description of the 1886 bill: VPRS 10265, unit 266, VPRO.
47 Letter from Page to Mr Wilson, 19 May 1884, VPRS 10265, unit 266, VPRO.
48 Letter from J. Bulmer to Hagenauer, 30 January 1889; letter from the Chief Secretary's Office to Hagenauer, 19 June 1890: VPRS 1694, unit 1, VPRO. Wilkinson also discusses this case in 'Fractured Families', pp. 15–16.
49 Minutes of Board meeting, 13 October 1897, B314, item 5, AA, Melbourne. Jan Critchett and Linda Wilkinson both discuss the Rawlings family: Critchett, *Our Land Till We Die*, p. 58; Wilkinson, 'Fractured Families', pp. 15–19.
50 *Age*, 6 February 1888, p. 6.
51 For example, the Board decided to send one such circular letter at its meeting on 3 September 1890: B314, item 4, AA, Melbourne.
52 Letter from Hagenauer to the Chief Secretary, 8 September 1892, VPRS 1694, unit 1, VPRO. The opinion of the Crown Solicitor is recorded in the minutes of Board meeting, 5 October 1892, B314, item 4, AA, Melbourne.
53 For the request that the Act be posted at police stations: memo from Page, 4 April 1887, B329/2, item 4, AA, Melbourne. For examples of letters seeking the removal of people from stations and reserves: see letters from Hagenauer to various police: 15 July 1890, 28 August 1890 and 22 June 1892, B329/2, item 5, AA, Melbourne.

54 Examples of the Board refusing requests for rations appear in the Board's minutes of meetings, 6 June 1894 and 6 March 1895, B314, item 4, AA, Melbourne.
55 The quote is from a letter written for the General Inspector to Rev. Bogisch, 4 December 1889, B329/2, item 5. Similar letters were sent around this time to other station managers.
56 Minutes of Board meeting, 6 June 1888, B314, item 4, AA, Melbourne. An almost identical quote appears in a letter from Page to Stähle, 11 June 1888, B329/2, item 4, AA, Melbourne.
57 Letter from Hagenauer to the Vice-Chairman of the Board, 19 November 1890, VPRS 1694, unit 1, VPRO.
58 Letter from Morrison to the Chief Secretary, 14 February 1890, VPRS 1694, unit 1, VPRO.
59 Letter from Morrison to the Chief Secretary, 15 March 1890, VPRS 1694, unit 1, VPRO.
60 'Thirty-third Report of the Board', *VPP*, 1897, vol. 1, p. 4.
61 *Age*, 8 June 1894, p. 7.
62 Minutes of Board meeting, 7 June 1899, B314, item 5, AA, Melbourne.
63 'Regulations Relating to Half-Castes', *Victorian Government Gazette*, 16 May 1890, pp. 1787–8. The September 1890 regulations appear in the *Victorian Government Gazette*, 12 September 1890, pp. 3719–22.
64 Letter from Page to Stähle, 28 August 1888, B329/2, item 4, AA, Melbourne.
65 An example of this power being exercised appears in a letter from Hagenauer to Stähle, 3 August 1892, B329/2, item 5, AA, Melbourne. Two other examples appear in one memorandum from the Board's Vice-Chairman, 14 March 1910, B329/2, item 8, AA, Melbourne.
66 'Twenty-fourth Report of the Board', *VPP*, 1888, vol. 3, p. 3, their emphasis.
67 Critchett, *Our Land Till We Die*, pp. 50–1.
68 'Twenty-eighth Report of the Board', *VPP*, 1892–93, vol. 5, p. 3.
69 'Thirty-first Report of the Board', *VPP*, 1895–96, vol. 4, p. 3. One of the occasional acts of leniency was evidenced by a letter from Hagenauer to Mrs B. Rawlings, in which Mrs Rawlings' son was granted a supply of clothes. Mrs Rawlings was told, however, that 'the Board cannot grant more in future': 31 May 1892, B329/2, item 5, AA, Melbourne.
70 Since 1869 the Governor had been empowered to make regulations concerning the care, custody and education of Aboriginal children: *An Act to Provide for the Protection and Management of the Aboriginal Natives of Victoria 1869* (Vic), section 2(v).
71 *Aborigines Protection Act 1886* (Vic), section 8; *Aborigines Act 1890* (Vic), section 6(x).
72 A letter from the Board to its New South Wales equivalent stated that in the years after 1886 children were 'sent out' as soon as possible after they reached 14 years of age: letter from the Board to the New South Wales Board for the Protection of Aborigines, 27 September 1910, B329/2, item 8, AA, Melbourne.
73 Letter from Hagenauer to Constable Weir, 26 May 1893, B329/2, item 6, AA, Melbourne.
74 Letter from W. Ditchburn to John Ross, 11 May 1891, B329/2, item 5, AA, Melbourne.
75 Letter from Hagenauer to the Secretary, Department for Neglected Children, 16 July 1895, B329/2, item 7, AA, Melbourne.
76 This letter to the *Warrnambool Standard*, dated 4 January 1889, is quoted in Critchett, *Our Land Till We Die*, p. 42.
77 Letter from the Board to the New South Wales Board for the Protection of Aborigines, 27 September 1910, B329/2, item 8, AA, Melbourne.
78 See *Victorian Government Gazette*, 1871, p. 338, regulation 13; *Aborigines Protection Act 1886* (Vic), section 8. Both powers were continued after the enactment of the consolidating *Aborigines Act 1890* (Vic): see section 6(xi) of the Act, and regulations 13 and 45, *Victorian Government Gazette*, 1890, pp. 3721–2. An instance of children being sent to an orphanage prior to their mother's death is evidenced by the letter from Hagenauer to a Brighton orphanage, 7 April 1897, B329/2, item 7, AA, Melbourne.

79 According to the 1886 and 1890 legislation, 'Every infant unable to earn his or her own living, the child of an aboriginal . . . living with such aboriginal' was deemed to be Aboriginal: *Aborigines Protection Act 1886* (Vic), section 4(4); *Aborigines Act 1890* (Vic), section 5(iv).
80 Minutes of Board meetings, 13 October 1897 and 13 October (sic) 1899, B314, item 5, AA, Melbourne. See also letter from the Board to Stähle, 17 July 1896, B329/2, item 7, AA, Melbourne.
81 Letter from Hagenauer to D. Slattery, 9 September 1897, B329/2, item 7, AA, Melbourne.
82 Letter from Hagenauer to Constable Akroyd, 3 September 1896, B329/2, item 7, AA, Melbourne.
83 *Victorian Government Gazette*, 1899, p. 4383, regulation 13.
84 Minutes of Board meeting, 5 September 1900, B314, item 5, AA, Melbourne.
85 'Thirty-sixth Report of the Board', *VPP*, 1900, vol. 3, p. 4.
86 'Thirty-sixth Report of the Board', p. 6, emphasis added.
87 The report of the Head of the Department for Neglected Children for the year 1900 is quoted at length in the 'Thirty-seventh Report of the Board', *VPP*, 1901, vol. 3, pp. 4–5.
88 See Wettenhall, 'Administrative Boards in Nineteenth Century Australia', especially p. 259.
89 Letter from Henry Jennings, Vice-Chairman of the Board, to the Chief Secretary, 12 June 1879, reprinted in the 'Fifteenth Report of the Board', *VPP*, 1879–80, vol. 3, p. 13.
90 'Twenty-fifth Report of the Board', *VPP*, 1889, vol. 4, p. 3.
91 Letter from Morrison to the Chief Secretary, 15 March 1890, VPRS 1694, unit 1, VPRO; letter from Morrison to the Chief Secretary, 5 March 1890, B2861/2, AA, Melbourne.
92 Barwick, 'A Little More than Kin', p. 110. For a good account of the fight to save Framlingham, see Critchett, *Our Land Till We Die*, pp. 36–48. Critchett's thesis, 'A History of Framlingham', on which the book is based, covers the topic in more depth.
93 Report from the Board to the Chief Secretary, 5 February 1902, reproduced in the 'Thirty-eighth Report of the Board', *VPP*, 1902–3, vol. 2, pp. 5–6.
94 Report from the Board to the Chief Secretary, 29 April 1902, reproduced in 'Thirty-eighth Report of the Board', pp. 6–7.
95 'Thirty-eighth Report of the Board', p. 7.
96 See Barwick, 'A Little More than Kin', pp. 119–23.
97 Barwick, 'A Little More than Kin', pp. 108, 116.
98 See Christie, *Aborigines in Colonial Victoria*, pp. 181ff; Critchett, *Our Land Till We Die*, pp. 36ff.
99 Minutes of Board meeting, 11 February 1908, B314, item 6, AA, Melbourne.
100 Memorandum from the Acting Secretary of the Board, W. Ditchburn, 17 June 1909, B329/2, item 8, AA, Melbourne. See also Wilkinson, 'Fractured Families', pp. 14–15.
101 Examples of exceptions to the policy being made for Aborigines who were dying or disabled are found in the minutes of Board meeting, 9 August 1906, B314, item 5, AA, Melbourne; and minutes of Board meeting, 7 April 1909, B314, item 6, AA, Melbourne.
102 *VPD*, Assembly, vol. 82, 19 August 1896, pp. 1324–8; 24 September 1896, pp. 2069–70. The quote appears at p. 2070. On Murray's sympathy with Aborigines at Framlingham, see Critchett, *Our Land Till We Die*, pp. 39–48, 52–60.
103 Letter from the Board to Miss Murray, 23 December 1909. Another exception is evidenced by the Board's letter to the Manager, Lake Condah Station, 15 February 1910. Both appear in B329/2, item 8, AA, Melbourne.
104 Letter from the Board to Murray, 8 March 1910, enclosing the Board's memorandum dated 14 February 1910; see also the Board's memorandum dated 24 March 1910: B329/2, item 8, AA, Melbourne.
105 Richard Broome, *Aboriginal Australians: Black Responses to White Dominance 1788–1994*, 1994, p. 82.

106 Letter from the Board to the Chief Secretary, 8 or 9 June 1910, B329/2, item 8, AA, Melbourne.
107 *Aborigines Act 1910* (Vic), section 2; minutes of Board meeting, 5 October 1910, B314, item 6, AA, Melbourne.
108 *VPD*, Assembly, vol. 125, 27 September 1910, p. 1386.
109 Minutes of Special Board Meeting, 23 September 1896, VPRS 1694, unit 1, VPRO.

2 Under the Law: Aborigines and Islanders in Colonial Queensland

1 *Commonwealth Parliamentary Debates* (hereafter *CPD*), Senate, vol. 10, 29 May 1902, p. 13005.
2 F. Lancaster Jones, *The Structure and Growth of Australia's Aboriginal Population*, 1970, p. 4.
3 See the comments of Sir Samuel Griffith at the Australasian Federal Convention in Sydney in 1891: *Official Record of the Debates of the Australasian Federal Convention*, Sydney 1891, pp. 898–9.
4 *CPD*, Senate, vol. 10, 29 May 1902, pp. 13004–5.
5 The speaker is Senator Glassey, *CPD*, Senate, vol. 9, 10 April 1902, p. 11596.
6 Noel Loos aptly uses the term 'era of protection' in 'A Chapter of Contact: Aboriginal–European Relations in North Queensland 1606–1992', in Henry Reynolds (ed.), *Race Relations in North Queensland*, 1993, p. 19.
7 See Les Malezer, Matt Foley and Paul Richards, *Beyond the Act*, 1979, p. 20.
8 C.D. Rowley, *The Destruction of Aboriginal Society*, 1972, p. 158. On Aboriginal resistance, see further Henry Reynolds and Noel Loos, 'Aboriginal Resistance in Queensland', *Australian Journal of Politics and History*, vol. 22, 1976, p. 214.
9 Suzanne Welborn, 'Politicians and Aborigines in Queensland and Western Australia 1897–1907', *Studies in Western Australian History*, vol. 2, 1978, p. 19.
10 On the Native Police Force, see Rowley, *Destruction*, pp. 158–72, 181. See also Raymond Evans, Kay Saunders and Kathryn Cronin, *Race Relations in Colonial Queensland: A History of Exclusion, Exploitation and Extermination*, 1988, pp. 55–66.
11 Malezer et al., *Beyond the Act*, p. 20.
12 Ross Fitzgerald, *A History of Queensland: From the Dreaming to 1915*, 1986, p. 214.
13 Noel Loos uses the term 'sea frontier' in 'A Chapter of Contact', p. 18. Elsewhere, Loos points out the difficulty of knowing how many Aborigines were kidnapped: Loos, 'Queensland's Kidnapping Act: The Native Labourers Protection Act of 1884', *Aboriginal History*, vol. 4, 1980, pp. 157–8.
14 *Native Labourers' Protection Act 1884* (Qld), sections 1, 2, 4, 5.
15 *Pearl-shell and Bêche-de-mer Fishery Act Amendment Act 1886* (Qld), section 5.
16 Rowley, *Destruction*, p. 175.
17 *Polynesian Laborers Act 1868* (Qld), sections 8, 9, Form D. *Pacific Islanders Protection Act 1872* (Imperial) and the *Pacific Islanders Protection Act 1875* (Imperial). *Pacific Island Labourers Act 1880* (Qld), section 14. See further Loos, 'Queenland's Kidnapping Act', pp. 150–1, 159, 170, 172. On the description of the Pacific Islander labour trade as a slave trade, see Fitzgerald, *A History of Queensland*, p. 236.
18 See Loos, 'Queensland's Kidnapping Act', p. 170. On the issue of Aboriginal and Islander labour threatening white labour, see the comments of the Premier, Samuel Griffith, during the second reading of the Pacific Island Labourers Act Amendment Bill, *Queensland Parliamentary Debates* (hereafter *QPD*), Assembly, vol. 41, 23 January 1884, p. 133.
19 See Fitzgerald, *A History of Queensland*, pp. 215–17; Patricia Grimshaw, Marilyn Lake, Ann McGrath and Marian Quartly, *Creating a Nation*, 1994, p. 139.
20 For such comments by parliamentarians, see *QPD*, Council, vol. 78, 8 December 1897, p. 1909; *QPD*, Assembly, vol. 87, 31 July 1901, p. 225.
21 *Oaths Act Amendment Act 1876* (Qld); *Oaths Act Amendment Act 1884* (Qld), section 2; *QPD*, Assembly, vol. 43, 31 July 1884, pp. 231–2. The quote is taken from Mr T. Campbell at p. 232.

22 *Elections Act 1885* (Qld), section 6; *Elections Acts Amendment Act 1905* (Qld), section 9; *Commonwealth Franchise Act 1902*, section 4. Unlike its Queensland counterpart, the Commonwealth exclusionary clause made an exception for 'aboriginal natives' from New Zealand. Maori people did have a limited franchise in New Zealand, and the desire not to jeopardise the possibility that New Zealand might enter the federation is the most likely reason why Maories in Australia were able to vote at the Commonwealth level: see *CPD*, Senate, vol. 10, 29 May 1902, pp. 13009–10.
23 This advice from the Secretary, Department of Home Affairs, Melbourne, is reproduced in the 'Annual Report of the Chief Protector of Aboriginals for 1905', *Queensland Parliamentary Papers* (hereafter *QPP*), 1906, vol. 2, pp. 30–1. See also Rosalind M. Kidd, Regulating Bodies: Administrations and Aborigines in Queensland 1840–1988, PhD Thesis, Griffith University, 1994, p. 250.
24 *Elections Acts Amendment Act 1930* (Qld), section 8.
25 Rowley, *Destruction*, p. 177; J.P.M. Long, *Aboriginal Settlements: A Survey of Institutional Communities in Eastern Australia*, 1970, p. 94.
26 Long, *Aboriginal Settlements*, pp. 92–4; Malezer et al., *Beyond the Act*, pp. 18–19; Loos, 'A Chapter of Contact', pp. 20–1; Horace Tozer, 'Measures Recently Adopted for the Amelioration of the Aborigines', *Votes and Proceedings of the Legislative Assembly* (Queensland), 1897, vol. 2, pp. 43–5. The Government had established several reserves with ration depots in 1875, although they did not last long: Rowley, *Destruction*, p. 174.
27 C.D. Rowley, *Outcasts in White Australia*, 1972, p. 109; Loos, 'A Chapter of Contact', p. 24.
28 Dawn May, 'Race Relations in Queensland 1897–1971', in Commissioner L.F. Wyvill, *Royal Commission into Aboriginal Deaths in Custody: Regional Report of Inquiry in Queensland*, 1991, p. 128.
29 See Evans et al., *Race Relations in Colonial Queensland*, pp. 118–19; Heather Wearne, *A Clash of Cultures: Queensland Aboriginal Policy (1824–1980)*, 1980, pp. 11–12.
30 *Australian Dictionary of Biography* (hereafter *ADB*), vol. 5, p. 243.
31 See N. Loos, *Invasion and Resistance: Aboriginal–European Relations on the North Queensland Frontier 1861–1897*, 1982, pp. 172–3.
32 Archibald Meston, 'Report on the Aboriginals of Queensland', *Votes and Proceedings of the Legislative Assembly* (Queensland), 1896, vol. 4, pp. 1–4, 13, his emphasis.
33 William Thorpe, 'Archibald Meston and Aboriginal Legislation in Colonial Queensland', *Historical Studies*, vol. 21, 1984, p. 64.
34 Meston, 'Report on the Aboriginals of Queensland', pp. 13–14. On Meston's report see also Rowley, *Destruction*, pp. 179–82.
35 Regina Ganter and Ros Kidd, 'The Powers of Protectors: Conflicts Surrounding Queensland's 1897 Aboriginal Legislation', *Australian Historical Studies*, vol. 25, 1993, p. 540.
36 W.E. Parry-Okeden, 'Report on the North Queensland Aborigines and the Native Police', *Votes and Proceedings of the Legislative Assembly* (Queensland), 1897, vol. 2, pp. 14–15.
37 Parry-Okeden, 'Report on the North Queensland Aborigines and the Native Police', pp. 18–19.
38 The Native Police would be used on conciliatory work only, such as the feeding and 'protection' of Aborigines, and the move to civil police followed soon after: see Edmund J.B. Foxcroft, *Australian Native Policy: Its History Especially in Victoria*, 1941, p. 119; Rowley, *Destruction*, p. 181.
39 Loos, 'A Chapter of Contact', p. 20.
40 Loos, 'A Chapter of Contact', p. 22; May, 'Race Relations in Queensland 1897–1971', p. 126.
41 See *Western Australia Parliamentary Debates*, Council, vol. 25, 4 October 1904, p. 557.
42 *Aboriginals Protection and Restriction of the Sale of Opium Act 1897* (Qld), sections 3, 4, 9, 31; *Aborigines Act 1905* (WA), sections 2, 3, 12, 60; *Northern Territory Aboriginals Act 1910* (SA), sections 2, 3, 16, 49; *Aborigines Act 1911* (SA), sections 3, 4, 17, 38. See Thorpe, 'Archibald Meston', p. 52; Rowley, *Destruction*, pp. 179, 218.

43 Previous Queensland legislation had restricted the sale of alcohol to Aborigines and 'half-castes'. See *Licensing Act 1885* (Qld), section 67.
44 *Aboriginals Protection and Restriction of the Sale of Opium Act 1897* (Qld) (hereafter *Aboriginals Protection Act 1897*), sections 3, 4, 9, 10; *Aboriginals Protection and Restriction of the Sale of Opium Act 1901* (Qld) (hereafter *Aboriginals Protection Act 1901*), section 2.
45 May, 'Race Relations in Queensland 1897–1971', p. 154.
46 *Aboriginals Protection Act 1897* (Qld), section 33.
47 *Aboriginals Protection Act 1897* (Qld), sections 6, 15. See May, 'Race Relations in Queensland 1897–1971', p. 127.
48 *Aboriginals Protection Act 1897* (Qld), section 31. See also Loos, 'A Chapter of Contact', p. 26; Loos, *Invasion and Resistance*, pp. 178–80.
49 Henry Reynolds and Dawn May, 'Queensland', in Ann McGrath (ed.), *Contested Ground: Australian Aborigines under the British Crown*, 1995, p. 182; Rowley, *Destruction*, p. 184. See also Ganter and Kidd, 'The Powers of Protectors', pp. 553–4.
50 Loos, 'A Chapter of Contact', p. 22.
51 See Loos, 'A Chapter of Contact', p. 27.
52 *QPD*, Assembly, vol. 78, 15 November 1897, p. 1546.
53 *QPD*, Assembly, vol. 78, 15 November 1897, pp. 1538, 1541.
54 *QPD*, Assembly, vol. 78, 15 November 1897, p. 1548.
55 *QPD*, Assembly, vol. 78, 18 November 1897, p. 1629. On the existence of a flicker of liberalism during these debates, see Welborn, 'Politicians and Aborigines in Queensland and Western Australia', p. 20; Loos, *Invasion and Resistance*, p. 181.
56 'Report of the Commissioner of Police for the Year 1897', *Votes and Proceedings of the Legislative Assembly* (Queensland), 1898, vol. 1, p. 5; May, 'Race Relations in Queensland 1897–1971', p. 127.
57 *Queensland Government Gazette*, vol. 72, 1899, p. 746, regulation 2; *ADB*, vol. 11, pp. 463–4.
58 *Queensland Government Gazette*, vol. 82, 1904, p. 1187, regulation 3; 'Annual Report of the Chief Protector of Aboriginals for 1904', *QPP*, 1905, vol. 1, p. 22; Welborn, 'Politicians and Aborigines in Queensland and Western Australia', p. 24; Peter Biskup, *Not Slaves Not Citizens: The Aboriginal Problem in Western Australia, 1898–1954*, 1973, p. 59.
59 *Aboriginals Protection Act 1897* (Qld), sections 10, 15.
60 *Queensland Government Gazette*, vol. 72, 1899, pp. 746–7, regulations 4–11.
61 Opinion of Crown Solicitor 'Re employment of aboriginals', attached to memo from Commissioner of Police, Brisbane, to Roth, April 1898, COL/142, QSA.
62 Roth, 'First Half-Yearly Report', 1 July 1898, COL/142, Queensland State Archives (hereafter QSA).
63 Letter from Police Department, Cooktown, to the Commissioner of Police, Brisbane, 10 March 1898, COL/142, QSA.
64 The number of permits issued in the north in 1901 was 1691; the figure for 1902 was 1418, and in 1903, 1745 permits were issued: 'Annual Report of the Northern Protector of Aboriginals for 1901', *QPP*, 1902, vol. 1, p. 1; 'Annual Report of the Northern Protector of Aboriginals for 1902', *QPP*, 1903, vol. 2, p. 1; 'Annual Report of the Northern Protector of Aboriginals for 1903', *QPP*, 1904, p. 1; Meston, 'General Statement of Work Done by Southern Protector', 30 March 1903, COL/144, QSA.
65 Opinion of Crown Solicitor 'Re employment of aboriginals', 20 January 1906, CRS/264, QSA. Opinion of Crown Solicitor 'Re employment of aboriginals', attached to memo from Commissioner of Police, Brisbane, to Roth, April 1898, COL/142, QSA. The position with regard to employees covered both by the *Native Labourers Protection Act 1884* (Qld) and the 1897 Act was clarified in 1901: *Aboriginals Protection Act 1901* (Qld), section 10(2).
66 Letter from E. Phayse, 25 May 1909, A/58656, QSA; letter from Chief Protector to V. Redwood, 31 July 1908, A/58655, QSA.
67 The Manager of the Gregory Downs Station alleged that 200 Aborigines in his district would be sacked unless changes were made in the administration of the Act: 'Extract from Annual Report of Inspector Galbraith, Normanton', 1904, A/58927, QSA.

68 *Aboriginals Protection Act 1901* (Qld), sections 10, 12.
69 Petition to James Forsyth, 28 August 1903, A/58850, QSA; 'Extract from Annual Report of Inspector Galbraith, Normanton', 1904, A/58927, QSA.
70 Letter from Meston to the Under Secretary, Home Office, 20 January 1903, COL/144, QSA.
71 *Queensland Government Gazette*, vol. 82, 1904, p. 187, regulations 11, 12.
72 *Post and Telegraph Act 1901* (Cwlth), section 16; *Sugar Bounty Act 1903* (Cwlth), section 2. The last Act was changed in 1905 so that the employment of 'any aboriginal native' would not prejudice a claim to a bounty. Such a clause also appeared in the wider *Bounties Act 1907* (Cwlth), which otherwise encouraged the use of white labour in the production of a range of goods: *Sugar Bounty Act 1905* (Cwlth), section 10; *Bounties Act 1907* (Cwlth), section 4. A Queensland regulation in 1909 briefly prevented the provision of work permits to Aborigines who sought work on sugar-cane plantations (other than as domestic servants). This was rescinded two weeks after it was gazetted: *Queensland Government Gazette*, vol. 92, 1909, pp. 111, 238.
73 See the 'Sugar Regulations' (made pursuant to the powers conferred by the *Excise Act 1901* and the *Sugar Bounty Act 1903*), *Commonwealth Government Gazette*, 1903, p. 640, regulation 1. Walter Roth considered these regulations in his 'Annual Report of the Northern Protector of Aboriginals for 1903', p. 3.
74 Reynolds and May, 'Queensland', p. 185.
75 Quoted in letter from Roth to the Commissioner of Police, Brisbane, 18 March 1898, COL/142, QSA.
76 May, 'Race Relations in Queensland 1897–1971', pp. 131–2.
77 *QPD*, Council, vol. 78, 8 December 1897, p. 1909.
78 *Aboriginals Protection Act 1897* (Qld), section 14.
79 Letter from Alex Gordon to the Home Secretary, 1 November 1899, COL/145, QSA.
80 'Report of the Northern Protector of Aboriginals for 1899', *Votes and Proceedings of the Legislative Assembly* (Qld), 1900, vol. 5, p. 10, our emphasis.
81 'Report of the Northern Protector of Aboriginals for 1899', p. 10.
82 'Annual Report of the Northern Protector of Aboriginals for 1901', p. 7.
83 'Annual Report of the Northern Protector of Aboriginals for 1902', p. 11. This is also referred to in Henry Reynolds (ed.), *Aborigines and Settlers: The Australian Experience 1788–1939*, 1972, p. 168.
84 *QPD*, Assembly, vol. 87, 31 July 1901, p. 215.
85 *Aboriginals Protection Act 1901* (Qld), section 19.
86 'Annual Report of the Chief Protector of Aboriginals for 1904', p. 10.
87 *Aboriginals Protection Act 1901* (Qld), section 2.
88 Quoted in 'Annual Report of the Northern Protector of Aboriginals for 1903', p. 13.
89 *Aboriginals Protection Act 1901* (Qld), section 14. *QPD*, Assembly, vol. 87, 31 July 1901, p. 225. See also Kidd, 'Regulating Bodies', pp. 196–7.
90 *QPD*, Assembly, vol. 87, 31 July 1901, p. 221.
91 *Aboriginals Protection Act 1901* (Qld), section 9. For information on white reactions to inter-racial marriage, see Loos, *Invasion and Resistance*, pp. 170–1.
92 The first quote is from a 'Circular Memo', received by the Home Secretary's Office on 26 September 1901, A/58764, QSA. Letter from Roth to the Commissioner of Police, Brisbane, 6 June 1898, COL/142, QSA. See also Roth, 'First Half-Yearly Report', 1 July 1898, COL/142, QSA. The second quote is from the 'Annual Report of the Northern Protector of Aboriginals for 1901', p. 9.
93 *Queensland Government Gazette*, vol. 79, 1902, p. 487.
94 *Queensland Government Gazette*, vol. 82, 1904, p. 1189, schedule L.
95 'Annual Report of the Chief Protector of Aboriginals for 1907', *QPP*, 1908, vol. 3, p. 14; 'Annual Report of the Chief Protector of Aboriginals for 1908', *QPP*, 1909, vol. 2, pp. 21–2.
96 Letter from Ashburner to the Commissioner of Police, 16 December 1904, A/58764, QSA. The offical position was noted at the bottom of this letter.
97 *QPD*, Assembly, vol. 87, 31 July 1901, p. 221.
98 *Aboriginals Protection Act 1901* (Qld), section 17.

99 *Mining Act 1898* (Qld), section 15 (which enabled the holder of a miner's right to take possession of crown land) and section 3 (which defined 'crown land' to include Aboriginal reserves); see also 'Report of the Northern Protector of Aboriginals for 1899', p. 6. From 1901 a miner needed a special permit from a district protector to enter Aboriginal reserves: *Aboriginals Protection Act 1901* (Qld), section 15.

100 See Ian O'Connor, 'Aboriginal Child Welfare Law, Policies and Practices in Queensland: 1865–1989', *Australian Social Work*, vol. 46, 1993, pp. 13–14. See also Richard Broome, *Aboriginal Australians: Black Response to White Dominance 1788–1980*, 1982, pp. 105–6, 110–11.

101 Commissioner Wyvill, quoted in O'Connor, 'Aboriginal Child Welfare Law', p. 14.

102 Rowley, *Destruction*, p. 247; Loos, 'A Chapter of Contact', pp. 24–5.

103 Long, *Aboriginal Settlements*, p. 96.

104 Meston, 'General Statement of Work Done by Southern Protector', 30 March 1903, COL/144, QSA. For an earlier statement, see 'Report of the Southern Protector of Aboriginals', *QPP*, 1902, vol. 1, p. 1.

105 'Annual Report of the Northern Protector of Aboriginals for 1901', pp. 12–13; see also Ganter and Kidd, 'The Powers of Protectors', p. 540.

106 Letter from Meston to the Home Secretary, 24 September 1902, COL/143, QSA.

107 'Annual Report of the Northern Protector of Aboriginals for 1902', p. 19.

108 *Aboriginals Protection Act 1901* (Qld), section 13. A weak limiting clause provided that the consent of Aborigines was required in order for these powers to be exercised 'except so far as may be necessary to provide for the due preservation of such property'.

109 *Queensland Government Gazette*, vol. 82, 1904, p. 1187, regulation 19.

110 *Queensland Government Gazette*, vol. 85, 1905, p. 1037.

111 See Loos, *Invasion*, pp. 167–8.

112 Ganter and Kidd, 'The Powers of Protectors', p. 541; see also Kidd, 'Regulating Bodies', p. 178; Jackie Huggins and Thom Blake, 'Protection or Persecution? Gender Relations in the Era of Racial Segregation', in Kay Saunders and Raymond Evans (eds), *Gender Relations in Australia: Domination and Negotiation*, 1992, p. 46.

113 Handwritten response, dated 1 December 1900, on letter of inquiry from a district protector to the Home Secretary's Department, 15 November 1900, COL/145, QSA.

114 *Aboriginals Protection Act 1897* (Qld), sections 4, 9, 10.

115 *QPD*, Assembly, vol. 78, 18 November 1897, p. 1630.

116 Letter from the Thursday Island Protector to the Chief Protector, 26 October 1904, A/58750, QSA.

117 Memo from Roth titled 'Synopsis of the Law Relating to Half-Castes', 6 February 1904, A/58751, QSA. Letter from Roth to the Under Secretary, Home Office, 20 November 1905, A/58751, QSA, emphasis added. Letter from Roth to the Commissioner of Police, Brisbane, 24 November 1905, A/58751, QSA.

118 *Aboriginals Protection Act 1897* (Qld), section 33; 'Annual Report of the Northern Protector of Aboriginals for 1903', p. 3; 'Annual Report of the Chief Protector of Aboriginals for 1907', p. 9; 'Annual Report of the Chief Protector of Aboriginals for 1908', p. 15; 'Annual Report of the Chief Protector of Aboriginals for 1909', *QPP*, 1910, vol. 3, p. 12. The quote is from the 1909 report.

119 *Industrial and Reformatory Schools Act 1865* (Qld), sections 6(7), 8, 9; see *QPD*, Assembly, vol. 87, 31 July 1901, p. 224; 'Annual Report of the Chief Protector of Aboriginals for 1905', *QPP*, 1906, vol. 2, p. 12. In 1906 section 6 was amended so that it no longer automatically deemed Aboriginal children to be neglected: *Industrial and Reformatory Schools Act Amendment Act 1906* (Qld), section 3. But it made little difference, since from 1897 most Aboriginal children (and from 1901 all Aboriginal children, including all 'half-caste' children) were able to be removed to reserves: *Aboriginals Protection Act 1897* (Qld), section 9; *Aboriginals Protection Act 1901* (Qld), section 2. See O'Connor, 'Aboriginal Child Welfare Law', p. 12.

120 'Annual Report of the Chief Protector of Aboriginals for 1905', p. 12.

121 'Annual Report of the Chief Protector of Aboriginals for 1904', pp. 9–10.

122 'Annual Report of the Chief Protector of Aboriginals for 1905', p. 13 (his emphasis).

123 'Annual Report of the Chief Protector of Aboriginals for 1905', p. 13.
124 This idea of Aborigines being victims of the law comes from Garth Nettheim, although he does not use the phrase in this particular context: Nettheim, *Victims of the Law: Black Queenslanders Today*, 1981. In Foucauldian terms, the rise of the new regime moved control over Aborigines from the realm of small 'p' power to that of Power: see D.A. King and A.W. McHoul, 'The Discursive Production of the Queensland Aborigine as Subject: Meston's Proposal, 1895', Social Analysis, no. 19, 1986, p. 36.

3 Is the Constitution to Blame?

1 Geoffrey Sawer, 'The Australian Constitution and the Australian Aborigine', *Federal Law Review*, vol. 2, 1966–67, p. 17.
2 Ann McGrath, ' "Beneath the Skin": Australian Citizenship, Rights and Aboriginal Women', in Renate Howe (ed.), *Women and the State: Australian Perspectives*, 1993, p. 99.
3 *Australian*, 11 August 1994.
4 Centenary of Federation Advisory Committee, *2001: A Report from Australia. A Report to the Council of Australian Governments by the Centenary of Federation Advisory Committee*, 1994, p. 3.
5 Margaret Foster, *Our Constitution*, 1996, p. 56 (emphasis added).
6 Sawer, 'The Australian Constitution and the Australian Aborigine', p. 18.
7 Sawer, 'The Australian Constitution and the Australian Aborigine', p. 17.
8 G.C. Bolton, 'Black and White after 1897', in C.T. Stannage (ed.), *A New History of Western Australia*, 1981, p. 124. See also Peter Biskup, *Not Slaves Not Citizens: The Aboriginal Problem in Western Australia 1898–1954*, 1973, p. 27.
9 *Aborigines Act 1890* (Vic), sections 5, 6.
10 *Aboriginals Protection and Restriction of the Sale of Opium Act 1897* (Qld), sections 4, 9, 12, 13; *Aboriginals Protection and Restriction of the Sale of Opium Act 1901* (Qld), section 2.
11 *An Act to allow the Aboriginal Natives of Western Australia to give information and evidence without the sanction of an Oath 1841* (WA) (the operation of this Act was extended by two later pieces of legislation, in 1843 and 1849); *An Act to further amend the Law of Evidence 1875* (WA); *An Act to prevent the enticing away the (sic) Girls of the Aboriginal Race from School, or from any Service in which they are employed 1844* (WA); *Pearl Shell Fishery Regulation Act 1873* (WA); *Aboriginal Offenders Act 1883* (WA); *Wines, Beer, and Spirit Sale Act 1880* (WA), section 56.
12 *Aborigines Protection Act 1886* (WA), sections 3, 16, 18, 43, 45.
13 *Aborigines Protection Act (Amendment) 1892* (WA), section 2.
14 *Aborigines Act 1897* (WA), sections 4, 5, 7.
15 *Aborigines Act 1889* (WA), section 8; *Land Act 1898* (WA), sections 6, 39.
16 *Constitution Act 1889* (WA), section 70 (this Act was *ultra vires* in some respects, a defect remedied by an Imperial Act the following year); *Aborigines Act 1897* (WA), section 2. See also Neville Green, 'Aborigines and White Settlers in the Nineteenth Century', in C.T. Stannage (ed.), *A New History of Western Australia*, pp. 109–10; Peter Johnston, 'The Repeals of Section 70 of the Western Australian Constitution Act 1889: Aborigines and Governmental Breach of Trust', *Western Australian Law Review*, vol. 19, 1989, pp. 318ff; Biskup, *Not Slaves Not Citizens*, pp. 25–6. See also Sandy Toussaint, 'Western Australia', in Ann McGrath (ed.), *Contested Ground: Australian Aborigines under the British Crown*, 1995, pp. 251–2.
17 *An Act to Allow the Aboriginal Natives of New South Wales to be received as Competent Witnesses in Criminal Cases 1839* (NSW); *An Act to Prohibit the Aboriginal Natives of New South Wales from Having Fire Arms or Ammunition in their Possession without the Permission of a Magistrate 1840* (NSW); *Liquor Act 1898* (NSW), section 48 (replacing earlier prohibitions on the supply of alcohol to Aborigines). The first two of these Acts were formally repealed only in 1924: *Statute Law Revision Act 1924* (NSW).

18 Heather Goodall, 'New South Wales', in McGrath (ed.), *Contested Ground*, p. 73; Bain Attwood, Winifred Burrage, Alan Burrage and Elsie Stokie, *A Life Together, A Life Apart: A History of Relations Bewteen Europeans and Aborigines*, 1994, pp. 4–5.
19 *An Ordinance to Provide for the Protection, Maintenance and Up-bringing of Orphans and other Destitute Children of the Aborigines 1844* (SA).
20 *An Ordinance to Facilitate the Admission of the Unsworn Testimony of the Aboriginal Inhabitants of South Australia and the parts adjacent 1848* (SA); *Licensed Victuallers Act 1880* (SA), section 81 (replacing earlier prohibitions on the sale of alcohol to Aborigines); *Opium Act 1895* (SA), section 3 (medicinal opium was exempted from the operations of this Act).
21 C.D. Rowley, *The Destruction of Aboriginal Society*, 1972, pp. 213, 216.
22 Ronald and Catherine Berndt, *From Black to White in South Australia*, 1951, pp. 54–5. See also Rowley, *Destruction*, pp. 206, 213.
23 *Constitution Acts Amendment Act 1899* (WA), sections 15, 26.
24 *Elections Act 1885* (Qld), section 6.
25 *Parliamentary Electorates and Elections Act 1893* (NSW), section 23(iv).
26 *Official Record of the Debates of the Australasian Federal Convention* (hereafter *Federation Debates*), Sydney 1891, p. 66.
27 *Federation Debates*, Sydney 1891, p. 274.
28 *Federation Debates*, Sydney 1891, p. 523.
29 *Federation Debates*, Sydney 1891, p. 525.
30 *Federation Debates*, Sydney 1891, pp. 702–3.
31 *Federation Debates*, Sydney 1891, pp. 898–9.
32 *Federation Debates*, Sydney 1891, pp. 898–9.
33 *Federation Debates*, Adelaide 1897, pp. 831–2.
34 *Federation Debates*, Adelaide 1897, p. 831.
35 *Federation Debates*, Adelaide 1897, p. 1020.
36 *Federation Debates*, Sydney 1897, p. 453.
37 *Federation Debates*, Melbourne 1898, p. 713.
38 *Federation Debates*, Melbourne 1898, pp. 713–14.
39 *Federation Debates*, Adelaide 1897, p. 715.
40 *Federation Debates*, Adelaide 1897, p. 717.
41 *Federation Debates*, Adelaide 1897, pp. 717–18.
42 *Federation Debates*, Adelaide 1897, p. 718.
43 *Federation Debates*, Adelaide 1897, p. 722.
44 *Federation Debates*, Adelaide 1897, p. 723.
45 *Federation Debates*, Adelaide 1897, p. 725.
46 *Federation Debates*, Adelaide 1897, p. 725.
47 *Federation Debates*, Adelaide 1897, p. 725.
48 *Federation Debates*, Adelaide 1897, p. 725.
49 *Federation Debates*, Adelaide 1897, p. 726.
50 *Federation Debates*, Adelaide 1897, pp. 730–1.
51 *Federation Debates*, Adelaide 1897, p. 731.
52 *Federation Debates*, Adelaide 1897, pp. 1193–4.
53 *Federation Debates*, Adelaide 1897, p. 1195.
54 *Federation Debates*, Adelaide 1897, p. 1197.
55 *Federation Debates*, Melbourne 1898, p. 1840.
56 *Federation Debates*, Melbourne 1898, pp. 1840–1.
57 *Federation Debates*, Melbourne 1898, p. 1841.
58 *Federation Debates*, Melbourne 1898, p. 1842.
59 *Federation Debates*, Melbourne 1898, pp. 1844–6.
60 *Federation Debates*, Adelaide 1897, p. 1020.
61 Pat Stretton and Christine Finnimore, 'Black Fellow Citizens: Aborigines and the Commonwealth Franchise', *Australian Historical Studies*, vol. 25, 1993, pp. 521–35, especially p. 530.
62 *The Queen v. Pearson; Ex Parte Sipka, Commonwealth Law Reports*, vol. 152, 1983, pp. 254ff.

63 Draft Constitution Bill (1891), chapter V, section 17.
64 John Quick and Robert Garran, *The Annotated Constitution of the Australian Commonwealth* 1976, [1901], p. 955.
65 *Australian Constitution*, section 117.
66 *Federation Debates*, Melbourne 1898, pp. 677, 682–3.
67 *Federation Debates*, Melbourne 1898, pp. 665–6.
68 W.K. Hancock, *Australia* 1961, [1930], p. 50.
69 See opinion of Geoffrey Sawer, Appendix III to the Commonwealth Parliament's 'Report from the Select Committee on Voting Rights of Aborigines. Part 1 – Report and Minutes of Proceedings', *Commonwealth Parliamentary Papers*, 1961, vol. 2, p. 37.
70 Commonwealth Parliament, 'Report from the Select Committee on Voting Rights of Aborigines', p. 3.
71 Commonwealth Parliament, 'Report from the Select Committee on Voting Rights of Aborigines', p. 3.
72 Sawer's opinion, Appendix III to the 'Report from the Select Committee on Voting Rights of Aborigines', p. 37.
73 Memorandum from the Secretary, Attorney-General's Department, to the Secretary, Department of Immigration, 27 June 1949, A432/81, 1949/576, Australian Archives, Canberra.

4 The Commonwealth Defines the Australian Citizen

1 *Commonwealth Franchise Act 1902*, section 4; *Naturalization Act 1903* (Cwlth), section 5; *Invalid and Old-Age Pensions Act 1908* (Cwlth), section 16(1)(c); *Maternity Allowance Act 1912* (Cwlth), section 6(2).
2 *Sugar Bounty Act 1905* (Cwlth), section 10; *Bounties Act 1907* (Cwlth), section 4.
3 *Emigration Act 1910* (Cwlth), section 3(1). 'Half-castes' were deemed to be Aboriginal by section 2 of this Act.
4 A similar piece of legislation, the Customs Tariff (British Preference) Bill 1906, was passed by both Houses of Commonwealth Parliament – and included a 'white labour' on British ships clause – but was reserved and stopped from receiving Royal assent by the Governor-General acting under section 58 of the Constitution, and was subsequently dropped by the government when it was discovered that the Act contravened Imperial policy and treaty obligations: G. Sawer, *Australian Federal Politics and Law 1901–1929*, 1972 [1956], p. 44.
5 *Defence Act 1903–1909* (Cwlth), section 138(1)(b); *Defence Act 1903–1910* (Cwlth), section 61(h).
6 See Alpheus Snow, *The Question of Aborigines in the Law and Practice of Nations*, 1921.
7 Snow, *The Question of Aborigines*, pp. 16–17.
8 Snow, *The Question of Aborigines*, p. 17.
9 Anthony Trollope, *Australia*, 1967 [1873], pp. 100–1.
10 *Commonwealth Franchise Act 1902* (Cwlth), section 3.
11 For evidence of this occurring in South Australia, see Pat Stretton and Christine Finnimore, 'Black Fellow Citizens: Aborigines and the Commonwealth Franchise', *Australian Historical Studies*, vol. 25, 1993, pp. 521–35, at pp. 529–30.
12 *Commonwealth Parliamentary Debates* (hereafter *CPD*), Senate, vol. 9, 10 April 1902, pp. 11580–1.
13 *CPD*, Senate, vol. 9, 10 April 1902, p. 11597.
14 *CPD*, Senate, vol. 9, 10 April 1902, pp. 11584–7.
15 *CPD*, Senate, vol. 9, 10 April 1902, pp. 11598–9.
16 *CPD*, Representatives, vol. 9, 24 April 1902, pp. 11977, 11980; Senate, vol. 10, 29 May 1902, pp. 13003, 13006.
17 Letter from the Commissioner of Maternity Allowances to the Assistant Minister, 31 May 1938, A571/97, 1938/883, Australian Archives (hereafter AA. All references in this chapter to the Australian Archives are to the Canberra office).

18 Deakin's opinion of 29 August 1901 is cited in Patrick Brazil and Bevan Mitchell (eds), *Opinions of Attorneys-General of the Commonwealth of Australia: With Opinions of Solicitors-General and the Attorney-General's Department: vol. 1, 1901–1914*, 1981, p. 24.
19 Memorandum from Garran, 30 September 1905; notation by Isaac Isaacs, dated 2 October 1905, A406/63, E1905/9383, AA.
20 Opinion of Garran, 17 April 1904, A96, vol. 1, AA.
21 Memorandum from Secretary, Department of External Affairs, 7 June 1904, A1, 1904/4979, AA. Section 7 allowed the executive to have the final discretion over the issue of a certificate, and reasons did not have to be given for its decisions.
22 Letter from R.A. Saleeby to Secretary, Department of External Affairs, 17 May 1904, A1, 1905/3040, AA.
23 Memorandum from Secretary, Department of External Affairs, 20 May 1904, A1, 1905/3040, AA.
24 Memorandum from Higgins to Minister for External Affairs, 9 June 1904, in Brazil and Mitchell (eds), *Opinions of Attorneys-General, vol. 1*, p. 218.
25 Opinion given by Garran, November 1912, in Brazil and Mitchell (eds), *Opinions of Attorneys-General, vol. 1*, p. 619 (emphasis added).
26 But this status as a British subject extended only within the bounds of the Australian Commonwealth. Only persons naturalised in Great Britain were naturalised British subjects throughout the Empire. This anomaly was only corrected by the *Nationality Act 1920* (Cwlth).
27 Opinion of Garran, 12 October 1904, in Brazil and Mitchell (eds), *Opinions of Attorneys-General, vol. 1*, pp. 319–20.
28 Letter from Glynn to the Prime Minister, 7 October 1909, in Brazil and Mitchell (eds), *Opinions of Attorneys-General, vol. 1*, pp. 454–6.
29 Australian Aborigines were not barred from naturalisation, but as British subjects by birth they had nothing to gain from being naturalised.
30 Opinion given by Garran, 3 March 1905, A659, 1943/1/1330, AA.
31 Opinion given by Garran, 4 April 1905, A659, 1943/1/1330, AA.
32 Opinion given by Garran, 5 July 1910, A659, 1943/1/1330, AA.
33 Opinion given by Garran, 27 June 1916, A659, 1943/1/1330, AA.
34 Opinion given by Garran, 3 January 1913, in Brazil and Mitchell (eds), *Opinions of Attorneys-General, vol. 1*, p. 626 (original emphasis).
35 Opinion given by Garran, 27 June 1922, in Brazil and Mitchell (eds), *Opinions of Attorneys-General of the Commonwealth of Australia: With Opinions of Solicitors-General and the Attorney-General's Department, vol. 2, 1914–1923*, pp. 870–1.
36 Letter from Deakin to the Minister for Trade and Customs, 4 April 1902, in Brazil and Mitchell (eds), *Opinions of Attorneys-General, vol. 1*, p. 75.
37 Memorandum from Garran to the Attorney-General, 30 September 1905, A1497/8, AA.
38 Letter from Garran to the Postmaster-General's Department, 15 November 1921, in Brazil and Mitchell (eds), *Opinions of Attorneys-General, vol. 2*, pp. 778–9.
39 By and large only whites could be naturalised (*Naturalization Act 1903* (Cwlth), section 5). Naturalised persons could still enjoy only a limited citizenship: viz the disfranchisement of naturalised ethnic Germans and other 'enemy' aliens during WWI.
40 Subject to one's racial status in a few cases, such as 'white labour' clauses.
41 *Passports Act 1920* (Cwlth), section 3.
42 Paper dated 1916 entitled 'Electoral Bill. Matters for Consideration with Law Department', A2863, 1918/27, AA.
43 Letter from the Crown Solicitor's Office to Oldham, 27 July 1916, A2863, 1918/27, AA.
44 This question from the Minister, posed in 1918, is referred to in the documents contained in A2863, 1918/27, AA.
45 See Brazil and Mitchell (eds), *Opinions of Attorneys-General, vol. 1*, pp. 318–20; see also document entitled 'Status of Asiatics', n.d., A406/62, E1945/1, part 1, AA.
46 *Nationality Act 1920* (Cwlth), section 7(3).

47 *Nationality Act 1920* (Cwlth), section 11.
48 Garran's opinion of 3 June 1921 is noted on an undated document entitled 'Status of Asiatics', A406/62, E1945/1, part 1, AA (original emphasis).
49 Memoranda from the Home and Territories Department, 6 and 9 January 1922, A659, 1943/1/1330, AA.
50 Memoranda from the Home and Territories Department, 21, 26, 27 January 1922, A659, 1943/1/1330, AA.
51 Memoranda from the Home and Territories Department, 11 May and 21 June 1923, A659, 1943/1/1330, AA.
52 See, for example, document entitled 'Status of Asiatics', n.d., A406/62, E1945/1, part 1, AA.
53 Memorandum from the Home and Territories Department, 19 October 1922, A6006, 1924/05/01, AA.
54 Document entitled 'Status of Asiatics', n.d., A406/62, E1945/1, part 1, AA.
55 Cabinet notes dated 21 February 1924 and 2 May 1924, A6006, 1924/05/01; see also documents contained in A1, 1922/18564, AA.
56 Document entitled 'For Cabinet', n.d., and attached memoranda, A981, India 16, AA.
57 Letter from Watt to the Governor-General, 10 April 1919, A981, India 16, AA.
58 Document entitled 'Grant of Invalid and Old-Age Pensions to British Indians', n.d., A981, India 16, AA.
59 A.B. Keith (ed.), *Speeches and Documents on the British Dominions 1918–1931: From Self-Government to National Sovereignty*, 1970 [1932], p. 64.
60 Keith (ed.), *Speeches and Documents*, p. 65.
61 Memorandum from Chief Electoral Officer, 18 February 1922, A406/62, E1945/1, part 1, AA.
62 This paper appears in A406/62, E1945/1, part 1, AA.
63 Letter from Hughes to Sastri, 1 July 1922, A981, India 16, AA.
64 Keith (ed.), *Speeches and Documents*, p. 145.
65 Memorandum from the Chief Electoral Officer, 4 March 1925, A406/62, E1945/1, part 2, AA.
66 Unsigned memorandum on 'Prime Minister' letterhead entitled 'Indians Domiciled in Australia – Enfranchisement of', 2 December 1924, A6006, 1924/12/03, AA.
67 Letter from Latham to the Prime Minister, 24 November 1924, A981, India 16, part 2, AA.
68 See documents contained in A1, 1924/28379, AA.
69 Cablegram from Secretary of State for the Colonies to Governor-General, 5 January 1925, and other documents contained in A981, India 16, part 2, AA.
70 At least two members of the High Court were known to favour a much broader reading of section 41 than that offered by the key Commonwealth adviser, Garran. For Isaacs' position, see Stretton and Finnimore, 'Black Fellow Citizens', pp. 526–7. For Higgins, see memorandum from Garran, 10 January 1925, A981, India 16, part 2, AA. Despite this, Garran's advice was that he saw 'no sufficient reason' to vary his opinion on section 41: Opinion given by Garran, 2 January 1925, Opinion Book 21, A1497, AA.
71 Handwritten note, 3 December 1924, A6006, 1924/12/03, AA.
72 Minutes of Cabinet meetings, 4 March and 10 August 1925, A2718/XM, vol. 1, part 2, AA. The *Commonwealth Electoral Act* was amended in 1925 to allow a 'native of British India' and 'a person to whom a certificate of naturalization has been issued' to be exempted from the 'aboriginal natives' ban, which otherwise remained in place. A similar change was made by the Commonwealth that year to the 'Northern Territory Electoral Regulations'. In 1926, the *Invalid and Old-Age Pensions Act* (Cwlth) was modified by the exemption of 'Indians born in British India' from the 'aboriginal natives' exclusion. In the same year, the word 'Asiatics' in the *Maternity Allowance Act* (Cwlth) was replaced with 'aliens'.
73 Handwritten note, 7 March 1921, A432/79, 1961/3180, AA.

74 The man asserted that his parents were of Greek descent. Opinion of Garran, 17 January 1923, in Brazil and Mitchell (eds), *Opinions of Attorneys-General, vol. 2*, p. 960.
75 *Jiro Muramats v. Commonwealth Electoral Officer for the State of Western Australia, Commonwealth Law Reports*, vol. 32, 1923, pp. 500–8.
76 *Electoral Act 1907* (WA), section 18.
77 *Commonwealth Law Reports*, vol. 32, 1923, pp. 503–5.
78 Higgins, at p. 505.
79 Higgins, at p. 505.
80 Higgins, at pp. 506–7.
81 Opinion of Garran, 16 February 1925, A6091/T1, NN, AA.
82 Handwritten note dated 21 October 1925, A1, 1925/23976, AA.
83 Letter from Minister for Home Affairs to the Attorney-General, 7 January 1929; memorandum from Garran, 25 January 1929, A1, 1934/4190, AA.
84 Memorandum from Chief Electoral Officer, 11 February 1928, A1, 1928/1706, AA.
85 Opinion given by Assistant Secretary of the Attorney-General's Department, 23 March 1928, A1, 1928/1706, AA.
86 Opinion given by Assistant Secretary of the Attorney-General's Department, 23 March 1928, A1, 1928/1706, AA.
87 The dates of these opinions are more likely to be 17 April 1904 and 29 March 1906: see opinion of Garran, 17 April 1904, A96, vol. 1, AA; and opinion of Isaacs, 29 March 1906, A96, vol. 2, AA. Both opinions related to the nationality of persons born in British dominions, the latter referring to the former. The discrepancy in the dates may relate to a delay between when the opinion was received and inserted into the relevant Opinion Book, and when it was actually written.
88 See documents relating to Katie's claim, A432/81, 1930/2016, AA.
89 See documents relating to Katie's claim, A432/81, 1930/2016, AA.
90 See documents relating to Katie's claim, A432/81, 1930/2016, AA.
91 See opinion given by Acting Solicitor-General, 11 November 1930, A432/81, 1930/2016, AA.
92 Garran's opinion appears in a handwritten note, 7 March 1921, A432/79, 1961/3180, AA.
93 See letter from Chief Protector of Aboriginals (Qld) to the Queensland Home Department, 13 February 1934, A1, 1934/4190, AA.
94 See letter from Chief Protector of Aboriginals (Qld) to the Queensland Home Department, 13 February 1934, A1, 1934/4190, AA.
95 Letter from Commonwealth Statistician to South Australia's Chief Protector of Aborigines, 12 July 1939, A432/81, 1939/883, AA.
96 Memorandum from Secretary of Attorney-General's Department, 6 September 1939, A432/81, 1939/883, AA.
97 Memorandum from the Returning Officer for the Northern Territory, to which Garran replied on 31 July 1928, A79, 2, AA.
98 Opinion given by Garran, 31 July 1928, A79, 2, AA.
99 This opinion was confirmed in 1933 when the Secretary of the Attorney-General's Department advised that 'half-caste' Aborigines in the Northern Territory would be deemed non-Aboriginal for the purposes of the *Workmen's Compensation Ordinance*, but Aboriginal for the purposes of the *Aboriginals Ordinance*. See memorandum from Secretary, Attorney-General's Department, to the Secretary, Department of the Interior, 9 June 1933, A79, 2, AA.
100 The Premier's comments are quoted in a letter from the Assistant Crown Solicitor to the Secretary, Attorney-General's Department, 10 February 1938, A432/81, 1938/114, AA.
101 Letter from the Assistant Crown Solicitor to the Secretary, Attorney-General's Department, 10 February 1938, A432/81, 1938/114, AA.
102 Letter from Hughes to W. Riordan, 23 August 1940, A432/85, 1940/317, AA.
103 See, for example, letter from British India Delegation, Indian Round-Table Conference, to the Prime Minister, 25 November 1930, A981, India 16, part 2, AA.

104 Memorandum from the Chief Electoral Officer, 18 February 1922, A406/62, E1945/1, part 1, AA.
105 Memorandum from the Office of the Prime Minister, 16 January 1934, A981, India 16, part 2, AA.
106 *Electoral Act Amendent Act 1934* (WA), section 2; *Constitution Acts Amendment Act 1934* (WA), section 2; *Elections Acts Amendment Act 1930* (Qld), section 7.
107 Memorandum from Commissioner of Pensions, 29 May 1939, A571/97, 1938/883, AA.
108 Memorandum from Commissioner of Pensions, 29 May 1939, A571/97, 1938/883, AA.
109 Letter from Minister for Social Services to Prime Minister, 5 June 1939, A571/97, 1938/883, AA.
110 Circular letter from the Federal Commissioner of Taxation to Protectors of Aboriginals and Superintendents of Government Settlements, 7 October 1943, R254, 1D/86, Queensland State Archives.
111 *Child Endowment Act 1941* (Cwlth), section 15; *Widows' Pensions Act 1942* (Cwlth), section 14.
112 *Unemployment and Sickness Benefits Act 1944* (Cwlth), section 19.
113 *Invalid and Old-Age Pensions (Reciprocity with New Zealand) Act 1943* (Cwlth), especially section 8.
114 *Social Services Consolidation Act 1947* (Cwlth), sections 19, 62, 86, 97, 111. This general exclusion could be waived for most of these benefits where an Aboriginal: (a) was for the time being exempt from State or Territory Aboriginal protection laws; or (b) resided in a State or Territory that did not make provision for such exemption, and the Director-General was satisfied that payment of the pension was desirable by reason of the claimant's 'character', 'standard of intelligence' and 'social development'.
115 Commonwealth of Australia, *Report of the Royal Commission on the Constitution together with Appendixes and Index*, 1929, p. 270.
116 A copy of the petition appears in A431, 1949/1591, AA. The number of signatories is referred to in a memorandum from the Minister for the Interior, 1 February 1938, in the same series.
117 See memorandum from Minister for the Interior, 1 February 1938, A431, 1949/1591, AA.
118 Knowles, in an opinion of 14 January 1938, argued that the Constitution precluded the Commonwealth from making a special 'aboriginal electorate' (following the New Zealand Maori electorate model) to cover nationally all Aborigines *qua* Aborigines, however, under the provision of section 122 it could do so for all Commonwealth Territories: A431, 1949/1591, AA. The electoral effect of section 122 had in fact been first examined in 1912 when Garran advised that the Commonwealth could grant whatever representation it liked to its Territories (then the Northern Territory and the Federal Capital Territory) and determine the rights and powers (if any) of these representatives (see documents contained in A202, 14/1865, AA).
119 Memorandum from McEwen, the Minister for the Interior, 1 February 1938, A431, 1949/1591, AA.
120 See, for example: A.P. Elkin, *Citizenship for the Aborigines: A National Aboriginal Policy*, 1944; 'Aborigines and the Franchise', *The Aborigines' Protector*, vol. 2(2), 1946, pp. 3–9; 'Is White Australia Doomed?' and 'Re-thinking the White Australia Policy', in W.D. Borrie et al., *A White Australia: Australia's Population Problem*, 1947. O. Pink, 'An open letter to defenders of the tribespeople anywhere in Australia', *Communist Review*, February 1950, pp. 444–7. A.G. Price, *What of our Aborigines?*, n.d. (mid-1940s). J.H. Sexton, *Legislation Governing the Australian Aborigines*, 1933; *Australian Aborigines*, 1942; *Bringing the Aborigines into Citizenship: How Western Australia is Dealing with the Problem*, n.d.; *Aboriginal Intelligence: Has the Full-blooded Aboriginal Sufficient Intelligence to Undertake the Responsibilities of Citizenship?*, n.d.
121 *Commonwealth Electoral Act 1949*, section 3.
122 *Commonwealth Electoral (War-Time) Act 1940*, section 6.

123 Memorandum from Garrett, Department of the Interior, to the Parliamentary Draftsman, Attorney-General's Department, 8 April 1941, A472, W2526, AA. A copy of the bill is also contained in this record series.
124 See, for example, the document entitled 'Notes Regarding British Nationality Citizenship of the United Kingdom and Colonies and Status of Aliens Bill', and other documents contained in A467/1, Bundle 82/SF40/9. See also documents contained in A467/1, Bundle 83/SF40/5; and A467/1, Bundle 82/SF40/13.
125 Draft letter, attached to memorandum from the Secretary, Attorney-General's Department, to the Secretary, Department of Immigration, 27 June 1949, A432/81, 1949/576, AA.

5 The States Confine the Aboriginal Non-citizen

1 The 'Apprentices (Half-Castes) Regulations' of February 1930 were reprinted in the *Ordinances of the Territory of North Australia, 1927 to 1931*, pp. 400–7. The quote is from regulation 3.
2 On this issue see Andrew Markus, *Governing Savages*, 1990, p. 6.
3 See, for example, Markus, *Governing Savages*, p. 12.
4 *Aborigines Act 1915* (Vic), sections 5, 6, 7, 9.
5 *Victoria Government Gazette*, vols. 159–60, 1916, pp. 3547–53, regulations 25(c), 56.
6 Quoted in Diane Barwick, 'Equity for Aborigines? The Framlingham Case', in Patrick N. Troy (ed.), *A Just Society? Essays on Equity in Australia*, 1981, p. 192.
7 *Aborigines Act 1928* (Vic), sections 5, 6.
8 *Licensing Act 1915* (Vic), section 177; *Licensing Act 1928* (Vic), section 177.
9 The quote is from *Victoria Government Gazette*, vol. 204, 1931, p. 1560, regulation 34(b). Reference to the Crown Solicitor's opinion is given in Charles McLean, 'Report upon the Operation of the Aborigines Act 1928 and the Regulations and Orders made thereunder', *Victorian Parliamentary Papers* (hereafter *VPP*), 1956–58, vol. 2, p. 12. See also D. Barwick, A Little More Than Kin: Regional Affiliation and Group Identity among Aboriginal Migrants in Melbourne, PhD Thesis, Australian National University, 1963, pp. 92–3.
10 'Forty-ninth report of the Board for the Protection of the Aborigines', *VPP*, 1922, vol. 2, p. 3.
11 'Forty-eighth report of the Board', *VPP*, 1912, vol. 2, p. 7; Phillip Pepper and Tess De Araugo, *The Kurnai of Gippsland. What did happen to the Aborigines of Victoria*, 1985, pp. 241–5, 255, 258.
12 Pepper and De Araugo, *The Kurnai of Gippsland*, p. 249.
13 *Victoria Government Gazette*, vol. 41, 1871, p. 338, regulation 2. The regulation also appeared in *Victoria Government Gazette*, vol. 204, 1931, p. 1558, regulation 2.
14 Barwick, 'A Little More Than Kin', p. 97; Pepper and De Araugo, *The Kurnai of Gippsland*, pp. 256, 258.
15 McLean, 'Report upon the Operation of the Aborigines Act 1928', p. 12.
16 McLean, 'Report upon the Operation of the Aborigines Act 1928', pp. 13–14.
17 Pepper and De Araugo, *The Kurnai of Gippsland*, p. 259.
18 A minor amendment in 1927 enabled the Queensland Executive to set aside waters in which Aborigines and Islanders alone could fish: *Aboriginals Protection and Restriction of the Sale of Opium Acts Amendment Act 1927* (Qld). Another amendment in 1928 extended the penalty for selling opium to Aborigines: *Aboriginals Protection and Restriction of the Sale of Opium Act Amendment Act 1928* (Qld).
19 See, for instance, *Sugar Works Act 1911* (Qld), section 9; *Pearl-shell and Bêche-de-Mer Fishery Acts Amendment Act 1913* (Qld), section 7.
20 *Aboriginals Protection and Restriction of the Sale of Opium Acts Amendment Act 1934* (Qld), sections 4, 5.
21 Henry Reynolds and Dawn May, 'Queensland', in Ann McGrath (ed.), *Contested Ground: Australian Aborigines under the British Crown*, 1995, p. 193.

22 *Dempsey v. Rigg, Queensland State Reports*, 1914, p. 248.
23 Letter from the Deputy Chief Protector of Aboriginals to the Home Secretary's Office, 23 May 1935, R254, 1A/267, Queensland State Archives (hereafter QSA). Notes were made at the end of this letter indicating that the wording of the legislation had achieved its purpose.
24 Dawn May, 'Race Relations in Queensland 1897–1971', in Commissioner L.F. Wyvill, *Royal Commission into Aboriginal Deaths in Custody. Regional Report of Inquiry in Queensland*, 1991, pp. 141–2. See also C.D. Rowley, *Outcasts in White Australia*, 1972, p. 115.
25 May, 'Race Relations in Queensland', p. 145.
26 *Aboriginals Protection and Restriction of the Sale of Opium Acts Amendment Act 1934* (Qld), sections 7, 13, 15. The quote is from section 21.
27 *Aboriginals Protection and Restriction of the Sale of Opium Acts Amendment Act 1934* (Qld), section 16.
28 Letter from the Anti-Slavery and Aborigines Protection Society to the Chief Secretary's Office, 27 July 1937, R254, 1A/267, QSA.
29 Letter from the Chief Protector of Aboriginals to the Home Secretary's Office, 13 September 1935, A/69499, QSA.
30 Commonwealth of Australia, *Aboriginal Welfare: Initial Conference of Commonwealth and State Aboriginal Authorities held at Canberra, 21st to 23rd April, 1937*, 1937, p. 6.
31 *Aboriginals Preservation and Protection Act 1939* (Qld), sections 4, 5, 6, 8.
32 'Director of Native Affairs – Information Contained in Report for the Year ended 31st December, 1939', *Queensland Parliamentary Papers*, 1940, p. 1077; see also Reynolds and May, 'Queensland', p. 194.
33 Heather Wearne, *A Clash of Cultures: Queensland Aboriginal Policy (1824–1980)*, 1980, p. 14. See also Reynolds and May, 'Queensland', p. 194.
34 *Aboriginals Preservation and Protection Act 1939* (Qld), sections 12, 14, 19, 22.
35 The Assistant Crown Solicitor gave this opinion in 1938 in determining the eligibility of Islander women for the maternity allowance. See memorandum from L. Lyons, Attorney-General's Department, 4 August 1961, A432/79, 1961/3180, Australian Archives (hereafter AA), Canberra.
36 *Torres Strait Islanders Act 1939* (Qld), sections 6, 11, 21, 22.
37 *Aboriginals Preservation and Protection Act Amendment Act 1946* (Qld); *Torres Strait Islanders Act Amendment Act 1946* (Qld).
38 'The Aboriginals Regulations of 1945', *Queensland Government Gazette*, vol. 164, 1945, pp. 1063–74, regulations 19, 21, 22, 32.
39 *Elections Act 1915* (Qld), section 11.
40 *Elections Acts Amendment Act 1930* (Qld), sections 7, 8.
41 Letter from J.W. Bleakley, Chief Protector of Aboriginals, to the Under Secretary, Home Department, 13 February 1934, A1, 1934/4190, AA, Canberra.
42 Memorandum from the Acting Chief Electoral Officer for the Commonwealth, 28 May 1934, A1, 1934/4190, AA, Canberra.
43 Sandy Toussaint, 'Western Australia', in McGrath (ed.), *Contested Ground*, p. 253.
44 *Aborigines Act 1905* (WA), sections 3, 4, 6, 7, 8, 12.
45 *Aborigines Act 1905* (WA), sections 17, 18, 33, 37, 39, 40, 42.
46 *Aborigines Act 1905* (WA), section 55; *Licensing Act 1911* (WA), sections 118, 119.
47 *Aborigines Act Amendment Act 1911* (WA), sections 3, 11. The quote is from section 3.
48 See Rowley, *Outcasts in White Australia*, p. 7.
49 *Aborigines Act Amendment Act 1936* (WA), sections 2, 3.
50 Anna Haebich, *For Their Own Good: Aborigines and Government in the Southwest of Western Australia, 1900–1940*, 1988, pp. 337–40, 343; Toussaint, 'Western Australia', pp. 254–5. See also Peter Biskup, *Not Slaves Not Citizens: The Aboriginal Problem in Western Australia, 1898–1954*, 1973, pp. 167–9.
51 *Aborigines Act Amendment Act 1936* (WA), sections 3, 7, 12, 29.
52 *Aborigines Act Amendment Act 1936* (WA), sections 25, 26.

53 *Aborigines Act Amendment Act 1936* (WA), sections 9, 31.
54 Biskup, *Not Slaves Not Citizens*, p. 190; Michael C. Howard, *Aboriginal Politics in Southwestern Australia*, 1981, p. 18.
55 *Native Administration Act Amendment Act 1941* (WA), section 2. A further amendment in 1947 clarified the Executive's power to proclaim certain places in which Aborigines were not permitted to go: *Native Administration Act Amendment Act 1947* (WA), section 2.
56 *Natives (Citizenship Rights) Act 1944* (WA), sections 4, 6.
57 *Natives (Citizenship Rights) Act 1944* (WA), section 4.
58 Toussaint, 'Western Australia', p. 256.
59 *Natives (Citizenship Rights) Act 1944* (WA), section 5.
60 *Natives (Citizenship Rights) Act 1944* (WA), section 7.
61 *Natives (Citizenship Rights) Act 1944* (WA), sections 5, 6.
62 *Electoral Act 1907–40* (WA), section 18; *Constitution Acts Amendment Act 1934* (WA), section 2. The quote comes from the former Act. These disqualifications did not apply to anyone who was a 'naturalised subject'.
63 Letter from K.H. Bailey to the Select Committee on Voting Rights of Aboriginals, 6 October 1961, A432/79, 1961/3180, AA, Canberra.
64 *Liquor Act 1898* (NSW), section 48; *Branch v. Sceats, New South Wales Weekly Notes*, vol. 20, 1903, p. 42.
65 *Liquor (Amendment) Act 1905* (NSW), section 8(4); *Ex Parte Willan, New South Wales Weekly Notes*, vol. 27, 1910, pp. 147–8.
66 *Aborigines Protection Act 1909* (NSW), sections 3, 4, 14, 20.
67 *Aborigines Protection Act 1909* (NSW), section 9; *Liquor Act 1912* (NSW), section 49; *Liquor (Amendment) Act 1946* (NSW), section 46(1)(l); *Aborigines Protection (Amendment) Act 1963* (NSW), section 2.
68 Letter from the Victorian Board for the Protection of Aborigines to the New South Wales Board for the Protection of Aborigines, 27 September 1910, B329/2, item 8, AA, Victoria; Rowley, *Outcasts in White Australia*, pp. 12–13.
69 *Parliamentary Electorates and Elections Act 1912* (NSW), section 20.
70 Letter from Chanter to the Commonwealth Electoral Office, 18 April 1904, A101, B1904/4739, AA, Canberra.
71 Letter from the Riverina Divisional Returning Officer to the Commonwealth Electoral Office, 26 February 1904, A101, B1904/4739, AA, Canberra.
72 Letter from the Riverina Divisional Returning Officer to the Commonwealth Electoral Office, 2 March 1904, A101, B1904/4739, AA, Canberra.
73 Letter from the Commonwealth Electoral Office to the Riverina Divisional Returning Officer, 21 March 1904; letter from the Commonwealth Electoral Office to the Deniliquin Divisional Returning Officer, 3 May 1904, A101, B1904/4739, AA, Canberra.
74 This figure included 'aboriginal natives' of Asia, Africa and Islands of the Pacific, as well as Australian Aborigines: memorandum provided at the request of the Chief Electoral Officer, 3 April 1922, A406/62, E1945/1, part 1, AA, Canberra.
75 *Aborigines Protection Amending Act 1915* (NSW), sections 3, 4.
76 Heather Goodall, 'New South Wales', in McGrath (ed.), *Contested Ground*, p. 80; see also Gillian Cowlishaw, *Black, White or Brindle: Race in Rural Australia*, 1988, p. 80; Peter Read, *The Stolen Generations: The Removal of Aboriginal Children in New South Wales 1883 to 1969*, 1982, pp. 5–6.
77 *Aborigines Protection (Amendment) Act 1918* (NSW), section 2.
78 Bain Attwood, Winifred Burrage, Alan Burrage and Elsie Stokie, *A Life Together, A Life Apart: A History of Relations between Europeans and Aborigines*, 1994, pp. 8–9.
79 Goodall, 'New South Wales', pp. 83–4.
80 Letter from the Australian Aborigines Progressive Association to the Prime Minister, 8 October 1925, A1, 1925/23976, AA, Canberra.
81 Memorandum from the Secretary, Department of Home and Territories, 21 October 1925, A1, 1925/23976, AA, Canberra.
82 *Aborigines Protection (Amendment) Act 1936* (NSW), section 2.

83 Goodall, 'New South Wales', pp. 85–6; Markus, *Governing Savages*, p. 11. Attwood et al. argue that the expansion of reserves amounted more to a policy of concentration than assimilation, in *A Life Together*, p. 9.
84 *Aborigines Protection (Amendment) Act 1936* (NSW), section 2; the quote from the Board member comes from Rowley, *Outcasts in White Australia*, p. 59. See also Richard Broome, *Aboriginal Australians: Black Response to White Dominance*, 1982, p. 163.
85 Goodall, 'New South Wales', p. 86. See also Goodall, 'Cryin' Out for Land Rights', in Verity Burgmann and Jenny Lee (eds), *Staining the Wattle: A People's History of Australia Since 1788*, 1988, p. 190.
86 Goodall, 'New South Wales', pp. 87–8; Richard Broome, 'Victoria', in McGrath (ed.), *Contested Ground*, p. 147.
87 Memorandum from the Minister for the Interior, 1 February 1938; a copy of the petition appears in the same group of papers in A431, 1949/1591, AA, Canberra.
88 Transcription of letter from Australian Aboriginal League to the Prime Minister, 26 October 1937, contained in Opinion of the Solicitor-General, 14 January 1938, A431, 1949/1591, AA, Canberra.
89 Opinion of the Solicitor-General, 14 January 1938, A431, 1949/1591, AA, Canberra.
90 Goodall, 'New South Wales', pp. 87–8; Broome, 'Victoria', p. 147.
91 Goodall, 'New South Wales', pp. 87–8; Russell McGregor, 'Protest and Progress: Aboriginal Activism in the 1930s', *Australian Historical Studies*, vol. 25, 1993, pp. 555–68; Markus, *Governing Savages*, pp. 178–9.
92 Rowley, *Outcasts in White Australia*, pp. 73, 77; J.P.M. Long, *Aboriginal Settlements: A Survey of Institutional Communities in Eastern Australia*, 1970, pp. 30–1.
93 *Aborigines Protection (Amendment) Act 1940* (NSW), sections 2, 3; *Aborigines Protection (Amendment) Act 1943* (NSW), section 2.
94 *Child Welfare Act 1939* (NSW), sections 72–93; Read, *The Stolen Generations*, p. 7.
95 *Aborigines Protection (Amendment) Act 1940* (NSW), section 3.
96 *Aborigines Protection (Amendment) Act 1943* (NSW), section 4.
97 *Aborigines Act 1911* (SA), sections 4, 8, 17, 26, 35.
98 *Aborigines Act 1911* (SA), sections 19, 27, 31, 33, 38.
99 Peggy Brock, 'South Australia', in McGrath (ed.), *Contested Ground*, p. 227; see also Fay Gale, *A Study of Assimilation: Part-Aborigines in South Australia*, 1964, pp. 106–8.
100 *Bray v. Milera, South Australian State Reports*, 1935, p. 210.
101 Brock, 'South Australia', p. 229.
102 *Aborigines Act 1934* (SA), sections 4, 47, 48; *Aborigines Act 1934 to 1939* (SA), section 4.
103 *Licensing Act 1917* (SA), section 169; *Dodd v. Walsh*, an unreported case of the South Australian Supreme Court, was discussed in *Amesbury v. Copeland, South Australian State Reports*, 1928, at pp. 487–8.
104 *Amesbury v. Copeland, South Australian State Reports*, 1928, p. 485. A similar case and decision occurred in *Williams v. Wight, South Australian State Reports*, 1943, p. 301.
105 *Aborigines Act 1934* (SA), sections 5, 7, 8, 9, 17, 19, 26, 35.
106 *Aborigines Act 1934* (SA), sections 27, 31.
107 *Aborigines Act 1934* (SA), sections 33, 42.
108 *Aborigines Act 1934 to 1939* (SA), sections 4A, 4C, 7, 11A, 17, 19, 35.
109 *Police Act 1936* (SA), section 85. In addition, the *Aborigines Act 1934 to 1939* (SA), section 34A, prohibited non-Aboriginal men from consorting or having sex with Aboriginal women. See Brock, 'South Australia', p. 231.
110 Pat Stretton and Christine Finnimore, *How South Australian Aborigines Lost the Vote: Some Side Effects of Federation*, 1991, pp. 5–6.
111 *Aborigines Act 1934* (SA), sections 7, 10, 38, 39; *Aborigines (Training of Children) Act 1923* (SA), sections 6, 7.
112 *Aborigines Act 1934 to 1939* (SA), sections 38, 39, 40A.
113 *Northern Territory Aboriginals Act 1910* (SA), sections 3, 7, 16, 43, 44, 45, 46.
114 *Northern Territory Aboriginals Act 1910* (SA), sections 22, 23.
115 Peter Read, 'Northern Territory', in McGrath (ed.), *Contested Ground*, p. 276.
116 *Commonwealth Government Gazette*, 1911, pp. 1898–9.

117 *Aboriginals Ordinance 1911* (NT) sections 3, 5, 9, schedule.
118 *Aboriginals Ordinance 1918* (NT), section 3; *Aboriginals Ordinance 1927* (NT), section 2.
119 *Aboriginals Ordinance 1918* (NT), sections 5, 7, 16.
120 *Aboriginals Ordinance 1918* (NT), sections 22, 23, 24, 26. The quote is from section 46.
121 *Aboriginals Ordinance 1918* (NT), sections 45, 53.
122 Ann McGrath, *'Born in the Cattle': Aborigines in Cattle Country*, 1987, p. 86.
123 *Aboriginals Ordinance 1918* (NT), sections 15, 17, 27, 55.
124 *Aboriginals Ordinance 1918* (NT), sections 11, 48, 67.
125 *Commonwealth Government Gazette*, 1919, p. 909, regulations 16, 17.
126 These regulations of December 1929 were reprinted in the *Ordinances of the Territory of North Australia 1927 to 1931*, pp. 397–400.
127 Read, 'Northern Territory', p. 277.
128 J.W. Bleakley, 'The Aboriginals and Half-Castes of Central Australia and North Australia', *Commonwealth Parliamentary Papers*, 1929, vol. 2, p. 29. For a good discussion of inter-racial sexual relations in the Northern Territory see McGrath, '*Born in the Cattle*', chapter 4.
129 Bleakley, 'The Aboriginals and Half-Castes of Central Australia and North Australia', pp. 30–31.
130 *Tuckiar v. the King*, *Commonwealth Law Reports*, vol. 52, 1934, p. 335. A summary of Elkin's and Rowley's comments are contained in C.D. Rowley, *The Destruction of Aboriginal Society*, 1972, pp. 290–7. For a good discussion of the case and the trial Judge, see Markus, *Governing Savages*, pp. 118–19. See also now Ted Egan, *Justice All Their Own: The Caledon Bay and Woodah Island Killings 1932–1933*, 1996.
131 McGrath, '*Born in the Cattle*', pp. 93–4.
132 The 'Apprentices (Half-Castes) Regulations' of February 1930 were reprinted in the *Ordinances of the Territory of North Australia, 1927 to 1931*, pp. 400–7. See regulations 2, 3, 8. The quote is from regulation 3.
133 *Aboriginals Ordinance 1936* (NT), section 2; *Aboriginals Ordinance 1943* (NT), section 2. The figure of 500 exempted Aborigines comes from a document entitled 'Citizenship. Legislation affecting Aboriginals', which exists with documents relating to the Native Welfare Council meeting in Canberra, September 1952, A452, 1951/1721, AA, Canberra.
134 *Workmen's Compensation Ordinance 1931* (NT), section 3; *Aboriginals Ordinance 1933* (NT), section 10; *Aboriginals Ordinance 1936* (NT), section 4; 'Aboriginals Regulations', *Commonwealth Government Gazette*, 1933, p. 941, regulations 30, 31.
135 Markus, *Governing Savages*, p. 9.
136 Commonwealth of Australia, *Aboriginal Welfare: Initial Conference of Commonwealth and State Aboriginal Authorities held at Canberra, 21st to 23rd April, 1937*, 1937, pp. 13–14. See also Read, 'Northern Territory', p. 281. For a good account of the 1937 conference see Rowley, *Destruction*, pp. 319–28.
137 Commonwealth of Australia, *Aboriginal Welfare: Initial Conference 1937*, p. 14. See also Read, 'Northern Territory', p. 281.
138 J. McEwen, 'The Northern Territory of Australia. Commonwealth Government's Policy with Respect to Aboriginals', 1939, R254, 1A/267, QSA. See also Read, 'Northern Territory', p. 281.
139 *Aboriginals Ordinance 1939* (NT), section 4; McEwen, 'The Northern Territory of Australia. Commonwealth Government's Policy with Respect to Aboriginals'.
140 *Native Administration Ordinance 1940* (NT), sections 3, 5, 7, 8, 9.
141 Read, 'Northern Territory', p. 284.
142 *Northern Territory Representation Act 1922* (Cwlth), section 7; 'Northern Territory Electoral Regulations', *Commonwealth Statutory Rules 1922*, no. 154, regulation 22.
143 Memorandum from the Returning Officer for the Northern Territory, 1928. Garran's opinion is dated 31 July 1928. Both documents are contained in A79, 2, AA, Canberra.
144 Memorandum from the Administrator of the Northern Territory, R.H. Weddell, 4 April 1933, A1, 1933/2419, AA, Canberra.

145 *Workmen's Compensation Ordinance 1931* (NT), section 3. Memorandum from the Secretary, Attorney-General's Department, to the Secretary, Department for the Interior, 9 June 1933, A79, 2, AA, Canberra.
146 *Licensing Act 1908* (Tas), section 34; *Cape Barren Island Reserve Act 1912* (Tas), sections 26, 29; *Cape Barren Island Reserve Act 1945* (Tas), sections 19, 22. See Ann McGrath, 'Tasmania: 1', in McGrath (ed.), *Contested Ground*, pp. 327–8.
147 Commonwealth of Australia, *Aboriginal Welfare: Initial Conference 1937*, p. 21.
148 Commonwealth of Australia, *Aboriginal Welfare: Initial Conference 1937*, p. 21.
149 Commonwealth of Australia, *Aboriginal Welfare: Initial Conference 1937*, p. 11.
150 See, for instance, *Victorian Parliamentary Debates*, Council, vol. 136, 8 July 1914, pp. 238–9; Markus, *Governing Savages*, p. 2.
151 Biskup, *Not Slaves Not Citizens*, pp. 193–4.
152 Commonwealth of Australia, *Aboriginal Welfare: Initial Conference 1937*, p. 34.
153 Document prepared by the Queensland Chief Protector of Aborigines, entitled 'Summary of Past Aboriginal Policy', 21 August 1936, A/69499, QSA. The Bishop's call had first been made in an article in the *Courier-Mail* in July 1935. See letter from Bleakley to the Home Secretary's Office, 16 August 1935, R254, 1A/267, QSA.
154 *Commonwealth Parliamentary Debates* (hereafter *CPD*), Representatives, vol. 177, 11 February 1944, pp. 136–7; vol. 173, 26 February 1943, p. 1091.
155 *CPD*, Representatives, vol. 177, 11 February 1944, p. 138. The quote is from vol. 177, 8 March 1944, p. 1102.
156 Constitution Alteration (War Aims and Reconstruction) Bill, October 1942; Constitution Alteration (Post-War Reconstruction) Bill, November 1942, section 2; A.P. Elkin, *Citizenship for the Aborigines: A National Aboriginal Policy*, 1944, p. 7; see also Biskup, *Not Slaves Not Citizens*, pp. 198–9.
157 Constitution Alteration (Post-War Reconstruction and Democratic Rights) 1944 Proposed Law, section 2.
158 The result of the referendum is reported in *Commonwealth Parliamentary Papers*, 1945–6, vol. 4, p. 1101; see also Scott Bennett, *Aborigines and Political Power*, 1989, p. 10.
159 See *CPD*, Senate, vol. 178, 22 March 1944, p. 1702.
160 *CPD*, Senate, vol. 178, 22 and 23 March 1944, p. 1865. Other observations that Aborigines had been treated better by the States than the Commonwealth were made in *CPD*, Representatives, vol. 172, 24 and 25 September 1942, p. 935; vol. 174, 12 March 1943, p. 1681; and vol. 177, 14 March 1944, p. 1267.

6 The Slow Path to Civil Rights

1 Letter from Attorney-General Garfield Barwick to Bryant, 9 July 1959, A432/81, 1966/3171, AA, Canberra (all references to AA in this chapter are to the Canberra office).
2 Draft opinion of Attorney-General Garfield Barwick, n.d. but probably May or June 1959, A432/81, 1966/3171, AA.
3 *Commonwealth Electoral (War-time) Act 1940*, section 6.
4 *Commonwealth Electoral Act 1949*, section 3. Letter from Secretary, Department of the Interior, to A.P. Elkin, 23 September 1948; letter from Elkin to the Secretary, Department of the Interior, 23 October 1948; A431, 1949/822, AA.
5 *Commonwealth Electoral Act 1949*, section 3.
6 Letter from the Chief Electoral Officer to the Secretary, Department of the Interior, 6 November 1941; memorandum from the Secretary, Department of the Interior, 13 March 1946; A431, 1949/822, AA.
7 *Commonwealth Electoral Act 1961*, section 4. Section 6 of this Act restated a person's eligibility to vote pursuant to section 41 of the Constitution, but this had ceased to be relevant to Aborigines following the linking of the federal franchise to State eligibility.
8 See memorandum from Chief Electoral Officer to Department of Territories, 7 September 1959, A406/62, E1957/1, part 4, AA; undated document entitled 'Aborigines – Northern Territory', A406/62, E1957/1, part 4, AA.

9 Memorandum from the Chief Electoral Officer to the Commonwealth Electoral Officers in all States, 5 September 1961, A406/62, E1957/1, part 2, AA.
10 Letter from the Commonwealth Electoral Officer for Queensland to the Chief Electoral Officer, 8 June 1961, A406/62, E1957/1, part 3, AA.
11 Memorandum from C.W. Harders to the Secretary, Prime Minister's Department, 7 July 1961, A432/79, 1961/3125, AA; memoranda from L.D. Lyons, Attorney-General's Department, 9 June 1961 and 4 August 1961, A432/79, 1961/3180, AA.
12 Memorandum from the Chief Electoral Officer to the Commonwealth Electoral Officers in all States, 5 September 1961, A406/62, E1957/1, part 2, AA.
13 Letter from the Commonwealth Electoral Officer for South Australia to the Sergeant at Arms, House of Represenatives, 29 June 1961, A406/62, E1957/1, part 2, AA.
14 Commonwealth Parliament, 'Report from the Select Committee on Voting Rights of Aborigines. Part I – Report and Minutes of Proceedings' (hereafter 'Report from the Select Committee on Voting Rights of Aborigines'), *Commonwealth Parliamentary Papers* (hereafter *CPP*), 1961, vol. 2, pp. 1, 2, 10.
15 'Report from the Select Committee on Voting Rights of Aborigines', p. 2.
16 'Report from the Select Committee on Voting Rights of Aborigines', pp. 4–5; see also the comments of Kim Beazley Snr in *Commonwealth Parliamentary Debates* (hereafter *CPD*), Representatives, vol. 35, 12 April 1962, p. 1702.
17 'Report from the Select Committee on Voting Rights of Aborigines', pp. 8, 38–41.
18 Transcript of evidence of Cornelius O'Leary to the Select Committee on Voting Rights of Aborigines, n.d., R254, 1A/554, Queensland State Archives (hereafter QSA).
19 Letter from the Director of Native Affairs (Queensland) to the Department of Health and Home Affairs, Brisbane, 5 June 1961, R254, 1A/554, QSA.
20 'Report from the Select Committee on Voting Rights of Aborigines', pp. 8–9. One view put forward by the Anglican Bishop of North Queensland was that eligibility for the franchise be determined by an education test: *Courier-Mail*, 21 June 1961, R254, 1A/554, QSA.
21 *CPD*, Representatives, vol. 33, 19 October 1961, p. 2247; vol. 35, 1 May 1962, p. 1771.
22 Confidential letter from Department of External Affairs and Department of Territories to Australian Diplomatic Posts, 24 January 1962, R254, 1A/345, QSA.
23 *Commonwealth Electoral Act 1962*, section 2.
24 *CPD*, Representatives, vol. 35, 12 April 1962, p. 1697.
25 Letter from G. Freeth to Prime Minister Menzies, 26 October 1961, A406/62, E1957/1, part 4, AA.
26 'Report from the Select Committee on Voting Rights of Aborigines', pp. 4, 8; *Commonwealth Electoral Act 1962*, section 3.
27 *Social Services Consolidation Act 1947* (Cwlth), sections 19(2), 47, 62(2), 76, 86(3), 91, 95(4), 97, 111. The policy quotation comes from a letter from the Prime Minister's Department to the Premier of Queensland, 26 July 1950, R254, 1A/467, QSA.
28 Opinion of P. Brazil, Attorney-General's Department, 22 February 1956; memorandum from L.D. Lyons to the Repatriation Commission, 20 April 1956; A432/75, 1955/3765, AA.
29 Letter from William McMahon, Minister for Social Services, to J.C. Knight, West Australian Native Welfare Council, 19 August 1955, A432/75, 1955/3765, AA.
30 Opinion of P. Brazil, Attorney-General's Department, 22 February 1956, A432/75, 1955/3765, AA.
31 Letter from H.J. Goodes, Department of Social Services, to the Secretary, Prime Minister's Department, January 1959, A432/70, 1967/3321, part 1, AA.
32 Letter from Acting Director, Department of Social Services, to the Department of Native Affairs, Brisbane, 2 October 1950, R254, 3A/207, QSA.
33 *Social Services Act 1959* (Cwlth), sections 6, 9, 11, 14, 16, 17, 18, 22. The quote is from section 24 (which inserted a new section 137A into the principal Act).
34 Statement by the Minister for Social Services, Hugh Roberton, 10 July 1959, R254, 1A/467, QSA.

35 Letter from the Department of Social Services to the Director of Native Affairs, Queensland, 16 December 1959, R254, 1A/467, QSA.
36 *Social Services Act 1966* (Cwlth), section 29. Section 26 of this Act also repealed the provision that had limited the payment of the child endowment only to Aboriginal children who were not dependent on State or Commonwealth support.
37 *Natives (Citizenship Rights) Act Amendment Act 1950* (WA), sections 2, 3; *Natives (Citizenship Rights) Act Amendment Act 1951* (WA), sections 5, 6.
38 *Natives (Citizenship Rights) Act Amendment Act 1951* (WA), section 8.
39 *Electoral Act Amendment Act 1951* (WA), section 3. See also the *Constitution Acts Amendment Act 1955* (WA), section 2.
40 *Natives (Citizenship Rights) Act Amendment Act 1958* (WA), sections 3, 4, 6. Another change to this legislation in 1964 allowed children named in their parents' Certificates of Citizenship to attain State citizenship at the age of 21: *Natives (Citizenship Rights) Act Amendment Act (No.2) 1964* (WA), section 2.
41 Commonwealth Parliament, 'Report from the Select Committee on Voting Rights of Aborigines. Part II – Minutes of Evidence' (hereafter 'Select Committee on Voting Rights of Aborigines – Minutes of Evidence'), *CPP*, 1961, vol. 2, pp. 170, 457.
42 *Native Administration Act Amendment Act 1954* (WA), section 2.
43 *Native Welfare Act 1905–1954* (WA), sections 4, 7, 8.
44 *Native Welfare Act 1954* (WA), sections 14, 18, 20, 41, 42, 43, 46, 60, 64.
45 Letters from S. McDonald to P. Hasluck, Minister for Territories, 12 February and March 1959; letter from Hasluck to Attorney-General Barwick, 5 May 1959; draft opinions of Attorney-General Garfield Barwick, n.d. but probably May or June 1959; A432/81, 1966/3171, AA.
46 *Electoral Act 1907–1953* (WA), section 18; *Constitution Acts Amendment Act 1955* (WA), section 2; *Native Welfare Act Amendment Act 1960* (WA), section 2. See also 'Report from the Select Committee on Voting Rights of Aborigines', p. 6.
47 For a discussion on this issue, dealing with similar 1951 changes to the citizenship legislation, see *Western Australia Parliamentary Debates* (hereafter *WAPD*), Assembly, vol. 129, 30 October 1951, p. 317.
48 Letter from K.H. Bailey to the Select Committee on Voting Rights of Aborigines, 6 October 1961, A432/79, 1961/3180, AA (his emphasis). See also Sawer in Appendix III of the 'Report from the Select Committee on Voting Rights of Aborigines', p. 37.
49 'Select Committee on Voting Rights of Aborigines – Minutes of Evidence', p. 169; 'Report from the Select Committee on Voting Rights of Aborigines', p. 6.
50 *Electoral Act Amendment Act 1962* (WA), section 3; *Constitution Acts Amendment Act (No. 2) 1962* (WA), section 3.
51 *WAPD*, Assembly, vol. 162, 16 October 1962, p. 1757.
52 *Criminal Code Amendment Act (No.2) 1963* (WA), section 3.
53 *Native Welfare Act 1963* (WA), sections 7, 10, 17, 18, 19, 20, 23, 29, 37, 38.
54 *Aborigines' and Torres Strait Islanders' Affairs Act 1965* (Qld), sections 6, 7.
55 *Aborigines' and Torres Strait Islanders' Affairs Act 1965* (Qld), sections 8, 16, 17, 18, 20, 23.
56 *Aborigines' and Torres Strait Islanders' Affairs Act 1965* (Qld), sections 8, 10, 16, 26, 34.
57 *Aborigines' and Torres Strait Islanders' Affairs Act 1965* (Qld), sections 27, 28.
58 'Aborigines' and Torres Strait Islanders' Regulations of 1966', *Queensland Government Gazette*, vol. 221, 1966, pp. 2105–34, regulation 15; see also C.D. Rowley, *Outcasts in White Australia*, 1973, pp. 358, 414.
59 *Aborigines' and Torres Strait Islanders' Affairs Act 1965* (Qld), sections 13, 44, 60. A minor amending Act in 1967 did not substantially affect any of the provisions we have detailed: *Aborigines' and Torres Strait Islanders' Affairs Act Amendment Act 1967* (Qld).
60 Quoted in C.M. Tatz, 'Queensland's Aborigines: Natural Justice and the Rule of Law', *Australian Quarterly*, vol. 35, no. 3, September 1963, pp. 33–49, at p. 43.
61 *Elections Acts Amendment Act 1959* (Qld), section 8; *Elections Acts 1915 to 1962* (Qld), sections 11, 11A.
62 See 'Report from the Select Committee on Voting Rights of Aborigines', p. 5.

63 Letter from the Director of Native Affairs (Queensland) to the Department of Health and Home Affairs, Brisbane, 5 June 1961, R254, 1A/554, QSA.
64 Submission by H.W. Noble, Minister for Health and Home Affairs, to Cabinet, n.d. but probably late 1961, R254, 1A/573, QSA.
65 Statement by H.W. Noble, Minister for Health and Home Affairs, circulated in December 1957, A/58919, QSA.
66 'Report of Special Committee enquiring into Legislation for the Promotion of the Well-being of Aborigines and Torres Strait Islanders in Queensland', 1964, R254, 1A/580, QSA.
67 *Elections Acts Amendment Act 1965* (Qld), sections 3, 4.
68 'The Aborigines' and Torres Strait Islanders' Regulations of 1966', regulation 70 (emphasis added).
69 Aborigines were, however, able to give evidence without oath: *Evidence Ordinances 1939* (NT), section 9A; this was repealed by *Evidence Ordinance 1967* (NT), section 3.
70 *Waters v. Commonwealth, Commonwealth Law Reports*, vol. 82, 1951, p. 188. The quotations appear at pp. 193, 195, 196.
71 Memorandum from the Administrator, Darwin, Northern Territory, to the Director of Northern Territory Affairs, Department of the Interior, 9 April 1951, A431, 1951/889, AA.
72 Memorandum from the Administrator, Darwin, Northern Territory, to the Director of Northern Territory Affairs, Department of the Interior, 9 April 1951, A431, 1951/889, AA.
73 Memorandum from the Administrator, Darwin, Northern Territory, to the Director of Northern Territory Affairs, Department of the Interior, 9 April 1951, A431, 1951/889, AA. Letter from the Australian Halfcaste Progressive Association to the Prime Minister, 12 March 1951, A431, 1951/889, AA.
74 Document entitled 'Commonwealth and States Conference on Native Welfare', Canberra, 3 to 4 September 1951, A452, 1951/1721, AA. See also Rowley, *Outcasts*, p. 398.
75 Statement by Paul Hasluck, Minister for Territories, Native Welfare Council Meeting, Canberra, 29 September 1952, A452, 1951/1721, AA. See also Hasluck in *CPD*, Representatives, vol. 218, 6 August 1952, pp. 44–6.
76 *Aboriginals Ordinance (No. 2) 1953* (NT), sections 3, 4. The definition of 'Aboriginal' was slightly more expanded for children.
77 *Centralian Advocate*, 2 October 1953, in A431, 1951/889, AA.
78 *Welfare Ordinance 1953* (NT), sections 4, 14.
79 *Welfare Ordinance 1953–1960* (NT), section 15.
80 'Report from the Select Committee on Voting Rights of Aborigines', p. 7. See also Peter Read, 'Northern Territory', in Ann McGrath (ed.), *Contested Ground: Australian Aborigines under the British Crown*, 1995, pp. 285–6.
81 *Welfare Ordinance 1953–1960* (NT), sections 17, 64, 67, 71B; *Police and Police Offences Ordinance 1961* (NT), section 5 (repealed by the *Police and Police Offences Ordinance 1964* (NT), section 5).
82 *Licensing Ordinance 1939–1960* (NT), sections 141, 142; *Licensing Ordinance (No. 2) 1962* (NT), section 2.
83 *Wards' Employment Ordinance 1953–1959* (NT), sections 32, 41.
84 *Wards' Employment Ordinance 1960* (NT), section 2; *Wards' Employment Ordinance Repeal Ordinance 1971* (NT), section 2. See Read, 'Northern Territory', p. 288.
85 Colin A. Hughes, 'The Marriage of Mick and Gladys: A Discretion without an Appeal', in B.B. Schaffer and D.C. Corbett (eds), *Case Studies in Australian Administration*, 1965.
86 Rowley, *Outcasts*, p. 400. The quotation appears at the same page.
87 *Social Welfare Ordinance 1964* (NT), sections 6, 7, 10.
88 Alcohol still remained illegal on Aboriginal reserves. See Rowley, *Outcasts*, p. 414.
89 'Northern Territory Electoral Regulations', *Commonwealth Statutory Rules 1947*, No. 148, regulation 22; *Commonwealth Statutory Rules 1949*, No. 61, regulation 3. See also document entitled 'Citizenship. Legislation Affecting Aboriginals', n.d., A452, 1951/1721, AA.

90 *Commonwealth Statutory Rules 1957*, No. 66 (the sole regulation); *Commonwealth Statutory Rules 1961*, No. 132, regulation 4; *Welfare Ordinance 1953–1960* (NT), section 14(2); *Commonwealth Statutory Rules 1962*, No. 49, regulation 1.
91 *CPD*, Representatives, vol. 37, 23 October 1962, p. 1779.
92 Charles McLean, 'Report Upon the Operation of the Aborigines Act 1928 and the Regulations and Orders made Thereunder', *Victorian Parliamentary Papers*, Legislative Assembly, 1956–58, vol. 2, pp. 11, 16, 19–21. The offences listed appeared in the following: *Aborigines Act 1928* (Vic), section 12; *Licensing Act 1928* (Vic), section 177; *Police Offences Act 1957* (Vic), section 69. See also Richard Broome, 'Victoria', in McGrath (ed.), *Contested Ground*, pp. 149–50.
93 *Aborigines Act 1957* (Vic), sections 3, 5, 6, 10, 11, 12. The quotes are from section 6. An *Aborigines Act 1958* (Vic) was passed one year later when the Victorian Government reprinted its statutes. No significant changes were made to the position that had existed the year before.
94 *Aboriginal Affairs Act 1967* (Vic), sections 2, 4, 10, 11, 18, 26, 42.
95 *Aborigines Protection (Amendment) Act 1963* (NSW), section 2; *Liquor (Amendment) Act 1946* (NSW), section 46(1)(l). See also Rowley, *Outcasts*, pp. 358, 407, 414.
96 Heather Goodall, 'New South Wales', in McGrath (ed.), *Contested Ground*, pp. 89–90, 94–5. The quote is from p. 94.
97 'Report from the Select Committee on Voting Rights of Aborigines', p. 5; 'Select Committee on Voting Rights of Aborigines – Minutes of Evidence', pp. 500–1.
98 *Aborigines Welfare Ordinance 1954* (ACT), sections 2, 3, 5, 7, 8, 11, 16, 17.
99 *Aborigines Welfare Repeal Ordinance 1965* (ACT), section 2.
100 *Juries Ordinance 1932–1951* (ACT), section 5. Repealed by *Juries Ordinance 1967* (ACT), section 5.
101 *Advisory Council Ordinance 1936–1938* (ACT), sections 5(3), (7).
102 'Australian Capital Territory Electoral Regulations', *Commonwealth Statutory Rules 1949*, No. 73, regulations 12, 14.
103 *Advisory Council Ordinance 1936–1959* (ACT), sections 3, 5. See also draft memorandum to the Secretary, Department of the Interior, July 1957, A432/77, 1957/3197, AA.
104 The ACT's franchise restrictions on Aboriginal natives of Asia, Africa and the Islands of the Pacific were removed in 1961: *Commonwealth Statutory Rules 1961*, No. 133, regulation 3.
105 *Aboriginal Affairs Act 1962* (SA), sections 4, 25, 26, 40.
106 Rowley, *Outcasts*, p. 358.
107 *Aboriginal Lands Trust Act 1966* (SA), sections 5, 6, 16, 18; *Aboriginal Affairs Act Amendment Act 1966–1967* (SA), section 3. The Aboriginal Reserve Councils had been set up by regulations under the *Aboriginal Affairs Act 1962* (SA): see *Aboriginal Lands Trust Act 1966* (SA), section 6.
108 *Aboriginal Affairs Act 1962* (SA), sections 5, 13, 15, 16, 17.
109 *Cape Barren Island Reserve Act 1945* (Tas); *Cape Barren Island Reserve Act 1950* (Tas); *Statute Law Revision Act 1958* (Tas), section 2; *Licensing Act 1932* (Tas), section 97(6). This last provision was repealed by the *Licensing Act 1958* (Tas), section 69(a).
110 Letter from Kim Beazley Snr to Prime Minister Chifley, 14 September 1949, A431, 1949/1591, AA.
111 Commonwealth Parliament, 'Report from the Joint Committee on Constitutional Review, 1958', *CPP*, 1958, vol. 6, p. 11; 'Report from the Joint Committee on Constitutional Review, 1959', *CPP*, 1959–1960, vol. 3, pp. 55–6.
112 For example, *CPD*, Representatives, vol. 30, 13 April 1961, p. 806; vol. 35, 12 April 1962, p. 1632; vol. 45, 1 April 1965, p. 528.
113 See, for instance, the comments of Gordon Bryant in *CPD*, Representatives, vol. 35, 12 April 1962, p. 1710.
114 *CPD*, Representatives, vol. 36, 30 August 1962, pp. 877–9.
115 *CPD*, Representatives, vol. 36, 30 August 1962, p. 880.
116 *CPD*, Representatives, vol. 42, 14 May 1964, p. 1902.
117 *CPD*, Representatives, vol. 48, 11 November 1965, pp. 2638–40.

118 *CPD*, Representatives, vol. 50, 10 March 1966, pp. 121, 123.
119 *CPD*, Representatives, vol. 54, 1 March 1967, pp. 263–4.
120 Commonwealth Parliament, 'Statistical Returns', *CPP*, 1968, vol. 3, p. 19.
121 The official 'Yes' case appears in Christopher Cunneen and Terry Libesman, *Indigenous People and the Law in Australia*, 1995, pp. 182–3. For an example of the argument that the referendum sought to 'transfer' responsibility for Aboriginal affairs from the States to the Commonwealth, see Goodall, 'New South Wales', p. 108.
122 Cunneen and Libesman, *Indigenous People and the Law in Australia*, p. 182.
123 See, for example, *CPD*, Representatives, vol. 36, 30 August 1962, pp. 879, 882; vol. 42, 14 May 1964, p. 1904; vol. 49, 23 November 1965, p. 3071.
124 Scott Bennett, *Aborigines and Political Power*, 1989, pp. 10–11. See also Verity Burgmann, *Power and Protest: Movements for Change in Australian Society*, 1993, p. 33; Ann McGrath, 'A National Story', in McGrath (ed.), *Contested Ground*, p. 46.
125 Faith Bandler, *Turning the Tide: A Personal History of the Federal Council for the Advancement of Aborigines and Torres Strait Islanders*, 1989, p. 98. Illustrating its significance, this story is referred to in Elliott Johnston, *Royal Commission into Aboriginal Deaths in Custody: National Report*, vol. 2, p. 519.
126 *Migration Act 1973* (Cwlth), section 6.
127 *Aboriginal Affairs (Arrangements with the States) Act 1973* (Cwlth), section 5.
128 *Aboriginal Development Commission Act 1980* (Cwlth), section 8.
129 *Commonwealth Electoral Legislation Amendment Act 1983*, section 28.
130 Both of these quotations appear in Bennett, *Aborigines and Political Power*, p. 79.
131 *Aboriginal Affairs Act 1962* (SA), section 17; *Aboriginal Affairs Act Amendment Act 1968* (SA), sections 5, 9.
132 *Evidence Act Amendment Act 1968* (SA), section 2; *Criminal Law Consolidation Act Amendment Act 1971* (SA), section 4.
133 *Community Welfare Act 1972* (SA), sections 5, 6, 84, 85.
134 *Liquor Act 1970* (WA), section 130. This provision was repealed in 1972 by the *Liquor Act Amendment Act 1972* (WA), section 32. See also Rowley, *Outcasts*, p. 358; Sandy Toussaint, 'Western Australia', in McGrath (ed.), *Contested Ground*, p. 259. *Natives (Citizenship Rights) Act Repeal Act 1971* (WA), section 2.
135 *Aboriginal Affairs Planning Authority Act 1972* (WA), sections 4, 6, 8, 10, 13, 18, 19, 20, 21, 23, 24, 33, 48, 49.
136 *Aboriginal Affairs Planning Authority Act Amendment Act 1973* (WA), section 3.
137 *Aboriginal Communities Act 1979* (WA), sections 4, 5, 7.
138 *Aborigines Act 1969* (NSW), sections 2, 4, 6, 8, 9, 10, 13, 14.
139 *Aborigines (Amendment) Act 1973* (NSW), sections 4, 5; *Aboriginal Land Rights Act 1983* (NSW).
140 *Aboriginal Affairs (Amendment) Act 1968* (Vic), section 4.
141 *Aboriginal Affairs (Transfer of Functions) Act 1974* (Vic), sections 2, 3, 7, 9.
142 *Aborigines Act 1971* (Qld), sections 5, 6, 7, 11, 12, 13, 18, 20, 29, 35, 37, 48, 49, 56; *Torres Strait Islanders Act 1971* (Qld), sections 5, 6, 11, 12, 13, 20, 30, 34, 61, 78. Amendments in 1974 specified that the management of an Aboriginal's or Islander's property by a district officer would terminate on the individual's request: *Aborigines Act and Torres Strait Islanders Act Amendment Act 1974* (Qld), sections 6, 12.
143 *Aborigines Act and other Acts Amendment Act 1975* (Qld).
144 *Aborigines and Islanders Acts Amendment Act 1979* (Qld), sections 4, 11, 23.
145 Quoted in Garth Nettheim, *Victims of the Law: Black Queenslanders Today*, 1981, p. 114.
146 Nettheim, *Victims of the Law*, p. 113.
147 *Aboriginal and Torres Strait Islanders (Queensland Reserves and Communities Self-Management) Act 1978* (Cwlth), sections 6, 7, 8.
148 *Community Services (Aborigines) Act 1984* (Qld), sections 6, 14, 17, 20, 25, 29, 39, 42, 43, 82; *Community Services (Torres Strait) Act 1984* (Qld), sections 6, 14, 17, 20, 23, 27, 37, 40, 41, 81; *Aborigines and Torres Strait Islanders (Land Holding) Act 1985* (Qld), sections 5, 6. See also Henry Reynolds and Dawn May, 'Queensland', in McGrath

(ed.), *Contested Ground*, pp. 199–200; and Will Sanders, *Reshaping Governance in Torres Strait: The Torres Strait Regional Authority and Beyond*, 1994, p. 9.

149 *Criminal Law Consolidation Ordinance (No. 2) 1968* (NT), section 3; *Wards' Employment Ordinance Repeal Ordinance 1971* (NT), section 2; *Liquor Act 1978* (NT), sections 74, 75, 76, 77, 81, 87; *Workmen's Compensation Ordinance (No. 3) 1968* (NT), section 2; *Status of Children Act 1978* (NT), section 3; *Family Provison Act 1979* (NT), section 4; *Administration and Probate Act 1979* (NT), section 5; *Motor Accidents (Compensation) Act 1979* (NT), section 4.

7 From Civil to Indigenous Rights

1 Address by Lois O'Donoghue, chairperson of the Aboriginal and Torres Strait Islander Commission, 11 February 1996, contained in 'ATSIC Report of the Constitutional Reform Conference Adelaide, 11–13 February 1996', p. 60.

2 Richard Broome, *Aboriginal Australians: Black Responses to White Dominance 1788–1994*, 1994, p. 177; Scott Bennett, *Aborigines and Political Power*, 1989, p. 12; Peter Read, 'Northern Territory', in Ann McGrath (ed.), *Contested Ground: Australian Aborigines under the British Crown*, 1995, p. 291; Stuart Macintyre, *Winners and Losers: The Pursuit of Social Justice in Australian History*, 1985, pp. 127–9.

3 Bennett, *Aborigines and Political Power*, p. 8; Broome, *Aboriginal Australians*, p. 176.

4 Bennett, *Aborigines and Political Power*, pp. 13–14; Broome, *Aboriginal Australians*, p. 184; Kevin Gilbert, *Because a White Man'll Never Do It*, 1994 [1973], pp. 26–30; Heather Goodall, *Invasion to Embassy: Land in Aboriginal Politics in New South Wales, 1770–1972*, 1996, pp. 338–40, 349–51.

5 Bennett, *Aborigines and Political Power*, p. 18; Steve Hawke and Michael Gallagher, *Noonkanbah: Whose Land, Whose Law?*, 1989, pp. 15–16.

6 *Racial Discrimination Act 1975* (Cwlth), sections 3, 9.

7 *International Convention on the Elimination of all forms of Racial Discrimination*, article 5, contained as the Schedule to the *Racial Discrimination Act 1975* (Cwlth).

8 *Commonwealth Parliamentary Debates* (hereafter *CPD*), Senate, vol. 58, 21 November 1973, p. 1976.

9 *Racial Discrimination Act 1975* (Cwlth), sections 10, 11, 12, 13; *Aboriginal and Torres Strait Islanders (Queensland Discriminatory Laws) Act 1975* (Cwlth), sections 5, 6.

10 Broome, *Aboriginal Australians*, p. 182.

11 *CPD*, Senate, vol. 64, 15 May 1975, p. 1515. *Koowarta v. Bjelke-Petersen and others, Commonwealth Law Reports* (hereafter *CLR*), vol. 153, 1982, p. 168.

12 *CPD*, Representatives, vol. 93, 6 March 1975, p. 1222; *CPD*, Senate, vol. 64, 15 May 1975, p. 1513.

13 Quoted in *CPD*, Senate, vol. 58, 21 November 1973, pp. 1976–7.

14 *CPD*, Senate, vol. 64, 15 May 1975, pp. 1543–4; 22 May 1975, pp. 1791–2.

15 *CPD*, Representatives, vol. 93, 13 February 1975, p. 285; Senate, vol. 64, 22 May 1975, p. 1803.

16 *Prohibition of Discrimination Act 1966* (SA), sections 3, 4, 5, 6, 7. Ten years later the South Australian parliament passed a new *Racial Discrimination Act 1976* (SA).

17 *Anti-Discrimination Act 1977* (NSW); *Viskauskas and another v. Niland, CLR*, vol. 153, 1982, pp. 280ff.

18 *Racial Discrimination Amendment Act 1983* (Cwlth).

19 *Anti-Discrimination Act 1977* (NSW) (as amended in 1996 reprint), sections 20C, 20D.

20 *Equal Opportunity Act 1984* (Vic), sections 4, 21, 29, 30; *Equal Opportunity Act 1984* (WA), sections 37, 46, 47.

21 *Anti-Discrimination Act 1991* (Qld); *Anti-Discrimination Act 1992* (NT); *Sex Discrimination Act 1994* (Tas).

22 *Crown Lands Ordinance (No. 3) 1969* (NT), section 8.

23 *Mining Ordinance 1970* (NT), section 7.

24 Aboriginal Land Rights Commission, 'Second Report April 1974', *Commonwealth Parliamentary Papers*, 1974, vol. 1, p. 9.

25 Aboriginal Land Rights Commission, 'Second Report April 1974', pp. 22, 63–4, 134–5, 161–79; Broome, *Aboriginal Australians*, pp. 185–6.
26 *Aboriginal Land Fund Act 1974* (Cwlth), sections 4, 19, 20.
27 Broome, *Aboriginal Australians*, p. 189.
28 *Aboriginal Land Rights (Northern Territory) Act 1976* (Cwlth); Elliott Johnston, *Royal Commission into Aboriginal Deaths in Custody: National Report* (hereafter *Deaths in Custody National Report*), vol. 2, p. 484; Broome, *Aboriginal Australians*, pp. 189–90.
29 *Aboriginal Land Ordinance 1978* (NT), sections 3, 4, 5, 6, 7, 11.
30 *Aboriginal Land Act 1979* (NT), section 9.
31 *Cobourg Peninsula Aboriginal Land and Sanctuary Act 1981* (NT); *Deaths in Custody National Report*, vol. 2, p. 484.
32 *Aboriginal Lands Trust Act 1966* (SA), sections 5, 6, 16.
33 *Pitjantjatjara Land Rights Act 1981* (SA), sections 15, 20; *Maralinga Tjarutja Land Rights Act 1984* (SA), sections 13, 21; *Deaths in Custody National Report*, vol. 2, pp. 491–3. *Gerhardy v. Brown*, *CLR*, vol. 159, 1984–5, pp. 70ff; See Nicola Nygh, 'Implications of Recent High Court Decisions for State Laws Dealing with Aborigines and Aboriginal Land: *Gerhardy v. Brown* and *Mabo v. Queensland*', *Public Law Review*, vol. 1, 1990, p. 329, at pp. 332–5.
34 *Aboriginal Lands Act 1970* (Vic), sections 8, 9; Broome, *Aboriginal Australians*, p. 176.
35 *Aboriginal Land (Lake Condah and Framlingham Forest) Act 1987* (Cwlth), preamble, sections 6–7; Bennett, *Aborigines and Political Power*, pp. 76–7.
36 *Aboriginal Lands (Aborigines' Advancement League) (Watt Street, Northcote) Act 1982* (Vic); *Aboriginal Land (Northcote Land) Act 1989* (Vic); *Aboriginal Lands Act 1991* (Vic); *Aboriginal Land (Manatunga Land) Act 1992* (Vic); *Deaths in Custody National Report*, vol. 2, p. 496.
37 *Aboriginal Affairs Planning Authority Act 1972* (WA), sections 20, 24; *Mining Act 1978* (WA), section 24.
38 Sandy Toussaint, 'Western Australia', in McGrath (ed.), *Contested Ground*, pp. 262–3; *Deaths in Custody National Report*, vol. 2, pp. 493–4.
39 *Leases (Wreck Bay Aboriginal Housing Company Limited) Ordinance 1977* (ACT), sections 2, 3, 6; see also John McCorquodale, *Aborigines and the Law: A Digest*, 1987, p. 18.
40 *Aboriginal Land Grant (Jervis Bay Territory) Act 1986* (Cwlth), sections 8, 9, 14.
41 *Aborigines (Amendment) Act 1973* (NSW), section 5.
42 *Aboriginal Land Rights Act 1983* (NSW), sections 28, 35, 36, 40; Broome, *Aboriginal Australians*, p. 209.
43 *Deaths in Custody National Report*, vol. 2, p. 487.
44 *Aurukun Associates Agreement Act 1975* (Qld); *Director of Aboriginal and Islanders Advancement v. Peinkinna and others*, *Australian Law Reports*, vol. 17, 1978, pp. 129ff.
45 *Aboriginal and Torres Strait Islanders (Queensland Reserves and Communities Self-Management) Act 1978* (Cwlth), sections 5, 6, 7; *Local Government (Aboriginal Lands) Act 1978* (Qld), sections 9, 10. See Frank Brennan, *Land Rights Queensland Style: The Struggle for Aboriginal Self-Management*, 1992, pp. 10–12.
46 *Local Government (Aboriginal Lands) Act 1978* (Qld), sections 4, 6, 23, 26, 30, 33; *Local Government (Aboriginal Lands) Act Amendment Act 1981* (Qld), section 4.
47 *Land Act (Aboriginal and Islander Land Grants) Amendment Act 1982* (Qld); Brennan, *Land Rights Queensland Style*, pp. 16–17, 25–6.
48 *Aborigines and Torres Strait Islanders (Land Holding) Act 1985* (Qld); Brennan, *Land Rights Queensland Style*, pp. 67–8, 70; *Deaths in Custody National Report*, vol. 2, p. 495.
49 *Aboriginal Land Act 1991* (Qld), preamble, sections 2.05, 2.06, 2.12, 3.01, 3.02, 4.02, 4.03, 4.06, 4.16, 5.01, 5.03, 5.17, 7.01, 8.01; *Torres Strait Islander Land Act 1991* (Qld), preamble, sections 2.04, 2.05, 2.08, 2.09, 3.01, 3.02, 4.02, 4.03, 4.06, 4.16, 5.01, 5.03, 5.17, 7.01, 8.01. See Brennan, *Land Rights Queensland Style*, pp. 158–60.
50 *Milirrpum and others v. Nabalco Pty Ltd and the Commonwealth of Australia*, *Federal Law Reports*, vol. 17, 1971, pp. 141–293, especially pp. 244–5.
51 *Mabo and others v. The State of Queensland (No. 2)*, *CLR*, vol. 175, 1992, pp. 1–217 (hereafter *Mabo (No. 2)*, referred to in the text as the *Mabo* decision).
52 Broome, *Aboriginal Australians*, p. 233.

53 *Queensland Coast Islands Declaratory Act 1985* (Qld); *Mabo and another v. The State of Queensland and another (No. 1), CLR,* vol. 166, 1988, pp. 186ff.
54 Quoted in Broome, *Aboriginal Australians,* p. 234.
55 Deane and Gaudron JJ., in *Mabo (No. 2),* p. 109.
56 Brennan J., in *Mabo (No. 2),* pp. 29–30. Toohey J., at p. 183, argued simply that a different line of reasoning was now 'more persuasive' than the previously established one.
57 *CPD,* Representatives, vol. 190, 16 November 1993, p. 2877.
58 *Native Title Act 1993* (Cwlth), sections 14, 107, 160, 161, 162, 163, 164, 165, 166, 167, 168, 169, 170.
59 *Native Title Act 1993* (Cwlth), sections 7(2), 18.
60 See Frank Brennan, *One Land, One Nation: Mabo – Towards 2001,* 1995, p. 103.
61 *Native Title Act 1993* (Cwlth), preamble; CPD, Representatives, vol. 190, 16 November 1993, p. 2878.
62 *Native Title Act 1993* (Cwlth), sections 19, 7(2).
63 *Land Titles Validation Act 1993* (Vic), sections 6, 7; *Land Titles Validation Act 1994* (Vic).
64 *Native Title (Queensland) Act 1993* (Qld), sections 8, 19; *Native Title (Queensland) Amendment Act 1994* (Qld), section 3.
65 *Native Title (New South Wales) Act 1994* (NSW), sections 8, 32, 76; *Native Title (Tasmania) Act 1994* (Tas); *Validation of Titles and Actions Act 1994* (NT); *Native Title Act 1994* (ACT); *Land Acquisition (Native Title) Amendment Act 1994* (SA); *Native Title (South Australia) Act 1994* (SA); *Environment, Resources and Development Court (Native Title) Amendment Act 1994* (SA).
66 *Land (Titles and Traditional Usage) Act 1993* (WA), section 7.
67 *State of Western Australia v. Commonwealth, Australian Law Reports,* vol. 128, 1995, pp. 1ff.
68 *Titles Validation Act 1995* (WA).
69 *Australian,* 10 October 1996.
70 *Re Waanyi People's Native Title Application, Australian Law Reports,* 1995, vol. 129, pp. 118ff.
71 *Wik and Thayorre v. Queensland,* as yet unreported.
72 Will Kymlicka, 'Introduction', in Will Kymlicka (ed.), *The Rights of Minority Cultures,* 1995, p. 13.
73 See Darlene M. Johnston, 'Native Rights as Collective Rights: A Question of Group Self-Preservation', in Kymlicka (ed.), *The Rights of Minority Cultures,* p. 194.
74 *Deaths in Custody National Report,* vol. 2, pp. 501–2. See Broome, *Aboriginal Australians,* p. 224.
75 *Deaths in Custody National Report,* vol. 2, pp. 504, 508.
76 Verity Burgmann, *Power and Protest: Movements for Change in Australian Society,* 1993, p. 28.
77 *Deaths in Custody National Report,* vol. 4, p. 7.
78 Lois O'Donoghue, 'Who's Accountable to Whom?', *Weekend Australian,* 15–16 June 1996.
79 *Aboriginal and Torres Strait Islander Commission Act 1989* (Cwlth), sections 27, 31, 46, 100, 101, 131.
80 *Deaths in Custody National Report,* vol. 4, pp. 7–12; see also Christine Fletcher, *Aboriginal Non Democracy: A Case for Aboriginal Self-Government and Responsive Administration,* 1994, pp. 13–14.
81 *Aboriginal and Torres Strait Islander Commission Amendment Act (No. 3) 1993* (Cwlth), section 118.
82 *Land Fund and Indigenous Land Corporation (ATSIC Amendment) Act 1995* (Cwlth).
83 *Aboriginal and Torres Strait Islander Commission Amendment Act (No. 3) 1993* (Cwlth), section 76. See W. Sanders, *Reshaping Governance in Torres Strait: The Torres Strait Regional Authority and Beyond,* 1994, pp. 1, 12, 14, 21.
84 O'Donoghue, 'Who's Accountable to Whom?'.
85 O'Donoghue, 'Who's Accountable to Whom?'.

86 *Age*, 22 June 1996.
87 *CPD*, Representatives, No. 8 1996, 10 September 1996, pp. 3860–1.
88 *Australian*, 31 October 1996.
89 *Coe v. Commonwealth of Australia and another*, *Australian Law Reports*, vol. 24, 1979, pp. 128–9, 132, 138.
90 *Coe (on behalf of the Wiradjuri tribe) v. Commonwealth of Australia and another*, *Australian Law Reports*, vol. 118, 1993, pp. 193ff, at p. 200. See also Brennan, *One Land, One Nation*, pp. 126–7.
91 Brennan, *One Land, One Nation*, pp. 127–8.
92 Henry Reynolds, *Aboriginal Sovereignty: Reflections on Race, State and Nation*, 1996, p. 15.
93 Bennett, *Aborigines and Political Power*, p. 155.
94 Quoted in Burgmann, *Power and Protest*, pp. 40–1; Kevin Gilbert, *Aboriginal Sovereignty Justice The Law and Land*, 1993 [1987], p. 51.
95 Bennett, *Aborigines and Political Power*, p. 155.
96 Broome, *Aboriginal Australians*, p. 222. A copy of the Barunga Statement appears in the *Public Law Review*, vol. 1, 1990, p. 340.
97 Burgmann, *Power and Protest*, p. 40.
98 John Howard, 'Treaty is a Recipe for Separatism', in Ken Baker (ed.), *A Treaty With the Aborigines?*, 1988, p. 6; Hugh Morgan, 'The Quest for Aboriginal Sovereignty', in Baker (ed.), *A Treaty with the Aborigines?*, p. 19.
99 See also Jeremy Beckett, *Torres Strait Islanders: Custom and Colonialism*, 1987, p. 16.
100 *Council for Aboriginal Reconciliation Act 1991* (Cwlth), sections 5, 6. A majority of the Council must be made up of Aborigines and Islanders, and the chair must be Aboriginal (section 14).
101 The preamble proposed by ATSIC is contained in Frank Brennan, *Securing a Bountiful Place for Aborigines and Torres Strait Islanders in a Modern, Free and Tolerant Australia*, 1994, pp. 20–1.
102 *CPD*, Senate, vol. 63, 20 February 1975, pp. 369–70.
103 *CPD*, Representatives, vol. 162, 23 August 1988, pp. 137, 151; Senate, vol. 128, 23 August 1988, pp. 56, 72. See Christopher Cunneen and Terry Libesman, *Indigenous People and the Law in Australia*, 1995, pp. 194–5.
104 'Speech by the Honourable Prime Minister, P.J. Keating MP, Australian Launch of the International Year for the World's Indigenous People, Redfern, 10 December 1992', *Aboriginal Law Bulletin*, vol. 3, no. 61, 1993, pp. 4–5.
105 *Council for Aboriginal Reconciliation Act 1991* (Cwlth), preamble; *Native Title Act 1993* (Cwlth), preamble; *Aboriginal and Torres Strait Islander Commission Amendment Act (No. 3) 1993* (Cwlth), section 118.

Bibliography

Primary Sources

Government Archives

Australian Archives Canberra
Documents contained in:
CRS A1:1904/4979; 1905/3040; 1922/18564; 1924/28379; 1925/23976; 1928/1706; 1933/2419; 1934/4190; CRS A79: 2; CRS A96: vols 1 and 2; CRS A101: B1904/4739; CRS A202: 14/1865; CRS A406/62: E1945/1 parts 1 and 2; E1957/1 parts 2 to 4; CRS A406/63: E1905/9383; CRS A431: 1947/392; 1949/822; 1949/1591; 1951/889; CRS A432/70: 1967/3321 part 1; CRS A432/75: 1955/3765; CRS A432/77: 1957/3197; CRS A432/79: 1961/3125; 1961/3180; CRS A432/81: 1930/2016; 1938/114; 1939/883; 1949/576; 1960/3289 part 2; 1966/3171; CRS A432/85: 1940/317; CRS A432/86: 1929/4353; CRS A452: 1951/1721; CRS A457/1: M110/1; CRS A467/1: Bundle 82/SF40/9; Bundle 82/SF40/13; Bundle 83/SF40/5; CRS A472: W2526; CRS A571/97:1938/883; CRS A659: 1943/1/1330; CRS A981: Imperial Relations 145A part 22; India 16; India 16 part 2; CRS A1497: Opinion Book 21; CRS A1497/8; CRS A1608/1:L45/2/1; CRS A2718/XM: vol.1 part 2; CRS A2863: 1918/27; CRS A6006: 1924/05/01; 1924/12/03; CRS A6091/T1: NN; CRS CP78/22:1925/569; CRS M1416/1: 58

Australian Archives Melbourne
Documents contained in:
CRS B314: 3 to 6; CRS B329/2: 3 to 8; CRS B2861/2

Queensland State Archives
Documents contained in:
A/58655; A/58656; A/58750; A/58751; A/58764; A/58804; A/58850; A/58919; A/58927; A/69470; A/69499; A/69735; A/69980; COL/142; COL/143; COL/144; COL/145; CRS/264; EDU/Z 1787; R254 1A/129; R254 1A/267; R254 1A/345; R254 1A/467; R254 1A/554; R254 1A/573; R254 1A/574; R254 1A/580; R254 1D/86; R254 3A/207

Victorian Public Record Office
Documents contained in:
VPRS 1694: 1; VPRS 10265: 266

Printed Government Sources

Australian Capital Territory
ACT Ordinances and Acts, 1932–1994

Commonwealth
Aboriginal Welfare: Initial Conference of Commonwealth and State Aboriginal Authorities, Canberra, 21st to 23rd April, 1937, Canberra 1937
Australian Law Reports, 1978–1995
Commonwealth Acts, 1901–1995
Commonwealth Government Gazette, 1901–1944
Commonwealth Law Reports, 1923–1992
Commonwealth Parliamentary Debates, 1901–1996
Commonwealth Parliamentary Papers, 1929–1974
Aboriginal Land Rights Commission, Second Report, 1974
Report by J.W. Bleakley on 'The Aboriginals and Half-Castes of Central Australia and North Australia', 1929
Report from the Joint Committee on Constitutional Review, 1958
Report from the Joint Committee on Constitutional Review, 1959
Report from the Select Committee on Voting Rights of Aborigines, parts 1 and 2, 1961
Statistical Returns in relation to Constitution Alteration (Aboriginals) 1967 Referendum, 1968
Statistical Returns in relation to Constitution Alteration (Post-War Reconstruction and Democratic Rights) 1944 Referendum, 1945
Commonwealth Statutory Rules, 1922–1962
Federal Law Reports, 1971
National Library of Australia, 'An Investigation of the Origins and Intentions of Section 51, Placitum XXVI, and Section 127 of the Constitution of the Commonwealth of Australia', Canberra 1961
Official Record of the Debates of the Australasian Federal Convention, 1891, 1897, 1898 (republished in 1986 by Legal Books, Sydney)
Report of the Royal Commission on the Constitution, Canberra 1929

New South Wales
New South Wales Acts, 1839–1994
New South Wales Weekly Notes, 1903–1910

Northern Territory
Northern Territory Ordinances and Acts, 1911–1994

Queensland
Queensland Acts, 1865–1994
Queensland Government Gazette, 1899–1966
Queensland Parliamentary Debates, 1884–1901
Queensland Parliamentary Papers, 1901–1940
Annual Reports of the Chief Protector of Aboriginals, 1904–1909

Annual Report of Director of Native Affairs, 1939
Annual Reports of the Northern Protector of Aboriginals, 1901–1903
Report of the Southern Protector of Aboriginals, 1902
Queensland State Reports, 1914
Votes and Proceedings of the Legislative Assembly, 1896–1900
Report by Archibald Meston on the Aboriginals of Queensland, 1896
Report of the Commissioner of Police, 1897
Report by Horace Tozer on Measures Recently Adopted for the Amelioration of the Aborigines, 1897
Report of the Northern Protector of Aboriginals, 1899
Report by W.E. Parry-Okeden on the North Queensland Aborigines and the Native Police, 1897

South Australia
South Australian Ordinances and Acts, 1844–1994
South Australian State Reports, 1928–1943

Tasmania
Tasmanian Acts, 1912–1994

Victoria
Victorian Acts, 1855–1994
Victorian Government Gazette, 1871–1931
Victorian Parliamentary Debates, 1886–1914
Victorian Parliamentary Papers, 1861–1959
Report of the Aborigines Welfare Board, 1958
Report of the Board appointed to Enquire into, and Report upon, the Present Condition and Management of the Coranderrk Aboriginal Station, 1882
Reports of the Board for the Protection of the Aborigines, 1872–1922
Reports of the Central Board appointed to Watch over the Interests of the Aborigines in the Colony of Victoria, 1861–1864
Report by Charles McLean upon the Operation of the Aborigines Act 1928 and the Regulations and Orders Made Thereunder, 1957
Royal Commission on the Aborigines. Report of the Commissioners, 1877
Victorian Year-Books, 1902–1958
Votes and Proceedings of the Legislative Assembly, 1859–1860
Report from the Select Committee upon Protection to the Aborigines, 1860
Votes and Proceedings of the Legislative Council, 1858–1859
Report of the Select Committee of the Legislative Council on the Aborigines, 1858–1859

Western Australia
West Australian Acts, 1841–1995
Western Australia Parliamentary Debates, 1904–1962

Newspapers

Age; *Argus*; *Australian*; *Courier-Mail*

Other Unpublished Material

Aboriginal and Torres Strait Islander Commission, Report of the Constitutional Reform Conference, Adelaide 11–13 February 1996.

Secondary Sources

Attwood, Bain, 'Off the Mission Stations: Aborigines in Gippsland 1860–1890', *Aboriginal History*, vol. 10, 1986, pp. 131–51.

—— , *The Making of the Aborigines*, Sydney: Allen and Unwin, 1989.

Attwood, Bain, Burrage, Winifred, Burrage, Alan and Stokie, Elsie, *A Life Together, A Life Apart: A History of Relations between Europeans and Aborigines*, Melbourne: Melbourne University Press, 1994.

Austin, Tony, *Simply the Survival of the Fittest: Aboriginal Administration in South Australia's Northern Territory 1863–1910*, Darwin: Historical Society of the Northern Territory, 1992.

Baker, Ken (ed.), *A Treaty with the Aborigines?*, Melbourne: Institute of Public Affairs, 1988.

Bandler, Faith, *Turning the Tide: A Personal History of the Federal Council for the Advancement of Aborigines and Torres Strait Islanders*, Canberra: Aboriginal Studies Press, 1989.

Barwick, Diane, A Little More than Kin: Regional Affiliation and Group Identity among Aboriginal Migrants in Melbourne, PhD thesis, Australian National University, 1963.

—— , 'Changes in the Aboriginal Population of Victoria, 1863–1966', in Mulvaney, D.J. and Golson, J. (eds), *Aboriginal Man and Environment in Australia*, Canberra: Australian National University Press, 1971.

—— , 'Coranderrk and Cumeroogunga: Pioneers and Policy', in Epstein, T. Scarlett and Penny, David H. (eds), *Opportunity and Response: Case Studies in Economic Development*, London: C. Hurst and Co., 1972.

—— , 'Equity for Aborigines? The Framlingham Case', in Troy, Patrick N. (ed.), *A Just Society? Essays on Equity in Australia*, Sydney: Allen and Unwin, 1981.

Beckett, Jeremy, *Torres Strait Islanders: Custom and Colonialism*, Cambridge: Cambridge University Press, 1987.

—— , 'Aboriginality, Citizenship and Nation State', *Social Analysis*, vol. 24, 1988, pp. 3–18.

Bennett, Scott, *Aborigines and Political Power*, Sydney: Allen and Unwin, 1989.

—— , 'Federalism and Aboriginal Affairs', *Australian Aboriginal Studies*, vol. 1, 1988, pp. 18–27.

Berndt, Ronald and Berndt, Catherine, *From Black to White in South Australia*, Melbourne: F.W. Cheshire, 1951.

—— (eds), *Aborigines of the West: Their Past and their Present*, Nedlands: University of Western Australia Press, 1979.

Biles, David and McDonald, David (eds), *Deaths in Custody Australia, 1980–1989: The Research Papers of the Criminology Unit of the Royal Commission into Aboriginal Deaths in Custody*, Canberra: Australian Institute of Criminology, 1992.

Biskup, Peter, *Not Slaves Not Citizens: The Aboriginal Problem in Western Australia, 1898–1954*, Brisbane: University of Queensland Press, 1973.

Bolton, G.C., 'Black and White after 1897', in Stannage, C.T. (ed.), *A New History of Western Australia*, Nedlands: University of Western Australia Press, 1981.

Borrie, W.D. et al., *A White Australia: Australia's Population Problem*, Sydney: Australasian Publishing in conjunction with the Australian Institute of Political Science, 1947.

Brazil, P. and Mitchell, B. (eds), *Opinions of Attorneys-General of the Commonwealth of Australia: With opinions of Solicitors-General and the Attorney-General's Department. Volume 1: 1901–1914*, Canberra: AGPS, 1981.

—— (eds), *Opinions of Attorneys-General of the Commonwealth of Australia: With opinions of Solicitors-General and the Attorney-General's Department. Volume 2: 1914–1923*, Canberra: AGPS, 1988.

Brennan, Frank, *Land Rights Queensland Style: The Struggle for Aboriginal Self-Management*, Brisbane: University of Queensland Press, 1992.

—— , *Securing a Bountiful Place for Aborigines and Torres Strait Islanders in a Modern, Free and Tolerant Australia*, Melbourne: Constitutional Centenary Foundation, 1994.

—— , *One Land, One Nation: Mabo – Towards 2001*, Brisbane: University of Queensland Press, 1995.

Brock, Peggy, 'South Australia', in McGrath, Ann (ed.), *Contested Ground: Australian Aborigines under the British Crown*, Sydney: Allen and Unwin, 1995.

Broome, Richard, *Aboriginal Australians: Black Response to White Dominance 1788–1980*, Sydney: Allen and Unwin, 1982.

—— , 'Why Use Koori?', *La Trobe Library Journal*, vol. 11, 1989, p. 5.

—— , *Aboriginal Australians: Black Responses to White Dominance 1788–1994*, Sydney: Allen and Unwin, 1994.

—— , 'Victoria', in McGrath, Ann (ed.), *Contested Ground: Australian Aborigines under the British Crown*, Sydney: Allen and Unwin, 1995.

Burgmann, Verity and Lee, Jenny (eds), *Staining the Wattle: A People's History of Australia Since 1788*, Melbourne: McPhee Gribble, 1988.

Burgmann, Verity, *Power and Protest: Movements for Change in Australian Society*, Sydney: Allen and Unwin, 1993.

Butlin, N.G., *Our Original Aggression: Aboriginal Populations of Southeastern Australia 1788–1850*, Sydney: Allen and Unwin, 1983.

Centenary of Federation Advisory Committee, *2001: A Report from Australia*, Canberra: AGPS, 1994.

Chandler, Mary J., 'From Half-Caste to Outcast', *Geo: Australasia's Geographical Magazine*, vol. 7(2), 1985, pp. 23–5.

Christie, M.F., *Aborigines in Colonial Victoria 1835–86*, Sydney: Sydney University Press, 1979.

—— , 'Aboriginal Literacy and Power: An Historical Case Study', *Australian Journal of Adult and Community Education*, vol. 30, 1990, pp. 116–21.

Clark, C.M.H., *A History of Australia vol. 5, The People Make Laws 1888–1915*, Melbourne: Melbourne University Press, 1981.

Cole, Keith, *The Aborigines of Victoria*, Bendigo: Keith Cole Publications, 1982.

—— , *The Lake Condah Aboriginal Mission*, Bendigo: Keith Cole Publications, 1984.

Corris, Peter, *Aborigines and Europeans in Western Victoria*, Canberra: Australian Institute of Aboriginal Studies, 1968.

Council for Aboriginal Reconciliation, *Walking Together: The First Steps. Report of the Council for Aboriginal Reconciliation 1991–94 to Federal Parliament*, Canberra: AGPS, 1994.

Cowlishaw, Gillian, *Black, White or Brindle: Race in Rural Australia*, Cambridge: Cambridge University Press, 1988.

Critchett, Jan, A History of Framlingham and Lake Condah Aboriginal Stations, 1860–1918, MA thesis, University of Melbourne, 1980.
——, *Our Land Till We Die: A History of the Framlingham Aborigines*, Warrnambool: Warrnambool Institute Press, 1980.
——, *'A Distant Field of Murder': Western District Frontiers 1834–1848*, Melbourne: Melbourne University Press, 1992.
Cronin, Kathryn, *Colonial Casualties: Chinese in Early Victoria*, Melbourne: Melbourne University Press, 1982.
Crowley, F.K., *Australia's Western Third: A History of Western Australia from the First Settlements to Modern Times*, London: Macmillan, 1960.
Cunneen, Christopher and Libesman, Terry, *Indigenous People and the Law in Australia*, Sydney: Butterworths, 1995.
Deverall, Myrna, 'Records of the Administration of Aborigines in Victoria, c. 1860–1968', *Aboriginal History*, vol. 2, 1978, pp. 108–13.
Duncanson, Ian and Kirkby, Diane (eds), *Law and History in Australia, vol. 2*, Bundoora: Legal Studies Department, La Trobe University, 1986.
Eckermann, Anne-Katrin, Half-Caste, Out-Cast: An Ethnographic Analysis of the Processes underlying Adaptation among Aboriginal People in Rural Town, South-West Queensland, PhD thesis, University of Queensland, 1977.
Egan, Ted, *Justice All Their Own: The Caledon Bay and Woodah Island Killings 1932–1933*, Melbourne: Melbourne University Press, 1996.
Elkin, A.P., *Citizenship for the Aborigines: A National Aboriginal Policy*, Sydney: Australasian Publishing, 1944.
——, 'Aborigines and the Franchise', *The Aborigines' Protector*, vol. 2(2), 1946, pp. 3–9.
——, 'Is White Australia Doomed?', in Borrie, W.D. et al., *A White Australia: Australia's Population Problem*, Sydney: Australasian Publishing in conjunction with the Australian Institute of Political Science, 1947.
——, 'Re-thinking the White Australia Policy', in Borrie, W.D. et al., *A White Australia: Australia's Population Problem*, Sydney: Australasian Publishing in conjunction with the Australian Institute of Political Science, 1947.
Epstein, T. Scarlett and Penny, David H. (eds), *Opportunity and Response: Case Studies in Economic Development*, London: C. Hurst and Co., 1972.
Evans, Heather, *The Aboriginal People of Victoria: Select Bibliography of Pre-1960 Printed Sources in the Collections of the State Library of Victoria*, Melbourne: State Library of Victoria, 1993.
Evans, Raymond, Saunders, Kay and Cronin, Kathryn, *Race Relations in Colonial Queensland: A History of Exclusion, Exploitation and Extermination*, Brisbane: University of Queensland Press, 1988.
Federal Council for Aboriginal Advancement, *Government Legislation and the Aborigines*, Bayswater NSW: Federal Council for Aboriginal Advancement, 1964.
Felton, Philip, 'Victoria: Lands Reserved for the Benefit of Aborigines 1835–1971', in Peterson, Nicolas (ed.), *Aboriginal Land Rights: A Handbook*, Canberra: Australian Institute of Aboriginal Studies, 1981.
Fitzgerald, Ross, *A History of Queensland: From the Dreaming to 1915*, Brisbane: University of Queensland Press, 1986.
Fletcher, Christine, *Aboriginal Politics: Intergovernmental Relations*, Melbourne: Melbourne University Press, 1992.
——, *Aboriginal Non Democracy: A Case for Aboriginal Self-Government and Responsive Administration*, Darwin: North Australia Research Unit Discussion Paper, 1994.

Forward, Roy (ed.), *Public Policy in Australia*, Melbourne: Cheshire Publishing, 1974.

Foster, Margaret, *Our Constitution*, Melbourne: Macmillan, 1996.

Foxcroft, Edmund J.B., *Australian Native Policy: Its History Especially in Victoria*, Melbourne: Melbourne University Press, 1941.

Gale, Fay, *A Study of Assimilation: Part-Aborigines in South Australia*, Adelaide: Libraries Board of South Australia, 1964.

—— , *Urban Aborigines*, Canberra: Australian National University Press, 1972.

Galligan, Brian, *A Federal Republic: Australia's Constitutional System of Government*, Cambridge: Cambridge University Press, 1995.

Ganter, Regina and Kidd, Ros, 'The Powers of Protectors: Conflicts Surrounding Queensland's 1897 Aboriginal Legislation', *Australian Historical Studies*, vol. 25, 1993, pp. 536–54.

Gilbert, Kevin, *Because a White Man'll Never Do It*, Sydney: Angus and Robertson, 1994 [1973].

—— , *Aboriginal Sovereignty Justice The Law and Land*, Canberra: Burrambinga Books, 1993.

Goddard, Elizabeth and Stannage, Tom, 'John Forrest and the Aborigines', in Reece, Bob and Stannage, Tom (eds), *European-Aboriginal Relations in Western Australian History*, Nedlands: University of Western Australia Press, 1984.

Goodall, Heather, 'Cryin' Out for Land Rights', in Burgmann, Verity and Lee, Jenny (eds), *Staining the Wattle: A People's History of Australia Since 1788*, Melbourne: McPhee Gribble, 1988.

—— , 'New South Wales', in McGrath, Ann (ed.), *Contested Ground: Australian Aborigines under the British Crown*, Sydney: Allen and Unwin, 1995.

—— , *Invasion to Embassy: Land in Aboriginal Politics in New South Wales, 1770–1972*, Sydney: Allen and Unwin, 1996.

Green, Neville, 'Aborigines and White Settlers in the Nineteenth Century', in Stannage, C.T. (ed.), *A New History of Western Australia*, Nedlands: University of Western Australia Press, 1981.

Greenway, John, *Bibliography of the Australian Aborigines and the Native Peoples of Torres Strait to 1959*, Sydney: Angus and Robertson, 1963.

Gribble, J.B., *Dark Deeds in a Sunny Land or Blacks and Whites in North-West Australia*, Nedlands: University of Western Australia Press, 1987 [1905].

Grimshaw, Patricia, Lake, Marilyn, McGrath, Ann and Quartly, Marian, *Creating a Nation*, Melbourne: McPhee Gribble, 1994.

Grimshaw, Patricia, 'A White Woman's Suffrage', in Irving, Helen (ed.), *A Woman's Constitution? Gender and History in the Australian Commonwealth*, Sydney: Hale and Iremonger, 1996.

Haebich, Anna, *For Their Own Good: Aborigines and Government in the Southwest of Western Australia, 1900–1940*, Nedlands: University of Western Australia Press, 1988.

Hancock, W.K., *Australia*, Brisbane: Jacaranda, 1961 [1930].

Hanks, Peter and Keon-Cohen, Bryan (eds), *Aborigines and the Law: Essays in Memory of Elizabeth Eggleston*, Sydney: Allen and Unwin, 1984.

Hasluck, Paul, *Black Australians: A Survey of Native Policy in Western Australia, 1829–1897*, Melbourne: Melbourne University Press, 1942.

—— , *Shades of Darkness: Aboriginal Affairs 1925–1965*, Melbourne: Melbourne University Press, 1988.

Hawke, Steve and Gallagher, Michael, *Noonkanbah: Whose Land, Whose Law?*, Fremantle: Fremantle Arts Centre Press, 1989.

Howard, John, 'Treaty is a Recipe for Separatism', in Baker, Ken (ed.), *A Treaty with the Aborigines?*, Melbourne: Institute of Public Affairs, 1988.

Howard, Michael C., *Aboriginal Politics in Southwestern Australia*, Nedlands: University of Western Australia Press, 1981.

Howe, Renate (ed.), *Women and the State: Australian Perspectives*, Bundoora: La Trobe University Press, 1993.

Huggins, Jackie, 'Response', in Janson, Susan and Macintyre, Stuart (eds), *Through White Eyes*, Sydney: Allen and Unwin, 1990.

Huggins, Jackie and Blake, Thom, 'Protection or Persecution? Gender Relations in the Era of Racial Segregation', in Saunders, Kay and Evans, Raymond (eds), *Gender Relations in Australia: Domination and Negotiation*, Sydney: Harcourt Brace Jovanovich, 1992.

Hughes, Colin A., 'The Marriage of Mick and Gladys: A Discretion Without an Appeal', in Schaffer, B.B. and Corbett, D.C. (eds), *Case Studies in Australian Administration*, Melbourne: F.W. Cheshire, 1965.

Hughes, Colin A. and Graham, B.D., *A Handbook of Australian Government and Politics 1890–1964*, Canberra: Australian National University Press, 1968.

Irving, Helen (ed.), *A Woman's Constitution? Gender and History in the Australian Commonwealth*, Sydney: Hale and Iremonger, 1996.

Jackson, Robert, Jackson, Doreen and Baxter-Moore, Nicolas (eds), *Contemporary Canadian Politics: Readings and Notes*, Scarborough: Prentice Hall, 1982.

Janson, Susan and Macintyre, Stuart (eds), *Through White Eyes*, Sydney: Allen and Unwin, 1990.

Johnston, Darlene M., 'Native Rights as Collective Rights: A Question of Group Self-Preservation', in Kymlicka, Will (ed.), *The Rights of Minority Cultures*, Oxford: Oxford University Press, 1995.

Johnston, Elliott, *Royal Commission into Aboriginal Deaths in Custody. National Report. Vols 2 and 4*, Canberra: AGPS, 1991.

Johnston, Peter W., 'The Repeals of Section 70 of the Western Australian Constitution Act 1889: Aborigines and Governmental Breach of Trust', *Western Australian Law Review*, vol. 19, 1989, pp. 318–51.

Jones, F. Lancaster, *The Structure and Growth of Australia's Aboriginal Population*, Canberra: Australian National University Press, 1970.

Keating, P.J., 'Speech by the Honourable Prime Minister, P.J. Keating MP. Australian Launch of the International Year for the World's Indigenous People', *Aboriginal Law Bulletin*, vol. 3, 1993, pp. 4–5.

Keith, Arthur Berriedale (ed.), *Speeches and Documents on the British Dominions 1918–1931: From Self-Government to National Sovereignty*, London: Oxford University Press, 1970 [1932].

Kidd, Rosalind M., Regulating Bodies: Administrations and Aborigines in Queensland 1840–1988, PhD Thesis, Griffith University, 1994.

King, D.A. and McHoul, A.W., 'The Discursive Production of the Queensland Aborigine as Subject: Meston's Proposal, 1895', *Social Analysis*, vol. 19, 1986, pp. 22–39.

King, Wayne, *Black Hours*, Sydney: Angus and Robertson, 1996.

Kingston, Beverley, *The Oxford History of Australia: Volume 3. 1860–1900. Glad, Confident Morning*, Melbourne: Oxford University Press, 1988.

Kymlicka, Will, 'Introduction', in Kymlicka, Will (ed.), *The Rights of Minority Cultures*, Oxford: Oxford University Press, 1995.

—— (ed.), *The Rights of Minority Cultures*, Oxford: Oxford University Press, 1995.

Kymlicka, Will and Norman, Wayne, 'Return of the Citizen: A Survey of Recent Work on Citizenship Theory', *Ethics*, vol. 104, 1994, pp. 352–81.

Langford, Ruby, *Don't Take Your Love to Town*, Melbourne: Penguin, 1988.

Langford Ginibi, Ruby, *Real Deadly*, Sydney: Angus and Robertson, 1992.

Long, J.P.M., *Aboriginal Settlements: A Survey of Institutional Communities in Eastern Australia*, Canberra: Australian National University Press, 1970.

Long, T., 'The Development of Government Aboriginal Policy: The Effect of Administrative Changes, 1829–1977', in Berndt, Ronald M. and Berndt, Catherine H. (eds), *Aborigines of the West: Their Past and their Present*, Nedlands: University of Western Australia Press, 1979.

Loos, Noel, 'Queensland's Kidnapping Act: The Native Labourers Protection Act of 1884', *Aboriginal History*, vol. 4, 1980, pp. 150–73.

—— , *Invasion and Resistance: Aboriginal–European Relations on the North Queensland Frontier 1861–1897*, Canberra: Australian National University Press, 1982.

—— , 'A Chapter of Contact: Aboriginal–European Relations in North Queensland 1606–1992', in Reynolds, Henry (ed.), *Race Relations in North Queensland*, Townsville: Department of History and Politics, James Cook University, 1993.

Lyons, Gregory, 'Official Policy Towards Victorian Aborigines 1957–1974', *Aboriginal History*, vol. 7, 1983, pp. 61–79.

McCorquodale, John, *Aborigines and the Law: A Digest*, Canberra: Aboriginal Studies Press, 1987.

McGrath, Ann, *'Born in the Cattle': Aborigines in Cattle Country*, Sydney: Allen and Unwin, 1987.

—— , '"Beneath the Skin": Australian Citizenship, Rights and Aboriginal Women', in Howe, Renate (ed.), *Women and the State: Australian Perspectives*, Bundoora: La Trobe University Press, 1993.

—— , 'A National Story' and 'Tasmania: 1', in McGrath, Ann (ed.), *Contested Ground: Australian Aborigines under the British Crown*, Sydney: Allen and Unwin, 1995.

—— (ed.), *Contested Ground: Australian Aborigines under the British Crown*, Sydney: Allen and Unwin, 1995.

McGregor, Russell, 'Protest and Progress: Aboriginal Activism in the 1930s', *Australian Historical Studies*, vol. 25, 1993, pp. 555–68.

Macintyre, Stuart, *Winners and Losers: The Pursuit of Social Justice in Australian History*, Sydney: Allen and Unwin, 1985.

Macintyre, Stuart, Boston, Ken and Pascoe, Susan (Civics Expert Group), *Whereas the People: Civics and Citizenship Education. Report of the Civics Expert Group*, Canberra: AGPS, 1994.

McLeod, D.W., *How the West was Lost: The Native Question in the Development of Western Australia*, Perth: D.W. McLeod, 1984.

Malezer, Les, Foley, Matt and Richards, Paul, *Beyond the Act*, Brisbane: Foundation for Aboriginal and Islander Research Action, 1979.

Marcard, Patricia, The Aborigines in Victoria, 1858 to 1884: Attitudes and Policies, BA Hons Thesis, History Department, University of Melbourne, 1963.

—— , 'Early Victoria and the Aborigines', *Melbourne Historical Journal*, vol. 4, 1964, pp. 23–9.

Marchant, Leslie R., *Aboriginal Administration in Western Australia, 1886–1905*, Canberra: Australian Institute of Aboriginal Studies, 1981.

Markus, Andrew, *From the Barrel of a Gun. The Oppression of the Aborigines, 1860–1900*, Melbourne: Victorian Historical Association, 1974.

——, *Governing Savages*, Sydney: Allen and Unwin, 1990.

——, *Australian Race Relations 1788–1993*, Sydney: Allen and Unwin, 1994.

Marshall, T.H., 'Citizenship and Social Class' [1950], in Marshall, T.H. and Bottomore, Tom, *Citizenship and Social Class*, London: Pluto Press, 1992.

Marshall, T.H. and Bottomore, Tom, *Citizenship and Social Class*, London: Pluto Press, 1992.

Massola, Aldo, *Aboriginal Mission Stations in Victoria: Yelta, Ebenezer, Ramahyuck, Lake Condah*, Melbourne: Hawthorn Press, 1970.

May, Dawn, 'Race Relations in Queensland 1897–1971', in Wyvill, L.F., *Royal Commission into Aboriginal Deaths in Custody. Regional Report of Inquiry in Queensland*, Canberra: AGPS, 1991.

Maykutenner (Matson-Green, Vicki), 'Tasmania: 2', in McGrath, Ann (ed.), *Contested Ground: Australian Aborigines under the British Crown*, Sydney: Allen and Unwin, 1995.

Morgan, Hugh, 'The Quest for Aboriginal Sovereignty', in Baker, Ken (ed.), *A Treaty with the Aborigines?*, Melbourne: Institute of Public Affairs, 1988.

Morgan, Sally, *My Place*, Fremantle: Fremantle Arts Centre Press, 1987.

Mulvaney, D.J. and Golson, J. (eds), *Aboriginal Man and Environment in Australia*, Canberra: Australian National University Press, 1971.

Nettheim, Garth, *Out Lawed: Queensland's Aborigines and Islanders and the Rule of Law*, Artarmon: Australia and New Zealand Book Co., 1973.

——, *Victims of the Law: Black Queenslanders Today*, Sydney: Allen and Unwin, 1981.

Neville, A.O., *Australia's Coloured Minority: Its Place in the Community*, Sydney: Curawong, n.d.

Nygh, Nicola, 'Implications of Recent High Court Decisions for State Laws Dealing with Aborigines and Aboriginal Land: Gerhardy v. Brown and Mabo v. Queensland', *Public Law Review*, vol. 1, 1990, pp. 329–37.

O'Connor, Ian, 'Aboriginal Child Welfare Law, Policies and Practices in Queensland: 1865–1989', *Australian Social Work*, vol. 46, 1993, pp. 11–22.

O'Donoghue, Lois, 'Who's Accountable to Whom?', *Weekend Australian*, 15–16 June 1996.

Paltiel, Khayyam Zev, 'Group Rights in the Canadian Constitution and Aboriginal Claims to Self-Determination', in Jackson, Robert, Jackson, Doreen and Baxter-Moore, Nicolas (eds), *Contemporary Canadian Politics: Readings and Notes*, Scarborough: Prentice Hall, 1982.

Pepper, Phillip and De Araugo, Tess, *The Kurnai of Gippsland. What did Happen to the Aborigines of Victoria*, Melbourne: Hyland House, 1985.

Perkins, Charles, *A Bastard Like Me*, Sydney: Ure Smith, 1975.

Peterson, Nicolas (ed.), *Aboriginal Land Rights: A Handbook*, Canberra: Australian Institute of Aboriginal Studies, 1981.

Pink, Olive M., 'An Open Letter to Defenders of the Tribespeople Anywhere in Australia', *Communist Review*, February 1950, pp. 444–7.

Pittock, A. Barrie and Lippmann, Lorna, 'Aborigines', in Forward, Roy (ed.), *Public Policy in Australia*, Melbourne: Cheshire Publishing, 1974.

Price, A.G., *What of our Aborigines?*, Adelaide: Rigby, n.d.

Quick, John, *The Legislative Powers of the Commonwealth and the States of Australia with Proposed Amendments*, Melbourne: Maxwell, 1919.

Quick, John and Garran, Robert, *The Annotated Constitution of the Australian Commonwealth*, Sydney: Legal Books, 1976 [1901].

Read, Peter, *The Stolen Generations: The Removal of Aboriginal Children in New South Wales 1883 to 1969*, Sydney: Occasional Paper No. 1, New South Wales Ministry of Aboriginal Affairs, n.d.

——, 'Northern Territory', in McGrath, Ann (ed.), *Contested Ground: Australian Aborigines under the British Crown*, Sydney: Allen and Unwin, 1995.

Reece, Bob and Stannage, Tom (eds), *European–Aboriginal Relations in Western Australian History*, Nedlands: University of Western Australia Press, 1984.

Reynolds, Henry (ed.), *Aborigines and Settlers: The Australian Experience 1788–1939*, Melbourne: Cassell, 1972.

——, *The Other Side of the Frontier: Aboriginal Resistance to the European Invasion of Australia*, Melbourne: Penguin, 1990.

——, *The Law of the Land*, Melbourne: Penguin, 1992 [1987].

—— (ed.), *Race Relations in North Queensland*, Townsville: Department of History and Politics, James Cook University, 1993.

——, *Fate of a Free People*, Melbourne: Penguin, 1995.

——, *Aboriginal Sovereignty: Reflections on Race, State and Nation*, Sydney: Allen and Unwin, 1996.

Reynolds, Henry and Loos, Noel, 'Aboriginal Resistance in Queensland', *Australian Journal of Politics and History*, vol. 22, 1976, pp. 214–26.

Reynolds, Henry and May, Dawn, 'Queensland', in McGrath, Ann (ed.), *Contested Ground: Australian Aborigines under the British Crown*, Sydney: Allen and Unwin, 1995.

Rhodes, David and Stocks, Robyn, 'Excavations at Lake Condah Aboriginal Mission 1984–85', *Historic Environment*, vol. 4, 1985, pp. 4–12.

Rowley, C.D., *The Destruction of Aboriginal Society*, Melbourne: Penguin, 1972.

——, *Outcasts in White Australia*, Melbourne: Penguin, 1973.

Rowse, Tim, 'Diversity in Indigenous Citizenship', *Communal/Plural*, vol. 2, 1993, pp. 47–63.

——, *After Mabo: Interpreting Indigenous Traditions*, Melbourne: Melbourne University Press, 1993.

Ryan, Lyndall, 'The Struggle for Recognition: Part-Aborigines in Bass Strait in the Nineteenth Century', *Aboriginal History*, vol. 1, 1977, pp. 27–51.

Sadler, Robert J., 'The Federal Parliament's Power to make Laws "With Respect to . . . the People of any Race . . . " ', *Sydney Law Review*, vol. 10, 1985, pp. 591–613.

Sanders, W., *Reshaping Governance in Torres Strait: The Torres Strait Regional Authority and Beyond*, Canberra: Centre for Aboriginal Economic Policy Research, Australian National University, 1994.

—— (ed.), *Mabo and Native Title: Origins and Institutional Implications*, Canberra: Centre for Aboriginal Economic Policy Research, Australian National University, 1994.

Saunders, Kay and Evans, Raymond (eds), *Gender Relations in Australia: Domination and Negotiation*, Sydney: Harcourt Brace Jovanovich, 1992.

Sawer, Geoffrey, 'The Australian Constitution and the Australian Aborigine', *Federal Law Review*, vol. 2, 1966–7, pp. 17–36.

——, *Australian Federal Politics and Law 1901–1929*, Melbourne: Melbourne University Press, 1972 [1956].

Schaffer, B.B. and Corbett, D.C. (eds), *Case Studies in Australian Administration*, Melbourne: F.W. Cheshire, 1965.

Sexton, J.H., *Legislation Governing the Australian Aborigines*, Adelaide: Aborigines' Friends' Association, 1933.

——, *Australian Aborigines*, Adelaide: Aborigines' Friends' Association, 1942.

——, *Bringing the Aborigines Into Citizenship: How Western Australia is Dealing With the Problem*, Adelaide: Aborigines' Friends' Association, n.d.

——, *Aboriginal Intelligence: Has the Full-blooded Aboriginal Sufficient Intelligence to Undertake the Responsibilities of Citizenship?*, Adelaide: Aborigines' Friends' Association, n.d.

Smith, L.R., *The Aboriginal Population of Australia*, Canberra: Australian National University Press, 1980.

Smyth, Rosaleen, 'The Aboriginal and Torres Strait Islander Population', in Biles, David and McDonald, David (eds), *Deaths in Custody Australia, 1980–1989: The Research Papers of the Criminology Unit of the Royal Commission into Aboriginal Deaths in Custody*, Canberra: Australian Institute of Criminology, 1992.

Snow, Alpheus Henry, *The Question of Aborigines in the Law and Practice of Nations*, New York: G.P. Putnam's Sons, 1921.

Stannage, C.T. (ed.), *A New History of Western Australia*, Nedlands: University of Western Australia Press, 1981.

Stevens, F.S., 'Parliamentary Attitudes to Aboriginal Affairs', in Stevens, F.S. (ed.), *Racism: The Australian Experience. A Study of Race Prejudice in Australia. vol. 2. Black versus White*, Sydney: Australia and New Zealand Book Co., 1972.

—— (ed.), *Racism: The Australian Experience. A Study of Race Prejudice in Australia. vol. 2. Black versus White*, Sydney: Australia and New Zealand Book Co., 1972.

Stone, Sharman N. (ed.), *Aborigines in White Australia: A Documentary History of the Attitudes Affecting Official Policy and the Australian Aborigine, 1697–1973*, Melbourne: Heinemann, 1974.

Stretton, Pat and Finnimore, Christine, *How South Australian Aborigines Lost the Vote: Some Side Effects of Federation*, Adelaide: Old Parliament House Research Paper, 1991.

——, 'Black Fellow Citizens: Aborigines and the Commonwealth Franchise', *Australian Historical Studies*, vol. 25, 1993, pp. 521–35.

Sykes, Roberta, *Black Majority*, Melbourne: Hudson, 1989.

Tatz, C.M., 'Queensland's Aborigines: Natural Justice and the Rule of Law', *Australian Quarterly*, vol. 35, 1963, pp. 33–49.

Thorpe, William, 'Archibald Meston and Aboriginal Legislation in Colonial Queensland', *Historical Studies*, vol. 21, 1984, pp. 52–67.

Toussaint, Sandy, 'Western Australia', in McGrath, Ann (ed.), *Contested Ground: Australian Aborigines under the British Crown*, Sydney: Allen and Unwin, 1995.

Trollope, Anthony, *Australia*, Brisbane: University of Queensland Press, 1967 [1873].

Troy, Patrick N. (ed.), *A Just Society? Essays on Equity in Australia*, Sydney: Allen and Unwin, 1981.

Tucker, Margaret, *If Everyone Cared: Autobiography of Margaret Tucker M.B.E.*, Sydney: Ure Smith, 1977.

Turner, Bryan S., *Citizenship and Capitalism: The Debate over Reformism*, London: Allen and Unwin, 1986.

——, 'Outline of a Theory of Citizenship', *Sociology*, vol. 24, 1990, pp. 189–217.

——, 'Rights and Communities: Prolegomenon to a Sociology of Rights', *Australian and New Zealand Journal of Sociology*, vol. 31, 1995, pp. 1–8.

Wearne, Heather, *A Clash of Cultures: Queensland Aboriginal Policy (1824–1980)*, Brisbane: Division of World Mission of the Uniting Church in Australia, 1980.

Welborn, Suzanne, 'Politicians and Aborigines in Queensland and Western Australia 1897–1907', *Studies in Western Australian History*, vol. 2, 1978, pp. 18–32.

Wettenhall, R.L., 'Administrative Boards in Nineteenth Century Australia', *Public Administration*, vol. 22, 1963, pp. 255–67.

Widders, Terry and Noble, Greg, 'On the Dreaming Track to the Republic: Indigenous People and the Ambivalence of Citizenship', *Communal/Plural*, vol. 2, 1993, pp. 95–112.

Wilkinson, Linda, 'Fractured Families, Squatting and Poverty: The Impact of the 1886 "Half-caste" Act on the Framlingham Aboriginal Community', in Duncanson, Ian and Kirkby, Diane (eds), *Law and History in Australia, vol. 2*, Bundoora: Legal Studies Department, La Trobe University, 1986.

Wyvill, L.F., *Royal Commission into Aboriginal Deaths in Custody. Regional Report of Inquiry in Queensland*, Canberra: AGPS, 1991.

Index